Birnbaum's WASHINGTON, DC 1993

Alexandra Mayes Birnbaum
EDITOR

Lois Spritzer
EXECUTIVE EDITOR

Laura L. Brengelman
Managing Editor

Mary Callahan
Jill Kadetsky
Susan McClung
Beth Schlau
Dana Margaret Schwartz
Associate Editors

Gene Gold
Assistant Editor

 HarperPerennial
A Division of HarperCollinsPublishers

To Stephen, who merely made all this possible.

BIRNBAUM'S WASHINGTON, DC 1993. Copyright © 1993 by HarperCollins Publishers.
All rights reserved. Printed in the United States of America. No part of this book may
be used or reproduced in any manner whatsoever without written permission except
in the case of brief quotations embodied in critical articles and reviews. For information
address HarperCollins*Publishers*, 10 East 53rd Street, New York, NY 10022.

FIRST EDITION

ISSN 0749-2561 (Stephen Birnbaum Travel Guides)
ISSN 1061-544X (Washington, DC)
ISBN 0- 06-278059-X (pbk.)

93 94 95 96 97 CWI 10 9 8 7 6 5 4 3 2

Contents

THE CITY

A thorough, qualitative guide to Washington, DC. Each section offers a comprehensive report on the city's most compelling attractions and amenities, designed to be used on the spot.

DIVERSIONS

A selective guide to more than 10 active and/or cerebral theme vacations, including the best places to pursue them.

For the Experience

For the Body

For the Mind

DIRECTIONS

Seven of the best walks in and around Washington, DC.

A Word from the Editor

I recall an early family vacation: My father was determined that his two daughters (then age about 10 and 11) were going to see our nation's capital. Come hell or high water — a distinct probability, given my recollection of the weather — we were dragged from monument to monument, from glimpses of one seminal document to another, from museum to foot-fatiguing museum. See it we did. Or so my father insisted.

Flash forward: Washington was the site of choice for my high school senior class trip. The timid teacher in charge shepherded a herd of ungrateful 1950s teenage girls to the same monuments, museums, and must-sees. The only must-see on *our* list was to catch a glimpse of a very young and handsome senator from Massachusetts, John F. Kennedy.

By the time that my husband Steve Birnbaum and I made our first trip together, to this — one of the most beautiful of American cities — I had absolutely no recollection of ever having seen anything other than the Washington Monument. (I had remembered that it was very tall.) And so we began the first of what turned into numerous pilgrimages to the capital, taking in and taking advantage of the history, beauty, and excitement of this city. Whether reading the Constitution or the names on the Vietnam Memorial; visiting the Library of Congress; seeing the cherry trees in bloom around the Tidal Basin; wandering around Georgetown, ice cream cone dripping in hand — we were the most dedicated of tourists, many a time hopping on the shuttle from New York just to see one or another of the extraordinary exhibits at the *National Gallery.* If youth was wasted on the young, later trips made up for it.

My own evolution as a traveler (which happily continues) is mirrored by the evolution of our guidebook series. When we began our series of modern travel guides, we logically began with "area" books, attempting to publish guides that would include the widest possible number of attractive destinations. When the public seemed to accept our new way of delivering travel data, we added titles covering only a single country, and when these became popular we began our newest expansion phase, which centers on a group of books that deal with only a single city. Now we can not only highlight our favorite urban destinations, but really describe how to get the very most out of a visit.

Such treatment of travel information only mirrors an increasingly pervasive trend among travelers — the frequent return to a treasured travel spot. Once upon a time, even the most dedicated travelers would visit distant parts of the world no more than once in a lifetime — usually as part of some sort of Grand Tour. But greater numbers of would-be sojourners are now availing themselves of the opportunity to visit a favored part of the world over and over again.

So where once it was routine to say you'd "seen" a particular city or country after a very superficial, once-over-lightly encounter, the more perceptive travelers of today recognize that it's entirely possible to have only skimmed the surface of a specific travel destination even after having visited that place more than a dozen times. Similarly, repeated visits to a single site permit true exploration of special interests, whether they be sporting, artistic, or intellectual.

For those of us who now have spent the last several years working out the special system under which we present information in this series, the luxury of being able to devote nearly as much space as we'd like to just a single city is as close to paradise for guide writers and editors as any of us expects to come. But clearly this is not the first guide to the glories of Washington, DC — one suspects that guides of one sort or another have existed at least since First Lady Abigail Adams complained of her new digs (the White House) — so a traveler might logically ask why a new one is suddenly necessary.

Our answer is that the nature of travel to the nation's capital — and even of the travelers who now routinely make the trip — has changed dramatically of late. For the past 200 years or so, travel to even a town within our own country was considered an elaborate undertaking, one that required extensive advance planning. But with the advent of jet air travel in the late 1950s and of increased-capacity, wide-body aircraft during the late 1960s, travel to and around once distant destinations became extremely common. Attitudes as well as costs have changed significantly in the last couple of decades.

Obviously, any new guidebook to Washington, DC, must keep pace with and answer the real needs of today's travelers. That's why we've tried to create a guide that's specifically organized, written, and edited for the more demanding modern traveler, one for whom qualitative information is infinitely more desirable than mere quantities of unappraised data. We think that this book, along with all the other guides in our series, represents a new generation of travel guides — one that is especially responsive to modern needs and interests.

For years, dating back as far as Herr Baedeker, travel guides have tended to be encyclopedic, seemingly much more concerned with demonstrating expertise in geography and history than with a real analysis of the sorts of things that actually concern a typical modern tourist. But today, when it is hardly necessary to tell a traveler where Washington, DC, is (in many cases, the traveler has been there nearly as often as the guidebook editors), it becomes the responsibility of those editors to provide new perspectives and to suggest new directions in order to make the guide genuinely valuable.

That's exactly what we've tried to do in this series. I think you'll notice a different, more contemporary tone to the text, as well as an organization and focus that are distinctive and more functional. And even a random reading of what follows will demonstrate a substantial departure from the standard guidebook orientation, for we've not only attempted to provide information of a more compelling sort, but we also have tried to present the data in a format that makes it particularly accessible.

Needless to say, it's difficult to decide just what to include in a guidebook of this size — and what to omit. Early on, we realized that giving up the encyclopedic approach precluded our listing every single route and restaurant, a realization that helped define our overall editorial focus. Similarly, when we discussed the possibility of presenting certain information in other than strict geographic order, we found that the new format enabled us to arrange data in a way that we feel best answers the questions travelers typically ask.

Large numbers of specific questions have provided the real editorial skeleton for this book. The volume of mail we regularly receive emphasizes that modern travelers want very precise information, so we've tried to organize our material in the most responsive way possible. Readers who want to know the best restaurants or the chicest shops in Washington will have no trouble extracting that data from this guide.

Travel guides are, understandably, reflections of personal taste, and putting one's name on a title page obviously puts one's preferences on the line. But I think I ought to amplify just what "personal" means. Like Steve, I don't believe in the sort of personal guidebook that's a palpable misrepresentation on its face. It is, for example, hardly possible for any single travel writer to visit thousands of restaurants (and nearly as many hotels) in any given year and provide accurate appraisals of each. And even if it were physically possible for one human being to survive such an itinerary, it would of necessity have to be done at a dead sprint, and the perceptions derived therefrom would probably be less valid than those of any other intelligent individual visiting the same establishments. It is, therefore, impossible (especially in a large, annually revised and updated guidebook *series* such as we offer) to have only one person provide all the data on the entire world.

I also happen to think that such individual orientation is of substantially less value to readers. Visiting a single hotel for just one night or eating one hasty meal in a random restaurant hardly equips anyone to provide appraisals that are of more than passing interest. No amount of doggedly alliterative or oppressively onomatopoeic text can camouflage a technique that is essentially specious. We have, therefore, chosen what I like to describe as the "thee and me" approach to restaurant and hotel evaluation and, to a somewhat more limited degree, to the sites and sights we have included in the other sections of our text. What this really reflects is a personal sampling tempered by intelligent counsel from informed local sources, and these additional friends-of-the-editor are almost always residents of the city and/or area about which they are consulted.

Despite the presence of several editors, writers, researchers, and local contributors, very precise editing and tailoring keep our text fiercely subjective. So what follows is the gospel according to Birnbaum, and it represents as much of our own taste and instincts as we can manage. It is probable, therefore, that if you like your cities stylish and prefer small hotels with personality to huge high-rise anonymities, we're likely to have a long and meaningful relationship. Readers with dissimilar tastes may be less enraptured.

I also should point out something about the person to whom this guidebook is directed. Above all, he or she is a "visitor." This means that such elements as restaurants have been specifically picked to provide the visitor with a representative, enlightening, stimulating, and above all pleasant experience. Since so many extraneous considerations can affect the reception and service accorded a regular restaurant patron, our choices can in no way be construed as an exhaustive guide to resident dining. We think we've listed all the best places, in various price ranges, but they were chosen with a visitor's enjoyment in mind.

Other evidence of how we've tried to tailor our text to reflect modern travel habits is most apparent in the section we call DIVERSIONS. Where once it was common for travelers to spend an urban visit in a determinedly passive state, the emphasis is far more active today. So we've organized every activity we could reasonably evaluate and arranged the material in a way that is especially accessible to activists of either athletic or cerebral bent. It is no longer necessary, therefore, to wade through a pound or two of superfluous prose just to find the very best crab cakes or the quaintest neighborhood within the city limits.

If there is a single thing that best characterizes the revolution in and evolution of current holiday habits, it is that most travelers now consider travel a right rather than a privilege. No longer is a family trip to the far corners of the world necessarily a once-in-a-lifetime thing; nor is the idea of visiting exotic, faraway places in the least worrisome. Travel today translates as the enthusiastic desire to sample all of the world's opportunities, to find that elusive quality of experience that is not only enriching but comfortable. For that reason, we've tried to make what follows not only helpful and enlightening, but the sort of welcome companion of which every traveler dreams.

Finally, I also should point out that every good travel guide is a living enterprise; that is, no part of this text is carved in stone. In our annual revisions, we refine, expand, and further hone all our material to serve your travel needs better. To this end, no contribution is of greater value to us than your personal reaction to what we have written, as well as information reflecting your own experiences while using the book. We earnestly and enthusiastically solicit your comments about this guide *and* your opinions and perceptions about places you have recently visited. In this way, we will be able to provide the most current information — including the actual experiences of recent travelers — and to make those experiences more readily available to others. Please write to us at 10 E. 53rd St., New York, NY 10022.

We sincerely hope to hear from you.

ALEXANDRA MAYES BIRNBAUM

How to Use This Guide

A great deal of care has gone into the special organization of this guidebook, and we believe it represents a real breakthrough in the presentation of travel material. Our aim is to create a new, more modern generation of travel books, and to make this guide the most useful and practical travel tool available today.

Our text is divided into four basic sections in order to present information in the best way on every possible aspect of a vacation to Washington, DC. This organization itself should alert you to the vast and varied opportunities available, as well as indicate all the specific data necessary to plan a successful visit. You won't find much of the conventional "swaying palms and shimmering sand" text here; we've chosen instead to deliver more useful and practical information. Prospective itineraries tend to speak for themselves, and with so many diverse travel opportunities, we feel our main job is to highlight what's where and to provide basic information — how, when, where, how much, and what's best — to assist you in making the most intelligent choices possible.

Here is a brief summary of the four basic sections of this book, and what you can expect to find in each. We believe that you will find both your travel planning and en route enjoyment enhanced by having this book at your side.

GETTING READY TO GO

This mini-encyclopedia of practical travel facts is a sort of know-it-all companion with all the precise information necessary to create a successful trip to Washington, DC. There are entries on about two dozen separate topics, including how to get where you're going, what preparations to make before leaving, what to expect, what your trip is likely to cost, and how to avoid prospective problems. The individual entries are specific, realistic, and where appropriate, cost-oriented.

We expect you to use this section most in the course of planning your trip, for its ideas and suggestions are intended to simplify this often confusing period. Entries are intentionally concise, in an effort to get to the meat of the matter with the least extraneous prose. These entries are augmented by extensive lists of specific sources from which to obtain even more specialized data, plus some suggestions for obtaining travel information on your own.

THE CITY

The individual report on Washington, DC, has been created with the assistance of researchers, contributors, professional journalists, and experts who live in the city. Although useful at the planning stage, THE CITY is really designed to be taken along and used on the spot. The reports offer a short-stay guide, including an essay introducing the city as a historic entity and as a contemporary place to visit. *At-a-Glance* material is actually a site-by-site survey of the most important, interesting, and sometimes most eclectic sights to see, and things to do. *Sources and Resources* is a concise listing of pertinent tourist information meant to answer myriad potentially pressing questions as they arise — from simple things such as the address of the local tourism office, how to get around, which sightseeing tours to take, and when special events occur to something more difficult, like where to find the best nightspot or hail a taxi, which are the chic places to shop, and where the best museums and theaters are to be found. *Best in Town* lists our collection of cost-and-quality choices of the best places to eat and sleep on a variety of budgets.

DIVERSIONS

This section is designed to help travelers find the best places in which to engage in a wide range of physical and cerebral activities, without having to wade through endless pages of unrelated text. This very selective guide lists the broadest possible range of activities, including all the best places to pursue them.

We start with a list of special places to stay and eat, move to activities that require some perspiration — sports preferences and other rigorous pursuits — and go on to report on a number of more spiritual vacation opportunities. In every case, our suggestions of a particular location — and often our recommendation of a specific hotel — is intended to guide you to that special place where the quality of experience is likely to be highest. Whether you seek a historic hotel or museum or the best place to shop or sail, each category is the equivalent of a comprehensive checklist of the absolute best in Washington, DC.

DIRECTIONS

Here are seven walks that cover the city, along its main thoroughfares and side streets, past its most spectacular landmarks and magnificent parks, and to nearby Old Town Alexandria, Virginia. This is the only section of the book that is organized geographically; itineraries can be "connected" for longer sojourns or used individually for short, intensive explorations.

Although each of the book's sections has a distinct format and a special function, they have all been designed to be used together to provide a complete inventory of travel information. To use this book to full advantage, take a few minutes to read the table of contents and random entries in each section to get a firsthand feel for how it all fits together.

Pick and choose needed information. Assume, for example, that you have always wanted to visit the nation's capital and partake of its spectacular seafood dinners — but you never really knew how to organize it or where to go. Choose specific restaurants from the selections offered in "Eating Out" in THE CITY, add some of those noted in each walking tour in DIRECTIONS, and cross-reference with those in the roundup of the best in the city in the *Capital Dining* section in DIVERSIONS.

In other words, the sections of this book are building blocks designed to help you put together the best possible trip. Use them selectively as a tool, a source of ideas, a reference work for accurate facts, and a guidebook to the best buys, the most exciting sights, the most pleasant accommodations, the tastiest food — *the best travel experience* that you can possibly have.

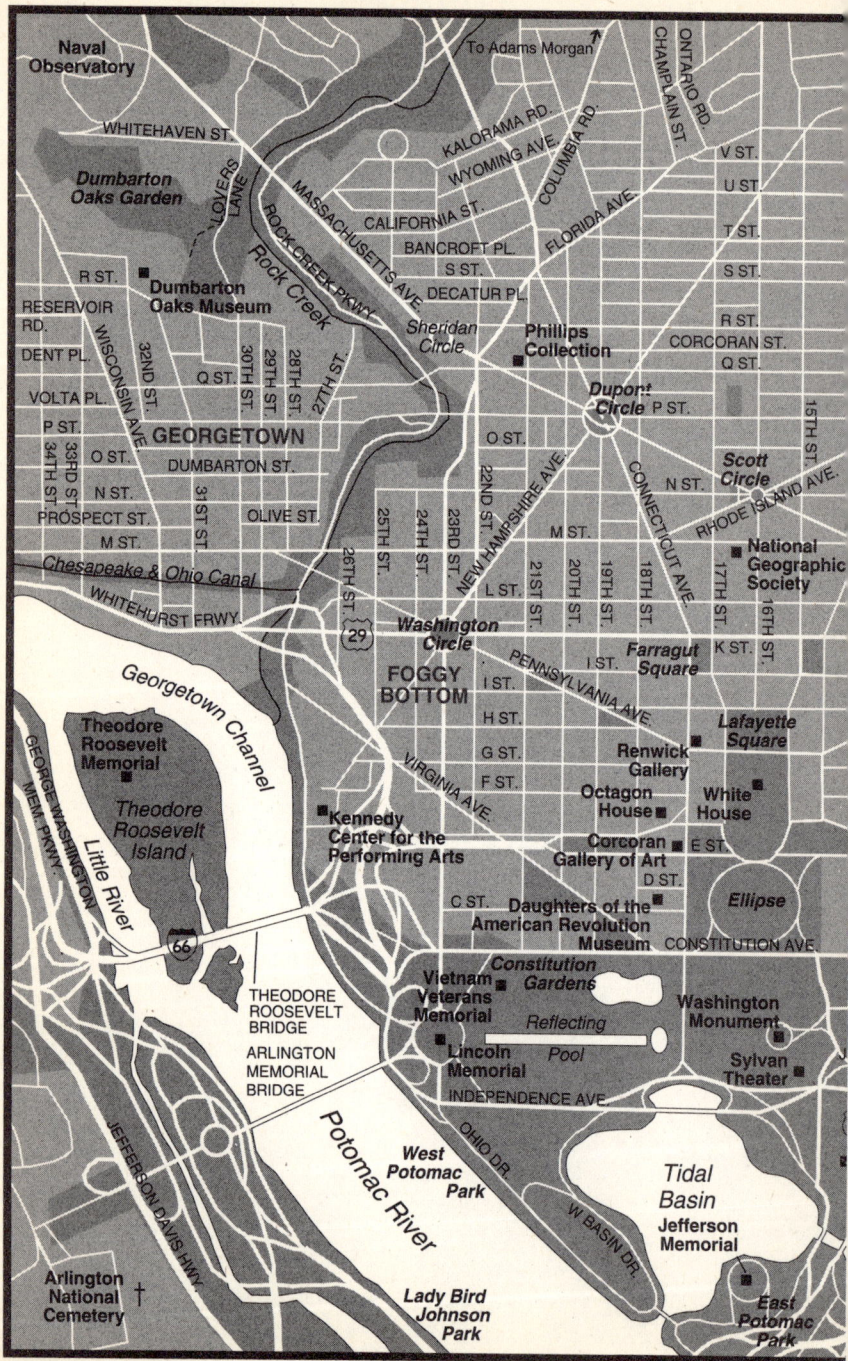

Naval Observatory

WHITEHAVEN ST.

Dumbarton Oaks Garden

LOVERS LANE

ROCK CREEK PKWY

Rock Creek

MASSACHUSETTS AVE.

To Adams Morgan

ONTARIO RD.

CHAMPLAIN ST.

KALORAMA RD.

WYOMING AVE.

COLUMBIA RD.

CALIFORNIA ST.

BANCROFT PL.

S ST.

DECATUR PL.

FLORIDA AVE.

V ST.

U ST.

T ST.

S ST.

R ST.

Dumbarton Oaks Museum

RESERVOIR RD.

DENT PL.

VOLTA PL.

WISCONSIN AVE.

32ND ST.

30TH ST.

29TH ST.

28TH ST.

31ST ST.

Sheridan Circle

Phillips Collection

Dupont Circle   P ST.

CORCORAN ST.

Q ST.

15TH ST.

Scott Circle

GEORGETOWN

DUMBARTON ST.

OLIVE ST.

33RD ST.

34TH ST.

P ST.

O ST.

N ST.

PROSPECT ST.

M ST.

31ST ST.

O ST.

22ND ST.

25TH ST.

24TH ST.

23RD ST.

26TH ST.

NEW HAMPSHIRE AVE.

CONNECTICUT AVE.

N ST.

M ST.

L ST.

21ST ST.

20TH ST.

19TH ST.

18TH ST.

RHODE ISLAND AVE.

17TH ST.

16TH ST.

National Geographic Society

Chesapeake & Ohio Canal

WHITEHURST FRWY.

29

Washington Circle

FOGGY BOTTOM

I ST.

H ST.

G ST.

F ST.

PENNSYLVANIA AVE.

Farragut Square

K ST.

Lafayette Square

Georgetown Channel

Theodore Roosevelt Memorial

GEORGE WASHINGTON MEM. PKWY.

Little River

Theodore Roosevelt Island

VIRGINIA AVE.

Kennedy Center for the Performing Arts

Renwick Gallery

Octagon House

Corcoran Gallery of Art   E ST.

White House

D ST.

66

C ST.

Daughters of the American Revolution Museum

Ellipse

CONSTITUTION AVE.

THEODORE ROOSEVELT BRIDGE

ARLINGTON MEMORIAL BRIDGE

JEFFERSON DAVIS HWY.

Vietnam Veterans Memorial

Constitution Gardens

Reflecting Pool

Washington Monument

Sylvan Theater

Lincoln Memorial

INDEPENDENCE AVE.

OHIO DR.

Arlington National Cemetery

Potomac River

West Potomac Park

W BASIN DR.

Tidal Basin

Jefferson Memorial

Lady Bird Johnson Park

East Potomac Park

Washington, DC

miles 0 — 1/4

N

FLORIDA AVE.
W ST.
V ST.
U ST.
T ST.
S ST.
R ST.
Q ST.

V ST.
U ST.
TODD PL.
T ST.

GEORGIA AVE.

RHODE ISLAND AVE.

VERMONT AVE.

SEATON PL.
S ST.
RANDOLPH PL.
R ST.
QUINCY ST.

Q ST.
BATES ST.
P ST.
O ST.
N ST.

FLORIDA AVE.

NEW YORK AVE.

Logan Circle

P ST.

9TH ST.
8TH ST.
7TH ST.
6TH ST.
5TH ST.
3RD ST.

13TH ST.

Thomas Circle

L ST.
K ST.

Franklin Square

NEW YORK AVE.

12TH ST.

11TH ST.

10TH ST.

Mt. Vernon Square

MASSACHUSETTS AVE.

CHINATOWN

NEW JERSEY AVE.

4TH ST.

1ST ST.

1ST ST.
M ST.
3RD ST.
4TH ST.
5TH ST.
6TH ST.

N CAPITOL ST.

Main Bus Station

L ST.
K ST.
I ST.
H ST.

2ND ST.

G ST.
F ST.
E ST.

National Portrait Gallery
Judiciary Square

National Theater
Peterson House
Ford's Theatre
J. Edgar Hoover Bldg.

PENNSYLVANIA AVE.

395

National Law Enforcement Officers' Memorial

John Marshall Park

Post Office
Union Station

D ST.
C ST.

LOUISIANA AVE.

DELAWARE AVE.

MARYLAND AVE.

Stanton Park

A ST.

National Museum of American History

Old Post Office
National Archives

National Museum of Natural History

National Gallery of Art

CONSTITUTION AVE.

N.W. | **N.E.**

Capitol Building

E CAPITOL ST.

Supreme Court Bldg.

Folger Shakespeare Library

Library of Congress

A ST.

Smithsonian Castle

MADISON DR.

THE MALL

JEFFERSON DR.

Reflecting Pool

National Air & Space Museum

S.W. | **S.E.**

Botanic Gardens

INDEPENDENCE AVE.

NEW JERSEY AVE.

C ST.

Folger Park

NORTH CAROLINA AVE.

SOUTH CAROLINA AVE.

D ST.

Freer Gallery
Arthur M. Sackler Gallery
Bureau of Engraving and Printing

D ST.

Arts & Industries Bldg.
Hirshhorn Museum

Hancock Park

National Museum of African Art

CANAL ST.

4TH ST.

E ST.

E ST.

395

G ST.

S CAPITOL ST.

Garfield Park

G ST.

VIRGINIA AVE.

395

Washington Channel

I ST.

GETTING READY TO GO

When and How to Go

When to Go

There isn't really a best time to visit Washington, DC, although the most popular vacation time traditionally is in the spring and summer. The city enjoys four distinct seasons, with an average temperature in the 80s in the humid summer and high 30s in the winter. Temperatures rarely drop much below freezing. The flowering spring and crisp autumn days are the most comfortable.

There are good reasons for visiting the nation's capital any time of the year. There are no real off-season periods when attractions are closed, so you aren't risking the disappointment of arriving at a sight and finding the gates locked. However, you can benefit from lower room rates if you visit during the late summer, from early August until mid-September, when Congress is in recess and business travel drops.

> ■·Note: When planning the timing of your visit, there is one period during which you must be careful. In the spring (the shortest tourist season), especially during cherry blossom time, hotels are at their most crowded and the majority of bargains disappear. During this period, make your bookings extra early — preferably 2 to 3 months ahead.

WEATHER: Travelers can get current readings and extended forecasts through the *Weather Channel Connection,* the worldwide weather report center of the *Weather Channel,* a cable TV station. By dialing 900-WEATHER and punching in either the first four letters of the city name or the area code (WASH or 202 for the capital) for over 600 cities in the US (including Puerto Rico and the US Virgin Islands), an up-to-date recording will provide such information as current temperature, barometric pressure, relative humidity, and wind speed, as well as a general 2-day forecast. Beach, boating, and highway reports are also provided for some locations. This 24-hour service can be accessed from any touch-tone phone in the US, and costs 95¢ per minute. The charge will show up on your phone bill. For additional information, write to the *Weather Channel Connection,* 2600 Cumberland Pkwy., Atlanta, GA 30339 (phone: 404-434-6800).

CULTURAL EVENTS: Much of the city's cultural life revolves around performances at the *Kennedy Center,* with the *National Symphony Orchestra*'s season there from September through June, the *Washington Opera*'s seven operas from November through March, the *Mostly Mozart Festival Concerts* in June, and various other performances throughout the year. The *Juilliard String Quartet* and other notable ensembles perform chamber music at the *Library of Congress Auditorium* in the spring and fall. During the summer there's music under the stars at *Wolf Trap Farm Park* and free concerts by the service bands in front of the Capitol or the Jefferson Memorial.

The city is also rich in theater, from the *Kennedy Center*'s 5 stages to *The National Theater,* the nation's third oldest still in operation, which features Broadway shows and tryouts as well as local premieres. The *Arena Stage* repertory company, the *Shakespeare*

Theater at the Folger, and a number of dinner-theaters provide evenings of theatrical pleasure. *Shear Madness,* an audience-participation whodunit comedy, is in its 6th year at the *Kennedy Center* and well on its way to becoming a local institution.

The museum roster is headed by the *Smithsonian Institution*'s 14 constituent parts (including the *National Air and Space Museum*), and the *National Gallery of Art.* Some of the other stars are the *Historical Society of Washington, DC, Hillwood, National Building Museum, National Museum of Women in the Arts,* and the *Phillips Collection.*

FESTIVALS: The year starts out with the quadrennial presidential festivities surrounding the inaugural on January 20. The *Cherry Blossom Festival* in early April is highlighted with a parade, a marathon, concerts, a Japanese lantern-lighting ceremony, a ball, and fireworks. The same month sees *White House Spring Garden Tours* and the *White House Easter Egg Roll* on Easter Monday for children under 8 accompanied by an adult. Other house, garden, and embassy tours are given in April and May, allowing entrance to some of Washington's most elegant interiors. For information on the tours, see the Weekend section in Friday's *Washington Post.* The *Twilight Tattoo* of military pageantry takes place in late July and August. The *Smithsonian* sponsors a *Festival of American Folklife* on the Mall in late June and early July. And, of course, the *Independence Day* celebrations in the capital are among the best in the country, with a parade, concerts, fireworks, and other entertainment. *Adams Morgan Day,* a neighborhood festival celebrating such diverse cultures as Spanish, Ethiopian, and central African, takes place in early September. There are more *White House Garden Tours* in October. The city is especially festive at *Christmas,* when special music programs are presented at the *Kennedy Center* and at many other spots around town.

Traveling by Plane

Flying is the quickest, most convenient means of travel between different parts of the country. It *sounds* expensive to travel across the US by air, but when all costs are taken into account for traveling any substantial distance, plane travel usually is less expensive per mile than traveling by car. It also is the most economical way to go in terms of time. Although touring by car, bus, or train certainly is a more scenic way to travel, air travel is far faster and more direct — and the less time spent in transit, the more time spent in Washington.

SCHEDULED FLIGHTS: Numerous airlines offer regularly scheduled flights to the capital's three airports: Washington National (DCA), 3 miles south of the city, handles only domestic air traffic, while Washington Dulles International (IAD), 22 miles west, and Baltimore-Washington International (BWI), 32 miles to the northeast, deal with both domestic and international flights.

Listed below are the major national air carriers serving Washington's airports and their toll-free telephone numbers:

American (serves all three area airports): 800-433-7300.

America West (DCA, BWI): 800-247-5692.

Continental (serves all three) and *Continental Express* (BWI, IAD): 800-525-0280.

Delta, Delta Shuttle (both serve all three) and *Delta Connection* (DCA): 800-221-1212.

Midwest Express (DCA): 800-452-2022.

Northwest (serves all three) and *NW Airlink* (BWI): 800-225-2525.

TWA (serves all three): 800-221-2000.

United (serves all three) and *United Express* (IAD): 800-241-6522.

USAir and *USAir Express* (both serve all three); *USAir Shuttle* (DCA): 800-428-4322.

Among the international carriers that serve Washington are *Aeroflot, Air France, British Airways, Icelandair, Japan Airlines, KLM,* and *Lufthansa.*

Tickets – When traveling on regularly scheduled flights, a full-fare ticket provides maximum travel flexibility. There are no advance booking or other ticketing requirements — except seat availability — although cancellation restrictions vary. It pays to check *before* booking your flight. It also is advisable to reserve well in advance during popular vacation periods and around holiday times.

Fares – Full-fare tickets are followed by a wide variety of discount fares, which even experts find hard to keep current. With these fares, the less you pay for your ticket, the more restrictions and qualifications are likely to be attached to the ticket purchase, including the months (and the days of the week) during which you must travel, how far in advance you must purchase your ticket, the minimum and maximum amount of time you may or must remain away, and your willingness to decide and stick with a return date at the time of booking. It is not uncommon for passengers sitting side by side on the same plane to have paid fares varying by hundreds of dollars.

In general, domestic airfares break down to four basic categories — first class, business class, coach (also called economy or tourist class), and excursion or discount fares. In addition, Advance Purchase Excursion (APEX) fares offer savings under certain conditions.

A **first class** ticket admits you to the special section of the aircraft with larger seats, more legroom, better (or more elaborately served) food, free drinks, free headsets for movies and music channels, and above all, personal attention. First class fares cost about twice those of full-fare (often called "regular") economy.

Behind first class often lies **business class**, usually a separate cabin or cabins. While standards of comfort and service are not as high as in first class, they represent a considerable improvement over conditions in the rear of the plane, with roomier seats, more leg and shoulder space between passengers, and fewer seats abreast. Free liquor and headsets, a choice of meal entrées, and a separate counter for speedier check-in are other inducements. Note that airlines often have their own names for their business class service — such as Ambassador Class on *TWA* and Medallion Class on *Delta.*

The terms of the **coach** or **economy** fare may vary slightly from airline to airline, and in fact from time to time airlines may be selling more than one type of economy fare. Coach or economy passengers sit more snugly, as many as 10 in a single row on a wide-body jet, behind the first class and business class sections. Normally, alcoholic drinks are not free, nor are the headsets.

In first, business class, and regular economy, passengers are entitled to reserve seats and are sold tickets on an open reservation system. They may travel on any scheduled flight they wish, buy a one-way or round-trip ticket, and have the ticket remain valid for a year. There are no requirements for a minimum or maximum stay or for advance booking and (often) no cancellation penalties — but beware, the rules regarding cancellation vary from carrier to carrier. The fare also allows free stopover privileges, although these can be limited in economy.

Excursion and other **discount** fares are the airlines' equivalent of a special sale and usually apply to round-trip bookings only. These fares generally differ according to the season and the number of travel days permitted. They are only a bit less flexible than full-fare economy tickets, and are, therefore, often useful for both business and holiday travelers. Most round-trip excursion tickets include strict minimum and maximum stay requirements and can be changed only within the specified time limits. So don't count on extending a ticket beyond the specified time of return or staying less time than required. Different airlines may have different regulations concerning the number of stopovers permitted, and sometime excursion fares are less expensive during midweek. The availability of these reduced-rate seats is most limited at busy times such as holidays. Discount or excursion fare ticket holders sit with the coach passengers and, for all intents and purposes, are indistinguishable from them. They receive all the same basic services, even though they may have paid anywhere between 30% and 55% less for the trip. Obviously, it's wise to make plans early enough to qualify for this less expensive transportation if possible.

These discount or excursion fares may masquerade under a variety of names and invariably have strings attached. A common requirement is that the ticket be purchased a certain number of days — usually between 7 and 21 days — in advance of departure, though it may be booked weeks or months in advance (it has to be "ticketed," or paid for, shortly after booking, however). The return reservation usually has to be made at the time of the original ticketing and often cannot be changed later than a certain number of days (again, usually 7 and 21 days) before the return flight. If events force a change in the return reservation after the date allowed, the passenger may have to pay the difference between the round-trip excursion rate and the round-trip coach rate, although some carriers permit such scheduling changes for a nominal fee. In addition, some airlines may allow passengers to use their discounted fares by standing by for an empty seat, even if the carrier doesn't otherwise have standby fares. Another common condition is the minimum and maximum stay requirement; for example, 1 to 6 days or 6 to 14 days (but including at least a Saturday night). Last, cancellation penalties of up to 50% of the full price of the ticket have been assessed — if a refund is offered at all — so check the specific penalty in effect when you purchase your discount/ excursion ticket.

On some airlines, the ticket bearing the lowest price of all the current discount fares is the ticket where no change at all in departure and/or return flights is permitted, and where the ticket price is totally nonrefundable. If you do buy such a nonrefundable ticket, you should be aware of a policy followed by some airlines that may make it easier to change your plans if necessary. For a fee — set by each airline and payable at the airport when checking in — you may be able to change the time or date of a return flight on a nonrefundable ticket. However, if the nonrefundable ticket price for the replacement flight is higher than that of the original (as often is the case when trading in a weekday for a weekend flight), you also will have to pay the difference. Any such change must be made a certain number of days in advance — in some cases as little as 2 days — of either the original or the replacement flight, whichever is earlier; restrictions are set by the individual carrier. (Travelers holding a nonrefundable or other restricted ticket who must change their plans due to a family emergency should know that some carriers may make special allowances in such situations.)

■ **Note:** Due to recent changes in many US airlines' policies, nonrefundable tickets are now available that carry none of the above restrictions. Although passengers still may *not* be able to obtain a refund for the price paid, the time or date of a departing or return flight may be changed at any time (assuming seats are available) for a nominal service charge.

There also is a newer, often less expensive, type of excursion fare, the **APEX**, or **Advanced Purchase Excursion** fare. As with traditional excursion fares, passengers paying an APEX fare sit with and receive the same basic services as any other coach or economy passengers, even though they may have paid 50% less for their seats. In return, they are subject to certain restrictions. In the case of domestic flights, the ticket usually is good for a minimum of 1 to 3 days away (including a Saturday) and a maximum, currently, of 1 to 6 months (depending on the airline and the destination); and as its name implies, it must be "ticketed," or paid for in its entirety, a certain period of time before departure — usually 21 days.

The drawback to APEX fares is that they penalize travelers who change their minds — and travel plans. Usually the return reservation must be made at the time of the original ticketing, and if for some reason you change your schedule, you will have to pay a penalty of $100 or 10% of the ticket value, whichever is greater, as long as you travel within the valid period of your ticket. More flexible APEX fares recently have been introduced which allow travelers to make changes in the date or time of their flights for a nominal charge (as low as $25).

With either type of APEX fare, if you change your return to a date less than the minimum stay or more than the maximum stay, the difference between the round-trip APEX fare and the full round-trip coach rate will have to be paid. There also is a penalty of anywhere from $50 to $100 or more for canceling or changing a reservation *before* travel begins — check the specific penalty in effect when you purchase your ticket.

In addition, most airlines offer package deals that may include a car rental, accommodations, and dining and/or sightseeing features along with the basic airfare, and the combined cost of packaged elements usually is considerably less than the cost of the exact same elements when purchased separately.

When you're satisfied that you've found the lowest price for which you can conveniently qualify, make your booking. You may have to call the airline more than once, because different airline reservations clerks have been known to quote different prices, and different fares will be available at different times for the same flight because of a relatively new computerized airline practice called yield management, which adds or subtracts low-fare seats to a given flight depending on how well it is selling.

To protect yourself against fare increases, purchase and pay for your ticket as soon as possible after you've received a confirmed reservation. Airlines generally will honor their tickets, even if the price at the time of your flight is higher than the price you paid. If fares go up between the time you reserve a flight and the time you pay for it, however, you likely will be out of luck. Finally, with excursion or discount fares, it is important to remember that when a reservations clerk says that you must purchase a ticket by a specific date, this is an absolute deadline. Miss the deadline and the airline usually will automatically cancel your reservation without telling you.

Frequent Flyers – Most of the leading carriers serving Washington, DC — including *American, Delta, Northwest, United,* and *USAir* — offer a bonus system to frequent travelers. After the first 10,000 miles, for example, a passenger might be eligible for a first class seat for the coach fare; after another 10,000 miles, he or she might receive a discount on his or her next ticket purchase. The value of the bonuses continues to increase as more miles are logged.

Bonus miles also may be earned by patronizing affiliated car rental companies or hotel chains, or by using one of the credit cards that now offers this reward. In deciding whether to accept such a credit card from one of the issuing organizations that tempt you with frequent flyer mileage bonuses on a specific airline, first determine whether the interest rate charged on the unpaid balance is the same as (or less than) possible alternate credit cards, and whether the annual "membership" fee also is equal or lower. If these charges are slightly higher than those of competing cards, weigh the difference against the potential value in airfare savings. Also ask about any bonus miles awarded just for signing up — 1,000 is common, 5,000 generally the maximum.

For the most up-to-date information on frequent flyer bonus options, you may want to send for the monthly *Frequent* newsletter. Issued by Frequent Publications, it provides current information about frequent flyer plans in general, as well as specific data about promotions, awards, and combination deals to help you keep track of the profusion — and confusion — of current and upcoming availabilities. For a year's subscription, send $33 to Frequent Publications, 4715-C Town Center Dr., Colorado Springs, CO 80916 (phone: 800-333-5937).

There also is a monthly magazine called *Frequent Flyer,* but unlike the newsletter mentioned above, its focus is primarily on newsy articles of interest to business travelers and other frequent flyers. Published by Official Airline Guides (PO Box 58543, Boulder, CO 80322-8543; phone: 800-323-3537), Frequent Flyer is available for $24 for a 1-year subscription.

Low-Fare Airlines – Increasingly, the stimulus for special fares is the appearance of airlines associated with bargain rates. On these airlines, all seats generally sell for the same price, which tends to be somewhat below the lowest discount fare offered by the larger, more established airlines. It is important to note that tickets offered by these smaller companies frequently are not subject to the same restrictions as some of the discounted fares offered by the more established carriers. They may not require advance purchase or minimum and maximum stays, may involve no cancellation penalties, and may be available one way or round trip. A disadvantage to some low-fare airlines, however, is that when something goes wrong, such as delayed baggage or a flight cancellation due to equipment breakdown, their smaller fleets and fewer flights mean that passengers may have to wait longer for a solution than they would on one of the equipment-rich major carriers.

Taxes and Other Fees – Travelers who have shopped for the best possible flight at the lowest possible price should be warned that a number of extras will be added to that price and collected by the airline or travel agent who issues the ticket. The 10% federal US Transportation Tax applies to travel within the US or US territories. Another fee is charged by some airlines to cover more stringent security procedures, prompted by recent terrorist incidents. Note that these taxes usually (but not always) are included in advertised fares and in the prices quoted by airlines reservations clerks.

Reservations – For those who don't have the time or patience to investigate personally all possible air departures and connections for a proposed trip, a travel agent can be of inestimable help. A good agent should have all the information on which flights go where and when, and which categories of tickets are available on each. Most have computerized reservation links with the major carriers, so that a seat can be reserved and confirmed in minutes. An increasing number of agents also possess fare-comparison computer programs, so they often are very reliable sources of detailed competitive price data. (For more information, see *How to Use a Travel Agent,* in this section.)

If making plane reservations through a travel agent, ask the agent to give the airline your home phone number, as well as your daytime business phone number. All too often the agent uses his or her agency's number as the official contact for changes in flight plans. Especially during the winter, weather conditions hundreds or even thousands of miles away can wreak havoc with flight schedules. The airlines are fairly reliable about getting this sort of information to passengers if they can reach them; diligence does little good at 10 PM if the airline has only the agency's or an office number.

Reconfirmation is not generally required on domestic flights. However, it always is wise to call ahead to make sure that the airline did not slip up in entering your original reservation, or in registering any changes you may have made since, and that it has your seat reservation and/or special meal request in the computer.

If you plan not to take a flight on which you hold a confirmed reservation, by all means inform the airline. Because the problem of "no-shows" is a constant expense for airlines, they are allowed to overbook flights, a practice that often contributes to the threat of denied boarding for a certain number of passengers (see "Getting Bumped," below).

Seating – For most types of tickets, airline seats usually are assigned on a first-come, first-served basis at check-in, although some airlines make it possible to reserve a seat at the time of ticket purchase. Always check in early for your flight, even with advance seat assignments. A good rule of thumb for domestic flights is to arrive at the airport at least 1 hour before the scheduled departure to give yourself plenty of time in case there are long lines.

Most airlines furnish seating charts, which make choosing a seat much easier, but there are a few basics to consider. You must decide whether you prefer a window, aisle, or middle seat. On those few domestic flights where smoking is permitted (see "Smoking," below), you also should indicate if you prefer the smoking or nonsmoking section.

The amount of legroom provided (as well as chest room, especially when the seat in front of you is in a reclining position) is determined by something called "pitch," a measure of the distance between the back of the seat in front of you and the front of the back of your seat. The amount of pitch is a matter of airline policy, not the type of plane you fly. First class and business class seats have the greatest pitch, a fact that figures prominently in airline advertising. In economy class or coach, the standard pitch ranges from 33 to as little as 31 inches — downright cramped.

The number of seats abreast, another factor determining comfort, depends on a combination of airline policy and airplane dimensions. First class and business class have the fewest seats per row. Economy generally has 9 seats per row on a DC-10 or an L-1011, making either one slightly more comfortable than a 747, on which there normally are 10 seats per row. A 727 has 6 seats per row.

Airline representatives claim that most craft are more stable toward the front and midsections, while the seats farthest from the engines are quietest. Passengers who have long legs and are traveling on a wide-body aircraft might request a seat directly behind a door or emergency exit, since these seats often have greater than average pitch, or a seat in the first row of a given section, which offers extra legroom — although these seats are increasingly being reserved for passengers who are willing (and able) to perform certain tasks in the event of emergency evacuation. It often is impossible, however, to see the movie from seats that are directly behind the plane's exits. Be aware that the first row of the economy section (called a "bulkhead" seat) on a conventional aircraft (not a widebody) does not offer extra legroom, since the fixed partition will not permit passengers to slide their feet under it, and that watching a movie from this first-row seat also can be difficult and uncomfortable. These bulkhead seats do, however, provide ample room to use a bassinet or safety seat and often are reserved for families traveling with small children.

A window seat protects you from aisle traffic and clumsy serving carts and also provides a view, while an aisle seat enables you to get up and stretch your legs without disturbing your fellow travelers. Middle seats are the least desirable, and seats in the last row are the worst of all, since they seldom recline fully. If you wish to avoid children on your flight or if you find that you are sitting in an especially noisy section, you usually are free to move to any unoccupied seat — if there is one.

If you are large, you may face the prospect of a long flight with special trepidation. Center seats in the alignments of wide-body 747s, L-1011s, and DC-10s are about 1½ inches wider than those on either side, so larger travelers tend to be more comfortable there.

Despite all these rules of thumb, finding out which specific rows are near emergency exits or at the front of a wide-body cabin can be difficult because seating arrangements on any two same-model planes usually vary from airline to airline. There is, however, a quarterly publication called the *Airline Seating Guide* that publishes seating charts for most major US airlines and many foreign carriers as well. Your travel agent should have a copy, or you can buy the US edition for $39.95 per year. Order from Carlson Publishing Co., PO Box 888, Los Alamitos, CA 90720 (phone: 800-728-4877 or 310-493-4877).

Simply reserving an airline seat in advance, however, actually may guarantee very little. Most airlines require that passengers arrive at the departure gate at least 45 minutes (sometimes more) ahead of time to hold a seat reservation. It pays to read the fine print on your ticket carefully and follow its requirements.

A far better strategy is to visit an airline ticket office (or one of a select group of travel agents) to secure an actual boarding pass for your specific flight. Once this has been issued, airline computers show you as checked in, and you effectively own the seat you have selected (although some carriers may not honor boarding passes of passengers arriving at the gate less than 10 minutes before departure). This also is good — but not foolproof — insurance against getting bumped from an overbooked flight and is, therefore, an especially valuable tactic at peak travel times.

Smoking – One decision regarding choosing a seat has been taken out of the hands of most domestic travelers who smoke. Effective February 25, 1990, the US government imposed a ban that prohibits smoking on all flights scheduled for 6 hours or less within the US and its territories. The new regulation applies to both domestic and international carriers serving these routes.

Only flights with a *continuous* flying time of over 6 hours between stops in the US or its territories are exempt. Even if the total flying time is longer, smoking is not permitted on segments of domestic flights where the time between US landings is under 6 hours — for instance, flights that include a stopover (even with no change of plane), or connecting flights. To further complicate the situation, several individual carriers ban smoking altogether on certain routes.

On those flights that do permit smoking, the US Department of Transportation has determined that nonsmoking sections must be enlarged to accommodate all passengers who wish to sit in one. The airline does not, however, have to shift seating to accommodate nonsmokers who arrive late for a flight or travelers flying standby. Cigar and pipe smoking are prohibited on all flights, even in the smoking sections.

For a wallet-size guide that notes in detail the rights of nonsmokers according to these regulations, send a self-addressed, stamped envelope to ASH (Action on Smoking and Health), Airline Card, 2013 H St. NW, Washington, DC 20006 (phone: 202-659-4310).

Meals – If you have specific dietary requirements, be sure to let the airline know well before departure time. The available meals include vegetarian, seafood, kosher, Muslim, Hindu, high-protein, low-calorie, low-cholesterol, low-fat, low-sodium, diabetic, bland, and children's menus (not all of these may be available on every carrier). There is no extra charge for this option. It usually is necessary to request special meals when you make your reservations — check-in time is too late. It's also wise to reconfirm that your request for a special meal has made its way into the airline's computer — the time to do this is 24 hours before departure. (Note that special meals generally are not available on shorter domestic flights, particularly on small local carriers. If this poses a problem, try to eat before you board, or bring a snack with you.)

Baggage – Though airline baggage allowances vary slightly, in general all passengers are allowed to carry on board, without charge, one piece of luggage that will fit easily under a seat of the plane or in an overhead bin, and whose combined dimensions (length, width, and depth) do not exceed 45 inches. A reasonable amount of reading material, camera equipment, and a handbag also are allowed. In addition, all passengers are allowed to check two bags in the cargo hold: one usually not to exceed 62 inches when length, width, and depth are combined, the other not to exceed 55 inches in combined dimensions. Generally no single bag may weigh more than 70 pounds.

Charges for additional, oversize, or overweight bags usually are made at a flat rate; the actual dollar amount varies from carrier to carrier. If you plan to travel with any special equipment or sporting gear, be sure to check with the airline beforehand. Most have specific procedures for handling such baggage, and you may have to pay for transport regardless of how much other baggage you have checked. Golf clubs and skis may be checked through as luggage (most airlines are accustomed to handling them), but tennis rackets should be carried onto the plane.

To reduce the chances of your luggage going astray, remove all airline tags from previous trips, label each bag inside and out — with your business address, rather than your home address, on the outside, to prevent thieves from knowing whose house might be unguarded. Lock everything and double-check the tag that the airline attaches to make sure that it is correctly coded DCA for Washington National Airport, IAD for Washington Dulles Airport, or BWI for Baltimore-Washington International Airport.

If your bags are not in the baggage claim area after your flight or if they're damaged, report the problem to airline personnel immediately. Keep in mind that policies regarding the specific time limit within which you have to make your claim vary from carrier to carrier. Fill out a report form on your lost or damaged luggage and keep a copy of it and your original baggage claim check. If you must surrender the check to claim a damaged bag, get a receipt for it to prove that you did, indeed, check your baggage on the flight. If luggage is missing, be sure to give the airline your destination and/or the telephone number where you can be reached. Also take the name and number of the person in charge of recovering lost luggage.

Most airlines have emergency funds for passengers stranded away from home without their luggage, but if it turns out that your bags are truly lost and not simply delayed, do not then and there sign any paper indicating you'll accept an offered settlement. Since the airline is responsible for the value of your bags within certain statutory limits ($1,250 per passenger for lost baggage on a US domestic flight), you should take the time to assess the extent of your loss (see *Insurance,* in this section). It's a good idea to keep records indicating the value of the contents of your luggage. A wise alternative is to take a photograph of the most valuable of your packed items just after putting them in your suitcase.

Considering the increased incidence of damage to baggage, now more than ever it's advisable to keep the sales slips that confirm how much you paid for your bags. These are invaluable in establishing the value of damaged luggage, and eliminate any arguments. A better way to protect your precious gear from the luggage-eating conveyers is to try to carry it on board whenever possible.

Getting Bumped – A special air travel problem is the possibility that an airline will accept more reservations (and sell more tickets) than there are seats on a given flight. This is entirely legal and is done to make up for "no-shows," passengers who don't show up for a flight for which they have made reservations and bought tickets. If the airline has oversold the flight and everyone does show up, there simply aren't enough seats. When this happens, the airline is subject to stringent rules designed to protect travelers.

In such cases, the airline first seeks ticket holders willing to give up their seats voluntarily in return for a negotiable sum of money or some other inducement, such as an offer of upgraded seating on the next flight or a voucher for a free trip at some other time. If there are not enough volunteers, the airline may bump passengers against their wishes.

Anyone inconvenienced in this way, however, is entitled to an explanation of the criteria used to determine who does and does not get on the flight, as well as compensation if the resulting delay exceeds certain limits. If the airline can put the bumped passengers on an alternate flight that is scheduled to arrive at their original destination within 1 hour of their originally scheduled arrival time, no compensation is owed. If the delay is more than 1 hour but less than 2 hours on a domestic US flight, they must be paid denied-boarding compensation equivalent to the one-way fare to their destination (but not more than $200). If the delay is more than 2 hours after the original arrival time on a domestic flight, the compensation must be doubled (not more than $400). The airline also may offer bumped travelers a voucher for a free flight instead of the denied-boarding compensation. The passenger may be given the choice of either the money or the voucher, the dollar value of which may be no less than the monetary compensation to which the passenger would be entitled. The voucher is not a substitute for the bumped passenger's original ticket; the airline continues to honor that as well. Keep in mind that the above regulations and policies are for US flights only.

To protect yourself as best you can against getting bumped, arrive at the airport early, allowing plenty of time to check in and get to the gate. If the flight is oversold, ask immediately for the written statement explaining the airline's policy on denied-boarding compensation and its boarding priorities. If the airline refuses to give you this information, or if you feel they have not handled the situation properly, file a complaint with both the airline and the appropriate government agency (see "Consumer Protection," below).

Delays and Cancellations – The above compensation rules also do not apply if the flight is canceled or delayed, or if a smaller aircraft is substituted due to mechanical problems. Each airline has its own policy for assisting passengers whose flights are delayed or canceled or who must wait for another flight because their original one was overbooked. Most airline personnel will make new travel arrangements if necessary. If the delay is longer than 4 hours, the airline may pay for a phone call or telegram, a meal, and in some cases, a hotel room and transportation to it.

■**Caution:** If you are bumped or miss a flight, be sure to ask the airline to notify other airlines on which you have reservations or connecting flights. When your name is taken off the passenger list of your initial flight, the computer usually cancels all of your reservations automatically, unless you take steps to preserve them.

CHARTER FLIGHTS: By booking a block of seats on a specially arranged flight, charter tour operators offer travelers air transportation for a substantial reduction over the full coach or economy fare. These operators may offer air-only charters (selling transportation alone) or charter packages (the flight plus a combination of land arrangements such as accommodations, meals, tours, or car rentals). Charters are especially attractive to people living in smaller cities or out-of-the-way places, because they frequently take off from nearby airports, saving travelers the inconvenience and expense of getting to a major gateway.

From the consumer's standpoint, charters differ from scheduled airlines in two main respects: You generally need to book and pay in advance, and you can't change the itinerary or the departure and return dates once you've booked the flight. In practice, however, these restrictions don't always apply. Today, although most domestic charter flights still require advance reservations, some permit last-minute bookings (when there are unsold seats available), and some even offer seats on a standby basis. Though charters almost always are round trip, and it is unlikely that you would be sold a one-way seat on a round-trip flight, on rare occasions one-way tickets on charters are offered.

Here are things to keep in mind about the charter game:

1. It cannot be repeated often enough that if you are forced to cancel your trip, you can lose much (and possibly all) of your money unless you have cancellation insurance, which is a *must* (see *Insurance,* in this section). Frequently, if the cancellation occurs far enough in advance (often 6 weeks or more), you may forfeit only a $25 or $50 penalty. If you cancel only 2 or 3 weeks before the flight, there may be no refund at all unless you or the operator can provide a substitute passenger.
2. Charter flights may be canceled by the operator up to 10 days before departure for any reason, usually underbooking. Your money is returned in this event, but there may be too little time for you to make new arrangements.

3. Most charters have little of the flexibility of regularly scheduled flights regarding refunds and the changing of flight dates; if you book a return flight, you must be on it or lose your money.

4. Charter operators are permitted to assess a surcharge, if fuel or other costs warrant it, of up to 10% of the airfare up to 10 days before departure.

5. Because of the economics of charter flights, your plane almost always will be full, so you will be crowded, though not necessarily uncomfortable. (There is, however, a new movement among charter airlines to provide flight accommodations that are more comfort-oriented, so this situation may change in the near future.)

To avoid problems, always choose charter flights with care. When you consider a charter, ask your travel agent who runs it and carefully check the company. The Better Business Bureau in the company's home city can report on how many complaints, if any, have been lodged against it in the past. Protect yourself with trip cancellation and interruption insurance, which can help safeguard your investment if you, or a traveling companion, are unable to make the trip and must cancel too late to receive a full refund from the company providing your travel services. (This is advisable whether you're buying a charter flight alone or a tour package for which the airfare is provided by charter or scheduled flight.)

Bookings – If you do fly on a charter, read the contract's fine print carefully and pay particular attention to the following:

Instructions concerning the payment of the deposit and its balance and to whom the check is to be made payable. Ordinarily, checks are made out to an escrow account, which means the charter company can't spend your money until your flight has safely returned. This provides some protection for you. To ensure the safe handling of your money, make out your check to the escrow account, the number of which must appear by law on the brochure, though all too often it is on the back in fine print. Write the details of the charter, including the destination and dates, on the face of the check; on the back, print "For Deposit Only." Your travel agent may prefer that you make out your check to the agency, saying that it will then pay the tour operator the fee minus commission. It is perfectly legal to write the check as we suggest, however, and if your agent objects too vociferously (he or she should trust the tour operator to send the proper commission), consider taking your business elsewhere. If you don't make your check out to the escrow account, you lose the protection of that escrow should the trip be canceled. Furthermore, recent bankruptcies in the travel industry have served to point out that even the protection of escrow may not be enough to safeguard a traveler's investment. More and more, insurance is becoming a necessity. The charter company should be bonded (usually by an insurance company), and if you want to file a claim against it, the claim should be sent to the bonding agent. The contract will set a time limit within which a claim must be filed.

Specific stipulations and penalties for cancellations. Most charters allow you to cancel up to 45 days in advance without major penalty, but some cancellation dates are 50 to 60 days before departure.

Stipulations regarding cancellation and major changes made by the charterer. US rules say that charter flights may not be canceled within 10 days of departure except when circumstances — such as natural disasters or political upheavals — make it physically impossible to fly. Charterers may make "major changes," however, such as in the date or place of departure or return, but you are entitled to cancel and receive a full refund if you don't wish to accept these changes. A price increase of more than 10% at any time up to 10 days before departure is considered a major change; no price increase at all is allowed during the last 10 days immediately before departure.

At the time of this writing, the following companies regularly offered charter flights within the US. As indicated, some of these companies sell charter flights directly to clients, while others are wholesalers and must be contacted through a travel agent.

Amber Tours (7337 W. Washington St., Indianapolis, IN 46251; phone: 800-225-9920). Retails to the general public.

Apple Vacations East (7 Campus Blvd., Newtown Sq., PA 19073; phone: 800-727-3400). This agency is a wholesaler, so use a travel agent.

Funway Holiday/Funjet, Inc. (PO Box 1460, Milwaukee, WI 53201-1460; phone: 800-558-3050). This agency is a wholesaler, so use a travel agent.

MLT Vacations (5130 Hwy. 101, Minnetonka, MN 55345; phone: 800-328-0025). This agency is a wholesaler, so use a travel agent.

Morris Air Service (260 E. Morris Ave., Salt Lake City, UT 84115-3200; phone: 800-444-5660). Retails to the general public.

MTI Vacations (1220 Kensington, Oak Brook, IL 60521; phone: 800-323-7285). This agency is a wholesaler, so use a travel agent.

Suntrips (2350 Paragon Dr., San Jose, CA 95131; phone: 800-SUNTRIP in California; 408-432-0700 elsewhere in the US). Retails to the general public.

Travel Charter (1120 E. Longlake Rd., Detroit, MI 48098; phone: 313-528-3570). This agency is a wholesaler, so use a travel agent.

You also may want to subscribe to the travel newsletter *Jax Fax,* which regularly features a list of charter companies and packagers offering seats on US charter flights. For a year's subscription send a check or money order for $12 to Jax Fax Publications, 397 Post Rd., Darien, CT 06820 (phone: 203-655-8746).

DISCOUNTS ON SCHEDULED FLIGHTS: Promotional fares often are called discount fares because they cost less than what used to be the standard airline fare — full-fare economy. Nevertheless, they cost the traveler the same whether they are bought through a travel agent or directly from the airline. Tickets that cost less if bought from some outlet other than the airline do exist, however. While it is likely that the vast majority of travelers flying within the US in the near future will be doing so on a promotional fare or charter rather than on a "discount" air ticket of this sort, it still is a good idea for cost-conscious consumers to be aware of the latest developments in the budget airfare scene. Note that the following discussion makes clear-cut distinctions among the types of discounts available based on how they reach the consumer; in actual practice, the distinctions are not nearly so precise.

Net Fare Sources – The newest notion for reducing the costs of travel services comes from travel agents who offer individual travelers "net" fares. Defined simply, a net fare is the bare minimum amount at which an airline or tour operator will carry a prospective traveler. It doesn't include the amount that normally would be paid to the travel agent as a commission. Traditionally, such commissions amount to about 10% on domestic fares — not counting significant additions to these commission levels that are paid retroactively when agents sell more than a specific volume of tickets or trips for a single supplier. At press time, at least one travel agency in the US was offering travelers the opportunity to purchase tickets and/or tours for a net price. Instead of earning its income from individual commissions, this agency assesses a fixed fee that may or may not provide a bargain for travelers; it requires a little arithmetic to determine whether to use the services of a net travel agent or those of one who accepts conventional commissions. One of the potential drawbacks of buying from agencies selling travel services at net fares is that some airlines refuse to do business with them, thus possibly limiting your flight options.

Travel Avenue is a fee-based agency that rebates its ordinary agency commission to the customer. They will find the lowest retail fare, then rebate 7% to 10% (depending on the airline) of that price, minus a ticket-writing charge of $10 for domestic flights. The ticket-writing charge is imposed per ticket; if the ticket includes more than eight separate flights, an additional $10 fee is charged. Customers using free flight coupons pay the ticket-writing charge, plus an additional $5 coupon-processing fee.

Travel Avenue will rebate its commissions on all tickets, including heavily discounted fares and senior citizen passes. Available 7 days a week, reservations should be made far enough in advance to allow the tickets to be sent by first class mail, since extra charges accrue for special handling. It's possible to economize further by making your own airline reservation, then asking *Travel Avenue* only to write/issue your ticket. For travelers outside the Chicago area, business may be transacted by phone and purchases charged to a credit card. For information, contact Travel Avenue at 641 W. Lake, Suite 201, Chicago, IL 60606-1012 (phone: 312-876-1116 in Illinois; 800-333-3335 elsewhere in the US).

Consolidators and Bucket Shops – Other vendors of travel services can afford to sell tickets to their customers at an even greater discount because the airline has sold the tickets to them at a substantial discount (usually accomplished by sharply increasing commissions to that vendor), a practice in which many airlines indulge, albeit discreetly, preferring that the general public not know they are undercutting their own "list" prices. Airlines anticipating a slow period on a particular route sometimes sell off a certain portion of their capacity at a very great discount to a wholesaler, or consolidator. The wholesaler sometimes is a charter operator who resells the seats to the public as though they were charter seats, which is why prospective travelers perusing the brochures of charter operators with large programs frequently see a number of flights designated as "scheduled service." As often as not, however, the consolidator, in turn, sells the seats to a travel agency specializing in discounting. Airlines also can sell seats directly to such an agency, which thus acts as its own consolidator. The airline offers the seats either at a net wholesale price, but without the volume-purchase requirement that would be difficult for a modest retail travel agency to fulfill, or at the standard price, but with a commission override large enough (as high as 50%) to allow both a profit and a price reduction to the public.

Travel agencies specializing in discounting sometimes are called "bucket shops," a term fraught with connotations of unreliability in this country. But in today's highly competitive travel marketplace, more and more conventional travel agencies are selling consolidator-supplied tickets, and the old bucket shops' image is becoming respectable. Agencies that specialize in discounted tickets exist in most large cities, and usually can be found by studying the smaller ads in the travel sections of local Sunday newspapers.

Before buying a discounted ticket, whether from a bucket shop or a conventional, full-service travel agency, keep the following considerations in mind: To be in a position to judge how much you'll be saving, first find out the "list" prices of tickets to your destination. Then do some comparison shopping among agencies. Also bear in mind that a ticket that may not differ much in price from one available directly from the airline may, however, allow the circumvention of such things as the advance-purchase requirement. If your plans are less than final, be sure to find out about any other restrictions, such as penalties for canceling a flight or changing a reservation. Most discount tickets are non-endorsable, meaning that they can be used only on the airline that issued them, and they usually are marked "nonrefundable" to prevent their being cashed in for a list-price refund.

A great many bucket shops are small businesses operating on a thin margin, so it's a good idea to check the local Better Business Bureau for any complaints registered against the one with which you're dealing — before parting with any money. If you still do not feel reassured, consider buying discounted tickets only through a conventional travel agency, which can be expected to have found its own reliable source of consolidator tickets — some of the largest consolidators, in fact, sell only to travel agencies.

A few bucket shops require payment in cash or by certified check or money order, but if credit cards are accepted, use that option. Note, however, if buying from a charter operator selling both scheduled and charter flights, that the scheduled seats are not protected by the regulations — including the use of escrow accounts — governing the charter seats. Well-established charter operators, nevertheless, may extend the same protections to their scheduled flights, and when this is the case, consumers should be sure that the payment option selected directs their money into the escrow account.

Listed below are some of the consolidators frequently offering discounted domestic fares:

Bargain Air (655 Deep Valley Dr., Suite 355, Rolling Hills, CA 90274; phone: 800-347-2345 or 213-377-2919).

Maharaja/Travel Consumer Wholesale (34 W. 33rd St., Suite 1014, New York, NY 10001; phone: 212-213-2020 in New York; 800-223-6862 elsewhere in the US).

TFI Tours International (34 W. 37th St., 12th Floor, New York, NY 10001; phone: 212-736-1140 in New York State; 800-825-3834 elsewhere in the US).

25 West Tours (2490 Coral Way, Miami, FL 33145; phone: 305-856-0810 in Florida; 800-252-5052 elsewhere in the US).

Unitravel (1117 N. Warson Rd., St. Louis, MO 63132; phone: 314-569-0900 in Missouri; 800-325-2222 elsewhere in the US).

Check with your travel agent for other sources of consolidator-supplied tickets.

■**Note:** Although rebating and discounting are becoming increasingly common, there is some legal ambiguity concerning them. Strictly speaking, it is legal to discount domestic tickets but not international tickets. On the other hand, the law that prohibits discounting, the Federal Aviation Act of 1958, is consistently ignored these days, in part because consumers benefit from the practice and in part because many illegal arrangements are indistinguishable from legal ones. Since the line separating the two is so fine that even the authorities can't always tell the difference, it is unlikely that most consumers would be able to do so, and in fact it is not illegal to *buy* a discounted ticket. If the issue of legality bothers you, ask the agency whether any ticket you're about to buy would be permissible under the above-mentioned act.

Last-Minute Travel Clubs – Still another way to take advantage of bargain airfares is open to those who have a flexible schedule. A number of organizations, usually set up as last-minute travel clubs and functioning on a membership basis, routinely keep in touch with travel suppliers to help them dispose of unsold inventory at discounts of between 15% and 60%. A great deal of the inventory consists of complete package tours and cruises, but some clubs offer air-only charter seats and, occasionally, seats on scheduled flights.

Members generally pay an annual fee and receive a toll-free hotline telephone number to call for information on imminent trips. In some cases, they also receive periodic mailings with information on bargain travel opportunities for which there is more advance notice. Despite the suggestive names of the clubs providing these services, last-minute travel does not necessarily mean that you cannot make plans until literally the last minute. Trips can be announced as little as a few days or as much as 2 months before departure, but the average is from 1 to 4 weeks' notice.

Among the organizations regularly offering such discounted travel opportunities in the US are the following:

Discount Travel International (Ives Building, 114 Forrest Ave., Suite 205, Narberth, PA 19072; phone: 800-334-9294 or 215-668-7184). Annual fee: $45 per household.

Encore/Short Notice (4501 Forbes Blvd., Lanham, MD 20706; phone: 301-459-8020; 800-638-0930 for customer service). Annual fee: $48 per family for Encore (main discount travel program; discounts on hotels), $36 per family for Short Notice program (discounts on tours and cruises).

Last Minute Travel (1249 Boylston St., Boston, MA 02215; phone: 800-LAST-MIN or 617-267-9800). No fee.

Moment's Notice (425 Madison Ave., New York, NY 10017; phone: 212-486-0503). Annual fee: $45 per family.

Traveler's Advantage (3033 S. Parker Rd., Suite 1000, Aurora, CO 80014; phone: 800-548-1116). Annual fee: $49 per family.

Vacations to Go (2411 Fountain View, Suite 201, Houston, TX 77057; phone: 800-338-4962). Annual fee: $19.95 per family.

Worldwide Discount Travel Club (1674 Meridian Ave., Miami Beach, FL 33139; phone: 305-534-2082). Annual fee: $40 per person; $50 per family.

Generic Air Travel – Organizations that apply the same flexible-schedule idea to air travel only and arrange for flights at literally the last minute also exist. Their service sometimes is known as "generic" air travel, and it operates somewhat like an ordinary airline standby service except that the organizations running it do not guarantee flights to a specific destination, but only to a general region, and offer seats on not one but several scheduled and charter airlines.

One pioneer of generic flights is *Airhitch* (2790 Broadway, Suite 100, New York, NY 10025; phone: 212-864-2000), which has been offering flights between the West Coast and the East Coast with its Calhitch program, now temporarily discontinued. When making travel plans, call to find out if the service has resumed. When Calhitch is operating, prospective travelers stipulate a range of at least 5 consecutive departure dates and their desired destination, along with alternate choices, and pay the fare in advance. They are then sent a voucher good for travel on a space-available basis on flights to their destination region (i.e., not necessarily the specific destination requested) during this time period. The week before this range of departure dates begins, travelers must contact *Airhitch* for specific information about flights on which seats may be available and instructions on how to proceed for check-in. (Return flights are arranged in the same manner as the outbound flights — a specified period of travel is decided upon, and a few days before this date range begins, prospective passengers contact *Airhitch* for details about flights that may be available.) If the client does not accept any of the suggested flights or cancels his or her travel plans after selecting a flight, the amount paid may be applied toward a future fare or the flight arrangements can be transferred to another individual (although, in both cases, an additional fee may be charged). No refunds are offered unless the prospective passenger does not ultimately get on any flight in the specified date range; in such a case, the full fare is refunded. (Note that *Airhitch*'s slightly more expensive Target program, which provides confirmed reservations on specific dates to specific destinations, offers passengers greater — but not guaranteed — certainty regarding destinations and other flight arrangements.) At press time, *Airhitch* did not serve the District of Columbia, but it might be worthwhile to call when planning a trip to see if it has expanded its service.

Bartered Travel Sources – Suppose a hotel buys advertising space in a newspaper. As payment, the hotel gives the publishing company the use of a number of hotel rooms in lieu of cash. This is barter, a common means of exchange among hotels, airlines, car rental companies, cruise lines, tour operators, restaurants, and other travel service companies. When a bartering company finds itself with empty airline seats (or excess hotel rooms, or cruise ship cabin space, and so on) and offers them to the public, considerable savings can be enjoyed.

Bartered travel clubs often can give discounts of up to 50% to members, who pay an annual fee (approximately $50 at press time) which entitles them to select from the flights, cruises, hotel rooms, or other travel services that the club obtained by barter. Members usually present a voucher, club credit card, or scrip (a dollar-denomination voucher negotiable only for the bartered product) to the hotel, which in turn subtracts the dollar amount from the bartering company's account.

Selling bartered travel is a perfectly legitimate means of retailing. One advantage to club members is that they don't have to wait until the last minute to obtain flight or room reservations.

Among the companies specializing in bartered travel, one frequently offers members travel services throughout the US:

Travel Guild (18210 Redmond Way, Redmond, WA 98052; phone: 206-861-1900). Annual fee: $48 per family.

OTHER DISCOUNT TRAVEL SOURCES: An excellent source of information on economical travel opportunities is the *Consumer Reports Travel Letter,* published monthly by Consumers Union. It keeps abreast of the scene on a wide variety of fronts, including package tours, rental cars, insurance, and more, but it is especially helpful for its comprehensive coverage of airfares, offering guidance on all the options, from scheduled flights on major or low-fare airlines to charters and discount sources. For a year's subscription, send $37 ($57 for 2 years) to Consumer Reports Travel Letter (PO Box 53629, Boulder, CO 80322-3629; phone: 800-999-7959). For information on other travel newsletters, see *For More Information,* in this section.

CONSUMER PROTECTION: Consumers who feel that they have not been dealt with fairly by an airline should make their complaints known. Begin with the customer service representative at the airport where the problem occurred. If your complaint cannot be resolved there to your satisfaction, write to the airline's consumer office. In a businesslike, typed letter, explain what reservations you held, what happened, the names of the employees involved, and what you expect the airline to do to remedy the situation. Send copies (never the originals) of the tickets, receipts, and other documents that back your claims. Ideally, all correspondence should be sent via certified mail, return receipt requested. This provides proof that your complaint was received.

Passengers with consumer complaints — lost baggage, compensation for getting bumped, violation of smoking and nonsmoking rules, deceptive practices by an airline — who are not satisfied with the airline's response should contact the Department of Transportation (DOT), Consumer Affairs Division (400 7th St. SW, Room 10405, Washington, DC 20590; phone: 202-366-2220). DOT personnel stress, however, that consumers initially should direct their complaints to the airline that provoked them.

Remember, too, that the federal Fair Credit Billing Act permits purchasers to refuse to pay for credit card charges for services that have not been delivered, so the onus of dealing with the receiver for a bankrupt airline, for example, falls on the credit card company. Do not rely on another airline to honor any ticket you're holding from a failed airline, since the days when virtually all major carriers subscribed to a default protection program that bound them to do so are long gone. Some airlines may voluntarily step forward to accommodate the stranded passengers of a fellow carrier, but this is now an entirely altruistic act.

The deregulation of US airlines has meant that travelers must find out for themselves what they are entitled to receive. The Department of Transportation's informative consumer booklet *Fly Rights* is a good place to start. To receive a copy, send $1 to the Superintendent of Documents (US Government Printing Office, Washington, DC 20402-9325; phone: 202-783-3238). Specify its stock number, 050-000-00513-5, and allow 3 to 4 weeks for delivery.

On Arrival

FROM THE AIRPORT TO THE CITY: Washington is served by three major airports. National is the city's primary facility, and the 20-minute drive to downtown by taxi will cost about $12 one way. The *Washington Flyer* (phone: 703-685-1400 for a tape recording, or 703-892-6800) provides limo service every half hour from National to the Downtown Airports Terminal at 1517 K St. NW and then shuttle bus service to most downtown and Capitol Hill hotels for $7; $12 round trip. The *Metro*'s blue and yellow lines connect downtown with the airport; *Metro Center* (11th and G Sts. NW; phone: 202-637-7000) is the system's main terminal.

Dulles International Airport is about 25 miles west of the city, in Virginia. The ride from Dulles to downtown District of Columbia usually takes about an hour, and cab fare should run about $35. The *Washington Flyer* (see above) leaves Dulles about every half hour for downtown; fare $14 one way, $22 round trip.

Baltimore/Washington International Airport, 28 miles away, also serves the DC area and is a 45-minute trip from downtown by car. Cab fare to the downtown area should run about $40. *The Airport Connection* (phone: 301-441-2345) offers bus service between the airport and the Downtown Airports Terminal at 1517 K St. NW every 90 minutes Sundays through Fridays and every 2½ hours on Saturdays. The fare is $13 one way, $23 round trip. The airport also has a rail station where travelers may board *Amtrak* (phone: 800-872-7245) or *Maryland Commuter* (*Marc;* phone: 800-325-7245) trains for Washington's Union Station.

CAR RENTAL: Unless planning to drive round trip from home, most travelers who want to drive while on vacation simply rent a car. They can rent a car through a travel agent or national rental firm before leaving home, or from a local company once they arrive in Washington. Another possibility, also arranged before departure, is to rent the car as part of a larger travel package.

It's tempting to wait until arrival to scout out the lowest-priced rental from the company located the farthest from the airport high-rent district and offering no pick-up services. But if your arrival coincides with a holiday or a peak travel period, you may be disappointed to find that even the most expensive car in the city was reserved months ago. Whenever possible, it is best to reserve in advance, anywhere from a few days in slack periods to a month or more during the busier seasons.

Often, the easiest place to rent (or at least pick up) the car is at the airport on arrival. The majority of the national car rental companies have locations at the 3 area airports, either in the terminals or reached by shuttle buses from each company that pick up clients and take them to the car rental locations. Travel agents can arrange rentals for clients, but it is just as easy to call and rent a car yourself. Listed below are the nationwide, toll-free telephone numbers of the major national rental companies that have locations in the District of Columbia:

Alamo: 800-327-9633
American International Rent-A-Car: 800-527-0202
Avis: 800-331-1212
Budget Rent-A-Car: 800-527-0700
Dollar Rent A Car: 800-800-4000
Hertz: 800-654-3131
National Car Rental: 800-CAR-RENT
Sears Rent-A-Car: 800-527-0770
Thrifty Rent-A-Car: 800-367-2277

Frequently, less expensive car rentals may be obtained from the lesser-known national and regional chains that in many cases limit their advertising to the yellow pages. These companies often do most of their business in insurance replacement but are happy to accommodate any tourists who come their way. Following is a list of such firms, many with nationwide 800 numbers. For the companies that do not have a nationwide reservations service, the number of the location nearest the airport has been provided, and they will provide details on other locations, if desired.

> *Agency Rent-A-Car:* 800-321-1972, nationwide.
> *Automate Car Rental:* 800-633-2824, nationwide.
> *Enterprise Rent-A-Car:* 800-325-8007, nationwide.
> *Payless Car Rental:* 800-PAYLESS, nationwide.
> *Reserve Rent-A-Car:* 800-346-6556, nationwide.

If you decide to wait until after you arrive, you'll find a number of small companies listed in the local yellow pages. One such company is *EASI Car Rentals,* located at the *Best Western* hotel in Arlington (2480 S. Glebe Rd., Arlington, VA 22206; phone: 703-521-0188). It makes free pick-ups at National Airport.

To economize on a car rental, also consider one of the firms that rent 3- to 5-year-old cars that are well worn but (presumably) mechanically sound; one such company is *Rent-A-Wreck* (615 Hungerford Dr., Rockville, MD; phone: 301-309-6767), whose local office is located 25 miles from both Dulles and National airports (the latter accessible by *Metro*). While the company cannot make airport pick-ups, it might well be worth the taxi ride.

Requirements – Whether you decide to rent a car in advance from a large national rental company or wait to rent from a local company, you should know that renting a car is rarely as simple as signing on the dotted line and roaring off into the night. If you are renting for personal use, you must have a valid driver's license and will have to convince the renting agency that (1) you are personally creditworthy, and (2) you will bring the car back at the stated time. This will be easy if you have a major credit card; most rental companies accept credit cards in lieu of a cash deposit, as well as for payment of your final bill. If you prefer to pay in cash, leave your credit card imprint as a "deposit," then pay your bill in cash when you return the car.

Note that *Avis, Budget, Hertz,* and other national companies usually *will* rent to travelers paying in cash and leaving either a credit card imprint or a substantial amount of cash as a deposit. This is not necessarily standard policy, however, as other national chains and a number of local companies will not rent to an individual who doesn't have a valid credit card. In this case, you will have to call around to find a company that accepts cash.

Also, keep in mind that although the minimum age to drive in most states is 16, the minimum age to rent a car is set by the rental company. (Restrictions vary from company to company, as well as at different locations.) Many firms have a minimum age requirement of 21 years, some raise that to 23 or 25 years, and for some models of cars it rises to 30 years. The upper age limit at many companies is between 69 and 75; others have no upper limit or may make drivers above a certain age subject to special conditions.

Costs – Finding the most economical car rental will require some telephone shopping on your part. As a *general* rule, expect to hear lower prices quoted by the smaller, strictly local companies than by the well-known international names.

Comparison shopping always is advisable, however. Even the international giants offer discount plans whose conditions are easy for most travelers to fulfill. For instance, *Budget* and *National* sometimes offer discounts of anywhere from 10% to 30% off their usual rates (according to the size of the car and the duration of the rental), provided that the car is reserved a certain number of days before departure (usually 7 to 14 days, but it can be less), is rented for a minimum period (5 days or, more often, a week), is paid for at the time of booking, and, in most cases, is returned to the same location that supplied it or to another in the same area. Similar discount plans include *Hertz*'s Leisure Rates and *Avis*'s Supervalue Rates.

If driving short distances for only a day or two, the best deal may be a per-day, per-mile rate: You pay a flat fee for each day you keep the car, plus a per-mile charge. An increasingly common alternative is to be granted a certain number of free miles each day and then be charged on a per-mile basis over that number.

Most companies also offer a flat per-day rate with unlimited free mileage; this certainly is the most economical rate if you plan to drive over 100 miles. Make sure that the low, flat daily rate that catches your eye, however, is indeed a per-day rate: Often the lowest price advertised by a company turns out to be available only with a minimum 3-day rental — fine if you want the car that long, but not the bargain it appears if you really intend to use it no more than 24 hours. Flat weekly rates also are available, as are some flat monthly rates that represent a further saving over the daily rate.

Another factor influencing the cost is the type of car you rent. Rentals are based on a tiered price system, with different sizes of cars — variations of budget, economy, regular, and luxury — often listed as A (the smallest and least expensive) through F, G, or H, and sometimes even higher. Charges may increase by only a few dollars a day through several categories of subcompact and compact cars — where most of the competition is — then increase by great leaps through the remaining classes of full-size and luxury cars and passenger vans. The larger the car, the more it costs to rent and the more gas it consumes, but for some people the greater comfort and extra luggage space of a larger car (in which bags and sporting gear can be safely locked out of sight) may make it worth the additional expense. Also more expensive are sleek sports cars, but again, for some people the thrill of driving such a car — for a week or a day — may be worth it.

Electing to pay for collision damage waiver (CDW) protection will add considerably to the cost of renting a car. (Some companies, such as *Hertz* and *Avis,* now call the option a loss damage waiver, or LDW.) You may be responsible for the full value of the vehicle being rented if it is damaged or stolen, but you can dispense with all of the possible liability by buying the offered waiver at a cost of around $5 to $13 a day. Before making any decisions about optional collision damage waivers, however, check with your own insurance agent and determine whether your personal automobile insurance policy covers rented vehicles; if it does, you probably won't need to pay for the waiver. Be aware, too, that increasing numbers of credit cards automatically provide CDW coverage if the car rental is charged to the appropriate credit card. However, the specific terms of such credit card coverage differ sharply among individual card companies, so check with the credit card company for information on the nature and amount of coverage provided. Business travelers also should be aware that, at the time of this writing, American Express had withdrawn its automatic CDW coverage from some corporate *Green* card accounts and limited the length of coverage — watch for similar cutbacks by other credit card companies.

When inquiring about CDW or LDW coverage and costs, be aware that a number of car rental companies now are automatically including the cost of this waiver in their quoted prices. This does not mean that they are absorbing this cost and you are receiving free coverage — in many cases total rental prices have increased to include the former CDW charge. The disadvantage of this inclusion is that you probably will not have the option to refuse this coverage, and will end up paying the added charge — even if you already are adequately covered by your own insurance policy or through a credit card company.

Another cost to be added to the price tag is drop-off charges or one-way service fees.

The lowest price quoted by any given company may apply only to a car that is returned to the same location from which it was rented. A slightly higher rate may be charged if the car is to be returned to a different location (even within the same city).

Package Tours

If the mere thought of buying a package for your visit to Washington conjures up visions of a trip spent marching in lockstep through the city's attractions with a horde of frazzled fellow travelers, remember that packages have come a long way. For one thing, not all packages necessarily are escorted tours, and the one you buy does not have to include any organized touring at all — nor will it necessarily include traveling companions. If it does, however, you'll find that people of all sorts — many just like yourself — are taking advantage of packages today because they are economical and convenient and save an immense amount of planning time. Given the high cost of travel these days, packages have emerged as a particularly wise buy.

In essence, a package is just an amalgam of travel services that can be purchased in a single transaction. A package (tour or otherwise) may include any or all of the following: round-trip transportation, local transportation (and/or car rentals), accommodations, some or all meals, sightseeing, entertainment, transfers to and from the hotel, taxes, tips, escort service, and a variety of incidental features that might be offered as options at additional cost. In other words, a package can be any combination of travel elements, from a fully escorted tour offered at an all-inclusive price to a simple fly/drive booking that allows you to move about totally on your own. Its principal advantage is that it saves money: The cost of the combined arrangements invariably is well below the price of all of the same elements if bought separately, and, particularly if transportation is provided by discount flight, the whole package could cost less than just a round-trip economy airline ticket on a regularly scheduled flight. A package provides more than economy and convenience: It releases the traveler from having to make individual arrangements for each separate element of a trip.

Tour programs generally can be divided into two categories — "escorted" (or locally hosted) and "independent." An escorted tour means that a guide will accompany the group from the beginning of the tour through to the return flight; a locally hosted tour means that the group will be met upon arrival at each location by a different local host. On independent tours, there generally is a choice of hotels, meal plans, and sightseeing trips, as well as a variety of special excursions. The independent plan is for travelers who do not want a totally set itinerary, but who do prefer confirmed hotel reservations. Whether choosing an escorted or an independent tour, always bring along complete contact information for your tour operator in case a problem arises, although tour operators often have local affiliates who can give additional assistance or make other arrangements on the spot.

To determine whether a package — or more specifically, *which* package — fits your travel plans, start by evaluating your interests and needs, deciding how much and what you want to spend, see, and do. Gather brochures on Washington tours. Be sure that you take the time to read each brochure *carefully* to determine precisely what is included. Keep in mind that they are written to entice you into signing up for a package tour. Often the language is deceptive and devious. For example, a brochure may quote the lowest prices for a package tour based on facilities that are unavailable during the off-season, undesirable at any season, or just plain nonexistent. Information such as "breakfast included" or "plus tax" (which can add up) should be taken into account. Note, too, that the prices quoted in brochures almost always are based on double occupancy: The rate listed is for each of two people sharing a double room, and if you travel alone, the supplement for single accommodations can raise the price considerably (see *Hints for Single Travelers,* in this section).

In this age of erratic airfares, the brochure most often will not include the price of an airline ticket in the price of the package, though sample fares from various gateway cities usually will be listed separately, as extras to be added to the price of the ground arrangements. Before figuring your actual costs, check the latest fares with the airlines, because the samples invariably are out of date by the time you read them. If the brochure gives more than one category of sample fares per gateway city — such as an individual tour-basing fare, a group fare, an excursion, APEX, or other discount ticket — your travel agent or airline tour desk will be able to tell you which one applies to the package you choose, depending on when you travel, how far in advance you book, and other factors. (An individual tour-basing fare is a fare computed as part of a package that includes land arrangements, thereby entitling a carrier to reduce the air portion almost to the absolute minimum. Though it always represents a saving over full-fare coach or economy, lately the individual tour-basing fare has not been as inexpensive as the excursion and other discount fares that also are available to individuals. The group fare usually is the least expensive fare, and it is the tour operator, not you, who makes up the group.) When the brochure does include round-trip transportation in the package price, don't forget to add the cost of round-trip transportation from your home to the departure city to come up with the total cost of the package.

Finally, read the general information regarding terms and conditions and the responsibility clause (usually in fine print at the end of the descriptive literature) to determine the precise elements for which the tour operator is — and is not — liable. Here the tour operator frequently expresses the right to change services or schedules as long as equivalent arrangements are offered. This clause also absolves the operator of responsibility for circumstances beyond human control, such as avalanches, earthquakes, or floods, or injury to you or your property. While reading, ask the following questions:

1. Does the tour include airfare or other transportation, sightseeing, meals, transfers, taxes, baggage handling, tips, or any other services? Do you want all these services?
2. If the brochure indicates that "some meals" are included, does this mean a welcoming and farewell dinner, two breakfasts, or every evening meal?
3. What classes of hotels are offered? If you will be traveling alone, what is the single supplement?
4. Does the tour itinerary or price vary according to the season?
5. Are the prices guaranteed; that is, if costs increase between the time you book and the time you depart, can surcharges unilaterally be added?
6. Do you get a full refund if you cancel? If not, be sure to obtain cancellation insurance.
7. Can the operator cancel if too few people join? At what point?

One of the consumer's biggest problems is finding enough information to judge the reliability of a tour packager, since individual travelers seldom have direct contact with the firm putting the package together. Usually, a retail travel agent is interposed between customer and tour operator, and much depends on his or her candor and cooperation. So ask a number of questions about the tour you are considering. For example:

- Has the travel agent ever used a package provided by this tour operator?
- How long has the tour operator been in business? Check the Better Business Bureau in the area where the tour operator is based to see if any complaints have been filed against it.
- Is the tour operator a member of the *United States Tour Operators Association* (*USTOA;* 211 E. 51st St., Suite 12B, New York, NY 10022; phone: 212-944-

5727)? *USTOA* will provide a list of its members on request; it also offers a useful brochure called *How to Select a Package Tour.*

● How many and which companies are involved in the package?

■ **A word of advice:** Purchasers of vacation packages who feel they're not getting their money's worth are more likely to get a refund if they complain in writing to the operator — and bail out of the whole package immediately. Alert the tour operator to the fact that you are dissatisfied, that you will be leaving for home as soon as transportation can be arranged, and that you expect a refund. They may have forms to fill out detailing your complaint; otherwise, state your case in a letter. Even if difficulty in arranging immediate transportation home detains you, your dated, written complaint should help in procuring a refund from the operator.

SAMPLE PACKAGES TO WASHINGTON, DC: Following is a list of some of the major tour operators that offer packages for our nation's capital. Most companies offer several departure dates, depending on the length of the tour and subject matter. Some operators offer flexible city stays that start with 1 hotel night, with a choice of locations and prices available, to which may be added more nights and a wide variety of options, such as sightseeing, transfers, car rental and, in some cases, dine-around plans. As indicated, some operators are wholesalers only, and will deal only with a travel agent.

Adventure Tours (9818 Liberty Rd., Randallstown, MD 21133; phone: 301-922-7000 in Baltimore; 800-638-9040 elsewhere in the US). Offers flexible city stays, including in Washington. This company is a wholesaler; consult a travel agent.

American Express Travel Related Services (offices throughout the US; phone: 800-241-1700 for information and local branch offices). Offers flexible city stays in Washington as well as independent and escorted tours throughout the US. The tour operator is a wholesaler, so use a travel agent.

Capitol Reservations (1730 Rhode Island Ave. NW, Suite 302, Washington, DC 20036; phone: 800-VISIT-DC or 202-452-1270). Offers year-round discounts at 70 Washington-area hotels.

Capitol Tours (PO Box 4241, Springfield, IL 62708; phone: 217-529-8166). Operates 7-day escorted motorcoach tours from Illinois during cherry blossom time and in June, July, and September.

Collette Tours (162 Middle St., Pawtucket, RI 02860; phone: 800-832-4656 or 800-752-2655 in New England). Has 4-day escorted program.

Corliss Tours (436 W. Foothill Blvd., Monrovia, CA 91016; phone: 818-359-5358). Offers 8-day Stay Put escorted program featuring the city and its environs. This company is a wholesaler, so consult a travel agent.

Dailey-Thorp (315 W. 57th St., New York, NY 10019; phone: 212-307-1555). Luxury tours focusing on opera and other music-related themes.

Dan Dipert Tours (PO Box 580, Arlington, TX 76004-0580; phone: 817-543-3710). Operates 6-day Washington/Williamsburg trip 3 times a year.

Domenico Tours (751 Broadway, PO Box 144, Bayonne, NJ 07002; phone: 800-554-8687, 201-823-8687, or 212-757-8687). Among its many programs are 3- and 4-day Washington Getaways and a 5-day Washington/Williamsburg tour combination.

GoGo Tours (69 Spring St., Ramsey, NJ 07446-0507; call any of the 75 local *GoGo* offices throughout the US; phone: 201-934-3500, to obtain location of nearest local office)). Offers land-only and air-inclusive city packages with sightseeing.

Grandtravel (6900 Wisconsin Ave., Suite 706; Chevy Chase, MD 20815; phone: 800-247-7651 or 301-986-0790). Specializing in tours for grandparents with their grandchildren, this company offers an 8-day program in the city and its environs that appeals to both ages.

Jefferson Tours (1206 Currie Ave., Minneapolis, MN 55403; phone: 800-767-7433 or 612-338-4174). Offers escorted Washington/Williamsburg motorcoach trips for 11 days from Minneapolis and Des Moines.

Maupintour (PO Box 807, Lawrence, KS 66044; phone: 800-255-4266). Offers a 1-week escorted motorcoach Washington-Williamsburg program.

Mayflower Tours (1225 Warren Ave., PO Box 490, Downers Grove, IL 60515; phone: 800-323-7604 outside of Illinois, or 708-960-3430). Operates an 8-day Washington-Williamsburg tour.

New England Vacation Tours (PO Box 560, West Dover, VT 05356; phone: 800-742-7669 or 802-464-2076). Offers 3-night escorted programs.

Panorama Tours (600 N. Sprigg St., Cape Giradeau, MO 63701; phone: 800-962-8687 or 314-335-7824). Operates 10-day Washington-Williamsburg motorcoach tours from Missouri, spring through fall.

SuperCities (Radisson Reservations Center, 11340 Blondo St., Omaha, NE 68164; phone: 800-333-1234). Offers highly flexible mix-and-match city packages. This tour operator is a wholesaler, so use a travel agent.

Travel Tours International (250 W. 49th St., Suite 600, New York, NY 10019; phone: 800-767-8777 or 212-262-0700). Offers air-inclusive and land-only city packages. They are a wholesaler, so contact your travel agent.

Yankee Holidays (20 Spring St., Saugus, MA 01906; phone: 800-225-2550 or 617-231-2884). Offers 2-night packages including sightseeing with extra nights available. This company is a wholesaler, so see your travel agent.

Many of the major air carriers maintain their own tour departments or subsidiaries to stimulate vacation travel to the cities they serve. In all cases, the arrangements may be booked through a travel agent or directly with the company. Air/hotel Washington packages are offered by the following tour operations of airlines serving the city:

American Airlines FlyAAway Vacations (Southern Reservation Center, Mail Drop 1000, Box 619619, Dallas/Ft. Worth Airport, TX 75261-9619; phone: 800-321-2121).

Continental's Grand Destinations (PO Box 1460, Milwaukee, WI 53201-1460; phone: 800-634-5555).

Whether visiting Washington independently or on one of the above city packages, if you would like to include some organized touring, the following tour operators offer 1-day or shorter guided tours of the city:

All About Town (519 6th St. NW, Washington, DC 20001; phone: 202-393-3696). Half-day and full-day tours, as well as a night tour.

Gray Line Sightseeing (Gray Line Terminal, Union Station, 50 Massachusetts Ave. NE, Washington, DC; phone: 202-289-1995). Features a wide variety of sightseeing tours, including a 12-hour excursion from New York on *Amtrak* that features lunch and 4 hours of sightseeing in the capital.

Old Town Trolley Tours of Washington (5225 Kilmer Pl., Hyattsville, MD 20781; phone: 301-985-3021). Offers a 2-hour narrated tour of Washington on trackless trolleys.

The Spirit of Washington (9 Pier 4, 6th & Water Sts. SW, Washington, DC 20024; phone: 202-554-8000 or 202-554-1542). Sightseeing and lunch and dinner cruises, March through December.

Tourmobile Sightseeing (1000 Ohio Dr. SW, Washington, DC 20024; phone: 202-554-7950). Shuttle trams visit 18 historic sights where visitors can get on and off at will, reboarding with their full-day tickets.

■ **Note:** Frequently, the best city packages are offered by the hotels, which are trying to attract guests during the weekends, when business travel drops off, and during other slow periods. These packages are sometimes advertised in local newspapers and sometimes in the Sunday travel sections of major metropolitan papers, such as *The Washington Post* (which is also the local paper) and *The New York Times,* which has a national edition available in most parts of the US. It's worth asking about packages, especially family and special-occasion offerings, when you call to make a hotel reservation. Calling several hotels can garner you a variety of options from which to choose.

Preparing

Calculating Costs

DETERMINING A BUDGET: A realistic appraisal of travel expenses is the most crucial bit of planning before any trip. It also is, unfortunately, one for which it is most difficult to give precise practical advice.

Estimating travel expenses for Washington, DC, depends on the mode of transportation you choose and how long you will stay, as well as the kind of trip you are planning.

When calculating costs, start with the basics, the major expenses being transportation, accommodations, and food. For Washington, that will mean $175 or more a night for a double at an expensive hotel, $100 to $170 for a moderate property, and somewhat under $95 for an inexpensive one. Dinner for two runs to over $75 at an expensive restaurant, $40 to $60 at a moderate one, and under $35 at an inexpensive one. Then there are breakfast and lunch to consider.

Don't forget such extras as local transportation, shopping, and such miscellaneous items as laundry and tips. The reasonable cost of these items often is a positive surprise to your budget. Ask about special discount passes on regular city or local transportation. The *Washington Metropolitan Area Transit Authority (Metro;* phone: 202-637-7000), for example, offers a 2-day Family/Tourist Pass good for unlimited travel on the *Metro* buses and subway for up to 4 persons. The $5 pass is available only at special *Metro* sales offices, the most convenient of which is the Center station at 12th and F Streets NW.

Other expenses, such as the cost of local sightseeing tours and other excursions, should be included. Tourist information offices and most of the better hotels will have someone at the front desk to provide a rundown on the cost of local tours and full-day excursions in and out of the District of Columbia. Travel agents also can provide this information.

In planning any travel budget, it also is wise to allow a realistic amount for both entertainment and recreation. Are you planning to spend time sightseeing and visiting local tourist attractions? Is tennis or golf a part of your plan? Are you traveling with children who want to visit every site? Finally, allow for the extra cost of nightlife, if such is your pleasure. This one item alone can add a great deal to your daily expenditures.

If at any point in the planning process it appears impossible to estimate expenses, consider this suggestion: The easiest way to put a ceiling on the price of all these elements is to buy a package tour with transportation, rooms, meals, sightseeing, local travel, tips, and a dinner show or two included and prepaid. This provides a pretty exact total of what the trip will cost beforehand, and the only surprise will be the one you spring on yourself by succumbing to some irresistible souvenir.

Planning a Trip

Travelers fall into two categories: those who make lists and those who do not. Some people prefer to plot the course of their trip to the finest detail, with contingency plans and alternatives at the ready. For others, the joy of a voyage is its spontaneity; exhaustive planning only lessens the thrill of anticipation and the sense of freedom.

For most travelers, however, a week-plus trip can be too expensive for an "I'll take my chances" attitude. At least some planning is crucial. This is not to suggest that you work out your itinerary in minute detail before you go, but it's still wise to decide certain basics at the very start: where to go, what to do, and how much to spend. These decisions require a certain amount of consideration. So before rigorously planning specific details, you might want to establish your general travel objectives:

1. How much time will you have for the entire trip, and how much of it are you willing to spend getting where you're going?
2. What interests and/or activities do you want to pursue while on vacation?
3. At what time of year do you want to go?
4. Do you want peace and privacy or lots of activity and company?
5. How much money can you afford to spend for the entire vacation?

You now can make almost all of your own travel arrangements if you have time to follow through with hotels, airlines, tour operators, and so on. But you'll probably save considerable time and energy if you have a travel agent make arrangements for you. The agent also should be able to advise you of alternative arrangements of which you may not be aware. Only rarely will a travel agent's services cost a traveler any money, and they may even save you some (see *How to Use a Travel Agent,* below).

Make plans early. During the spring and summer months and holidays, make hotel reservations at least a month in advance. If you are flying at these times and want to benefit from savings offered through discount fares, purchase tickets as far ahead as possible. Many hotels require deposits before they will guarantee reservations, and this most often is the case during peak travel periods. (Be sure to get a receipt for any deposit or, better yet, charge the deposit to a credit card.)

When packing, make a list of any valuable items you are carrying with you, including credit card numbers and the serial numbers of your traveler's checks. Put copies in your purse or pocket, and leave other copies at home. Put a label with your name and home address on the inside of your luggage for identification in case of loss. Put your name and business address — *never your home address* — on a label on the outside of your luggage. (Those who run businesses from home should use the office address of a friend or relative.)

Review your travel documents. If you are traveling by air, check that your ticket has been filled in correctly. The left side of the ticket should have a list of each stop you will make (even if you are stopping only to change planes), beginning with your departure point. Be sure that the list is correct, and count the number of copies to see that you have one for each plane you will take. If you have confirmed reservations, be sure that the column marked "status" says "OK" beside each flight. Have in hand vouchers or proof of payment for any reservation for which you've paid in advance; this includes hotels, transfers to and from the airport, sightseeing tours, car rentals, and tickets to special events.

Although policies vary from carrier to carrier, it's still smart to reconfirm your flight 48 to 72 hours before departure, both going and returning. If you are traveling by car, bring your driver's license, car registration, and proof of insurance, as well as gasoline credit cards and auto service card (if you have them).

Finally, you always should bear in mind that despite the most careful plans, things do not always occur on schedule. If you maintain a flexible attitude and try to accept minor disruptions as less than cataclysmic, you will enjoy yourself a lot more.

How to Use a Travel Agent

T.A. A reliable travel agent remains the best source of service and information for planning a trip, whether you have a specific itinerary and require an agent only to make reservations or you need extensive help in sorting through the maze of airfares, tour offerings, hotel packages, and the scores of other arrangements that may be involved in your trip.

Know what you want from a travel agent so that you can evaluate what you are getting. It is perfectly reasonable to expect your travel agent to be a thoroughly knowledgeable travel specialist, with information about your destination and, even more crucial, a command of current airfares, ground arrangements, and other wrinkles in the travel scene.

Most travel agents work through computer reservations systems (CRS). These are used to assess the availability and cost of flights, hotels, and car rentals, and through them they can book reservations. Despite reports of "computer bias," in which a computer may favor one airline over another, the CRS should provide agents with the entire spectrum of flights available to a given destination and the complete range of fares, in considerably less time than it takes to telephone the airlines individually — and at no extra cost to the client.

Make the most intelligent use of a travel agent's time and expertise; understand the economics of the industry. As a client, traditionally you pay nothing for the agent's services; with few exceptions it's all free, from hotel bookings to advice on package tours. Any money the travel agent makes on the time spent arranging your itinerary — booking hotels, resorts, or flights, or suggesting activities — comes from commissions paid by the suppliers of these services — the airlines, hotels, and so on. These commissions generally run from 10% to 15% of the total cost of the service, although suppliers often reward agencies that sell their services in volume with an increased commission called an override.

A travel agent sometimes may charge a fee for special services. These chargeable items may include long-distance telephone costs incurred in making a booking, for reserving a room in a place that does not pay a commission (such as a small, out-of-the-way hotel), or for a special attention such as planning a highly personalized itinerary. A fee also may be assessed in instances of deeply discounted airfares.

Choose a travel agent with the same care with which you would choose a doctor or lawyer. You will be spending a good deal of money on the basis of the agent's judgment, so you have a right to expect that judgment to be mature, informed, and interested. At the moment, unfortunately, there aren't many standards within the travel agent industry to help you gauge competence, and the quality of individual agents varies enormously.

At present, only nine states have registration, licensing, or other forms of travel agent–related legislation on their books. Rhode Island licenses travel agents; Florida, Hawaii, Iowa, and Ohio register them; and California, Illinois, Oregon, and Washington have laws governing the sale of transportation or related services. While state licensing of agents cannot absolutely guarantee competence, it can at least ensure that an agent has met some minimum requirements.

Perhaps the best-prepared agents are those who have completed the CTC Travel Management program offered by the Institute of Certified Travel Agents (ICTA) and carry the initials CTC (Certified Travel Counselor) after their names. This indicates a relatively high level of expertise. For a free listing of CTCs in your area, send a self-addressed, stamped, #10 envelope to ICTA, 148 Linden St., PO Box 56, Wellesley,

MA 02181 (phone: 617-237-0280 in Massachusetts; 800-542-4282 elsewhere in the US).

An agent's membership in the *American Society of Travel Agents (ASTA)* can be a useful guideline in making a selection. But keep in mind that *ASTA* is an industry organization, requiring only that its members be licensed in those states where required; be accredited to represent the suppliers whose products they sell, including airline and cruise tickets; and adhere to its Principles of Professional Conduct and Ethics code. *ASTA* does not guarantee the competence, ethics, or financial soundness of its members, but it does offer some recourse if you feel you have been dealt with unfairly. Complaints may be registered with *ASTA* (Consumer Affairs Dept., 1101 King St., Alexandria, VA 22314; phone: 703-739-2782). First try to resolve the complaint directly with the supplier. For a list of *ASTA* members in your area, send a self-addressed, stamped, #10 envelope to *ASTA* (Public Relations Dept.) at the address above.

There also is the *Association of Retail Travel Agents (ARTA),* a smaller but highly respected trade organization similar to *ASTA.* Its member agencies and agents similarly agree to abide by a code of ethics, and complaints about a member can be made to *ARTA*'s Grievance Committee, 1745 Jefferson Davis Hwy., Suite 300, Arlington, VA 22202-3402 (phone: 800-969-6069 or 703-553-7777).

Perhaps the best way to find a travel agent is by word of mouth. If the agent (or agency) has done a good job for your friends over a period of time, it probably indicates a certain level of commitment and competence. Always ask for the name of the company *and* for the name of the specific agent with whom your friends dealt, for it is that individual who will serve you, and quality can vary widely within a single agency.

Insurance

It is unfortunate that most decisions to buy travel insurance are impulsive and usually are made without any real consideration of the traveler's existing policies. Therefore, the first person with whom you should discuss travel insurance is your own insurance broker, not a travel agent or the clerk behind the airport insurance counter. You may discover that the insurance you already carry — homeowner's policies and/or accident, health, and life insurance — protects you adequately while you travel and that your real needs are in the more mundane areas of excess value insurance for baggage or trip cancellation insurance.

TYPES OF INSURANCE: To make insurance decisions intelligently, however, you first should understand the basic categories of travel insurance and what they cover. Then you can decide what you should have in the broader context of your personal insurance needs, and you can choose the most economical way of getting the desired protection: through riders on existing policies; with onetime, short-term policies; through a special program put together for the frequent traveler; through coverage that's part of a travel club's benefits; or with a combination policy sold by insurance companies through brokers, automobile clubs, tour operators, and travel agents.

There are seven basic categories of travel insurance:

1. Baggage and personal effects insurance
2. Personal accident and sickness insurance
3. Trip cancellation and interruption insurance
4. Default and/or bankruptcy insurance
5. Flight insurance (to cover injury or death)
6. Automobile insurance (for driving your own or a rented car)
7. Combination policies

Baggage and Personal Effects Insurance – Ask your insurance agent if baggage and personal effects are included in your current homeowner's policy, or if you will need a special floater to cover you for the duration of a trip. The object is to protect your bags and their contents in case of damage or theft anytime during your travels, not just while you're in flight, where only limited protection is provided by the airline. Baggage liability varies from carrier to carrier, but generally speaking, on domestic flights, luggage usually is insured to $1,250 — that's per passenger, not per bag. This limit should be specified on your airline ticket, but to be awarded any amount, you'll have to provide an itemized list of lost property, and if you're including new and/or expensive items, be prepared for a request that you back up your claim with sales receipts or other proof of purchase.

If you are carrying goods worth more than the maximum protection offered by the airlines, consider excess value insurance. Additional coverage is available from airlines at an average, currently, of $1 to $2 per $100 worth of coverage, up to a maximum of $5,000. This insurance can be purchased at the airline counter when you check in, though you should arrive early to fill out the necessary forms and to avoid holding up other passengers.

Major credit card companies provide coverage for lost or delayed baggage — and this coverage often also is over and above what the airline will pay. The basic coverage usually is automatic for all cardholders who use the credit card to purchase tickets, but to qualify for additional coverage, cardholders generally must enroll.

American Express: Provides $500 coverage for checked baggage; $1,250 for carry-on baggage; and $250 for valuables, such as cameras and jewelry.

Carte Blanche and Diners Club: Provide $1,250 free insurance for checked or carry-on baggage that's lost or damaged.

Discover Card: Offers $500 insurance for checked baggage and $1,250 for carry-on baggage — but to qualify for this coverage cardholders first must purchase additional flight insurance (see "Flight Insurance," below).

MasterCard and Visa: Baggage insurance coverage set by the issuing institution.

Additional baggage and personal effects insurance also is included in certain of the combination travel insurance policies discussed below.

■**A note of warning:** Be sure to read the fine print of any excess value insurance policy; there often are specific exclusions, such as cash, tickets, furs, gold and silver objects, art, and antiques. Insurance companies ordinarily will pay only the depreciated value of the goods rather than their replacement value. The best way to protect your property is to take photos of your valuables, and keep a record of the serial numbers of such items as cameras, typewriters, laptop computers, radios, and so on. If an airline loses your luggage, you will be asked to fill out a Property Irregularity Report before you leave the airport. Also report the loss to the police (since the insurance company will check with the police when processing the claim).

Personal Accident and Sickness Insurance – This covers you in case of illness during your trip or death in an accident. Most policies insure you for hospital and doctors' expenses, lost income, and so on. In most cases, it is a standard part of existing health insurance policies (especially where domestic travel is concerned), though you should check with your insurance broker to be sure of the conditions for which your policy will pay. If your coverage is insufficient, take out a separate vacation accident policy or an entire vacation insurance policy that includes health and life coverage.

Trip Cancellation and Interruption Insurance – Most package tour passengers pay for their travel well before departure. The disappointment of having to miss a vacation because of illness or any other reason pales before the awful prospect that not

all (and sometimes none) of the money paid in advance might be returned. So cancellation insurance for any package tour is a must.

Although cancellation penalties vary (they are listed in the fine print of every tour brochure, and before you purchase a package tour you should know exactly what they are), rarely will a passenger get more than 50% of this money back if forced to cancel within a few weeks of scheduled departure. Therefore, if you book a package tour, you should have trip cancellation insurance to guarantee full reimbursement or refund should you, a traveling companion, or a member of your immediate family get sick, forcing you to cancel your trip or return home early.

The key here is *not* to buy just enough insurance to guarantee full reimbursement for the cost of the package in case of cancellation. The proper amount of coverage should include reimbursement for the cost of having to catch up with a tour after its departure or having to travel home at the full economy airfare if you have to forgo the return flight tied to the package. There usually is quite a discrepancy between an excursion or other special airfare and the amount charged to travel the same distance on a regularly scheduled flight at full economy fare.

Trip cancellation insurance is available from travel agents and tour operators in two forms: as part of a short-term, all-purpose travel insurance package (sold by the travel agent); or as specific cancellation insurance designed by the operator for a specific tour. Generally, tour operators' policies are less expensive, but also less inclusive. Cancellation insurance also is available directly from insurance companies or their agents as part of a short-term, all-inclusive travel insurance policy.

Before you decide on a policy, read each one carefully. (Either type can be purchased from a travel agent when you book the package tour.) Be sure to check the fine print for stipulations concerning "family members" and "pre-existing medical conditions," as well as allowances for living expenses if you must delay your return due to injury or illness.

Default and/or Bankruptcy Insurance – Although trip cancellation insurance usually protects you if you are unable to complete — or begin — your trip, a fairly recent innovation is coverage in the event of default and/or bankruptcy on the part of the tour operator, airline, or other travel supplier. In some travel insurance packages, this contingency is included in the trip cancellation portion of the coverage; in others, it is a separate feature. Either way, it is becoming increasingly important. Whereas sophisticated travelers have long known to beware of the possibility of default or bankruptcy when buying a tour package, in recent years more than a few respected airlines have unexpectedly revealed their shaky financial condition, sometimes leaving hordes of stranded ticket holders in their wake. While default/bankruptcy insurance will not ordinarily result in reimbursement in time to pay for new arrangements, it can ensure that you will get your money back, and even independent travelers buying no more than an airplane ticket may want to consider it.

Flight Insurance – US airlines' liability for injury or death to passengers on domestic flights currently is determined on a case-by-case basis in court — this means potentially unlimited liability. But remember, this liability is not the same thing as an insurance policy; every penny that an airline eventually pays in the case of death or injury likely will be subject to a legal battle.

But before you buy last-minute flight insurance from an airport vending machine, consider the purchase in light of your total existing insurance coverage. A careful review of your current policies may reveal that you already are amply covered for accidental death. Be aware that airport insurance, the kind typically bought at a counter or from a vending machine, is among the most expensive forms of life insurance coverage, and that even within a single airport, rates for approximately the same coverage vary widely.

If you buy your plane ticket with a major credit card, you generally receive automatic

insurance coverage at no extra cost. Additional coverage usually can be obtained at extremely reasonable prices, but a cardholder must sign up for it in advance.

Automobile Insurance – If you have an accident in a state that has "no fault" insurance, each party's insurance company pays his or her expenses up to certain specified limits. When you rent a car, the rental company is required to provide you with collision protection.

In your car rental contract, you'll see that for about $10 to $13 a day, you may buy optional collision damage waiver (CDW) protection. Some companies, such as *Hertz* and *Avis,* call the option a loss damage waiver (LDW). (If partial coverage with a deductible is included in the rental contract, the CDW will cover the deductible in the event of an accident, and can cost as much as $25 per day.) If you do not accept the CDW coverage, you may be liable for as much as the full retail value of the rental car if it is damaged or stolen; by paying for the CDW, you are relieved of all responsibility for any damage to the car. Before agreeing to this coverage, however, check with your own broker about your own existing personal automobile insurance policy. It very well may cover your entire liability exposure without any additional cost, or you automatically may be covered by the credit card company to which you are charging the cost of your rental. To find out the amount of rental car insurance provided by major credit cards, contact the issuing institutions.

Combination Policies – Short-term insurance policies, which may include a combination of any or all of the types of insurance discussed above, are available through retail insurance agencies, automobile clubs, and many travel agents. These combination policies are designed to cover you for the duration of a single trip.

The following companies provide such coverage for the insurance needs discussed above:

Access America International: A subsidiary of the Blue Cross/Blue Shield plans of New York and Washington, DC, now available nationwide. Contact *Access America,* PO Box 90310, Richmond, VA 23230 (phone: 800-284-8300 or 804-285-3300).

Carefree: Underwritten by The Hartford. Contact *Carefree Travel Insurance,* Arm Coverage, PO Box 310, Mineola, NY 11501 (phone: 800-645-2424 or 516-294-0220).

NEAR Services: In addition to a full range of travel services, this organization offers a comprehensive travel insurance package. An added feature is coverage for lost or stolen airline tickets. Contact *NEAR Services,* 450 Prairie Ave., Suite 101, Calumet City, IL 60409 (phone: 708-868-6700 in the Chicago area; 800-654-6700 elsewhere in the US and Canada).

Tele-Trip: Underwritten by the Mutual of Omaha Companies. Contact *Tele-Trip Co.,* PO Box 31685, 3201 Farnam St., Omaha, NE 68131 (phone: 402-345-2400 in Nebraska; 800-228-9792 elsewhere in the US).

Travel Assistance International: Provided by Europe Assistance Worldwide Services, and underwritten by Transamerica Occidental Life Insurance Company. Contact *Travel Assistance International,* 1133 15th St. NW, Suite 400, Washington, DC 20005 (phone: 202-331-1609 in Washington, DC; 800-821-2828 elsewhere in the US).

Travel Guard International: Underwritten by the Insurance Company of North America, it is available through authorized travel agents; or contact *Travel Guard International,* 1145 Clark St., Stevens Point, WI 54481 (phone: 715-345-0505 in Wisconsin; 800-826-1300 elsewhere in the US).

Travel Insurance PAK: Underwritten by The Travelers. Contact *The Travelers Companies,* Ticket and Travel Plans, One Tower Sq., Hartford, CT 06183-5040 (phone: 203-277-2319 in Connecticut; 800-243-3174 elsewhere in the US).

Wallach & Co.: This organization offers two health insurance plans as well as other coverage. Contact *Wallach & Co.,* 243 Church St. NW, Suite 100-D, Vienna, VA 22180 (phone: 703-281-9500 in Virginia; 800-237-6615 elsewhere in the US).

Hints for Handicapped Travelers

From 40 to 50 million people in the US alone have some sort of disability, and over half this number are physically handicapped. Like everyone else today, they — and the uncounted disabled millions around the world — are on the move. More than ever before, they are demanding facilities they can use comfortably, and they are being heard. With the 1990 passage of the Americans with Disabilities Act, the physically handicapped increasingly will be finding better access to places and services throughout the US. The provisions of the act relating to public accommodations and transportation, which took effect in January 1992, mandate that means of access be provided except where the cost would be prohibitive, and creative alternatives are being encouraged. As the impact of the law spreads across the country, previous barriers to travel in the US should be somewhat ameliorated.

PLANNING A TRIP: Make your travel arrangements well in advance and specify to services involved the exact nature of your condition or restricted mobility, as your trip will be much more comfortable if you know that there are accommodations and facilities to suit your needs.

One of the best sources of information on facilities for the disabled in Washington, DC, is the Information, Protection and Advocacy Center for Handicapped Individuals (4455 Connecticut Ave. NW, Suite B-100, Washington, DC 20008; phone: 202-966-8081 for voice; 202-966-2500 for TDD — telecommunications device for the deaf). This organization helps disabled visitors in emergencies such replacing missing wheelchair parts or locating short-notice attendants. It also publishes a useful book, *A Guide to Metropolitan Washington for the Physically Disabled,* which costs $6 including shipping and handling and may be obtained by writing the center at the above address.

It is also advisable to call the hotel you are considering and ask specific questions. If you require a corridor of a certain width to maneuver a wheelchair or if you need handles on the bathroom walls for support, ask the manager (many large hotels have rooms especially designed for the handicapped). A travel agent or the local chapter or national office of the organization that deals with your particular disability — for example, the *American Foundation for the Blind* or the *American Heart Association* — will supply the most up-to-date information on the subject.

The following organizations also offer general information on access:

ACCENT on Living (PO Box 700, Bloomington, IL 61702; phone: 309-378-2961). This information service for persons with disabilities provides a free list of travel agencies specializing in arranging trips for the disabled; for a copy send a self-addressed, stamped envelope. It also offers a wide range of publications, including a quarterly magazine ($10 per year; $17.50 for 2 years) for persons with disabilities.

Direct Link (PO Box 1036, Solvang, CA 93463; phone: 805-688-1603). This company provides an on-line computer service and links the disabled and their families with a wide range of information, including accessibility, attendant care, transportation, and travel necessities.

Disabled Individuals Assistance Line (DIAL; 100 W. Randolph St., Suite 8-100, Chicago, IL 60601; 800-233-DIAL; both voice and TDD). This toll-free hotline provides information about public and private resources available to people with disabilities.

Information Center for Individuals with Disabilities (Ft. Point Pl., 1st Floor, 27-43 Wormwood St., Boston, MA 02210; phone: 800-462-5015 in Massachusetts; 617-727-5540/1 elsewhere in the US; both numbers provide voice and TDD). The center offers information and referral services on disability-related issues, publishes fact sheets on travel agents, tour operators, and other travel resources, and can help you research your trip.

Mobility International USA (MIUSA; PO Box 3551, Eugene, OR 97403; phone: 503-343-1284; both voice and TDD). This US branch of *Mobility International* (the main office is at 228 Borough High St., London SE1 1JX, England; phone: 011-44-71-403-5688), a nonprofit British organization with affiliates worldwide, offers members advice and assistance — including information on accommodations and other travel services, and publications applicable to the traveler's disability. *Mobility International* also offers a quarterly newsletter and a comprehensive sourcebook, *A World of Options for the 90s: A Guide to International Education Exchange, Community Service and Travel for Persons with Disabilities* ($14 for members; $16 for non-members). Membership includes the newsletter and is $20 a year; subscription to the newsletter alone is $10 annually.

National Rehabilitation Information Center (8455 Colesville Rd., Suite 935, Silver Spring, MD 20910; phone: 301-588-9284). A general information, resource, research, and referral service.

Paralyzed Veterans of America (PVA; PVA/ATTS Program, 801 18th St. NW, Washington, DC 20006; phone: 202-416-7708 in Washington, DC; 800-424-8200 elsewhere in the US). The members of this national service organization all are veterans who have suffered spinal cord injuries, but it offers advocacy services and information to all persons with a disability. *PVA* also sponsors Access to the Skies (ATTS), a program that coordinates the efforts of the national and international air travel industry in providing airport and airplane access for the disabled. Members receive several helpful publications, as well as regular notification of conferences on subjects of interest to the disabled traveler.

Society for the Advancement of Travel for the Handicapped (SATH; 347 Fifth Ave., Suite 610, New York, NY 10016; phone: 212-447-7284). To keep abreast of developments in travel for the handicapped as they occur, you may want to join *SATH,* a nonprofit organization whose members include consumers, as well as travel service professionals who have experience (or an interest) in travel for the handicapped. For an annual fee of $45 ($25 for students and travelers who are 65 and older), members receive a quarterly newsletter and have access to extensive information and referral services. *SATH* also offers two useful publications: *Travel Tips for the Handicapped* (a series of informative fact sheets) and *The United States Welcomes Handicapped Visitors* (a 48-page guide covering domestic transportation and accommodations, as well as useful hints for travelers with disabilities); to order, send a self-addressed, #10 envelope and $1 per title for postage.

Travel Information Service (Moss Rehabilitation Hospital, 1200 W. Tabor Rd., Philadelphia, PA 19141-3099; phone: 215-456-9600 for voice; 215-456-9602 for TDD). This service assists physically handicapped people in planning trips and supplies detailed information on accessibility, for a nominal fee.

Blind travelers should contact the *American Foundation for the Blind* (15 W. 16th St., New York, NY 10011; phone: 800-829-0500 or 212-620-2147) and *The Seeing Eye* (Box 375, Morristown, NJ 07963-0375; phone: 201-539-4425); both provide useful information on resources for the visually impaired.

In addition, there are a number of publications — from travel guides to magazines — of interest to handicapped travelers. Among these are the following:

Access to the World, by Louise Weiss, offers sound tips for the disabled traveler. Published by Facts on File (460 Park Ave. S., New York, NY 10016; phone: 212-683-2244 in New York State; 800-322-8755 elsewhere in the US; 800-443-8323 in Canada), it costs $16.95 and is available only in paperback. Check with your local bookstore; it also can be ordered by phone with a credit card.

The Diabetic Traveler (PO Box 8223 RW, Stamford, CT 06905; phone: 203-327-5832) is a useful quarterly newsletter for travelers with diabetes. Each issue highlights a single destination or type of travel and includes information on general resources and hints for diabetics. A 1-year subscription costs $18.95. When subscribing, ask for the free fact sheet including an index of special articles; back issues are available for $4 each.

Guide to Traveling with Arthritis, a free brochure available by writing to the Upjohn Company (PO Box 307-B, Coventry, CT 06238), provides lots of good, commonsense tips on planning your trip and how to be as comfortable as possible when traveling by car, bus, train, cruise ship, or plane.

Handicapped Travel Newsletter is regarded as one of the best sources of information for the disabled traveler. It is edited by wheelchair-bound Vietnam veteran Michael Quigley, who has traveled to 93 countries around the world. Issued every 2 months (plus special issues), a subscription is $10 per year. Write to *Handicapped Travel Newsletter,* PO Box 269, Athens, TX 75751 (phone: 903-677-1260).

Handi-Travel: A Resource Book for Disabled and Elderly Travellers, by Cinnie Noble, is a comprehensive travel guide full of practical tips for those with disabilities affecting mobility, hearing, or sight. To order this book, send $12.95, plus shipping and handling, to the *Canadian Rehabilitation Council for the Disabled,* 45 Sheppard Ave. E., Suite 801, Toronto, Ontario M2N 5W9, Canada (phone: 416-250-7490; both voice and TDD).

The Itinerary (PO Box 2012, Bayonne, NJ 07002-2012; phone: 201-858-3400). This quarterly travel magazine for people with disabilities includes information on accessibility, listings of tours, news of adaptive devices, travel aids, and special services, as well as numerous general travel hints. A subscription costs $10 a year.

The Physically Disabled Traveler's Guide, by Rod W. Durgin and Norene Lindsay, rates accessibility of a number of travel services and includes a list of organizations specializing in travel for the disabled. It is available for $9.95, plus shipping and handling, from Resource Directories, 3361 Executive Pkwy., Suite 302, Toledo, OH 43606 (phone: 419-536-5353 in the Toledo area; 800-274-8515 elsewhere in the US).

Ticket to Safe Travel offers useful information for travelers with diabetes. A reprint of this article is available free from local chapters of the *American Diabetes Association.* For the nearest branch, contact the central office at 1660 Duke St., Alexandria, VA 22314 (phone: 703-549-1500 in Virginia; 800-232-3472 elsewhere in the US).

Travel for the Patient with Chronic Obstructive Pulmonary Disease, a publication of the George Washington University Medical Center, provides some sound practical suggestions for those with emphysema, chronic bronchitis, asthma, or other lung ailments. To order, send $2 to Dr. Harold Silver, 1601 18th St. NW, Washington, DC 20009 (phone: 202-667-0134).

Traveling Like Everybody Else: A Practical Guide for Disabled Travelers, by Jacqueline Freedman and Susan Gersten, offers the disabled tips on traveling

by car, cruise ship, and plane, as well as lists of accessible accommodations, tour operators specializing in tours for disabled travelers, and other resources. It is available for $11.95, plus postage and handling, from Modan Publishing, PO Box 1202, Bellmore, NY 11710 (phone: 516-679-1380).

Travel Tips for Hearing-Impaired People, a free pamphlet for deaf and hearing-impaired travelers, is available from the *American Academy of Otolaryngology* (One Prince St., Alexandria, VA 22314; phone: 703-836-4444). For a copy, send a self-addressed, stamped, business-size envelope to the academy.

Travel Tips for People with Arthritis, a free 31-page booklet published by the *Arthritis Foundation,* provides helpful information regarding travel by car, bus, train, cruise ship, or plane, planning your trip, medical considerations, and ways to conserve your energy while traveling. It also includes listings of helpful resources, such as associations and travel agencies that operate tours for disabled travelers. For a copy, contact your local *Arthritis Foundation* chapter, or send $1 to the national office, PO Box 19000, Atlanta, GA 30326 (phone: 404-872-7100).

The Wheelchair Traveler, by Douglass R. Annand, lists accessible hotels, motels, restaurants, and other sites by state throughout the US. This valuable resource is available directly from the author. For the price of the most recent edition, contact Douglass R. Annand, 123 Ball Hill Rd., Milford, NH 03055 (phone: 603-673-4539).

A few more basic resources to look for are *Travel for the Disabled,* by Helen Hecker ($19.95), and by the same author, *Directory of Travel Agencies for the Disabled* ($19.95). *Wheelchair Vagabond,* by John G. Nelson, is another useful guide for travelers confined to a wheelchair (hardcover, $14.95; paperback, $9.95). All three titles are published by Twin Peaks Press, PO Box 129, Vancouver, WA 98666 (phone: 800-637-CALM or 206-694-2462). The publisher also offers a catalogue of 26 other books on travel for the disabled for $2.

PLANE: The US Department of Transportation (DOT) has ruled that US airlines must accept all passengers with disabilities. As a matter of course, US airlines were pretty good about accommodating handicapped passengers even before the ruling, although each airline has somewhat different procedures. Ask for specifics when you book your flight.

Disabled passengers always should make reservations well in advance and should provide the airline with all relevant details of their conditions. These details include information on mobility and equipment that you will need the airline to supply — such as a wheelchair for boarding or portable oxygen for in-flight use. Be sure that the person to whom you speak fully understands the degree of your disability — the more details provided, the more effective help the airline can give you.

On the day before the flight, call back to make sure that all arrangements have been prepared, and arrive early on the day of the flight so that you can board before the rest of the passengers. It's a good idea to bring a medical certificate with you, stating your specific disability or the need to carry particular medicine.

Because most airports have jetways (corridors connecting the terminal with the door of the plane), a disabled passenger usually can be taken as far as the plane, and sometimes right onto it, in a wheelchair. If not, a narrow boarding chair may be used to take you to your seat. Your own wheelchair, which will be folded and put in the baggage compartment, should be tagged as escort luggage to assure that it's available at planeside upon landing rather than in the baggage claim area. Travel is not quite as simple if your wheelchair is battery-operated: Unless it has non-spillable batteries, it might not be accepted on board, and you will have to check with the airline ahead of time to find out how the batteries and the chair should be packaged for the flight.

Usually people in wheelchairs are asked to wait until other passengers have disembarked. If you are making a tight connection, be sure to tell the attendant.

Passengers who use oxygen may not use their personal supply in the cabin, though it may be carried on the plane as cargo (the tank must be emptied) when properly packed and labeled. If you will need oxygen during the flight, the airline will supply it to you (there is a charge) provided you have given advance notice — 24 hours to a few days, depending on the carrier.

The free booklet *Air Transportation of Handicapped Persons* explains the general guidelines that govern air carrier policies. For a copy, write to the US Department of Transportation (Distribution Unit, Publications Section, M-443-2, Washington, DC 20590) and ask for "Free Advisory Circular #AC-120-32." *Access Travel: A Guide to the Accessibility of Airport Terminals,* a free publication of the Airport Operators Council International, provides information on more than 500 airports worldwide and offers ratings of 70 features, such as accessibility to bathrooms, corridor width, and parking spaces. For a copy, contact the Consumer Information Center (Dept. 563W, Pueblo, CO 81009; phone: 719-948-3334).

The following airlines have TDD toll-free lines in the US for the hearing-impaired:

American: 800-582-1573 in Ohio; 800-543-1586 elsewhere in the US
America West: 800-526-8077
Continental: 800-343-9195
Delta: 800-831-4488
Northwest: 800-328-2298
TWA: 800-252-0622 in California; 800-421-8480 elsewhere in the US
United: 800-942-8819 in Illinois; 800-323-0170 elsewhere in the US
USAir: 800-242-1713 in Pennsylvania; 800-245-2966 elsewhere in the US

GROUND TRANSPORTATION: Perhaps the simplest solution to getting around is to travel with an able-bodied companion who can drive. If you are accustomed to driving your own hand-controlled car and want to rent one, you are in luck. Some rental companies will fit cars with hand controls. *Avis* (phone: 800-331-1212) can convert a car to hand controls with as little as 24 hours' notice, though it's a good idea to arrange for one more than a day in advance. *Hertz* (phone: 800-654-3131) requires 2 days to install the controls. Neither company charges extra for hand controls, but *Avis* will fit them only on a full-size car, and both request that you bring your handicapped driver's permit with you. Other car rental companies provide hand-control cars at some locations; however, as there usually are only a limited number available, call well in advance.

A relatively new company, *Wheelchair Getaways,* rents vans accommodating one or two wheelchairs and up to five passengers. Each vehicle has straps to secure wheelchairs, air-conditioning, and stereo. The renter provides the driver. The Pennsylvania-based company (PO Box 819, Newtown, PA 18940; phone: 800-642-2042 or 215-579-9120) has franchises in a number of US cities, although at press time, nothing in the Washington area. It would be worthwhile, however, to call the headquarters when making travel plans to find out if the company has extended service to the District of Columbia.

The *American Automobile Association (AAA)* publishes a useful booklet, *The Handicapped Driver's Mobility Guide.* Contact the central office of your local *AAA* club for availability and pricing, which may vary at different branch offices.

TOURS: Programs designed for the physically impaired are run by specialists who have researched hotels, restaurants, and sites to be sure they present no insurmountable obstacles. The following travel agencies and tour operators specialize in making group and individual arrangements for travelers to Washington, DC, with physical or other disabilities:

Access: The Foundation for Accessibility by the Disabled (PO Box 356, Malverne, NY 11565; phone: 516-887-5798). A travelers' referral service that acts as an intermediary with tour operators and agents worldwide, and provides information on accessibility at various locations.

Accessible Journeys (412 S. 45th St., Philadelphia, PA 19104; phone: 215-747-0171). Arranges for traveling companions who are medical professionals — registered or licensed practical nurses, therapists, or doctors (all are experienced travelers). Several prospective companions' profiles and photos are sent to the client for perusal, and if one is acceptable, the "match" is made. The client usually pays all travel expenses for the companion, plus a certain amount in "earnings" to replace wages the companion would be making at his or her usual job.

Accessible Tours/Directions Unlimited (720 N. Bedford Rd., Bedford Hills, NY 10507; phone: 914-241-1700 in New York State; 800-533-5343 elsewhere in the continental US). Arranges group or individual tours for disabled persons traveling in the company of able-bodied friends or family members. Accepts the unaccompanied traveler if completely self-sufficient.

Dahl Good Neighbor Travel Service (124 S. Main St., Viroqua, WI 54665: phone: 608-637-2128; and 535 N. St. Mary's Rd., Libertyville, IL 60048; phone: 708-362-0129). This agency can arrange a full range of services and provide necessities to travelers with any special needs, mental or physical.

Evergreen Travel Service (4114 198th St. SW, Suite 13, Lynnwood, WA 98036-6742; phone: 800-435-2288 or 206-776-1184 throughout the continental US and Canada). Offers tours, including to Washington, and makes individual arrangements for the disabled (Wings on Wheels Tours), sight impaired/blind (White Cane Tours), hearing impaired/deaf (Flying Fingers Tours). Most programs are first class or deluxe, and include a trained escort.

First National Travel Ltd. (Thornhill Sq., 300 John St., Suite 302, Thornhill, Ontario L3T 5W4, Canada; phone: 416-731-4714). Handles individual arrangements.

Flying Wheels Travel (143 W. Bridge St., Box 382, Owatonna, MN 55060; phone: 507-451-5005 or 800-535-6790). Handles both tours and individual arrangements.

Guided Tour (613 W. Cheltenham Ave., Suite 200, Melrose Park, PA 19126-2414; phone: 215-782-1370). Arranges tours, including to the District of Columbia, for people with developmental and learning disabilities and sponsors separate tours for members of the same population who also are physically disabled or who simply need a slower pace.

Hinsdale Travel (201 S. Ogden Ave., Hinsdale, IL 60521; phone: 708-325-1335 or 708-469-7349). Janice Perkins, the tour leader, has been in a wheelchair for years and leads an active life. She takes groups of handicapped travelers on the road, making arrangements to meet their special needs.

Prestige World Travel (5710X High Point Rd., Greensboro, NC 27407; phone: 800-476-7737 or 919-292-6690). Owner Kay Jones arranges for the handicapped, including the wheelchair-bound, to travel on her regular tour programs; she will also design independent travel programs.

Sprout (893 Amsterdam Ave., New York, NY 10025; phone: 212-222-9575). Arranges travel programs, including ones to Washington, for mildly and moderately developmentally disabled teens and adults.

USTS Travel Horizons (11 E. 44th St., New York, NY 10017; phone: 800-487-8787 or 212-687-5121). Travel agent and registered nurse Mary Ann Hamm designs trips for individual travelers requiring all types of kidney dialysis and handles arrangements for the dialysis.

Weston Travel Agency (134 N. Cass Ave., PO Box 1050, Westmont, IL 60559; phone: 800-633-3725 outside of Illinois, or 708-968-2513). This agency specializes in travel services for people with cerebral palsy and those who are wheelchair-bound.

Travelers who would benefit from being accompanied by a nurse or physical therapist also can hire a companion through *Traveling Nurses' Network,* a service provided by Twin Peaks Press (PO Box 129, Vancouver, WA 98666; phone: 800-637-CALM or 206-694-2462). For a $10 fee, clients receive the names of three nurses, whom they can then contact directly; for a $125 fee, the agency will make all the hiring arrangements for the client. Travel arrangements also may be made in some cases — the fee for this further service is determined on an individual basis.

A similar service is offered by *MedEscort International* (ABE International Airport, PO Box 8766, Allentown, PA 18105; phone: 800-255-7182 in the continental US; elsewhere, call 215-791-3111). Clients can arrange to be accompanied by a nurse, paramedic, respiratory therapist, or physician through *MedEscort.* The fees are based on the disabled traveler's needs. This service also can assist in making travel arrangements.

Hints for Single Travelers

Just about the last trip in human history on which the participants were neatly paired was the voyage of Noah's Ark. Ever since, passenger lists and tour groups have reflected the same kind of asymmetry that occurs in real life, as countless individuals set forth to see the world unaccompanied (or unencumbered, depending on your outlook) by spouse, lover, friend, companion, or relative.

The truth is that the travel industry is not very fair to people who vacation by themselves. People traveling alone almost invariably end up paying more than individuals traveling in pairs. Most travel bargains, including package tours, accommodations, resort packages, and cruises, are based on double occupancy rates. This means that the per-person price is offered on the basis of two people traveling together and sharing a double room (which means they each will spend a good deal more on meals and extras). The single traveler will have to pay a surcharge, called a single supplement, for exactly the same package. In extreme cases, this can add as much as 35% to the basic per-person rate.

Don't despair, however. Throughout the US, there are scores of smaller hotels and other hostelries where, in addition to a cozier atmosphere, prices still are quite reasonable for the single traveler.

The obvious, most effective alternative is to find a traveling companion. Even special "singles' tours" that promise no supplements usually are based on people sharing double rooms. Perhaps the most recent innovation along these lines is the creation of organizations that "introduce" the single traveler to other single travelers. Some charge fees, while others are free, but the basic service offered is the same: to match an unattached person with a compatible travel mate. Among such organizations are the following:

Jane's International (2603 Bath Ave., Brooklyn, NY 11214; phone: 718-266-2045). This service puts potential traveling companions in touch with one another. It has started a new organization, *Sophisticated Women Travelers,* to create groups for single women to travel together. No age limit, no fee for either.

Partners-in-Travel (PO Box 491145, Los Angeles, CA 90049; phone: 213-476-4869). Members receive a list of singles seeking traveling companions; prospective companions make contact through the agency. The membership fee is $40 per year and includes a chatty newsletter (6 issues per year).

Travel Companion Exchange (PO Box 833, Amityville, NY 11701; phone: 516-454-0880). This group publishes a newsletter for singles and a directory of individuals looking for travel companions. On joining, members fill out a lengthy questionnaire and write a small listing (much like an ad in a personal column). Based on these listings, members can request copies of profiles and contact prospective traveling companions. It is wise to join well in advance of your planned vacation so that there's enough time to determine compatibility and plan a joint trip. Membership fees, including the newsletter, are $30 for 6 months or $60 a year for a single-sex listing; $66 and $120, respectively, for a complete listing. Subscription to the newsletter alone costs $24 for 6 months or $36 per year.

In addition, a number of tour packages cater to single travelers. These companies offer packages designed for individuals interested in vacationing with a group of single travelers or in being matched with a traveling companion. Among the better established of these agencies are the following:

Gallivanting (515 E. 79 St., Suite 20F, New York, NY 10021; phone: 800-933-9699 or 212-988-0617). Offers matching service for singles ages 25 through 55 willing to share accommodations in order to avoid paying single supplement charges, with the agency guaranteeing this arrangement if bookings are paid for at least 75 days in advance.

Marion Smith Singles (611 Prescott Pl., N. Woodmere, NY 11581; phone: 516-791-4852, 516-791-4865, or 212-944-2112). Specializes in tours for singles ages 20 to 50, who can choose to share accommodations to avoid paying single supplement charges.

Odyssey Network (118 Cedar St., Wellesley, MA 02181; phone: 800-487-6059 or 617-237-2400). Originally founded to match single female travelers, this company now includes men in its enrollment. *Odyssey* offers a quarterly newsletter for members who are seeking a travel companion and makes independent arrangements for them. A $50 membership fee includes the newsletter.

Saga International Holidays (120 Boylston St., Boston, MA 02116; phone: 800-343-0273 or 617-451-6808). A subsidiary of a British company specializing in older travelers, many of them single, *Saga* offers a broad selection of packages for people age 60 and over or those 50 to 59 traveling with someone 60 or older. Recent offerings included a Behind the Scenes tour of Washington. Although anyone can book a *Saga* trip, a $15 club membership includes a subscription to their newsletter, as well as other publications and travel services — such as a matching service for single travelers.

Travel in Two's (239 N. Broadway, Suite 3, N. Tarrytown, NY 10591; phone: 914-631-8409). For city programs, this company matches up solo travelers and then customizes programs for them. The firm also puts out a quarterly *Singles Vacation Newsletter,* which costs $7.50 per issue or $20 per year.

A good book for single travelers is *Traveling On Your Own,* by Eleanor Berman, which offers tips on traveling solo and includes information on trips for singles. Available in bookstores, it also can be ordered by sending $12.95, plus postage and handling, to Random House, Order Dept., 400 Hahn Rd., Westminster, MD 21157 (phone: 800-733-3000).

Single travelers also may want to subscribe to *Going Solo,* a newsletter that offers helpful information on going on your own. Issued eight times a year, a subscription costs $36. Contact Doerfer Communications, PO Box 1035, Cambridge, MA 02238 (phone: 617-876-2764).

Those interested in a particularly cozy type of accommodation should consider going the bed and breakfast route. Though a single person will likely pay more than half of the rate quoted for a couple even at a bed and breakfast establishment, the prices still are quite reasonable, and the homey atmosphere will make you feel less conspicuously alone.

Another possibility is the *United States Servas Committee* (11 John St., Room 407, New York, NY 10038; phone: 212-267-0252), which maintains a list of hosts around the world, including in Washington, who are willing to take visitors into their homes as guests. *Servas* will send an application form and a list of interviewers at the nearest locations for you to contact. After the interview, if you are accepted as a *Servas* traveler, you'll receive a membership certificate. The membership fee is $45 per year for an individual, with a $15 deposit to receive the host list, refunded upon its return.

Hints for Older Travelers

Special discounts and more free time are just two factors that have given Americans over age 65 a chance to see the world at affordable prices. Senior citizens make up an ever-growing segment of the travel population, and the trend among them is to travel more frequently and for longer periods of time.

PLANNING: When planning a vacation, prepare your itinerary with one eye on your own physical condition and the other on your interests. One important factor to keep in mind is not to overdo anything and to be aware of the effects that the weather may have on your capabilities.

Older travelers may find the following publications of interest:

Discount Guide for Travelers Over 55, by Caroline and Walter Weintz, is an excellent book for budget-conscious older travelers. Published by Penguin USA, it is currently out of print; check your local library.

International Health Guide for Senior Citizen Travelers, by Dr. W. Robert Lange, covers such topics as trip preparations, food and water precautions, adjusting to weather and climate conditions, finding a doctor, motion sickness, jet lag, and so on. Also includes a list of resource organizations that provide medical assistance for travelers. It is available for $4.95 postpaid from Pilot Books, 103 Cooper St., Babylon, NY 11702 (phone: 516-422-2225).

Mature Traveler is a monthly newsletter that provides information on travel discounts, places of interest, useful tips, and other topics of interest for travelers 49 and up. To subscribe, send $24.50 to GEM Publishing Group, PO Box 50820, Reno, NV 89513 (phone: 702-786-7419).

Senior Citizen's Guide to Budget Travel in the US and Canada, by Paige Palmer, provides specific information on economical travel options for senior citizens. To order, send $4.95, plus $1 for postage and handling, to Pilot Books (address above).

Take a Camel to Lunch and Other Adventures for Mature Travelers, by Nancy O'Connell, offers offbeat and unusual adventures for travelers over 50. Available for $8.95 at bookstores or directly from Bristol Publishing Enterprises (include $2.75 for shipping and handling), PO Box 1737, San Leandro, CA 94577 (phone: 800-346-4889 or 510-895-4461).

Travel Easy: The Practical Guide for People Over 50, by Rosalind Massow, discusses a wide range of subjects — from trip planning, transportation options, and preparing for departure to avoiding and handling medical problems en route. The book is out of print, so check your local library.

Unbelievably Good Deals & Great Adventures That You Absolutely Can't Get

Unless You're Over 50, by Joan Rattner Heilman, offers travel tips for older travelers, including discounts on accommodations and transportation, as well as a list of organizations for seniors. It is available for $7.95, plus shipping and handling, from Contemporary Books, 180 N. Michigan Ave., Chicago, IL 60601 (phone: 312-782-9181).

HEALTH: Pre-trip medical and dental checkups are strongly recommended. In addition, be sure to take along any prescription medication you need, enough to last *without a new prescription* for the duration of your trip; pack all medications with a note from your doctor for the benefit of airport authorities. If you have specific medical problems, bring prescriptions and a "medical file" composed of the following:

1. A summary of your medical history and current diagnosis.
2. A list of drugs to which you are allergic.
3. Your most recent electrocardiogram, if you have heart problems.
4. Your doctor's name, address, and telephone number.

DISCOUNTS AND PACKAGES: Since guidelines change from place to place, it is a good idea to inquire in advance about discounts on transportation, hotels, concerts, movies, museums, and other activities. For instance, the National Park Service has a Golden Age Passport, which entitles people over 62 (and those in the car with them) to free entrance to all national parks and monuments (available by showing a Medicare card or driver's license as proof of age at any national park).

Many hotel chains, airlines, cruise lines, bus companies, car rental companies, and other travel suppliers offer discounts to older travelers. For instance, *United* offers senior citizen coupon books — with either four or eight coupons each — that can be exchanged for tickets on domestic flights of up to 2,000 miles. These coupons are good 7 days a week for travel in all 50 states, although some peak travel periods are omitted. Other airlines also offer discounts for passengers age 60 (or 62) and over, which may be applicable to one traveling companion per senior. Among the airlines that often offer such discounted airfares are *America West, Continental,* and *TWA.* Given the continuing changes in the airline industry, however, these discounted fares may not be available when you purchase your tickets. For information on current prices and applicable restrictions, contact the individual carriers.

Some discounts, however, are extended only to bona fide members of certain senior citizens organizations. Because the same organizations frequently offer package tours to both domestic and international destinations, the benefits of membership are twofold: Those who join can take advantage of discounts as individual travelers and also reap the savings that group travel affords. In addition, because the age requirements for some of these organizations are quite low (or nonexistent), the benefits can begin to accrue early.

In order to take advantage of these discounts, you should carry proof of your age (or eligibility). A driver's license, membership card in a recognized senior citizens organization, or a Medicare card should be adequate. Among the organizations dedicated to helping older travelers see the world are the following:

American Association of Retired Persons (AARP; 601 E St. NW, Washington, DC 20049; phone: 202-434-2277). The largest and best known of these organizations. Membership is open to anyone 50 or over, whether retired or not; dues are $8 a year, $20 for 3 years, or $45 for 10 years, and include spouse. The *AARP* Travel Experience Worldwide program, available through *American Express Travel Related Services,* offers members tours and other travel programs designed exclusively for older travelers. For example, it offers an independent Washington, DC, city program. Members can book these services by calling *American Express* at 800-927-0111 for land and air travel.

Mature Outlook (Customer Service Center, 6001 N. Clark St., Chicago, IL 60660; phone: 800-336-6330). Through its *Travel Alert,* tours, cruises, and other vacation packages are available to members at special savings. Hotel and car rental discounts and travel accident insurance also are available. Membership is open to anyone 50 years of age or older, costs $9.95 a year, and includes a bimonthly newsletter and magazine, as well as information on package tours.

National Council of Senior Citizens (1331 F St. NW, Washington, DC 20005; phone: 202-347-8800). Here, too, the emphasis is on keeping costs low. This nonprofit organization offers members a different roster of package tours each year, as well as individual arrangements through its affiliated travel agency *(Vantage Travel Service).* Although most members are over 50, membership is open to anyone (regardless of age) for an annual fee of $12 per person or couple. Lifetime membership costs $150.

Certain travel agencies and tour operators offer special trips geared to older travelers. Among them are the following:

Evergreen Travel Service (4114 198th St. SW, Suite 13, Lynnwood, WA 98036-6742; phone: 800-435-2288 or 206-776-1184 throughout the continental US and Canada). This specialist in trips for persons with disabilities recently introduced Lazybones Tours, a program offering leisurely tours for older travelers, including to Washington, DC. Most programs are first class or deluxe, and include an escort.

Gadabout Tours (700 E. Tahquitz Canyon Way, Palm Springs, CA 92262; phone: 619-325-5556 or 800-521-7309 in California; 800-952-5068 elsewhere in the US). Offers escorted tours to a number of destinations, including the District of Columbia.

Saga International Holidays (120 Boylston St., Boston MA 02116; phone: 800-343-0273 or 617-451-6808). A subsidiary of a British company catering to older travelers, *Saga* offers a broad selection of packages for people age 60 and over or those 50 to 59 traveling with someone 60 or older. Although anyone can book a *Saga* trip, a $15 club membership includes a subscription to their newsletter, as well as other publications and travel services.

One company providing a charming and unusual travel experience for older travelers is *Grandtravel* (6900 Wisconsin Ave., Suite 706; Chevy Chase, MD 20815; phone: 800-247-7651 or 301-986-0790), which specializes in tours for grandparents with their grandchildren. It offers an 8-day program in the city and its environs that appeals to both ages.

Many travel agencies, particularly the larger ones, are delighted to make presentations to help a group of senior citizens select destinations. A local chamber of commerce should be able to provide the names of such agencies. Once a time and place are determined, an organization member or travel agent can obtain group quotations for transportation, accommodations, meal plans, and sightseeing. Larger groups usually get the best breaks.

Another choice open to older travelers is a trip that includes an educational element. *Elderhostel,* a nonprofit organization, offers programs at educational institutions in the US, including Washington, and worldwide. The domestic programs generally last 1 week and include double-occupancy accommodations in hotels or student residence halls and all meals. Travel to the programs usually is by designated scheduled flights, and participants can arrange to extend their stay at the end of the program. Elderhostelers must be at least 60 years old (younger if a spouse or companion qualifies), in good health, and not in need of special diets. For a free catalogue describing the program and current offerings, write to *Elderhostel* (75 Federal St., Boston, MA 02110; phone: 617-426-7788). Those interested in the program also can borrow slides at no charge or purchase an informational videotape for $5.

Hints for Traveling with Children

What better way to encounter Washington's historic past than in the company of the young, wide-eyed members of your family? Their presence does not have to be a burden or an excessive expense. The current generation of discounts for children and family package deals can make a trip together quite reasonable.

A family trip to Washington, DC, will be an investment in your children's future, making geography and the history of the early years of our country come alive to them and leaving a memory that will be among the fondest you will share with them someday. Their insights will be refreshing to you; their impulses may take you to unexpected places with unexpected dividends. The experience will be invaluable to them at any age.

PLANNING: Here are several hints for making a trip with children easy and fun:

1. Children, like everyone else, will derive more pleasure from a trip if they know something about their destination before they arrive. Begin their education about a month before you leave. Using maps, travel magazines, and books, give children a clear idea of where you are going and how far away it is.
2. Children should help to plan the itinerary, and where you go and what you do should reflect some of their ideas. If they already know something about the city and the sites they will visit, they will have the excitement of recognition when they arrive.
3. Give children specific responsibilities: The job of carrying their own flight bags and looking after their personal things, along with some other light chores, will give them a stake in the journey.
4. Give each child a travel diary or scrapbook to take along.

Children's books about the nation's capital and its place in the history of our country provide an excellent introduction and can be found at children's bookstores (see "Books and Bookstores" in *For More Information,* in this section), many general bookstores, and in libraries.

And for parents, *Travel With Your Children* (*TWYCH;* 80 Eighth Ave., New York, NY 10011; phone: 212-206-0688) publishes a newsletter, *Family Travel Times,* that focuses on families with young travelers and offers helpful hints. An annual subscription (10 issues) is $35 and includes a copy of the "Airline Guide" issue (updated every other year), which focuses on the subject of flying with children. This special issue is available separately for $10.

Another newsletter devoted to family travel is *Getaways.* This quarterly publication provides reviews of family-oriented literature, activities, and useful travel tips. To subscribe, send $25 to Getaways, Att. Ms. Brooke Kane, PO Box 8282, McLean, VA 22107 (phone: 703-534-8747).

Also of interest to parents traveling with their children is *How to Take Great Trips With Your Kids,* by psychologist Sanford Portnoy and his wife, Joan Flynn Portnoy. The book includes helpful tips from fellow family travelers, tips on economical accommodations and touring by car, as well as over 50 games to play with your children en route. It is available for $8.95, plus shipping and handling, from Harvard Common Press, 535 Albany St., Boston, MA 02118 (phone: 617-423-5803). Another title worth looking for is *Great Vacations with Your Kids,* by Dorothy Jordan (Dutton; $12.95).

Another book on family travel, *Travel with Children* by Maureen Wheeler, offers a wide range of practical tips on traveling with children. It is available for $10.95, plus shipping and handling, from Lonely Planet Publications, Embarcadero W., 112 Linden St., Oakland, CA 94607 (phone: 510-893-8555).

Also look for the Washington, DC, volume of the "Kidding Around" series on US cities, published by John Muir Publications. It starts with an overview of the city, along with some interesting background information, and then it is divided into areas, with descriptions of the various attractions in the general order in which you might encounter them. The book can be ordered for $9.95, plus shipping, from John Muir Publications, PO Box 613, Santa Fe, NM 87504, or by calling 800-888-7504 or 505-982-4078.

Finally, parents arranging a trip with their children may want to deal with an agency specializing in family travel, such as *Let's Take the Kids* (1268 Devon Ave., Los Angeles, CA 90024; phone: 800-726-4349 or 213-274-7088). In addition to arranging and booking trips for individual families, this group occasionally organizes trips for single-parent families traveling together. They also offer a parent travel network, whereby parents who have been to a particular destination can evaluate it for others.

PLANE: Begin early to investigate all available family discount flights, as well as any package deals and special rates offered by the major airlines. When you make your reservations, tell the airline that you are traveling with a child. Children ages 2 through 11 generally travel at about a 20% to 30% discount off regular full-fare adult ticket prices on domestic flights. This children's fare, however, usually is much higher than the excursion fare, which may be used by any traveler, regardless of age. An infant under 2 years of age usually can travel free if it sits on an adult's lap. A second infant without a second adult would pay the fare applicable to children ages 2 through 11.

Although some airlines will, on request, supply bassinets for infants, most carriers encourage parents to bring their own safety seat on board, which then is strapped into the airline seat with a regular seat belt. This is much safer — and certainly more comfortable — than holding the child in your lap. If you do not purchase a seat for your baby, you have the option of bringing the infant restraint along on the off-chance that there might be an empty seat next to yours — in which case some airlines will let you use that seat at no charge for your baby and infant seat. However, if there is no empty seat available, the infant seat no doubt will have to be checked as baggage (and you may have to pay an additional charge), since it generally does not fit under the airplane seats or in the overhead racks. The safest bet is to pay for a seat.

Be forewarned: Some safety seats designed primarily for use in cars do not fit into plane seats properly. Although nearly all seats manufactured since 1985 carry labels indicating whether they meet federal standards for use aboard planes, actual seat sizes may vary from carrier to carrier. At the time of this writing, the FAA was in the process of reviewing and revising the federal regulations regarding infant travel and safety devices — it was still to be determined if children should be *required* to sit in safety seats and whether the airlines will have to provide them.

If using one of these infant restraints, you should try to get bulkhead seats, which will provide extra room to care for your child during the flight. You also should request a bulkhead seat when using a bassinet — again, this is not as safe as strapping the child in. On some planes the bassinet hooks into a bulkhead wall; on others it is placed on the floor in front of you. (Note that bulkhead seats often are reserved for families traveling with small children.) As a general rule, babies should be held during takeoff and landing.

Request seats on the aisle if you have a toddler or if you think you will need to use the bathroom frequently. Carry onto the plane all you will need to care for and occupy your children during the flight — formula, diapers, a sweater, books, favorite stuffed animals, and so on. Dress your baby simply, with a minimum of buttons and snaps, because the only place you may have to change a diaper is at your seat or in a small lavatory.

You also can ask for a hot dog or hamburger instead of the airline's regular dinner if you give at least 24 hours' notice. Some, but not all, airlines have baby food aboard, and the flight attendant can warm a bottle for you. While you should bring along toys from home, also ask about children's diversions. Some carriers have terrific free packages of games, coloring books, and puzzles.

When the plane takes off and lands, make sure your baby is nursing or has a bottle, pacifier, or thumb in its mouth. This sucking will make the child swallow and help to clear stopped ears. A piece of hard candy will do the same for an older child.

Parents traveling by plane with toddlers, children, or teenagers may want to consult *When Kids Fly,* a free booklet published by Massport (Public Affairs Dept., 10 Park Plaza, Boston, MA 02116-3971; phone: 617-973-5600), which includes helpful information on airfares for children, infant seats, what to do in the event of overbooked or canceled flights, and so on.

■ **Note:** Newborn babies, whose lungs may not be able to adjust to the altitude, should not be taken aboard an airplane. And some airlines may refuse to allow a pregnant woman in her 8th or 9th month to fly. Check with the airline ahead of time, and carry a letter from your doctor stating that you are fit to travel — and indicating the estimated date of birth.

Things to Remember

1. If you are visiting many sites, pace the days with children in mind. Break the trip into half-day segments, with running around or "doing" time built in.
2. Don't forget that a child's attention span is far shorter than an adult's. Children don't have to see every sight or all of any sight to learn something from their trip; watching, playing with, and talking to other children can be equally enlightening.
3. Let your children lead the way sometimes; their perspective is different from yours, and they may lead you to things you would never have noticed on your own.
4. Remember the places that children love to visit: aquariums, zoos, amusement parks, beaches, nature trails, and so on. Among the activities that may pique their interest are bicycling, horseback riding, boat trips, visiting planetariums and children's museums, and viewing natural habitat exhibits. The perennial Washington attractions for children include the *National Zoo,* the *National Learning Center Capital Children's Museum, Tech 2000,* and the *National Air and Space Museum.*

On the Road

Credit Cards and Traveler's Checks

It may seem hard to believe, but one of the greatest (and least understood) costs of travel is money itself. Your one single objective in relation to the care and retention of your travel funds is to make them stretch as far as possible. When you do spend money, it should be on things that expand and enhance your travel experience, with no buying power lost due to carelessness or lack of knowledge. This requires more than merely ferreting out the best airfare or the most charming budget hotel. It means being canny about the management of money itself. Herewith, a primer on making money go as far as possible while traveling.

TRAVELER'S CHECKS: It's wise to carry traveler's checks while on the road instead of (or in addition to) cash, since it's possible to replace them if they are stolen or lost; in the US, you usually can receive partial or full replacement funds the same day if you have your purchase receipt and proper identification. Issued in various denominations, with adequate proof of identification (credit cards, driver's license, passport), traveler's checks are as good as cash in most hotels, restaurants, stores, and banks. Don't assume, however, that restaurants, small shops, and other establishments are going to be able to change checks of large denominations. More and more establishments are beginning to restrict the face amount of traveler's checks they will accept or cash, so it is wise to purchase at least some of your checks in small denominations — say, $10 and $20.

Every type of traveler's check is legal tender in banks around the world, and each company guarantees full replacement if checks are lost or stolen. After that the similarity ends. Some charge a fee for purchase, while others are free; you can buy traveler's checks at almost any bank, and some are available by mail. Most important, each traveler's check issuer differs slightly in its refund policy — the amount refunded immediately, the accessibility of refund locations, the availability of a 24-hour refund service, and the time it will take you to receive replacement checks. For instance, *American Express* offers a 3-hour replacement of lost or stolen traveler's checks at any *American Express* office — other companies may not be as prompt. (Note that *American Express*'s 3-hour policy is based on the traveler's being able to provide the serial numbers of the lost checks. Without these numbers, refunds can take much longer. *American Express*'s offices in Washington are located at 1150 Connecticut Ave. NW (phone: 202-457-1300); 5300 Wisconsin Ave. NW (phone: 202-362-4000); and 1001 G St. NW (phone: 393-0095).

We cannot overemphasize the importance of knowing how to replace lost or stolen checks. All of the traveler's check companies have agents throughout the US, both in their own name and at associated agencies (usually, but not necessarily, banks), where refunds can be obtained during business hours. Most of them also have 24-hour toll-free telephone lines, and some even will provide emergency funds to tide you over on a Sunday.

Be sure to make a photocopy of the refund instructions that will be given to you by the issuing institution at the time of purchase. To avoid complications should you need to redeem lost checks (and to speed up the replacement process), keep the purchase receipt and an accurate list, by serial number, of the checks that have been spent or cashed. You may want to incorporate this information in an "emergency packet," also including the numbers of the credit cards you are carrying, and any other bits of information you shouldn't be without. Always keep these records separate from the checks and the original records themselves (you may want to give them to a traveling companion to hold).

Several of the major traveler's check companies charge 1% for the acquisition of their checks; others don't. To receive fee-free traveler's checks you may have to meet certain qualifications — for instance, *Thomas Cook*'s checks issued in US currency are free if you make your travel arrangements through its travel agency. *American Express* traveler's checks are available without charge to members of the *American Automobile Association (AAA)*. Holders of some credit cards (such as the *American Express Platinum* card) also may be entitled to free traveler's checks. The issuing institution (e.g., the particular bank at which you purchase them) may itself charge a fee. If you purchase traveler's checks at a bank in which you or your company maintains significant accounts (especially commercial accounts of some size), the bank may absorb the 1% fee as a courtesy.

American Express, Bank of America, Citicorp, MasterCard, Thomas Cook, and *Visa* all offer traveler's checks. Here is a list of the major companies issuing traveler's checks and the numbers to call to report lost or stolen checks throughout the US:

> *American Express:* 800-221-7282
> *Bank of America:* 800-227-3460
> *Citicorp:* 800-645-6556
> *MasterCard:* Note that *Thomas Cook Mastercard* (below) is now handling all *MasterCard* traveler's check inquiries and refunds.
> *Thomas Cook MasterCard:* 800-223-7373
> *Visa:* 800-227-6811

CREDIT CARDS: Some establishments you may encounter during the course of your travels may not honor any credit cards and some may not honor all cards, so there is a practical reason to carry more than one. The following is a list of credit cards that enjoy wide domestic and international acceptance:

> *American Express:* Cardholders can cash personal checks for traveler's checks and cash at *American Express* or its representatives' offices in the US up to the following limits (within any single 21-day period): $1,000 for *Green* and *Optima* cardholders; $5,000 for *Gold* cardholders; and $10,000 for *Platinum* cardholders. Check cashing also is available to cardholders who are guests at participating hotels (up to $250), and for holders of airline tickets at participating airlines (up to $50). Free travel accident, baggage, and car rental insurance is provided if the ticket or rental is charged to the card; additional insurance also is available for additional cost. For further information or to report a lost or stolen *American Express* card, call 800-528-4800 throughout the continental US.
>
> *Carte Blanche:* Free travel accident, baggage, and car rental insurance if ticket or rental is charged to card; additional insurance also is available at additional cost. For medical, legal, and travel assistance, call 800-356-3448 throughout the US. For further information or to report a lost or stolen *Carte Blanche* card, call 800-525-9135 throughout the US.
>
> *Diners Club:* Emergency personal check cashing for cardholders staying at participating hotels and motels (up to $250 per stay). Free travel accident, baggage, and car rental insurance if ticket or rental is charged to card; additional insurance also is available for an additional fee. For medical, legal, and travel assis-

tance worldwide, call 800-356-3448 throughout the US. For further information or to report a lost or stolen *Diners Club* card, call 800-525-9135 throughout the US.

Discover Card: Offered by a subsidiary of Sears, Roebuck & Co., it provides cardholders with cash advances at numerous automatic teller machines and *Sears* stores throughout the US. For further information or to report a lost or stolen *Discover* card, call 800-DISCOVER throughout the US.

MasterCard: Cash advances are available at participating banks worldwide. Check with your issuing bank for information. *MasterCard* also offers a 24-hour emergency lost card service; call 800-826-2181 throughout the US.

Visa: Cash advances are available at participating banks worldwide. Check with your issuing bank for information. *Visa* also offers a 24-hour emergency lost card service; call 800-336-8472 throughout the US.

SENDING MONEY: If you have used up your traveler's checks, cashed as many emergency personal checks as your credit card allows, drawn on your cash advance line to the fullest extent, and still need money, have it sent to you via one of the following services:

American Express (phone: 800-543-4080). Offers a service called "Moneygram," completing money transfers in as little as 15 minutes. The sender can go to any *American Express* office in the US and transfer money by presenting cash, a personal check, money order, or credit card — *Discover, Mastercard, Visa,* or *American Express Optima* (no other *American Express* or other credit cards are accepted). *American Express Optima* cardholders also can arrange for this transfer over the phone. The minimum transfer charge is $12, which rises with the amount of the transaction; the sender can forward funds of up to $10,000 per transaction (credit card users are limited to the amount of their pre-established credit line). To collect at the other end, the receiver must show identification (driver's license or other picture ID) at an *American Express* branch office. The company's offices in Washington are listed above in the "Traveler's Checks" section.

Western Union Telegraph Company (phone: 800-325-4176 throughout the US). A friend or relative can go, cash in hand, to any *Western Union* office in the US, where, for a *minimum* charge of $13 (it rises with the amount of the transaction), the funds will be transferred to a centralized *Western Union* account. When the transaction is fully processed — generally within 30 minutes — you can go to any *Western Union* branch office to pick up the transferred funds; for an additional fee of $2.95 you will be notified by phone when the money is available. For a higher fee, the sender may call *Western Union* with a *MasterCard* or *Visa* number to send up to $2,000, although larger transfers will be sent to a predesignated location. Two convenient locations in Washington are at 1150 Connecticut Ave. NW (phone: 429-2222) and 801 14th St. NW (phone: 624-0100).

CASH MACHINES: Automatic teller machines (ATMs) are increasingly common throughout the US. If your bank participates in one of the international ATM networks (most do), the bank will issue you a "cash card" along with a personal identification code or number (also called a PIC or PIN). You can use this card at any ATM in the same electronic network to check your account balances, transfer monies between checking and savings accounts, and — most important for a traveler — withdraw cash instantly. Network ATMs generally are located in banks, commercial and transportation centers, and near major tourist attractions.

Some financial institutions offer exclusive automatic teller machines for their own customers only at bank branches. At the time of this writing, ATMs that *are* connected generally belong to one of the following two international networks:

CIRRUS: Has over 70,000 ATMs in more than 45 countries, including over 65,000 locations in the US — more than 150 in Washington. *MasterCard* holders also may use their cards to draw cash against their credit lines. For further information on the *CIRRUS* network, call 800-4-CIRRUS.

PLUS SYSTEM: Has over 70,000 automatic teller machines worldwide, including over 50,000 locations in the US — about 140 of them in the District of Columbia. *MasterCard* and *Visa* cardholders also may use their cards to draw cash against their credit lines. For further information on the *PLUS* system network, call 800-THE-PLUS.

Information about the *CIRRUS* and *PLUS* systems also is available at member bank branches, where you can obtain free booklets listing the locations worldwide. Note that a recent change in banking regulations permits financial institutions to subscribe to *both* the *CIRRUS* and *PLUS* systems, allowing users of either network to withdraw funds from ATMs at participating banks.

Time Zone and Business Hours

TIME ZONE: Washington is in the Eastern time zone and observes daylight saving time beginning on the first Sunday in April and continuing until the last Sunday in October.

BUSINESS HOURS: The District of Columbia maintains business hours that are fairly standard throughout the country: 9 AM to 5 PM, Mondays through Fridays.

Banks generally are open weekdays from 9 AM to 3 PM, and 24-hour "automatic tellers" or "cash machines" are common (for information on national networks, see *Credit Cards and Traveler's Checks,* in this section).

Retail stores usually are open from 9:30 or 10 AM to 5:30 or 6 PM, Mondays through Saturdays. Some of the larger stores are open until 9 PM Wednesdays through Saturdays in warm weather, with Thursday being the most common late-closing night in winter. Many retail establishments also remain open on Sundays until 5 PM or so.

Mail, Telephone, and Electricity

MAIL: Most post offices are open 24 hours a day, with at least a self-service section for weighing packages and buying stamps. In Washington the main post office is located at 900 N. Brentwood Rd. NE (phone: 202-636-1532). While the lobby is open 24 hours, window service is provided from 8 AM to 8 PM weekdays and from noon to 6 PM on Saturdays. The National Capital branch (across from Union Station at 2 Massachusetts Ave. NE; phone: 202-523-2628) is open from 8 AM to midnight weekdays and 7 AM to 8 PM on Saturdays.

Stamps also are available at most hotel desks. There are vending machines for stamps in drugstores, transportation terminals, and other public places. Stamps cost more from these machines than they do at the post office. Two convenient post offices for visitors are located at 1125 19th St. NW (phone: 202-523-2506; open from 8 AM to 6 PM during the week; closed Saturdays) and 1215 31st St. NW in Georgetown (phone: 202-523-2405; open 8 AM to 5:30 PM on weekdays and 8:30 AM to 2 PM on Saturdays).

For rapid, overnight delivery to other cities, *Federal Express* can be useful. The phone number to call for pick-up in Washington is 301-953-3333, while convenient drop-off addresses include 1825 K St. NW, 1 Dupont Circle NW, and 1025 Thomas Jefferson St. NW in Georgetown. The pick-up number for another service, *DHL,* is 800-225-5345.

TELEPHONE: Public telephones are available just about everywhere — including transportation terminals, hotel lobbies, restaurants, drugstores, libraries, post offices, and other municipal buildings, as well as major tourist centers.

The Washington area code is 202; the adjoining Maryland suburbs are in the 301 area, while the nearby places in Virginia are in the 703 area.

Although you can use a telephone company credit card number on any phone, pay phones that take major credit cards (*American Express, MasterCard, Visa,* and so on) are increasingly common, particularly in transportation and tourism centers. Also now available is the "affinity card," a combined telephone calling card/bank credit card that can be used for domestic and international calls. Cards of this type include the following:

> *AT&T/Universal* (phone: 800-662-7759)
> *Executive Telecard International* (phone: 800-950-3800).

Similarly, *MCI VisaPhone* (phone: 800-866-0099) can add phone card privileges to the services available through your existing *Visa* card. This service allows you to use your *Visa* account number, plus an additional code, to charge calls on any touch-tone phone.

You must first dial 1 to indicate that you are making a long-distance call. The nationwide number for information is 555-1212. If you need a number in another area code, dial 1 + the area code + 555-1212. (If you don't know the area code, simply dial 0 for an operator who will tell you.)

Long-distance rates are charged according to when the call is placed: weekday daytime; weekday evenings; and nights, weekends, and holidays. Least expensive are the calls you dial yourself from a private phone at night and on weekends and major holidays. It generally is more expensive to call from a pay phone than it is to call from a private phone, and you must pay for a minimum 3-minute call. If the operator assists you, calls are more expensive. This includes credit card, bill-to-a-third-number, collect, and time-and-charge calls, as well as person-to-person calls, which are the most expensive. Rates are fully explained in the front of the white pages of every telephone directory.

Hotel Surcharges – Before calling from any hotel room, inquire about any surcharges the hotel may impose. These can be excessive, but are avoidable by calling collect, using a telephone credit card (see above), or calling from a public pay phone. (Note that when calling from your hotel room, even if the call is made collect or charged to a credit card number, some establishments still may add on a nominal line usage charge — so ask before you call.)

Emergency Number – As in most cities, 911 is the number to dial in the event of an emergency in Washington. Operators at this number will get you the help you need from the police, fire department, or ambulance service. It is, however, a number that should be used for real emergencies only.

■**Note:** An excellent resource for planning your trip is *AT&T's Toll-Free 800 Directory,* which lists thousands of companies with 800 numbers, both alphabetically (white pages) and by category (yellow pages), including a wide range of travel services — from travel agents to transportation and accommodations. Issued in a consumer edition for $9.95 and a business edition for $14.95, both are available from *AT&T Phone Centers* or by calling 800-426-8686. Other useful directories for use before you leave and on the road include the Toll-Free Travel & Vacation Information Directory ($4.95 postpaid from Pilot Books, 103 Cooper St., Babylon, NY 11702; phone: 516-422-2225) and The Phone Booklet, which lists the nationwide, toll-free (800) numbers of travel information sources and suppliers — such as major airlines, hotel and motel chains, car rental companies, and tourist information offices (send $2 to Scott American Corp., Box 88, West Redding, CT 06896).

ELECTRICITY: All 50 US states have the same electrical current system: 110 volts, 60 cycles, alternating current (AC). Appliances running on standard current can be used throughout the US without adapters or converters.

Staying Healthy

The surest way to return home in good health is to be prepared for medical problems that might occur en route. Below, we've outlined everything about which you need to think before you go.

BEFORE YOU GO: Older travelers or anyone suffering from a chronic medical condition, such as diabetes, high blood pressure, cardiopulmonary disease, asthma, or ear, eye, or sinus trouble, should consult a physician before leaving home. Those with conditions requiring special consideration when traveling should conside seeing, in addition to their regular physician, a specialist in travel medicine. For a referral in a particular community, contact the nearest medical school or ask a local doctor to recommend such a specialist. Dr. Leonard Marcus, a member of the American Committee on Clinical Tropical Medicine and Travelers' Health, provides a directory of more than 100 travel doctors across the country. For a copy, send a 9-by-12-inch, self-addressed, stamped envelope to Dr. Marcus at 148 Highland Ave., Newton, MA 02165 (phone: 617-527-4003).

Also be sure to check with your insurance company ahead of time about the applicability of your hospitalization and major medical policies while you're away. If your medical policy does not protect you while you're traveling, there are comprehensive combination policies specifically designed to fill the gap. (For a discussion of medical insurance and a list of inclusive combination policies, see *Insurance,* in this section.)

FIRST AID: Put together a compact, personal medical kit including Band-Aids, first-aid cream, antiseptic, nose drops, insect repellent, aspirin or non-aspirin pain reliever, an extra pair of prescription glasses or contact lenses (and a copy of your prescription for glasses or contact lenses), sunglasses, over-the-counter remedies for diarrhea, indigestion, and motion sickness, a thermometer, and a supply of those prescription medicines you take regularly.

In a corner of your kit, keep a list of all the drugs you have brought and their purpose, as well as duplicate copies of your doctor's prescriptions (or a note from your doctor). As brand names may vary in different parts of the US, it's a good idea to ask your doctor for the generic name of any drugs you use so that you can ask for their equivalent should you need a refill.

It also is a good idea to ask your doctor to prepare a medical identification card that includes such information as your blood type, your social security number, any allergies or chronic health problems you have, and your medical insurance information. Considering the essential contents of your medical kit, keep it with you, rather than in your checked luggage.

MEDICAL ASSISTANCE: If a bona fide emergency occurs, dial 911, the emergency number, and immediately state the nature of your problem and your location. If you are able to, another alternative is to go directly to the emergency room of the nearest hospital.

In Washington, a major medical institution with top emergency facilities is *George Washington University Medical Center* at 901 23rd St. NW (phone: 202-994-3884). Another one is *Georgetown University Hospital* at 3800 Reservoir Rd. NW (phone: 202-784-2000).

For other medical emergencies, *Peoples Drug Stores,* open 24 hours a day, 7 days a week, has several locations, including 1121 Vermont Ave. NW (phone: 202-628-0720), 1009 Connecticut Ave. NW (phone: 202-223-8777), and 7 Dupont Circle (phone: 202-785-1466). Pharmacists in the District of Columbia will generally fill non-narcotic out-of-state prescriptions.

If a doctor is needed for something less than an emergency, there are several ways to find one. If you are staying in a hotel, ask for help in reaching a doctor or other emergency services, or for the house physician, who may visit you in your room or ask you to visit an office. When you check in at a hotel, it's not a bad idea to include your home address and telephone number; this will facilitate the process of notifying friends, relatives, or your own doctor in case of an emergency.

Medical assistance also is available for travelers who have chronic ailments or whose illness requires them to return home. If you have a health condition that may not be readily perceptible to the casual observer — one that might result in a tragic error in an emergency situation — *MedicAlert Foundation* (2323 N. Colorado, Turlock, CA 95380; phone: 800-ID-ALERT or 209-668-3333) offers identification emblems specifying such conditions. The foundation also maintains a computerized central file from which your complete medical history is available 24 hours a day by phone (the telephone number is clearly inscribed on the emblem). The onetime membership fee (between $25 and $45) is based on the type of metal from which the emblem is made — the choices range from stainless steel to 10K gold-filled.

■**Note:** Those who are unable to take a reserved flight due to personal illness or who must fly home unexpectedly due to a family emergency should be aware that airlines may offer a discounted airfare (or arrange a partial refund) if the traveler can demonstrate that his or her situation is indeed a legitimate emergency. Your inability to fly or the illness or death of an immediate family member usually must be substantiated by a doctor's note or the name, relationship, and funeral home where the deceased will be buried. In such cases, airlines often will waive certain advance purchase restrictions or you may receive a refund check or voucher for future travel at a later date. Be aware, however, that this bereavement fare may not necessarily be the least expensive fare available and, if possible, it is best to have a travel agent check all possible flights through a computer reservations system (CRS).

HELPFUL PUBLICATIONS: Practically every phase of health care — before, during, and after a trip — is covered in *The New Traveler's Health Guide,* by Drs. Patrick J. Doyle and James E. Banta. It is available for $4.95, plus postage and handling, from Acropolis Books Ltd., 13950 Park Center Rd., Herndon, VA 22071 (phone: 800-451-7771 or 703-709-0006).

The Traveling Healthy Newsletter, which is published six times a year, also is brimming with healthful travel tips. For an annual subscription, which costs $24, contact Dr. Karl Neumann (108-48 70th Rd., Forest Hills, NY 11375; phone: 718-268-7290). Dr. Neumann also is the editor of the useful free booklet, *Traveling Healthy,* which is available by writing to the Travel Healthy Program (PO Box 10208, New Brunswick, NJ 08906-9910; phone: 908-732-4100).

Legal Aid

LEGAL AID: The best way to begin looking for legal aid in an unfamiliar area is to call your own lawyer. If you don't have, or cannot reach, your own attorney, most cities offer legal referral services (sometimes called attorney referral services) maintained by county bar associations. Such referral services see that anyone in need of legal representation gets it. (Attorneys also are listed in the yellow pages.) In Washington, DC, contact the *DC Bar Lawyer Referral Service* (1707 L St. NW, 6th Floor; phone: 202-331-4365). They can match you with an attorney and set up an appointment for you. If your case goes to court, you are entitled to court-appointed representation if you can't get a lawyer or can't afford one.

In the case of minor traffic accidents (such as fender benders), it is often most expedient to settle the matter before the police get involved. If you get a traffic or parking ticket, pay it. For most violations, you will receive a citation at most, and be required to appear in court on a specified date.

Drinking and Drugs

DRINKING: As in all 50 states, the legal drinking age in the District of Columbia is 21. Liquor may be served in restaurants, bars, and lounges from 8 AM until 2 AM Mondays through Thursdays and until 3 AM on Fridays and Saturdays. The Sunday hours are from 10 AM to 2 AM.

For retail purchases, liquor, wine, and beer are sold at package stores, which are closed on Sundays. Beer and wine may be purchased at supermarkets and convenience stores, while wine also is available at wine shops.

DRUGS: Despite the US government's intensified and concerted effort to stamp out drugs, illegal narcotics still are prevalent in the US, as elsewhere. Enforcement of drug laws is becoming increasingly strict throughout the nation, however, and local narcotics officers are renowned for their absence of understanding and lack of a sense of humor.

Possession of a small amount of marijuana is usually at best a misdemeanor, while being caught with crack, cocaine or heroin brings exposure to a felony charge, with conviction leading to jail terms of several years. It is important to bear in mind that the quantity of drugs involved is of minor importance. The best advice we can offer is this: Don't carry, use, buy, or sell illegal drugs.

To avoid difficulties during spot luggage inspections at the airport, if you carry medicines that contain such controlled drugs as codeine or codeine derivatives, be sure to bring along a current doctor's prescription.

Tipping

While tipping is at the discretion of the person receiving the service, 50¢ is the rock-bottom tip for anything, and $1 is the current customary minimum for small services. In restaurants, tip between 10% and 20% of the bill. For average service in an average restaurant, a 15% tip to the waiter is reasonable, although one should never hesitate to penalize poor service or reward excellent and efficient attention by leaving less or more.

Although it's not necessary to tip the maître d' of most restaurants — unless he has been especially helpful in arranging a special party or providing a table (slipping him something may, however, get you seated sooner or procure a preferred table) — when tipping is desirable or appropriate, the least amount should be $5. In the finest restaurants, where a multiplicity of servers are present, plan to tip 5% to the captain in addition to the gratuity left for the waiter. The sommelier (wine waiter) is tipped approximately 10% of the price of the bottle of wine.

In allocating gratuities at a restaurant, pay particular attention to what has become the standard credit card charge form, which now includes separate places for gratuities for waiters and/or captains. If these separate boxes are not on the charge slip, simply ask the waiter or captain how these separate tips should be indicated. In some establishments, tips indicated on credit card receipts may not be given to the help, so you may want to leave tips in cash.

In a large hotel, where it is difficult to determine just who out of a horde of attendants actually performed particular services, it is perfectly proper for guests to ask to have an extra 10% to 15% added to their bill. For those who prefer to distribute tips themselves, a chambermaid generally is tipped at the rate of around $1 a day. Tip the concierge or hall porter for specific services only, with the amount of such gratuities dependent on the level of service provided. For any special service you receive in a hotel, a tip is expected — $1 being the minimum for a small service.

Bellhops, doormen, and porters at hotels and transportation centers generally are tipped at the rate of $1 per piece of luggage, along with a small additional amount if a doorman helps with a cab or car. Taxi drivers should get about 15% of the total fare.

Miscellaneous tips: Sightseeing tour guides should be tipped. If you are traveling in a group, decide together what you want to give the guide and present it from the group at the end of the tour ($1 per person is a reasonable tip). If you have been individually escorted, the amount paid should depend on the degree of your satisfaction, but it should not be less than 10% of the tour price. Museum and monument guides also are usually tipped a few dollars. Coat checks are worth about 50¢ to $1 a coat, and washroom attendants are tipped — there usually is a little plate with a coin already in it suggesting the expected amount. In barbershops and beauty parlors, tips also are expected, but the percentages vary according to the type of establishment — 10% in the most expensive salons; 15% to 20% in less expensive establishments. (As a general rule, the person who washes your hair should get a small additional tip.)

Tipping always is a matter of personal preference. In the situations covered above, as well as in any others that arise where you feel a tip is expected or due, feel free to express your pleasure or displeasure. Again, never hesitate to reward excellent and efficient attention or to penalize poor service. Give an extra gratuity and a word of thanks when someone has gone out of his or her way for you. Either way, the more personal the act of tipping, the more appropriate it seems. And if you didn't like the service — or the attitude — don't tip.

Religion on the Road

The surest source of information on religious services in an unfamiliar community is the desk clerk of the hotel or resort in which you are staying; the local tourist information office or a church of another religious affiliation also may be able to provide this information. For a full range of options, joint religious councils often provide circulars with the addresses and times of services of other houses of worship in the area. These often are printed as part of general tourist guides provided by the local tourist and convention center, or as part of a "what's going

GETTING READY / Religion   63

on" guide to the city. Many newspapers also offer a listing of religious services in their area in weekend editions.

You may want to use your vacation to broaden your religious experience by joining an unfamiliar faith in its service. This can be a moving experience, especially if the service is held in a church, synagogue, or temple that is historically significant or architecturally notable. You almost always will find yourself made welcome and comfortable.

Sources and Resources

Tourist Information

The Washington, DC, Convention and Visitors Association is located at 1212 New York Ave. NW, Washington, DC 20005 (phone: 202-789-7007). For local tourist information, see *Sources and Resources* in THE CITY.

For More Information

BOOKS AND BOOKSTORES: The variety and scope of books and other travel information in and on the United States today is astounding. Every city and region are represented, so before you leave on your journey you can prepare by perusing books relevant to your special travel interests. These can usually be found in bookshops devoted to travel, among them the following:

Book Passage (51 Tamal Vista Blvd., Corte Madera, CA 94925; phone: 415-927-0960 in California; 800-321-9785 elsewhere in the US). Travel guides and maps to all areas of the world. A free catalogue is available.

The Complete Traveller (199 Madison Ave., New York, NY 10016; phone: 212-685-9007). Travel guides and maps. A catalogue is available for $2.

Forsyth Travel Library (PO Box 2975, Shawnee Mission, KS 66201-1375; phone: 800-367-7984 or 913-384-3440). Travel guides and maps, old and new, to all parts of the world. Ask for the "Worldwide Travel Books and Maps" catalogue.

Gourmet Guides (2801 Leavenworth Ave., San Francisco, CA 94133; phone: 415-771-9948). Travel guides and maps, along with cookbooks. Mail-order lists available on request.

Phileas Fogg's Books and Maps (87 Stanford Shopping Center, Palo Alto, CA 94304; phone: 800-533-FOGG or 415-327-1754). Travel guides and maps.

Powell's Travel Store (Pioneer Courthouse Sq., 701 SW 6th Ave., Portland, OR 97204; phone: 503-228-1108). A wealth of travel-related books (over 15,000 titles) and reference materials (globes, an extensive selection of maps, for example), as well as luggage and travel accessories (travel irons, and the like). There is even a travel agency on the premises.

Tattered Cover (2955 E. First Ave., Denver, CO 80206; phone: 800-833-9327 or 303-322-7727). The travel department alone of this enormous bookstore carries over 7,000 books, as well as maps and atlases. No catalogue is offered (the list is too extensive), but a newsletter, issued three times a year, is available on request.

Thomas Brothers Maps & Travel Books (603 W. Seventh St., Los Angeles, CA

90017; phone: 213-627-4018). Maps (including road atlases, street guides, and wall maps), guidebooks, and travel accessories.

Traveller's Bookstore (22 W. 52nd St., New York, NY 10019; phone: 212-664-0995). Travel guides, maps, literature, and accessories. A catalogue is available for $2.

MAGAZINES: As sampling the regional fare is likely to be one of the highlights of any visit, you will find reading about local edibles worthwhile before you go or after you return. *Gourmet,* a magazine specializing in food, frequently features mouth-watering articles on food and restaurants in the US, although its scope is much broader than domestic fare alone. It is available at newsstands nationwide for $2.50 an issue or for $18 a year from *Gourmet,* PO Box 53780, Boulder, CO 80322 (phone: 800-365-2454).

There are numerous additional magazines for every special interest available; check at your library information desk for a directory of such publications, or look over the selection offered at a well-stocked newsstand.

NEWSLETTERS: One of the very best sources of detailed travel information is *Consumer Reports Travel Letter.* Published monthly by Consumers Union (PO Box 53629, Boulder, CO 80322-3629; phone: 800-999-7959), it offers comprehensive coverage of the travel scene on a wide variety of fronts. A year's subscription costs $37; 2 years, $57.

In addition, the following travel newsletters provide useful up-to-date information on travel services and bargains:

Entree (PO Box 5148, Santa Barbara, CA 93150; phone: 805-969-5848). Monthly; a year's subscription costs $59. Subscribers also have access to a 24-hour hotline providing information on restaurants and accommodations around the world. This newsletter caters to a sophisticated, discriminating traveler with the means to explore the places mentioned.

The Hideaway Report (Harper Associates, Subscription Office: PO Box 300, Whitefish, MO 59937; phone: 406-862-3480; Editorial Office: PO Box 50, Sun Valley, ID 83353; phone: 208-622-3193). This monthly source highlights retreats — including domestic idylls — for sophisticated travelers. A year's subscription costs $90.

Romantic Hideaways (217 E. 86th St., Suite 258, New York, NY 10028; phone: 212-969-8682). This newsletter leans toward those special places made for those traveling in twos. A year's subscription to this monthly publication costs $65.

Travel Smart (Communications House, 40 Beechdale Rd., Dobbs Ferry, NY 10522; phone: 914-693-8300 in New York; 800-327-3633 elsewhere in the US). This monthly newsletter covers a wide variety of trips and travel discounts. A year's subscription costs $44.

COMPUTER SERVICES: Anyone who owns a personal computer and a modem can subscribe to a database service providing everything from airline schedules and fares to restaurant listings. Two such services to try:

CompuServe (5000 Arlington Center Blvd., Columbus, OH 43220; phone: 800-848-8199 or 614-457-8600). It costs $39.95 to join, plus hourly usage fees of $6 to $12.50.

Prodigy Services (445 Hamilton Ave., White Plains, NY 10601; phone: 800-822-6922 or 914-993-8000). A month's subscription costs $12.95, plus variable phone charges.

■ **Note:** Before using any computer bulletin-board services, be sure to take precautions to prevent downloading of a computer "virus." First install one of the programs designed to screen out such nuisances.

Cameras and Equipment

Vacations (and even some business trips) are everybody's favorite time for taking pictures and home movies. After all, most of us want to remember the places we visit — and to show them off to others. Here are a few suggestions to help you get the best results from your travel photography or videography.

BEFORE THE TRIP

If you're taking your camera or camcorder out after a long period in mothballs, or have just bought a new one, check it thoroughly before you leave to prevent unexpected breakdowns or disappointing pictures.

1. Still cameras should be cleaned carefully and thoroughly, inside and out. If using a camcorder, run a head cleaner through it. You also may want to have your camcorder professionally serviced (opening the casing yourself will violate the manufacturer's warranty). Always use filters to protect your lens while traveling.
2. Check the batteries for your camera's light meter and flash, and take along extras just in case yours wear out during the trip. For camcorders, bring along extra Nickel-Cadmium (Ni-Cad) batteries; if you use rechargeable batteries, a recharger will cut down on the extras.
3. Using all the settings and features, shoot at least one test roll of film or one videocassette, using the type you plan to take along with you.

EQUIPMENT TO TAKE ALONG

Keep your gear light and compact. Items that are too heavy or bulky to be carried comfortably on a full-day excursion will likely remain in your hotel room.

1. Invest in a broad camera or camcorder strap if you now have a thin one. It will make carrying the camera much more comfortable.
2. A sturdy canvas, vinyl, or leather camera or camcorder bag, preferably with padded pockets (not an airline bag), will keep your equipment organized and easy to find. If you will be doing much shooting around the water, a waterproof case is best.
3. For cleaning, bring along a camel's hair brush that retracts into a rubber squeeze bulb. Also take plenty of lens tissue, soft cloths, and plastic bags to protect equipment from dust and moisture.

FILM AND TAPES: If you are concerned about airport security X-rays damaging rolls of undeveloped still film (X-rays do not affect processed film) or tapes, store them in one of the lead-lined bags sold in camera shops. This possibility is not as much of a threat as it used to be, however. In the US, incidents of X-ray damage to unprocessed film (exposed or unexposed) are few because low-dosage X-ray equipment is used virtually everywhere. If you're traveling without a protective bag, you may want to ask to have your photo equipment inspected by hand. One type of film that should never be subjected to X-rays is the very high speed ASA 1000 film; there are lead-lined bags made especially for it — and, in the event that you are refused a hand inspection, this is the only way to save your film. The walk-through metal detector devices at airports do not affect film, though the film cartridges may set them off.

You should have no problem finding film or tapes in Washington. When buying film, tapes, or photo accessories the best rule of thumb is to stick to name brands with which you are familiar. The availability of film processing labs and equipment repair shops will vary.

For tips on some of Washington's most photogenic spots, see *A Shutterbug's Washington* in DIVERSIONS.

THE CITY

WASHINGTON, DC

In the 1950s, during one of the thaws in the Cold War, President Eisenhower was showing the visiting Nikita Khrushchev around Washington. Every time Eisenhower pointed out a government building, the Soviet leader would claim that the Russians had one bigger and better that had taken only half as long to build. Eisenhower, so the story goes, got pretty weary of this civic one-upmanship, and when they passed the Washington Monument he said nothing, forcing Khrushchev to ask what the structure was. Eisenhower replied, "It's news to me. It wasn't here yesterday."

Well, the story may be apocryphal, but it does indicate something important about Washington: It is a city filled with imperial architecture — grand, expansive, deliberate — of a kind that simply doesn't happen overnight or by chance. And yet it is a city that did, indeed, happen almost by chance; a city that until World War II seemed to resist almost in its bones being what it has become today: the international showplace of the United States.

A walk along the Mall will remove any doubts you have about the quality of Washington's cityscape. The Mall is the grand promenade of the capital, connecting the Capitol to the Lincoln Memorial by 2 miles of open green and reflecting pools, lined by several of the superb *Smithsonian* museums. Gleaming marble and massive, columned buildings on and surrounding this expanse signify that this is the seat of the sovereign power of the United States of America. These structures, familiar to everyone from picture postcards, take on real dimensions and fulfill the promise of grandeur (particularly at night, when they are bathed in floodlights). But this city of wide tree-lined avenues offers enough open space for varied architectural styles to appear highly consistent. Newer government buildings of modern design and neat rows of townhouses fit in with Federal and Greek Revival structures. And Washington will retain its impressive mien. A city ordinance limits the height of buildings to 13 stories, so the Capitol remains the city's tallest building. Though others approach it, none surpasses the splendor of this domed edifice.

The fact that Washington is so impressive is especially remarkable if you consider its stormy birth at the turn of the 18th century. Its future then couldn't have looked more bleak. Were it not for a band of disgruntled Continental soldiers who marched into Philadelphia on June 20, 1783, to demand back pay, Congress might well have remained in that most civilized of American cities, and Washington would probably still be a marshy swamp.

For the next 7 years, Congress wrangled over the location of the new federal city. In 1790, as a result of a compromise between the North and the South, a site on the Potomac shore was selected, far enough inland to protect against surprise attack, yet accessible to ocean vessels and at the head of a tidewater. Maryland agreed to give 69.25 square miles of land and Virginia 30.75 square miles to form the square to be known as the District of Columbia. The city was named for George Washington, who as first president was authorized to oversee its development.

Washington appointed Major Pierre L'Enfant, a French engineer, to lay out the city. L'Enfant arrived on the scene in 1791 and on viewing Jenkins Hill, the present Capitol Hill, he pronounced it "a pedestal waiting for a monument." He also set about designing avenues 160 feet wide which were to radiate out from circles crowned with sculpture. The city's two focal points were to be the Capitol and the president's house, with Pennsylvania Avenue the principal ceremonial street between.

L'Enfant soon became involved in a controversy over the sale of lots that were to have raised money to finance construction of government buildings, and he was fired before the year was out. He spent the rest of his life in relative obscurity, living off the charity of friends. George Washington died in 1799 before the development of the federal city was assured. But President John Adams's resolve was firm and Congress was pried from its comfortable surroundings in Philadelphia to the howling wilderness of Washington in November of 1800. Abigail Adams was none too happy with the choice, and wrote to her sister from the new White House: "Not one room or chamber of the whole is finished. . . . We have not the least fence, yard or other convenience without, and the great unfinished audience room I make a drying room of, to hang the clothes in." Abigail was displeased by the White House, and nobody was pleased with the city. The streets were unpaved and mud-rutted, the sewers nonexistent, and the swampy surroundings infested with mosquitoes (better to stay in the drying room).

During the War of 1812 the city underwent a devastating setback when British troops marched in and succeeded in burning the White House and gutting the Capitol. A torrential thunderstorm saved the city from total destruction, but much was burned beyond repair.

Ironically, for the showplace of democracy, just about the most constructive period of the capital's history took place 50 years later, when Alexander "Boss" Shepherd, Governor of the District of Columbia, decided to make Washington worthy of being the capital city in fact as well as in name. Between 1871 and 1874 he succeeded in having the streets paved, gas, sewer mains, and street lights installed, and parks laid out. He thought big, lived high, and used cronyism as his modus operandi. The results were spectacular, as was the debt — $20 million — which left the city bankrupt. The "Boss" was fired; he fled to Mexico, but returned later to a hero's welcome.

Events did not turn out so badly after all for Pierre L'Enfant — or at least for his plans (he, unfortunately, died a pauper in 1825). In 1901 the McMillan Commission was instituted to resurrect L'Enfant's original plans and treat the capital as a work of civic art. Railroad tracks were removed from the Mall, plans were made for the construction of the Lincoln Memorial and Arlington Bridge, and 640 acres of swampland were converted into Potomac parklands. The remains of Pierre L'Enfant were transferred to a grave in Arlington National Cemetery overlooking the city that still bears the stamp of his magnificent design.

First-time visitors to Washington may well wonder if there's a life in Washington beyond the monuments, buildings, fountains, and statues. Behind the handsome façades lie many Washingtons, but it would take the combined skills of a historian, political analyst, city planner, expert on international, race, and social relations, and master satirist to explain each one. The writer Ben Bagdikian observes: "In many respects, Washington, DC, is a perfectly normal American city. Its rivers are polluted. The air is periodically toxic from exhaust fumes. It has traffic jams, PTA meetings, and other common hazards of urban life. . . . Beyond its official buildings the natives rise each morning, crowd into buses and car pools, go to work, return at night, to the naked eye no different from the inhabitants of Oklahoma City or Pawtucket, Rhode Island."

All true, but Washington has something no other city has — the federal government. The District is something of a one-industry town, but the industry is government, and that makes all the difference. Nearly half of the 700,000 people living in Washington and its immediate surroundings work for some branch of government (the population of the entire metropolitan area is over 3.5 million). As civil servants, they earn relatively high incomes, a factor that provides a solid economic base for the city. Contrary to popular opinion, the population is relatively stable. Even during a change of administration, only about 3,000 officeholders are unseated. In addition to the permanent government employees, diplomats from more than 150 countries serve in Washington — considered to be the world's top post. The embassies lend a cultural sophistication to the capital and further diversify the population.

In response to these influences, Washington has developed as a major cosmopolitan center. Restaurants offer nearly as wide a representation of nationalities as do the embassies, and in some cases, even wider — you can eat in a Cuban restaurant, but try to find the Cuban embassy (if you do, it's news to us; it wasn't there yesterday). In the *Smithsonian Institution*'s museums you can see anything and everything, including the film *To Fly* (at the *National Air and Space Museum*), projected on a huge screen with dazzling camerawork that scans the countryside and the globe from dizzying heights, as if the viewer were in the cockpit of a plane or a spacecraft. The cultural picture has never been brighter (remember that it used to be an "event" to have a visiting ballet troupe squeeze onto the stage of a downtown movie theater or a post-Broadway road show visit Washington's only theater, the *National*). But today the *Kennedy Center* draws star artists and provides a home for music, theater, and dance companies. And what better proof of being an established cultural center than having branches of *Bloomingdale's, I. Magnin,* and *Neiman Marcus?*

Still, there are some long shadows across the Washington horizon. The city has a sufficiently high crime rate to have caused it to be dubbed "Murder City," though the business and tourist areas, as well as most of the western end of the city, are relatively safe. It is highly unadvisable, however, to walk around alone after dark. The District's resident population, which is largely black, suffers from a distressingly high rate of unemployment, particularly among unskilled workers and teenagers, and the drug problem is epidemic. Drug-related crime has risen enormously in the last few years, and the arrest and conviction, in 1990, of former Mayor Marion Barry on drug charges is testament to how deep and pervasive the problem is. The combination of distrust in local elected officials and high crime figures precipitated a "white flight" to the suburbs, but recently there is some evidence of families returning to the city to renovate homes in once-seedy neighborhoods that are becoming more stable, integrated communities. Many of the city's worst slums, particularly in the southwest section, have been torn down and replaced by apartment houses, theaters, restaurants, townhouses, and a redeveloped waterfront area.

The forecast remains murky. With home rule a reality (since 1973), Washington abandoned its status as "the last colony." Though residents now can vote for president, a mayor, a city council, and a non-voting representative to Congress, civic corruption has meaningfully impeded reform and renewal. Still, the city a visitor sees has never been more vital and vibrant.

And so it goes with Pierre L'Enfant's city. It is the Washington he envisioned that you see today. Every visitor to the Capitol should stand on its west terrace and appreciate one of the finest cityscapes in the world. And as you gaze, you might contemplate the words of Henry Adams. Over a century ago, he wrote, "One of these days this will be a very great city if nothing happens to it." Something has, but nevertheless it is.

WASHINGTON AT-A-GLANCE

SEEING THE CITY: The 555-foot Washington Monument commands a panorama of the capital in all its glory. To the north stands the White House, below stretches the green Mall, with the Lincoln Memorial in the west and the Capitol perfectly aligned with it to the east. Beyond to the south and west flows the Potomac River, and across the river lies Virginia.

SPECIAL PLACES: In Washington, all roads lead to the Capitol. The building marks the center of the District. North–south streets are numbered in relation to it, east–west streets are lettered, and the four quadrants into which Washington is divided (NW, NE, SW, and SE, designated after addresses) meet here. Note: A surprising number of remarkable attractions in this city have no admission charge.

An easy way to get around the principal sightseeing area, which includes Arlington National Cemetery (across the Potomac in Arlington, VA), is by *Tourmobile.* These 88-passenger shuttle trams allow you to buy your ticket (good all day) as you board, get on or off at any of the 18 stops, listen to highlights of the sights along the way, and set your own pace. *Tourmobiles* pass each stop every 30 minutes. For complete information contact the office at 1000 Ohio Dr. SW (phone: 554-7950).

Old Town Trolley Tours offers 2-hour group charter tours or individual tours of the District (phone: 301-985-3021). *Gray Line* offers guided, narrated bus tours of the District and outlying areas (phone: 289-1995 or 301-386-8300). Museum tours as well as special group tours emphasizing historic Washington are run by *National Fine Arts Associates* (4801 Massachusetts Ave. NW; phone: 966-3800). The *Spirit of Washington* runs sightseeing boats from March to December on the Potomac and the *Spirit of Mt. Vernon* runs from March to mid-October to Mount Vernon (6th and Water Sts. SW; phone: 554-8000 or 554-1542).

CAPITOL HILL AREA

The Capitol – The Senate and House of Representatives are housed in the Capitol, which is visible from almost every part of the city. When the French architect L'Enfant first began to plan the city, he noted that Jenkins Hill (now called Capitol Hill) was "a pedestal waiting for a monument." And though Washington laid the cornerstone in 1793, the pedestal had to wait through some 150 years of additions, remodelings, and fire (it was burned by the British in 1814) to get the monument we know today. The 258-foot cast-iron dome, topped by Thomas Crawford's statue of Freedom, was erected during the Civil War; beneath it, the massive Rotunda is a veritable art gallery of American history featuring Constantino Brumidi's fresco *The Apotheosis of Washington* in the eye of the dome, John Trumbull's Revolutionary War paintings on the walls, and statues of Washington, Lincoln, Jefferson, and others. The rest of the building also contains many artworks, and though you are free to wander about, the 40-minute guided tours that leave from the Rotunda every quarter hour are excellent and provide access to the visitors galleries of Congress (congressional sessions start at noon). Open daily from 9 AM to 4:30 PM (last tour at 3:45 PM). Between the first week of May and *Labor Day,* the Rotunda is open until 8 PM. No admission charge. You also can ride the monorail subway that joins the House and Senate wings with the congressional office buildings and try the famous bean soup in the Senate dining room (see also *Quintessential Washington, DC* in DIVERSIONS). 1st St. between Constitution and Independence Aves. (phone: 224-3121). *Metro:* Capitol South or Union Station.

Supreme Court Building – This neo-classical white marble structure, surrounded by Corinthian columns and with the inscription on its pediment "Equal Justice Under Law," was designed by Cass Gilbert and completed in 1935. Until then, however, the highest judicial body in the nation and one of three equal branches of government met in makeshift quarters in the basement of the Capitol. Now the Court receives equal treatment under the law and meets in an impressive courtroom flanked by Ionic columns when it is in session, intermittently from the first Monday in October through June. Sessions are open to the public on a first-come, first-served basis. Open weekdays; courtroom presentations are every hour on the half hour from 9:30 AM to 3:30 PM except when court is in session. No admission charge. 1st St. between Maryland Ave. and E. Capitol St. NE (phone: 479-3000). *Metro:* Capitol South or Union Station.

Library of Congress – These magnificent Italian Renaissance buildings house the world's largest and richest library. Originally designed as a research aid to Congress, the Library serves the public as well with 84 million items in 470 languages, including manuscripts, maps, photographs, motion pictures, and music. The exhibition hall displays include Jefferson's first draft of the Declaration of Independence and Lincoln's first two drafts of the Gettysburg Address. Among the Library's other holdings are one of three extant copies of the Gutenberg Bible, Pierre L'Enfant's original design for Washington, and the oldest-known existing film — the 3-second *Sneeze* by Thomas Edison. Forty-five-minute guided tours are offered on weekdays from 10 AM to 4 PM, Saturdays from 10 AM to 3 PM, and Sundays at 1, 2, and 3 PM. Open weekdays from 8:30 AM to 9:30 PM, Saturdays from 8:30 AM to 5 PM, Sundays from 1 to 5 PM. No admission charge. 1st St. between E. Capitol and Independence Sts. SE (phone: 707-5458). *Metro:* Capitol South.

Folger Shakespeare Library – The nine bas-reliefs on the façade depict scenes from Shakespeare's plays, and inside you can find out anything you want to know about Shakespeare and the English Renaissance. The world's finest collection of rare books, manuscripts, and research materials relating to the foremost English-language playwright is here. The library, an oak-paneled, barrel-vaulted Elizabethan palace, also has a model of the *Globe Theatre* and a full-scale replica of an Elizabethan theater complete with a trapdoor (called the "heavens" and used for special effects). Visitors can see how productions were mounted in Shakespeare's day and how they are done today. The bookstore features the fine *Folger* series on the Elizabethan period as well as editions of Shakespeare's plays. Open 10 AM to 4 PM (tours at 11 AM) daily except Sundays. No admission charge. 201 E. Capitol St. SE (phone: 546-4600). *Metro:* Capitol South or Union Station.

Botanic Gardens – If you feel as if you are overdosing on history, the Botanic Gardens provides a pleasant antidote with its azaleas, orchids, and tropical plants — and we're not even going to tell you how big they are or where they're from. Open daily, 9 AM to 7:30 PM from September through November; 9 AM to 5 PM all other months. Closed *Christmas.* No admission charge. 1st St. and Maryland Ave. SW, at the foot of Capitol Hill (phone: 225-8333). *Metro:* Federal Center Southwest.

Union Station – This 82-year-old landmark recently was restored to its former Beaux Arts grandeur. Modeled after the Diocletian Baths and the triumphal Arch of Constantine in Rome, its marble floors, granite walls, bronze grilles, and classic statuary dazzle visitors. In front of *Amtrak*'s rail terminal is a complex of chic boutiques and dining areas. (*Sfuzzi Washington* is one of our favorites; see *Eating Out.*) The main concourse, once the largest room under a single roof, has been divided into a series of levels and mezzanines for stores and eateries. The lower level houses movie theaters and a score of fast-food outlets. 50 Massachusetts Ave. NE (phone: 371-9441). *Metro:* Union Station.

THE WHITE HOUSE AREA

White House – Probably the most historic house in America because George Washington never slept here, though every president since has. It has been the official residence of the head of state since 1800. Designed originally by James Hoban, the White House still looks like an Irish country mansion from the outside; inside there are elegant parlors decorated with portraits of the presidents and first ladies, antique furnishings of many periods, and many innovations added by various presidents, like the revolving tray in the Green Room — an invention of Thomas Jefferson's that revolved between pantry and dining room, allowing him to serve such novelties as macaroni and ice cream and waffles without fear of eavesdropping servants. The five state rooms on the first floor are open to the public, and though you actually won't see the business of government going on, you'll be very close to it.

Visitors line up at the East Gate on E. Executive Avenue. (Tickets, required during summer months, are available from the kiosk on the Ellipse.) Congressional tours of seven rooms, instead of the usual five, are available by writing to your congressman in advance. Be sure to specify alternate dates. Open Tuesdays through Saturdays from 10 AM to noon. No admission charge. 1600 Pennsylvania Ave. NW (phone: 456-7041 or 472-3669). *Metro:* McPherson Square.

Lafayette Square – If you do not enter the White House, you can get a fine view of it from this square, which was originally proposed by city planner L'Enfant as the mansion's front yard. Statues commemorate Andrew Jackson and the foreign heroes of the American Revolution — Lafayette, de Rochambeau, von Steuben, and Kosciusko. Flanking the square are two early-19th-century buildings designed by Benjamin Latrobe, Washington's first public architect. St. John's Church, constructed along classically simple lines, is better known as the Church of Presidents because every president since Madison has attended services here. Open daily. No admission charge. 16th and H Sts. NW (phone: 347-8766). The Decatur House, built for Commodore Stephen Decatur and occupied after his death by a succession of diplomats, is a Federal townhouse featuring handsome woodwork, a spiral staircase, and furniture of the 1820s. Open Tuesdays through Fridays, 10 AM to 2 PM; weekends, noon to 4 PM. Admission charge. 748 Jackson Pl. NW (phone: 842-0920). Near the southwest corner of the square is Blair House, the president's official guesthouse since 1942 (not open to the public; 1651-1653 Pennsylvania Ave. NW). *Metro:* Farragut West.

Ellipse – This grassy 32-acre expanse is the location of the zero milestone from which all distances in Washington are measured, the site of everything from demonstrations and ball games to the national *Christmas* tree. 1600 Constitution Ave. NW. *Metro:* Farragut West.

Corcoran Gallery of Art – If you think you've seen the Athenaeum portraits of George Washington before, you're probably not experiencing déjà vu. Check your wallet and with luck you'll see several more reproductions, and maybe a few of Jackson, too. This outstanding collection of American art contains some less familiar works as well, including a beardless portrait of Lincoln (a $5 bill won't help you here). The *Corcoran* also offers the opulent Grand Salon from the *Hôtel d'Orsay* in Paris, built by Boucher d'Orsay during the reign of Louis XVI and moved and reconstructed here in its entirety. The recently renovated 1,850-square-foot semicircular Hemicycle Hall features an impressive gallery of special exhibitions by Washington artists. Open 10 AM to 5 PM, Tuesdays through Sundays; until 9 PM on Thursdays. No admission charge. 17th St. and E St. NW (phone: 638-3211). *Metro:* Farragut West.

Renwick Gallery – The nation's first art museum, this beautiful French Second Empire building was designed by *Smithsonian* "Castle" architect James Renwick in 1859 to house W. W. Corcoran's art collection. Now run by the *Smithsonian Institution,* it is worth a visit for its changing exhibitions of contemporary American crafts and design. The gallery's other noteworthy sights are the entrance foyer, with its impressive staircase, and the 1870 Grand Salon, with overstuffed Louis XV sofas and potted palms. Open daily, 10 AM to 5:30 PM. No admission charge. Pennsylvania Ave. at 17th St. NW (phone: 357-2531). *Metro:* Farragut North or West.

Daughters of the American Revolution Museum – Though any member of the DAR must prove that she is descended from those who served the cause of American independence with "unfailing loyalty," the museum is open to everyone regardless of the color of his or her skin. Exhibitions feature 33 period rooms, including the parlor of a 19th-century Mississippi River steamboat. There's also an extensive genealogical library. Open weekdays from 8:30 AM to 4 PM, Sundays from 1 to 5 PM (closed Saturdays); State Rooms open from 9 AM to 4 PM.. No admission charge. 1776 D St. NW (phone: 628-1776). *Metro:* Farragut West.

Octagon House – This stately red brick townhouse is a notable example of Federal architecture. The house in which President James and Dolley Madison lived for 6 months after the British burned down the White House in 1814 is maintained as a museum to give a picture of the high style of the early 19th century and features American antique furnishings from the Federal period. Open Tuesdays through Fridays from 10 AM to 4 PM, weekends noon to 4 PM. Donations suggested. 1799 New York Ave. NW (phone: 638-3105). *Metro:* Farragut West.

Organization of American States – In the Pan American Union Building. Its architects, Paul Cret and Albert Kelsey, have blended the styles of North and South America in this building of imposing formality and inviting elegance. Open 9 AM to 5 PM weekdays. The *Art Museum of the Americas* is just behind the Aztec Garden. Open daily except Sundays from 10 AM to 5 PM. No admission charge. 17th St. and Constitution Ave. NW (phone: 458-6016). *Metro:* Farragut West.

THE MALL AREA

This 2-mile stretch of green from the Lincoln Memorial to the Capitol forms something of the grand avenue envisioned by Pierre L'Enfant in his original plans for the city.

■ **Note:** Due to extensive repairs to the Lincoln and Jefferson memorials, visitors will be seeing more scaffolding than monuments for the next several years. The statues themselves, however, will not be obstructed. Although both will remain open to the public, walking around the colonnades will be prohibited until repairs are completed, sometime in 1996.

Lincoln Memorial – From the outside, this columned white marble building looks like a Greek temple; inside the spacious chamber with its colossal seated statue of Lincoln, sculpted by Daniel French, it is as inspiring. Carved on the walls are the words of the Gettysburg Address and Lincoln's Second Inaugural Address. National Park Service guides present brief talks at regular intervals. Open 24 hours a day; park rangers are on duty until midnight. No admission charge. Memorial Circle between Constitution and Independence Aves. (phone: 426-6841). *Metro:* Farragut West.

Washington Monument – Dominating the Mall is the 555-foot marble and granite obelisk designed by Robert Mills (completed in 1888) to commemorate George Washington. The top (reached by elevator) commands an excellent panoramic view of the city. On National Park Service tours on weekends, you can walk down the 897 steps, where you see many stones donated by such groups as the "Citizens of the US residing in Foo Chow Foo, China." Open daily, 8 AM to midnight, from the first Sunday in April through *Labor Day;* 9 AM to 5 PM the rest of the year. No admission charge. 15th St. between Independence and Constitution Aves. (phone: 426-6841). *Metro:* Smithsonian.

Vietnam Veterans Memorial – Maya Ying Lin, while a Yale architecture student, designed this simple but immensely moving memorial to the American soldiers who died or are missing as a result of the Vietnam War. The two arms of the long, V-shaped, polished black granite walls point toward the Washington Monument and the Lincoln Memorial. On the 492-foot-long wall are inscribed the names of more than 58,000 men and women who were killed in the war or are still missing. A sculpture by Frederick Hart, depicting three soldiers, stands a short distance from the memorial. Under construction nearby is a memorial honoring the estimated 10,000 women who served in the Vietnam War. The memorial, a bronze sculpture by Gienna Goodacre, will depict two women in uniform attending a wounded male soldier; it will be dedicated this year on *Veterans Day* (November 11). Constitution Ave. NW and Henry Bacon Dr. (phone: 634-1568). *Metro:* Foggy Bottom.

Jefferson Memorial – Dominating the south bank of the Tidal Basin, this domed temple-like structure (designed by John Russell Pope) is a tribute to our third president and the drafter of the Declaration of Independence. The bronze statue of Jefferson was executed by Rudolph Evans, and inscribed on the walls are quotations from Jefferson's writings. This is the place to be for the most dramatic view of the cherry blossoms in early spring. Open daily. No admission charge. South Basin Dr. SW (phone: 426-6822). *Metro:* L'Enfant Plaza.

Bureau of Engraving and Printing – If you're interested in money and how it is really made, the 25-minute self-guided tour that follows the entire process of paper currency production will prove enlightening if not enriching. Everything of a financial character from the 1-cent postage stamp to the $500-million Treasury Note is designed, engraved, and printed here. Though it costs only a penny to produce a single note, there are no free samples. Open weekdays, 9 AM to 2 PM. No admission charge. 14th and C Sts. SW (phone: 874-3316). *Metro:* Smithsonian.

J. Edgar Hoover Building – If you want to find out a little more about an organization that already knows everything about you, take a tour of the FBI. In addition to a film on some past investigative activities, you'll get to see the laboratory and a firearms demonstration. Open weekdays, 8:45 AM to 4:15 PM. This popular 1-hour FBI tour is given every 20 minutes. Line up early. No admission charge. Pennsylvania Ave. between 9th and 10th Sts. NW (phone: 324-3447). *Metro:* Metro Center or Gallery Place.

National Archives – The repository for all major American records. The 76 Corinthian columns supporting this handsome building designed by John Russell Pope are nothing compared to the contents. Inside, in special helium-filled glass and bronze cases, reside the very pillars of our democracy — the Declaration of Independence, the Constitution, and the Bill of Rights. Open daily, 10 AM to 5:30 PM; April through *Labor*

Day, 10 AM to 9 PM. No admission charge. Constitution Ave. between 7th and 9th Sts. NW (phone: 501-5205). *Metro:* Archives.

US Navy Memorial Plaza – The plaza, dedicated in October 1987, has a statue of a lone US sailor overlooking the US portion of a granite world map. The visitors' center, which opened last year, includes a gift shop, IMAX theater, and museum. Military bands perform during spring and summer evenings; pick up a brochure at any hotel or call for schedule. Pennsylvania Ave. between 7th and 9th Sts. NW (phone: 737-2300 or 800-821-8892). *Metro:* Archives/Navy Memorial.

National Gallery of Art – One of the larger jewels in Washington's rich cultural crown, this gift to the nation by Andrew Mellon, financier and former Secretary of the Treasury, houses one of the world's finest collections of Western art from the 13th century to the present. Among the masterpieces in this huge and opulent white marble gallery are a grand survey of Italian painting including da Vinci's *Ginevra de' Benci* (the only da Vinci in the US), Fra Filippo Lippi's *The Adoration of the Magi,* Raphael's *Saint George and the Dragon,* works of French Impressionists, a self-portrait by Rembrandt, Renoir's *Girl With a Watering Can,* Picasso's *The Lovers,* and an extensive American collection. The 7-story East Building, designed by I. M. Pei, is something of an architectural masterpiece itself. An intriguing structure of interlocking triangular forms, it houses the Center for Advanced Study in the Visual Arts as well as exhibition halls. Several visits are necessary to see the whole gallery; there also are tours, films, lectures, and weekly concerts. Major exhibitions scheduled for this year (dates were unavailable at press time; call ahead) include "Art of the American Indian Frontier: The Collection of Chandler and Pohrt," "Steiglitz in the Darkroom," "Helen Frankenthaler Prints," and the "Reinstallation of Twentieth-Century Art." Open Mondays through Saturdays from 11 AM to 6 PM, Sundays from noon to 9 PM. No admission charge. Between 3rd and 7th Sts. and Constitution Ave. NW (phone: 737-4215). *Metro:* Judiciary Square Federal Center or Archives.

Smithsonian Institution – Before James Smithson died in 1829 he willed his entire fortune of half a million dollars "to found on Washington . . . an establishment for the increase and diffusion of knowledge among men." The wealthy English scientist had never even been to America and probably had no idea how much knowledge would be increased and diffused here in his name. Today the *Smithsonian* administers numerous museums, galleries, and research organizations, and has an operating budget of over $90 million, a staff of over 4,000, and 75 million items in its total collection. The *Smithsonian's* $73-million, 3-floor complex just south of the Castle on Independence Avenue SW is a bit controversial because it is underground. Opened in autumn 1987, it houses two museums — the *Arthur M. Sackler Gallery,* featuring Asian art (including bronzes, jades, paintings, lacquerware, and sculpture; see below), and the *National Museum of African Art* (see below), which was moved from its former Capitol Hill location. The third floor houses the International Center for exhibitions, and atop it all is the Enid A. Haupt Garden, a $3-million Victorian delight built around a 100-year-old linden tree. Entry to the museums is through kiosks in the garden. The Romanesque red sandstone building known as the Castle is the best place to get visitor information on any of the *Institution's* activities. All buildings are open daily, 10 AM to 5:30 PM. Extended summer hours. No admission charge. 1000 Jefferson Dr. SW (phone: 357-2700, for information on all 14 *Smithsonian* museums). Also for the young — and young-at-heart — is the beautiful 50-year-old carousel set in the shadow of the Smithsonian Castle; it operates in the warm weather between 10 AM and 5:30 PM. *Metro:* Smithsonian.

Among the *Smithsonian Museums* on the Mall are the following:

    National Museum of African Art – The most extensive collection of African art in this country, and the only one dedicated exclusively to the arts of sub-

Saharan Africa. Exhibitions include figures, masks, and sculptures in ivory, wood, bronze, and clay from 20 African nations; also color panels and audiovisual presentations on the people and environment of Africa. One gallery has an intriguing display concerning the influence of Africa's cultural heritage on modern European and American art. Delightful gift shop. 950 Independence Ave. SW, next to the *Sackler Gallery of Art* (phone: 357-4600). *Metro:* Smithsonian.

Arthur M. Sackler Gallery – Donated by Dr. Arthur M. Sackler, a New York medical researcher, the extensive collection of over 1,000 pieces of Eastern art includes Chinese bronzes from the Shang (1523–1028 BC) through Han (206 BC–AD 220) dynasties, Chinese jade that dates to 3000 BC, and numerous Near Eastern works in silver, gold, bronze, and lesser ores. There are also Persian and Indian paintings, Chinese Ming Dynasty furniture, and more. 1050 Independence Ave. SW (phone: 357-2700). *Metro:* Smithsonian.

Freer Gallery – An eclectic collection of Asian art, plus late-19th- and early-20th-century American art. Wealthy Detroit businessman Charles Lang Freer donated the works from his personal collection. *The Peacock Room,* painted by Freer's friend, James McNeill Whistler, is a must-see. Jefferson Dr. at 12th St. SW (phone: 357-2104). *Metro:* Smithsonian.

National Museum of Natural History – Only 1% of the museum's collection is on display but, with a total of some 118 million specimens, there's still plenty to see. Features eyefuls of the biggest and the best of most everything from the largest elephant on record — 12 tons from the African bush — to the precious Hope Diamond, at a hefty 45.5 karats, the largest blue diamond known (its only flaw is that it has brought tragedy to all its possessors). The Dinosaur Hall has mammoth skeletons. And there's even Martha, who died in the Cincinnati Zoo in 1914 and now is stuffed, the last of the extinct passenger pigeons. 10th St. and Constitution Ave. NW. *Metro:* Smithsonian or Federal Triangle.

National Museum of American History – Everything that has to do with American ingenuity in craftsmanship, design, and industry can be found here, along with some things that bear only the most tenuous link. (That's where the real fun begins.) Hall after hall features such items as Eli Whitney's cotton gin, a gargantuan pendulum that was used by French physicist Jean Foucault to demonstrate the rotation of the earth, Radar's teddy bear (from the TV series "MASH"), Dorothy's ruby slippers (from the film *The Wizard of Oz*), and a full gallery of First Lady mannequins dressed in Inaugural Ball gowns. 12th to 14th Sts. and Constitution Ave. NW. *Metro:* Smithsonian or Federal Triangle.

National Air and Space Museum – The largest of the *Smithsonian*'s museums, with displays of aircraft in its vast, lofty interior. Exhibitions include the Wright Brothers' plane, Charles Lindbergh's *Spirit of St. Louis,* the Apollo 11 command module, and a walk-through model of a Skylab orbital station. The films *To Fly, The Dream Is Alive, Living Player,* and *Flyers,* shown on a huge screen, are as spectacular as they are dizzying. Planetarium shows are presented in the *Albert Einstein Planetarium.* 6th St. and Independence Ave. SW. *Metro:* L'Enfant Plaza.

Hirshhorn Museum and Sculpture Garden – Smaller but also superb is this collection donated in 1974 by a Latvian immigrant and self-made millionaire. The *Hirshhorn,* designed by Gordon Bunshaft, is worth a visit not only for its fine collection but also for the building itself, a circular concrete structure with an open core in which a bronze fountain shoots water 82 feet into the air. Displays include 19th- and 20th-century European and American works, and an attractive sculpture garden that features Rodin's *The Burghers of Calais* and Picasso's *Baby Carriage.* Independence Ave. and 7th St. SW. *Metro:* L'Enfant Plaza.

Arts and Industries Building – Just east of the Castle, this is the second-oldest

Smithsonian building on the Mall. The *Centennial Exhibition,* displayed in Philadelphia in 1876, has been re-created with marvelous displays of fashions, furnishings, and machinery. Jefferson Dr. and Independence Ave. at 9th St. SW. *Metro:* Smithsonian.

DOWNTOWN

National Portrait Gallery and National Museum of American Art – Inside the *National Portrait Gallery,* an excellent example of Greek Revival architecture, many Americans who have gone down in the history of this country have gone up on the walls (in portrait form, that is). Among those hanging are all the American presidents, Pocahontas, Horace Greeley, and Harriet Beecher Stowe. The *National Museum of American Art* features American painting, sculpture, and graphic arts, including Catlin's paintings of the Indians and a choice group of works of the American Impressionists. Both museums (also administered by the *Smithsonian*) are open daily. No admission charge. 8th St. at F and G Sts. NW. *Metro:* Gallery Place.

Ford's Theatre – The site of Abraham Lincoln's assassination by John Wilkes Booth is a national monument, and in the 1960s it was restored and decorated as it appeared on the fatal night of April 14, 1865. In the basement is a museum of Lincoln memorabilia, including displays showing his life as a lawyer, statesman, husband and father, and president, and the clothes he was wearing when he was shot, the derringer used by Booth to shoot him, and the assassin's personal diary. Theater performances are held throughout the year. For theater tickets, call 347-4833. Open daily, 9 AM to 5 PM. Admission charge for shows only. 511 10th St. NW (phone: 426-6924). *Metro:* Metro Center, 11th St. exit.

Peterson House – Directly across the street from the theater and museum is the house in which Lincoln died the morning after the shooting. The small, sparsely furnished house appears much the way it did in 1865. Open daily from 9 AM to 5 PM. No admission charge. 516 10th St. NW (phone: 426-6830). *Metro:* Metro Center.

National Law Enforcement Officers' Memorial – Dedicated in late 1991, this new monument honors federal, state, and local law enforcement officers who have died in the line of duty, dating as far back as 1794. The enclosed plaza has walled pathways that encircle a terraced pool, and are guarded on each side by majestic bronze lions. E St. NW, between 4th and 5th Sts. (phone: 703-827-0518). *Metro:* Judiciary Square.

ADAMS MORGAN

This funky, international neighborhood is now rivaling Georgetown as the area for after-hours fun and frolicking in the nation's capital. Long the bohemian section of town, it has been home to many Salvadoran, Ethiopian, and African immigrants. Surrounding Columbia Road and 18th Street NW are foreign-language book and record stores; clothing boutiques with products from Asia and Africa; Ethiopian and Vietnamese restaurants; reggae bars; and hot nightspots. *Adams Morgan Day,* an annual cultural street fair held in early September, is alive with music from all over the world; chefs from the local restaurants provide a host of international foods to satisfy any palate. *Metro:* Dupont Circle.

GEORGETOWN

Once the Union's major tobacco port, the only tobacco left in this area is in the smoke shops. This area of Washington, still holding fast to its own identity, is particularly nice in the spring when it's pleasant to walk along the Chesapeake and Ohio Canal. The whole area's great for strolling. And in the summer, it's possible to catch a slow-moving barge up the canal. Tickets can be purchased at the *Foundry Mall* (1055 Thomas Jefferson St. NW; phone: 472-4376). Beside the Canal (between Jefferson and 31st Sts.), the streets off Wisconsin Avenue house the city's social and political elite in beautiful restored townhouses with prim gardens and lovely magnolia trees. Many of the buildings are on the National Register of Historic Places and are well worth seeing. The main drags — Wisconsin Avenue and M Street — are where most of the action is. In addition to boasting a serene shopping mall and some of the hottest nightlife (including sports and blues bars) in town, the area is rich with boutiques, movie theaters, and restaurants offering a vast variety of food — from Vietnamese to Indian to French.

In the area at the top of the hill (along R Street east of Wisconsin Avenue), large 18th-century country estates mingle with smaller, more modern row houses. The Dumbarton Oaks Garden has beautiful formal grounds, and the *Dumbarton Oaks Museum* has a fine collection of early Christian and Byzantine art. The museum is open Tuesdays through Sundays from 2 to 5 PM; no admission charge. The gardens are open daily from 2 to 5 PM; admission charge from April through October (phone: 342-3200 or 338-8278). The entrance to the museum is at 1703 32nd St. NW; the entrance to the gardens is at 31st and R Sts. NW.

On 37th and O Streets is the campus of Georgetown University. Established in 1789, it is the oldest Jesuit university in the United States and is renowned for its schools of foreign service and languages, as well as one of the best law schools in the country.

■**EXTRA SPECIAL:** Just 16 miles south of Washington on George Washington Memorial Parkway is Mount Vernon, George Washington's estate from 1754 to 1799 and his final resting place. This lovely 18th-century plantation is interesting because it shows a less familiar aspect of the military-political man — George Washington as the rich Southern planter. The mansion, overlooking the Potomac, and the outbuildings that housed the shops that made Mount Vernon a self-sufficient economic unit have been authentically restored and refurnished. Some 500 of the original 8,000 acres remain; all are well maintained, and the parterre gardens and formal lawns provide a magnificent setting. There's also a museum with Washington memorabilia; the tomb of George and Martha lies at the foot of the hill. During the spring or the summer, start out early to avoid big crowds. Bicycle paths lead from the DC side of Memorial Bridge to Mount Vernon — a lovely ride along the Potomac. Open daily, 9 AM to 5 PM, March through October; to 4 PM the rest of the year. Admission charge (phone: 703-780-2000).

Also beautifully landscaped and overlooking the Potomac, but with many more tombs and monuments, is Arlington National Cemetery, a solemn reminder of this country's turbulent history. Here lie the bodies of many who served in the military forces — or in other ways served their country, among them Admiral Richard Byrd, General George C. Marshall, Robert F. Kennedy, Justice Oliver Wendell Holmes, and John F. Kennedy, whose grave is marked by an Eternal Flame. The Tomb of the Unknown Soldier, a 50-ton block of white marble, commemorates the dead of World Wars I and II and the Korean, Vietnam, and Persian Gulf wars and is always guarded by a solitary soldier. Changing of the guard takes place every hour on the hour (every half hour during summer months). The grounds of the cemetery once were the land of Robert E. Lee's plantation but were confiscated by the Union after Lee joined the Confederacy. Lee's home, Arlington House, has been restored and is open for public inspection. Cars are not allowed in the cemetery, but you can park at the visitors' center and go on foot or pay and ride the *Tourmobile* (phone: 554-7950). The house is open daily, 9:30 AM to 4:30 PM from October to March, to 6 PM the rest of the year. No admission charge (phone: 703-557-0613). The cemetery is open daily from 8 AM to 5 PM; April to October to 7 PM (phone: 703-692-0931). Directly west of Memorial Bridge in Arlington, Virginia. *Metro:* Arlington Cemetery.

SOURCES AND RESOURCES

TOURIST INFORMATION: The Washington, DC, Convention and Visitors Association (1212 New York Ave. NW, Washington, DC 20005) coordinates all Washington tourism information and runs the visitors' center (at 1455 Pennsylvania Ave. NW; phone: 789-7038). The center (open daily except Sundays, 9 AM to 5 PM) provides free maps and information on where to stay, eat, and shop. Contact the District of Columbia's hotline (phone: 789-7000) for maps, calendars of events, health updates, and travel advisories.

Local Coverage – The *Washington Post,* morning daily; The *Washington Times,* morning daily; and *Washingtonian* magazine, monthly, all are available at newsstands. *City Paper,* a free weekly highlighting cultural events in the area, is available in shops and restaurants. *Museum and Arts Washington* lists current museum exhibits, and *Regardie's* is a monthly business magazine.

Television Stations – WRC Channel 4–NBC; WJLA Channel 7–ABC; WUSA Channel 9–CBS; Channel 13–CNN; WETA Channel 26–PBS.

Radio Stations – AM: WFMD 930 (adult contemporary music); WNTR 1050 (news/talk); WTOP 1500 (news). FM: WPFW 89.3 (jazz/community radio); WKYS 93.9 (urban contemporary); WMZQ 98.7 (country); WGAY 99.5 (easy listening); WAVA 105.1 (top 40); WCXR 105.9 (classic rock).

Food – *Best Restaurants and Others* by Phyllis Richman (101 Productions, $8.95) lists fine dining places in Washington, DC, and environs. *Washingtonian* magazine also has good restaurant listings.

TELEPHONE: The area code for the District is 202; for Maryland, 301; and for Virginia, 703.

SALES TAX: The city sales tax is 6%; there is an 11% tax on hotel rooms.

GETTING AROUND: Train – More than 50 *Amtrak* trains daily pull into historic Union Station on Capitol Hill, including the *Metroliner,* linking the capital to New York and other Northeast-corridor cities. For reservations and information, call 800-872-7245.

Bus – The *Metro Bus* system serves the entire District and the surrounding area. Transfers within the District are free; the rates increase when you go into Maryland and Virginia. For complete route information call the *Washington Metropolitan Area Transit Authority* office (phone: 637-7000). *Greyhound/Trailways* runs to and from its main bus station at 1st and L St. NE (phone: 310-565-2662).

Car Rental – For information on renting a car, see *On Arrival,* in GETTING READY TO GO.

Subway – The fastest way to get around Washington is by *Metrorail,* the subway system. The lines that are in operation provide a quick and quiet ride. New lines to the suburbs and other areas of the city open as they are completed, and buses deposit or pick up passengers at these stations. Transfers to the bus system are free. Be sure to pick up a transfer at your boarding station (not the exiting station). Children ages 5 and under ride free. *Metro* hours are 6 AM to midnight, weekdays; 8 AM to midnight, Saturdays; and 10 AM to midnight, Sundays. Inquire about discount passes; for example, a 2-day Family/Tourist Pass, costing $5, is good for unlimited travel on the Metro buses and subway for up to 4 persons. For complete route and travel information and a map of the system, contact the *Washington Metropolitan Area Transit Authority* office, 600 5th St. NW (phone: 637-7000).

Taxi – Cabs in the District charge by zone. Sharing cabs is common, but ask the driver whether there is a route conflict if you join another passenger. Cabs may be hailed in the street, picked up outside stations and hotels, or ordered on the phone, but there is an extra charge of $1.50 for phone dispatch. By law, basic rates must be posted in all taxis. Major cab companies are *Yellow* (phone: 544-1212) and *Diamond* (phone: 387-6200).

Tourmobile – This shuttle bus operates in the downtown sightseeing area between the Lincoln Memorial and Capitol area (the Mall). Tickets can be purchased from the driver or from a booth near the tour sites. Passengers get on and off as often as they wish. The *Tourmobile* (phone: 554-7950) also goes to Arlington National Cemetery.

LOCAL SERVICES: Audiovisual Equipment – *Avcom* (1006 6th St. NW; phone: 638-1513); *Total Audio-Visual Systems* (303 H St. NW; phone: 737-3900).

Baby-sitting – *Kids First,* 15th and K Sts. (phone: 289-5437).

Business Services – *Echo Temporary Services,* 1441 K St. NW (phone: 457-1848).

Dry Cleaner/Tailor – *Bergmann's* offers pickup and delivery at several locations (2318 Rhode Island Ave. NE; phone: 529-2440; 1301 E. Capitol St. SE; phone: 547-0418; and 714 6th St. NW; phone: 737-6925).

Limousine – *International Limousine Service,* multilingual drivers, sedans also (phone: 388-6800); *Congressional Limousine,* 24-hour service (phone: 966-6000).

Mechanic – *Call Carl,* gas 24 hours and repairs 7:30 AM to 5 PM, 5030 Connecticut Ave. (phone: 364-6360).

Medical Emergency – *George Washington University Medical Center,* 901 23rd St. NW (phone: 994-3884).

Messenger Services – *Central Delivery Service* (phone: 783-8020).

National/International Courier – *Federal Express* (phone: 301-953-3333); *DHL Worldwide Courier Express* (phone: 800-225-5345).

Pharmacy – *Peoples Drug Stores,* open 24 hours, has several locations, including 1121 Vermont Ave. NW (phone: 628-0720).

Photocopies – *City Duplicating Center* (1617 I St. NW; phone: 296-0700); *Beaver Press,* pickup and delivery service (1333 H St. NW; phone: 347-6400; and 1800 M St. NW; phone: 466-4830).

Post Office – National Capitol Station, open from 7 AM to midnight, N. Capitol St. and Massachusetts Ave. (phone: 523-2337).

Professional Photographer – *Garrison Studio,* 52 O St. NW (phone: 265-5168).

Secretary/Stenographer – *Courtesy Associates,* 655 15th St. NW, Suite 300 (phone: 347-5900).

Teleconference Facilities – *Four Seasons* (2800 Pennsylvania Ave., NW; phone: 342-0444 or 800-332-3442) and at *Loews L'Enfant Plaza* (480 L'Enfant Plaza SW; phone: 484-1000 or 800-243-1166).

Translator – *Berlitz,* written translations only (1050 Connecticut Ave. NW; phone: 331-1160); *International Translation Center* (1660 L St. NW, Room 613; phone: 296-1344).

Typewriter Rental – *Shields Business Machines* (22560 Glenn Dr., Suite 116, Sterling, VA; phone: 703-450-6161); *North's Office Machines* (2101 K St. NW; phone: 466-2000).

Western Union/Telex – Many offices are located around the city (phone: 624-0100).

Other – *The Capital Informer,* convention and meeting planning, 3240 Prospect St. NW (phone: 965-7420).

SPECIAL EVENTS: Any town that inaugurates a new president every 4 years is in good standing when it comes to special events. The president takes the oath of office every 4th year on January 20. Usually the swearing-in is followed by a parade down Pennsylvania Avenue.

In between inaugurations there's plenty to keep the District going for 4 more years. The publications above list exact dates. When you start noticing white single blossoms and a flood of pink double blossoms, it's *Cherry Blossom* time in Washington. In early April, a big festival celebrates the coming of the blossoms and the spring with concerts, parades, balls, and the lighting of the Japanese Lantern at the Tidal Basin.

Around the same time (give or take a few blossoms) is the *Easter Monday Egg Rolling,* when scads of children descend on the White House lawn; adults are admitted only if accompanied by a child.

House, garden, and embassy tours are given in April and May, allowing entrance to some of Washington's most elegant interiors. For information on the tours, see the Weekend section in Friday's *Washington Post.*

During the summer, the *Festival of American Folklife,* sponsored by the *Smithsonian Institution,* sets up its tents on the Mall near the reflecting pool, and groups from all regions of the country do their stuff with jug bands, blues, Indian dance, and handicraft demonstrations. In midsummer the *Twilight Tattoo* features military pageantry. And the *Fourth of July* celebrations in the capital are among the best in the country, with a parade, concerts, fireworks, and other entertainment.

In early September celebrate *Adams Morgan Day,* a neighborhood festival with cultural diversity from Spanish, Ethiopian, and African influences, including music, crafts, and food from 11 AM to dusk. 18th St., Columbia Rd., and Florida Ave. NW.

The city is especially festive at *Christmas.* Special music programs are presented at the *Kennedy Center* and at many other spots around town.

MUSEUMS: When it comes to museums, Washington is one of the nation's major showplaces, with the *Smithsonian Institution*'s outstanding museums leading the way. In addition to those described in *Special Places,* other notable museums include the following:

Hillwood – Exquisite 18th- and 19th-century French and Russian icons, portraits, and Fabergé creations are housed in the elegant former home of cereal heiress Marjorie Merriweather Post. Other buildings on the 25-acre site include a dacha, or Russian country house, with a small collection of Russian art; the C. W. Post collection of paintings, sculpture, and furnishings; and a lodge housing American Indian artifacts. Be sure to stroll around the Rose Garden, French Garden, and Japanese Garden. Closed Sundays and Mondays. Tours by appointment only; call well in advance for reservations. Admission charge. 4155 Linnean Ave. NW (phone: 686-8500). *Metro:* Van Ness–UDC.

Historical Society of Washington, DC – A museum devoted to Washington, DC, history, housed in the spectacular Victorian mansion of brewer Christian Heurich. Library open to the public Wednesdays, Fridays, and Saturdays from 10 AM to 4 PM; tours on the hour Wednesdays through Saturdays from noon to 3 PM. Admission charge. 1307 New Hampshire Ave. NW (phone: 785-2068). *Metro:* Dupont Circle.

National Building Museum – Housed in the old and wonderful Pension Building, this museum has permanent and changing exhibits relating to architecture, building, engineering, and design. Presidential inaugural balls are held in its Great Hall. Open Mondays through Saturdays, 10 AM to 4 PM, Sundays from noon to 4 PM. No admission charge. 401 F St. NW (phone: 272-2448). *Metro:* Judiciary Square.

National Geographic Society Explorers Hall – Headquarters for the society; exhibits here document research and discoveries made by its explorers and documentarians. Open Mondays through Saturdays, 9 AM to 5 PM; Sundays from 10 AM to 5 PM. No admission charge. 17th and M Sts. NW (phone: 857-7588). *Metro:* Farragut North.

National Learning Center Capital Children's Museum – A hands-on museum where children can dress up in period costumes, feed animals, and work on high-tech equipment. Open daily from 10 AM to 5 PM. Admission charge. 800 3rd St. NE (phone: 543-8600). *Metro:* Union Station.

National Museum of Women in the Arts – In a former Masonic temple is a permanent collection of 500 pieces of pictorial, sculpted, and ceramic art spanning 400 years of women's work. Open Mondays through Saturdays from 10 AM to 5 PM; Sundays, noon to 5 PM. Admission charge. 1250 New York Ave. at 13th St. NW (phone: 783-5000). *Metro:* Metro Center.

Phillips Collection – Nineteenth- and 20th-century French and American paintings plus changing exhibits. Open Mondays through Saturdays, 10 AM to 5 PM; Sundays from noon to 7 PM. 1600 21st St. and Q St. NW (phone: 387-0961). *Metro:* Dupont Circle.

Tech 2000 – The world's first permanent gallery of interactive multimedia technology designed as a showcase, a learning lab, and a research center. Housed midway between the Capitol and the White House, this airy hall has been turned into an electronic playhouse for adults and children with a representation of over 60 applications of computer technology. Open Tuesdays through Sundays, 11 AM to 5 PM. Admission charge. 800 K St. NW (phone: 842-0500). *Metro:* Gallery Place or Metro Center.

Textile Museum – A diverse collection of fabrics from around the world, in a large former mansion. Open Mondays through Saturdays from 10 AM to 5 PM and Sundays from 1 to 5 PM. Admission charge. 2320 S St. NW (phone: 667-0441). *Metro:* Dupont Circle.

Washington Doll's House and Toy Museum – This private collection of dollhouse historian Floragill Jacobs displays antique dollhouses and toys, including a section of presidents' games that includes the "Game of Politics or Race for the Presidency," a board game published by W. S. Reed of Leominster, MA, in 1887; the "Game of Presidents," a card game by Parker Bros. dating to the early 20th century; and the "Myriopticon Rebellion," a historical diorama, by Bradley Co. of Springfield, MA. Open Tuesdays through Saturdays, 10 AM to 5 PM; Sundays from noon to 5 PM. Admission charge. One block west of Wisconsin Ave., between Jennifer and Harrison Sts. 5236 44th St. NW (phone: 244-0024). *Metro:* Friendship Heights.

Woodrow Wilson House – Home to Woodrow Wilson from 1921 to 1924, and to Mrs. Wilson until her death in 1961, this is now a memorial to our 28th president and his wife. On exhibit are gifts of state, presidential memorabilia, and other items from the 1920s. Open Tuesdays through Sundays, 10 AM to 4 PM. Admission charge. 2340 S St. NW (phone: 387-4062 or 673-4034). *Metro:* Dupont Circle North.

MAJOR COLLEGES AND UNIVERSITIES: Washington has several universities of high national standing — American University (Massachusetts and Nebraska Aves. NW; phone: 885-1000); Gallaudet University — for the deaf (7th St. and Florida Ave. NE; phone: 651-5000); Georgetown University (37th and O Sts. NW; phone: 687-5055); George Washington University (19th to 24th Sts. NW, F St. to Pennsylvania Ave.; phone: 994-1000); and Howard University (2000 6th St. NW; phone: 806-6100).

SHOPPING: When you've had your fill of monuments (for the moment), the nation's capital has enough shopping venues to satisfy even "shop-till-you-drop" appetites. Following the sprucing up of Pennsylvania Avenue some years ago, Washington is now home to a number of excellent shopping malls. For unique gifts, the city's impressive museums are the best bet. Most museums, shrines, and churches have their own shops, some offering reproductions of priceless treasures at very affordable prices. Here's a capital shoppers' guide:

SHOPPING MALLS

Connecticut Connection – This 3-story shopping and dining emporium is conveniently located atop the Farragut North *Metro* station. Connecticut Ave. and L St. NW (no main phone number).

Eastern Market – An open-air extravaganza on weekends with fresh produce, flowers, and the like. Pennsylvania Ave. and 7th St. SE.

F Street Plaza – Home to, among other shops, Washington's traditional department stores: *Hecht's* (phone: 628-6661) and *Woodward and Lothrop* (phone: 347-5300). 11th and F Sts. NW.

Georgetown Park Mall – The centerpiece of Georgetown shopping, this handsome brick complex, with its magnificent Victorian interior, houses more than 100 elegant shops, including *Ann Taylor, F.A.O. Schwarz,* and *Williams-Sonoma* (see below), and restaurants. 3222 M St. NW at Wisconsin Ave. (phone: 342-8190).

International Square – In this 12-story atrium with a cascading fountain are 30 retail shops, restaurants, and fast-food eateries. 1850 K St. NW (phone: 223-1850).

Mazza Gallerie – On the north end of Wisconsin Avenue, this enclosed mall features high-fashion shops and specialty stores such as *Neiman Marcus.* 5300 Wisconsin Ave. NW (phone: 966-6144).

National Place – A prime shoppers' paradise including *Victoria's Secret, Sharper Image,* and *Express.* 13th and F Sts. NW (phone: 783-9090).

Old Post Office Pavilion – The city's oldest Federal building, complete with a bell tower and skylight, has shops, cafés, and restaurants on its lower floors. 12th St. and Pennsylvania Ave. NW (phone: 289-4224).

2000 Pennsylvania Avenue – On the edge of the George Washington University campus, this mall, located within a brick townhouse complex, has a variety of specialty shops. Between 20th and 21st Sts. NW (phone: 822-8460).

Union Station – The capital's Beaux Arts train station has been restored to its former glory and contains varied and numerous shops as well as unique and entertaining eating spots. 50 Massachusetts Ave. NE (phone: 371-9441).

Washington Harbour – This expansive office/retail/residential complex on the Potomac River features unique architectural designs, with fountain-filled courtyards and specialty shops and restaurants. 3000 K St. NW, under the Whitehurst Freeway in Georgetown (phone: 944-4140).

Watergate – A prestigious shopping arcade in the Watergate complex, including *Yves St. Laurent, Gucci, Valentino,* and *Guy Laroche.* New Hampshire and Virginia Aves. NW (phone: 298-5500).

Willard Inter-Continental – Several designer boutiques are within this historic hotel. Pennsylvania Ave. and 14th St. (phone: 628-9100).

■**DISCOUNT ALERT:** Thirty minutes south of Washington is *Potomac Mills,* one of the world's largest outlet malls, and a big attraction for Washington shoppers on weekends. Among the almost 200 discount stores are outlets of such well-known retailers as *Eddie Bauer, Laura Ashley, Nordstrom's,* and *Benetton.* Open Mondays through Saturdays, 10 AM to 9:30 PM; Sundays, 11 AM to 6 PM. On I-95S, exit 52, in Prince William, VA (phone: 703-490-5948 or 800-VA-MILLS).

DOWNTOWN SHOPS

Ann Taylor – Classic women's wear. *Union Station,* 50 Massachusetts Ave. NE (phone: 371-8010).

Britches of Georgetown – Casual menswear and women's wear. 1219 Connecticut Ave. NW (phone: 347-8994).

Brookstone – Wide variety of unique and practical items from gardening tools and outdoor games to desk and automotive accessories. *Union Station,* 50 Massachusetts Ave. NE (phone: 289-3553).

Burberrys Ltd. – Raincoats, woolens, and umbrellas from the British isles. 1155 Connecticut Ave. NW (phone: 463-3000).

Caswell-Massey – Soaps, bath gels, and other fine bath products. *Old Post Office Pavilion,* 12th St. and Pennsylvania Ave. NW (phone: 898-1833).

Earl Allen – Office clothing for women. *International Sq.,* 1850 K St. NW (phone: 466-3437).

Jena-rue – British chocolates. 13th and F Sts. NW (phone: 783-8029).

Kramerbooks – Wide selection of classics and new titles; *Afterwords,* an all-night café, is in the rear of the store. Two locations: 1517 Connecticut Ave. NW and at *International Square,* 1850 K St. NW (phone: 387-1400 for both).

Nature Company – Minerals, bird feeders, binoculars, and books on the outdoors. *Union Station,* 50 Massachusetts Ave. NE (phone: 842-3700).

Post Office Exchange – Designer and souvenir Washington T-shirts. *Old Post Office Pavilion,* 12th St. and Pennsylvania Ave. NW (phone: 389-4224).

Paper on Parade – Stationery galore. *Old Post Office Pavilion,* 12th St. and Pennsylvania Ave. NW (phone: 389-4224).

Raleigh's – One of Washington's own department stores, with everything from clothes to housewares. 1133 Connecticut Ave. NW (phone: 833-0120).

Sharper Image – Expensive designer gadgets. National Press Bldg., 13th and F Sts. NW (phone: 626-6340).

Tannery West – Leather and suede clothing and bags. *Union Station,* 50 Massachusetts Ave. NE (phone: 371-1705).

Windsor Shirt Company – Men's shirts. *International Square,* 1850 K St. NW (phone: 887-0011).

GEORGETOWN

Abercrombie & Fitch – Menswear including dress shirts and sportswear. *Georgetown Park Mall,* Wisconsin Ave. and M St. NW (phone: 965-6500).

Ann Taylor – Classic women's clothing. *Georgetown Park Mall,* Wisconsin Ave. and M St. NW (phone: 938-5290).

Appalachian Spring – Handmade crafts, quilts, and jewelry from all over the US. 1415 Wisconsin Ave. NW (phone: 337-5780).

Conran's Habitat – Housewears and furniture. *Georgetown Park Mall,* Wisconsin Ave. and M St. NW (phone: 298-8300).

F.A.O. Schwarz – Upscale toys for all ages. *Georgetown Park Mall,* Wisconsin Ave. and M St. NW (phone: 342-2285).

Hats in the Belfry – Funny, unusual, elegant, and antique toppers for all occasions. 1237 Wisconsin Ave. NW (phone: 342-2006).

J. Crew – Casual wear for men and women. *Georgetown Park Mall,* Wisconsin Ave. and M St. NW (phone: 965-4091).

Little Caledonia – Unusual furnishings, fabrics, and stationery. 1419 Wisconsin Ave. NW (phone: 333-4700).

Orpheus Records – Specializes in vintage and rare recordings. 3249 M St. NW (phone: 337-7970).

Phoenix – Mexican jewelry, crafts, and clothing. 1514 Wisconsin Ave. NW (phone: 338-4404).

Polo/Ralph Lauren – Superb sportswear for men and women. *Georgetown Park Mall*, Wisconsin Ave. and M St. NW (phone: 965-0904).

Santa Fe Style – Crafts and art from the American Southwest. 1525 Wisconsin Ave. NW (phone: 333-3747).

Talbots – Conservative clothing for women. *Georgetown Park Mall*, Wisconsin Ave. and M St. NW (phone: 338-3510).

Threepenny Bit – Irish items — including hand-knit sweaters, shorts, shirts, ties, and shoes. 3122 M St. NW (phone: 338-1338).

Victoria's Secret – Lingerie and bath products. *Georgetown Park Mall*, Wisconsin Ave. and M St. NW (phone: 965-5457).

Williams-Sonoma – Upscale kitchenware. *Georgetown Park Mall*, Wisconsin Ave. and M St. NW (phone: 965-3422).

MUSEUM SHOPS

Some of the most memorable souvenirs of your visit to the nation's capital are found in its museum shops. From T-shirts to Lincoln memorabilia, the variety is virtually endless.

Arts and Industries Building – Stocks items shown in the *Smithsonian* mail-order gift catalogue. Jefferson Dr. and Independence Ave. at 9th St. NW (phone: 357-2700).

Bethune Museum Gift Shop – Books on such famous black women as Harriet Tubman and Josephine Baker. 1318 Vermont Ave. NW (phone: 322-1233).

Corcoran Gallery of Art – Art reproductions. 17th St. and E St. NW (phone: 638-3211).

Dumbarton Oaks – The private collection of Byzantine and pre-Columbian jewelry is reproduced for sale. R and 32nd Sts. NW (phone: 342-3200).

Ford's Theatre – The book and gift store here stocks materials pertaining to President Lincoln, his assassination, and the Civil War. 511 10th St. NW (phone: 426-0179).

Friends of the Kennedy Center – Jewelry, tote bags, T-shirts, scarves, cards, cookbooks, and more. New Hampshire Ave. and Rock Creek Pkwy. NW (phone: 416-8343).

Hirshhorn Museum – Contemporary jewelry and art reproductions. Independence Ave. and 7th St. SW (phone: 357-2700).

Mt. Vernon Estate – Replicas of George Washington memorabilia, books, and prints. George Washington Memorial Pkwy. (phone: 703-780-2000).

National Air and Space Museum – NASA flight jackets, US rocket model kits, and astronaut freeze-dried dinners. 6th St. and Independence Ave. SW (phone: 357-2700).

National Geographic Society – Offers some of the best bargains around in atlases and maps. 17th and M Sts. NW (phone: 857-7588).

National Museum of African Art – Arts and crafts, jewelry, books, graphics, posters, and postcards. 950 Independence Ave. SW (phone: 357-4600).

National Museum of American Art – Books, prints, postcards, and jewelry. 8th St. at F and G Sts. NW (phone: 357-2700).

National Museum of Natural History – Everything from a reproduction of the Hope Diamond to First Lady dolls. 14th St. and Constitution Ave. NW (phone: 357-2700).

National Portrait Gallery – Busts of past presidents. 8th St. at F and G Sts. NW (phone: 357-2700).

National Trust for Historic Preservation – Books, scarves, replicas of antique furniture. Decatur House, Lafayette Sq. NW (phone: 673-4000).

National Shrine of the Immaculate Conception – Religious items. 4th and Michigan Sts. NE (phone: 526-4433).

Renwick Gallery – Pieces by American crafts artists, including ceramics, woodcarvings, clocks, scarves, and quilting. Pennsylvania Ave. at 7th St. NW (phone: 357-2531).

Washington Doll's House and Toy Museum – Replicas of dolls and president's games. 5236 44th St. NW (phone: 244-0024).

Washington National Cathedral – An extensive gift shop. Massachusetts and Wisconsin Sts. NW (phone: 537-6200).

SPORTS AND FITNESS: Basketball – The NBA's *Bullets* hold court from October to April at the *Capital Centre* (Capital Beltway and Central Ave., in Landover, MD; phone: 301-350-3400). Tickets can be ordered by calling NBA-DUNK.

Bicycling – Rent from *Metropolis Bike & Scooter* (709 8th St. SE; phone: 543-8900); *Big Wheel Bikes* (M St. NW, Georgetown; phone: 337-0254); or *Thompson's Boat Center* (Virginia Ave. at Rock Creek Pkwy. NW; phone: 333-4861). The towpath of the Chesapeake and Ohio Canal, starting at the barge landing in Georgetown, is a good place to ride.

Fitness Center – Most major hotels have health and fitness centers (see *Checking In*).

Football – The NFL's 1992 *Super Bowl* champion *Redskins* play at *Robert F. Kennedy Stadium* from September through December. Tickets during the season are hard to come by and there usually is a waiting list for season tickets, but if you're in town during late July or August for pre-season games, chances are much better. Try *TicketMaster* (phone: 432-7328), or the stadium box office (E. Capitol and 22nd Sts. SE; phone: 547-9077).

Golf – The best public golf course is *East Potomac Park*. In East Potomac Park off Ohio Dr. (phone: 863-9007).

Hockey – The *Capitals*, Washington's pro hockey team, play at *Capital Centre* from October to April. Tickets are available at *TicketCenter* outlets or by calling 301-350-3400.

Jogging – Join plenty of others in making a round trip from the Lincoln Memorial to the Capitol (4 miles); also run in Rock Creek Park and in Georgetown, along the C&O Canal.

Skating – From November to April you can skate on the rink on the Mall, between 7th St. and Constitution Ave. NW (phone: 371-5340).

Swimming – Year-round facilities are available at the *East Capitol Natatorium*, 635 North Carolina Ave. SE (phone: 724-4495). Many of the hotels also have pools (see *Checking In*).

Tennis – Washington has some fine public courts; the best bets are the District tennis facilities at 16th and Kennedy Sts. NW (phone: 722-5949).

THEATER: The *Kennedy Center for the Performing Arts* (opened in 1971) gives the District its cultural cachet (off Virginia Ave. on New Hampshire Ave. NW; phone: 467-4600). The center's *Eisenhower Theater* offers musical and dramatic productions, including Broadway previews and road shows (phone: 467-4600). The *Terrace Theater,* on the top floor, offers many different productions — modern dance, ballet, dramas, poetry recitals, and so on (phone: 254-9895). The *National Theater* presents major productions throughout the year (1321 Pennsylvania Ave. NW; phone: 628-6161). The *Arena Stage,* the *Kreeger Theater,* and *The Old Vat Room* host classical and original plays year-round (6th St. and Maine Ave. SW;

phone: 554-9066; box office, 488-3300), and *Ford's Theatre* offers American productions (511 10th St. NW; phone: 347-4833). The *Shakespeare Theatre Group* offers
innovative interpretations of the bard's plays as well as more contemporary works at
the *Folger Theater* (201 E. Capitol St. SE; phone: 544-4600). Washington also has what
one theater critic calls the "off-off Kennedy Center movement" — a network of small
avant-garde houses on or near the stretch of 14th Street NW above Thomas Circle:
Studio Theater (1333 P St. NW; phone: 265-8412); *Woolly Mammoth Theater Company* (phone: 393-3939) and *Horizons Theater* (phone: 265-6574), which have separate
stages at the same address (1401 Church St. NW); and *Source Theater* (1835 14th St.
NW; phone: 462-1073). During the summer the *Olney Theater,* about a half-hour drive
from the District, offers summer stock with well-known casts (Rte. 108, Olney, MD;
phone: 301-924-3400). In winter, the *Barns at Wolf Trap,* a 350-seat theater, holds
performances indoors (1624 Trap Rd., off Rte. 7 near Vienna, VA, accessible via Dulles
Airport toll road Rte. 267 and by *Metro* to West Falls Church; phone: 703-938-2404).
Unsold theater and concert tickets are available on the day of the performance at half
price from the *TICKETplace* stand (in F Street Plaza, 12th and F Sts. NW; phone:
842-5387). A unique dinner-theater experience is a Saturday at *Mystery on the Menu.*
The evening includes a play that centers around a Georgetown wedding reception for
a senator and his bride, during which a murder occurs and where all guests get a chance
to solve the crime; three-course meal with glass of champagne included. Reservations
necessary. *Georgetown Holiday Inn,* 2101 Wisconsin Ave. NW (phone: 333-6875).

MUSIC: The *National Symphony Orchestra,* conducted by Mstislav Ros-
tropovich, performs at the *Kennedy Center Concert Hall* from September
through June (phone: 467-4600); in June there's also a *Mostly Mozart Festival.* Concerts are also given at the city's *former* premier venue, *Constitution
Hall,* which is renowned for its acoustics (18th and C Sts. NW; phone: 638-2661). The
Washington Opera (phone: 857-0900) presents seven operas a year, between November
and March, at the *Kennedy Center Opera House.* The *Juilliard String Quartet* and other
notable ensembles perform chamber music concerts on Stradivarius instruments at the
Library of Congress's *Coolidge Auditorium* (1st St. between E. Capitol St. and Independence Ave. SE, Thursday and Friday evenings in the spring and fall; for tickets, call
707-5500). During the summer, the *Wolf Trap Farm Park for the Performing Arts*
presents musicals, ballet, pop concerts, and symphonic music in a lovely outdoor setting
(bring a picnic; 1624 Trap Rd. off Rte. 7 near Vienna, VA, accessible via Dulles Airport
toll road Rte. 267 and by *Metro* to West Falls Church; phone: 703-255-1868). There
are free concerts by the service bands on the plaza at the West Front of the Capitol
or in front of the Jefferson Memorial. Consult newspapers for where and when. *Army
and Navy Band* concerts are presented at different locations in the winter (phone:
433-2416). During the first 2 weeks in June, the *British Embassy Players* delight
audiences with old-fashioned music hall performances. The British Embassy's Reception Hall is magically transformed into a cabaret, with most of the staff — and other
"Brits" living in the area — providing the entertainment. Tickets are limited and must
be reserved well in advance (3100 Massachusetts Ave. NW; phone: 703-271-0172).

NIGHTCLUBS AND NIGHTLIFE: For some, Washington is an early-to-bed
town, but there's plenty of pub crawling, jazz, bluegrass, soul, rock, and folk
music going on after dark. You just have to know where to look for it, and
best bets are Georgetown, lower Connecticut Avenue, and the Capitol Hill
areas. Current favorites: *Blues Alley,* for mainstream jazz and Dixieland (1073 Wisconsin Ave. NW; phone: 337-4141); *Jenkins Hill,* for the District's longest bar, where
everyone from public servants to students slakes his or her thirst (223 Pennsylvania
Ave. SE; phone: 544-6600); the *Dubliner Restaurant and Pub,* with old Irish and Celtic

tunes and jigs (520 N. Capitol St. NW; phone: 737-3773); *Market Inn*, a popular steak and seafood house on Capitol Hill where live jazz is featured nightly (200 E St. SW; phone: 554-2100); and *Cities*, a watering hole–cum–restaurant–cum–nightclub in what once was a 3-story auto dealership (2424 18th St. NW; phone: 328-7194). *Cities*, which changes its city theme every 6 months, is located in the heart of Washington's newest nightlife scene — Adams Morgan, a funky mélange of bars, dance clubs, ethnic restaurants, and shops radiating from the intersection of Columbia Road and 18th Street NW. In recent years Adams Morgan has come to rival Georgetown as "the" place to see and be seen after dark in the capital.

On Saturday nights, the *Bayou* in Georgetown presents *Bushcapades*, a production of *Gross National Product*, a satirical and sometimes ridiculous political revue targeting Washington politicians in the spotlight. Reservations necessary (3135 K St. NW; phone: 783-7212). Political satirist Mark Russell also performs occassionally in local nightspots (check local newspapers for details). The *Comedy Café* features nationally known comedians in an informal, downtown club (1520 K St. NW; phone: 638-5653). The dining room staff at Georgetown's *La Niçoise* not only serves French fare while on roller skates, but the talented crew also presents an amusing after-dinner cabaret (1720 Wisconsin Ave. NW; phone: 965-9300). *Déjà Vu* is a lively dance club with music from the 1960s to today (2119 M St. NW; phone: 452-1966). *Joe and Mo's* is a hopping weekday disco spot but on weekends turns into a ballroom–dance hall where dancers swing to the sounds of the 1920s and 1930s played by Eric Felten and his orchestra (1211 Connecticut Ave. NW; phone: 659-1211). *West End Café* is a popular piano bar where classical and jazz music is featured (*One Washington Circle Hotel*, One Washington Circle; phone: 293-5390). For rock 'n' roll lovers, the *Hard Rock Café* is an all-time favorite (999 E St. NW; phone: 737-7625).

■ **Bar None:** Because Washingtonians are serious about their sports teams, especially the *Redskins*, sports bars are scattered around the area and are prime spots for game nights (if you don't have seats at *RFK Stadium*). Try *Champions*, a Georgetown favorite (1206 Wisconsin Ave. NW; phone: 333-3700); *Bottom Line*, a rugby bar popular with local players and their cheering squads (1716 I St. NW; phone: 298-8488); *Poor Robert's*, which offers satellite TV for special sporting events (3419 Connecticut Ave. NW; phone: 363-1839); and *Joe Theismann's*, a sports bar owned by the former, fabulous *Redskins* quarterback (1800 Diagonal Rd., Alexandria, VA; phone: 703-739-0777). The capital is also a major saloon town, and some of the best stomping grounds are on the "Hill." *Bullfeathers*, where the Congressional crowd hangs out, has a bar that doesn't quit (410 1st St. SE; phone: 543-5005). The *Hawk and Dove*, a dark, rustic bar, is perfect for after work (or after play), and crowded with both Capitol Hillers and law students (329 Pennsylvania Ave. SE; phone: 543-3300). *Clyde's* in Georgetown is your typical wood and brass fern bar, with cozy pub decor (3236 M St., NW; phone: 333-9180), and *Hamburger Hamlet*, also in Georgetown, offers a casual, warm atmosphere, great summer drinks, and crayons for drawing on the paper tablecloths (3112 M St. NW; phone: 897-5350).

BEST IN TOWN

CHECKING IN: Washington currently enjoys a wealth of good-quality hotel establishments because of a building boom in the late 1980s. Still, accommodations at the best stopping places can dwindle fast, so reservations should be made in advance. Visitors in town for only a few days should stay downtown to make the best use of their limited time; weekends offer the best package deals. Inexpensive taxis, the *Metro* system, and buses facilitate getting around without a car, which is difficult and expensive to park. However, if you have a car, major motel chains have facilities at all principal entry points to the district — Silver Spring and Bethesda in Maryland; Arlington, Rosslyn, and Alexandria in Virginia. Expect to pay $175 and up (sometimes way up) for a double room in the expensive range, $100 to $170 in the moderate range, and $70 to $100 in the inexpensive category. For information about bed and breakfast accommodations, contact *The Bed and Breakfast League/ Sweet Dreams & Toast* (PO Box 9490, Washington, DC 20016; phone: 363-7767). *Washington, DC, Accommodations* provides assistance with hotel reservations according to visitors' needs. This free service is available by calling 800-554-2220. All telephone numbers are in the 202 area code unless otherwise indicated. All accommodations receive CNN except where noted.

Ana – This link in the Westin chain is as elegant inside as it is outside. There is a lovely interior garden, and 415 luxuriously appointed rooms that include 36 Executive Club rooms and 26 suites; 3 Executive Premier King suites have cable TV, 3 phones, voice mail, and terry cloth robes. There are 3 nonsmoking floors and 9 rooms equipped for the handicapped. The *Colonnade* is a fine restaurant for formal dining, and there's a more casual brasserie and a lobby lounge in a glass loggia just off the garden. As if all this were not enough, there is a professionally staffed fitness center, complete with pool, Jacuzzi, sauna, squash courts, aerobics room, weights, and state-of-the-art exercise equipment, plus a beauty salon and juice bar. Facilities include 14 meeting rooms, A/V equipment, photocopiers, computers, and secretarial services. Round-the-clock room service, a concierge desk, and express checkout complete the picture. Children under 18 stay free. 24th and M Sts. NW (phone: 429-2400 or 800-228-3000; fax: 457-5010). Expensive.

Canterbury – Near the downtown business district and not far from the White House, this small place has 99 suites with a stocked bar in each. Amenities include a complimentary continental breakfast, underground parking, nightly turn-down service, complimentary cocktail each evening in the *Union Jack Pub,* and *Chaucer's* restaurant. Lower weekend package rates are available. Room service is available until 10 PM. There's a helpful concierge desk, and business amenities include 6 meeting rooms, secretarial services, A/V equipment, photocopiers, and computers. 1733 N St. NW (phone: 393-3000 or 800-424-2950; fax: 785-9581). Expensive.

Capital Hilton – One of Washington's most luxurious hostelries is also one of the most conveniently located, just a few minutes from the White House. Recently renovated, it has 549 expansive rooms, designed in soft color schemes with woven fabrics. Each room has a marble foyer, 2 telephones, a TV set, fully stocked mini-bar, and terry cloth robes. The Deluxe Towers' rooms on the top 4 floors also have VCRs, electric trouser press, and a separate concierge and check-in area. Restaurants include *Trader Vic's,* which serves Chinese and Polynesian fare, the sophisticated *Twigs Grill,* and the lobby bar. There is a state-of-the-art fitness center with treadmills, Nautilus, steamrooms, and saunas. Business services include 14 meeting rooms, 24-hour room service, a concierge, foreign currency exchange, secretarial services, A/V equipment, photocopiers, foreign language translation, computers, fax machines, and express checkout. 1001 16th and K Sts. NW (phone: 393-1000; fax: 393-7992). Expensive.

Carlton – Host to many presidents and dignitaries, Harry Truman conducted his affairs of state here while the White House was being redone, and Jimmy Carter announced his intention to run here. The Italian Renaissance lobby is elegant, the 197 rooms comfortable, and the bar good enough to win approval from feisty *Newsday* columnist Jimmy Breslin. The *Allegro* dining room is excellent and has a terrific Sunday brunch (see *Eating Out*), and there's also a cocktail lounge.

Business services include secretarial and concierge assistance, 7 meeting rooms, A/V equipment, photocopiers, C-SPAN, computers and express checkout. There's also 24-hour room service. 923 16th St. NW (phone: 638-2626 or 800-325-3535; fax: 638-4321). Expensive.

Four Seasons – On the edge of Georgetown, it looks a lot like a penitentiary from the outside, but the interior is bright and beautiful, and the appeal of its rooms has got visitors returning whenever possible. The *Aux Beaux Champs* restaurant deserves high praise (see *Eating Out*), as does *Le Petit Champs,* a private nightclub for guests and members. There's also afternoon tea in the sunlit indoor *Garden Terrace.* A traditional concierge offers many personal services including mail delivery. Around-the-clock room service is available, as is C-SPAN, 6 meeting rooms, secretarial services, A/V equipment, photocopiers, and computers, express checkout, and complimentary limo service on weekdays. Other special services include overnight pressing, shoeshine, and laptop computers. A new fitness center boasts exercise machines equipped with color television sets, VCRs, and Walkmans (with an audio and video library) to enjoy while working out, a lap pool, a Jacuzzi, a massage therapist, and a juice bar. Complimentary for guests; for non-guests, the fitness center charges $25 and is available from 9 AM to 4 PM. 2800 Pennsylvania Ave. NW (phone: 342-0444 or 800-332-3442; fax: 342-1673). Expensive.

Grand – A distinctive copper dome wedged between walls of brick and granite marks this West End hostelry. In architecture and ambience, it is reminiscent of a small European hotel: A white marble staircase cascades through the lobby, the inner courtyard is meticulously landscaped, and all 263 rooms feature Italian marble baths, 3 phones, remote-control TV sets, and working fireplaces in some suites. The elegant *Mayfair* serves *cuisine courante,* a step beyond nouvelle, with a menu that changes daily; the *Promenade Lounge* features breakfast, lunch, dinner, and afternoon tea in a more informal atmosphere. Besides a multilingual concierge and currency conversion service, there is 24-hour room service, valet and dry cleaning, valet parking, and Godiva chocolates accompanying the nightly turn-down service. Other pluses include 10 meeting rooms, secretarial services, A/V equipment, photocopiers, computers, and concierge services. 2350 M St. NW (phone: 429-0100 or 800-848-0016; fax: 429-9759). Expensive.

Grand Hyatt Washington – Located in the heart of downtown DC, across from the *Washington Convention Center,* this property has 907 rooms, including 60 suites, and a Regency Club floor with a private lounge and concierge service. The suites, all with living areas, wet bars, and lots of greenery, also have saunas and marble baths. All rooms have turn-down service, free cable television with HBO and ESPN, and full-service honor bars. Dining facilities include the *Zephyr Deli,* a New York–style deli; the *Grande Café,* an informal eatery for breakfast, lunch, and dinner; the more formal *Hamilton's; Palladio's,* a 3-level lobby bar; and *Grand Slam,* a sports bar with two large-screen television sets. Business facilities include 13 meeting rooms, the Independence Ballroom and Constitution Ballroom, 24-hour room service, A/V equipment, secretarial services on request, modem hookups in rooms, and express checkout. There's also a health club with an exercise room, a sauna, a Jacuzzi, a lap pool, and aerobics classes. 1000 H St. NW (phone: 582-1234; telex: 897118; fax: 637-4781). Expensive.

Hay-Adams – At an incomparable location just off Lafayette Square, within a silver dollar's throw of the White House. This 143-room hotel retains its Old World dignity and maintains the standards of the neighborhood with antique furnishings, a paneled lobby, and 3 fine dining rooms — the formal *Adams Room* for breakfast and lunch (see *Eating Out*), the *John Hay Room* with traditional English decor and original paneling from Warwick Palace for tea and cocktails, and the informal

Eagle Bar & Grill for soup and salad. Room service is available 24 hours a day. There's also a concierge desk, 3 meeting rooms, A/V equipment, secretarial service, photocopiers, computers, and express checkout. 16th and H Sts. NW (phone: 638-6600 or 800-424-5054; fax: 638-2716). Expensive.

Hyatt Regency Crystal City – Conveniently located near the airport and only 15 minutes from downtown DC, this establishment is popular with business folks. There are 685 rooms and suites built around a 5-story atrium — all with central air conditioning and each equipped with color TV sets, ESPN, complimentary HBO, and radios. The Regency Club Level offers a private concierge, complimentary breakfast, evening cocktails and hors d'oeuvres, and turndown cordials. The *Chesapeake Grill* serves seafood for lunch and dinner and the *Cinnabar* restaurant serves three meals daily in a casual setting. There is an outdoor swimming pool, a health club, and a Jacuzzi. Business facilities include 25 meeting rooms and 14 conference parlors; translation equipment, A/V equipment, computer hookups, and secretarial services on request. 2799 Jefferson Davis Hwy., Arlington, VA (phone: 703-418-1234 or 800-228-9000; fax: 703-416-1289). Expensive.

Hyatt Regency Washington – Located on Capitol Hill, and within walking distance of the Library of Congress, the House and Senate Buildings, and the Mall museums, it has 803 rooms and 31 suites, including 2 Presidential suites. All rooms have cable television with HBO, ESPN, and C-SPAN, and a complimentary newspaper weekdays. There are 3 restaurants, a lounge, and a bar, plus a heated pool with indoor/outdoor decks, a health club with modern exercise equipment, saunas, and steamrooms. Business facilities include 3 ballrooms for up to 1,500, a conference theater, 2 boardrooms, and 8 meeting suites; A/V equipment, computer, fax machines, photocopiers, secretarial services on request, and express checkout. 400 New Jersey Ave. NW (phone: 737-1234 or 800-233-1234; fax: 393-7927). Expensive.

Jefferson – A clubby place and a favorite of many politicians. Located near the White House and the shops on Connecticut Avenue, it has a low-key, traditional atmosphere and outstanding service. The *Jefferson* dining room is a series of cozy alcoves serving "new Virginia cuisine" made with local ingredients (specialties include plantation corncakes with smoked salmon and chive cream, crab-and-lobster cakes, and spicy pan-fried Chincoteague oysters). The 69 rooms and 35 suites offer stereos with CD players, mini-bars, and at least two phone lines that are fax and computer compatible. Jazz on Saturday and Sunday nights. There are 3 meeting rooms, 24-hour concierge and secretarial services, A/V equipment, photocopiers, and computers. Round-the-clock room service and express checkout round out the amenities. 16th and M Sts. NW (phone: 347-2200 or 800-368-5966; fax: 331-7982). Expensive.

J.W. Marriott – A significant step above other members of this chain. Connected to a mall complex of 160 stores and the *National Theater,* it has 772 rooms, an indoor pool, and a health spa. The Marquis floors (14 and 15) are especially nice. The Concierge Level includes breakfast, complimentary hors d'oeuvres, and a private lounge on the 14th floor. There also is a Grand Ballroom for up to 2,000 people, and the Capital Ballroom, which can accommodate up to 800. Room service is available around the clock. Among the business services are concierge and secretarial services, 10 meeting rooms, A/V equipment, photocopiers, computers, and express checkout. 1331 Pennsylvania Ave. NW (phone: 393-2000 or 800-228-9290; fax: 626-6991). Expensive.

Loews L'Enfant Plaza – A recent multimillion-dollar face-lift keeps this imposing, modernistic structure — occupying the top floors of an office complex — one of Washington's best. A flower garden graces the plaza in front of the building; below the hotel area is a large shopping mall with chic boutiques and a *Metro* station, and on the 12th floor there's an indoor/outdoor swimming pool. The service is high quality, the location conveniently near the Mall. There are 370 rooms, a restaurant (*Café Pierre*), and 2 bars. All rooms have VCRs and there is a new fitness center with state-of-the-art Nautilus machines, free weights, aerobic classes, and personal trainers. Special children's programs are available, which include tours of the hotel kitchens, and pet programs — your pet's food arrives on a silver tray, and 5% of your room rate goes to the ASPCA. Equally advantageous is an obliging concierge, secretarial services, room service (6 AM to midnight), A/V equipment, photocopiers, computers, 4 meeting rooms, C-SPAN, and express checkout. 480 L'Enfant Plaza SW (phone: 484-1000 or 800-243-1166; fax: 646-4456). Expensive.

Madison – With 374 luxurious rooms, excellent service by a well-trained staff, amid gracious Federal decor; extras including interpreters, refrigerators, and bathroom phones. There is also a health club. The *Montpelier Room* is quite a good restaurant; it serves a buffet on weekdays and brunch on Sundays. The *Retreat* restaurant is open from 6 AM to 11 PM, and the lobby bar has nightly entertainment. Afternoon tea is offered in the *Retreat* from 3 to 5 PM weekdays. In addition to 24-hour room service, there also are concierge and secretarial services available, as well as 15 meeting rooms, A/V equipment, photocopiers, computers, C-SPAN, and express checkout. 15th and M Sts. NW (phone: 862-1600 or 800-424-9577; fax: 785-1255). Expensive.

Omni Shoreham – Host to many world leaders and a site of inaugural balls since Franklin Roosevelt's time, this is one of the city's older luxury establishments. The 770 rooms — including 55 suites — are decorated in shades of burgundy, gray, and blue, amenities include marble bathrooms, cable television, and video checkout. There is a French-style brasserie, a garden court lounge, the *Marquee Cabaret* with nightly entertainment, and a snack bar. Other pluses include an Olympic-size pool, 3 lighted clay tennis courts, and a new fitness center with Nautilus and Lifecycle equipment. Meeting facilities include 30 meeting rooms (6 of which are luxurious ballrooms, plus 7 executive conference rooms for up to 2,400 people), A/V equipment, and 24-hour room service. 2500 Calvert St. NW (phone: 234-0700 or 800-THE-OMNI; fax: 322-1322). Expensive.

Pullman Highland – A new hostelry, the first North American link in this European chain, opened in the former *Highland* hotel following a $6-million renovation. It has 145 spacious rooms elegantly decorated with traditional furniture and muted peach colors. All rooms have TV sets, fax and computer hookups, mini-bar, safe, and coffee maker. There are 2 restaurants, plus a fully equipped business center with 4 meeting rooms, a resource library, fax machines, computers, photocopiers, secretarial, and translation services. There's also a multilingual concierge, access to a health club, tennis, and golf, and 24-hour room service. Located in the heart of the embassy district. 1914 Connecticut Ave. NW (phone: 797-2000 or 800-424-2464; fax: 462-0944). Expensive.

Ramada Renaissance – This large hostelry is part of "Tech 2000," a 2.5-million-square-foot multipurpose complex across the street from the *Washington Convention Center*. The 801 rooms and 61 suites are decorated in a sophisticated contemporary style, and there are 2 restaurants, a swimming pool, and on-site parking. There is also a full health club. A Club Level is available with a private lounge, complimentary breakfast, hors d'oeuvres, and a full bar. Business services include 24-hour room service, 19 meeting rooms, a concierge, secretarial services, A/V equipment, photocopiers, computers, 2 ballrooms, an exhibition hall, an auditorium, and express checkout. 999 9th St. NW (phone: 898-9000 or 800-228-9898; fax: 289-0947). Expensive.

Ritz-Carlton – Restored to an elegance beyond even its original standard. This is as close to an evocation of a classic European hostelry as exists in Washington. There are 230 rooms, the *Jockey Club* restaurant (see *Eating Out*), and the *Fairfax Bar*, as well as a ballroom and a new health club with weights and cardiovascular machines. Standard business amenities include 24-hour room service, a concierge and secretarial assistance, 7 meeting rooms, A/V equipment, photocopiers, and computers. 2100 Massachusetts Ave. NW (phone: 293-2100 or 800-241-3333; fax: 466-9867). Expensive.

Stouffer Concourse – Located in Arlington near Washington National Airport, this popular convention hotel has 386 rooms and 7 suites, with 3 Club Floors. All rooms have color TV sets with complimentary HBO, ESPN, the Disney Channel, radio, and direct-dial phones with message alert. Complimentary coffee and newspaper accompany wake-up calls. The *Ondine* restaurant serves American fare and is open for breakfast, lunch, and dinner, and Sunday brunch; the more casual *Ondine* lounge has a lighter menu and entertainment nightly except Sundays. There is also a bar, an indoor swimming pool, saunas, a sun deck, an exercise room, and a gameroom. Guest services provide free shuttle service to the *Pentagon City Mall*, where shoppers will find *Macy's* and *Nordstrom's*. Business facilities include 20 meeting rooms, 3 ballrooms, 4 meeting suites, 24-hour room service, photocopiers, A/V equipment, and computers on request. 2399 Jefferson Davis Hwy., Arlington, VA (phone: 703-418-3763 or 800-HOTELS-1; fax: 703-418-3763). Expensive.

Stouffer Mayflower – Four blocks from the White House, this 658-room (78 are suites) property hosted Calvin Coolidge's inaugural ball (it's undergone a complete face-lift since then). The flower-filled lobby and public areas are light and airy, and there also are two excellent restaurants: The elegant *Nicholas* specializes in nouvelle American cuisine with a wide variety of seafood and vegetarian dishes, and the less formal *Café Promenade* serves breakfast, lunch, and dinner daily and has a buffet lunch with scrumptious desserts on Sundays. The *Town and Country* cocktail lounge has nightly entertainment and complimentary hors d'oeuvres from 5 to 7 PM and also serves a light lunch. Amenities include overnight pressing and a host of complimentary perks: limo service within 3 miles, overnight shoeshine, and coffee and newspaper with wake-up calls. The hotel also offers collect, toll-free, and credit card calls with no connecting charge, and low fax charges. All rooms have 31-inch TV sets with C-SPAN and HBO, 3 phones, hair dryers, robes, and twice-daily room service; there also are 17 meeting rooms, and A/V equipment, photocopiers, and computers to cater to guests' business needs. There is a multilingual concierge, and express checkout. 1127 Connecticut Ave. NW (phone: 347-3000 or 800-HOTELS-1; fax: 466-9082). Expensive.

Vista Washington – François Mitterrand and Elizabeth Taylor are among those who have stayed at this recently renovated, 399-room hostelry, only 6 blocks from the White House. Its six 1-bedroom suites, designed by Givenchy, sport full-length mirrors, large private balconies, and bathrooms in opalescent tile with Jacuzzis, and are completely separate from the rest of the hotel — sharing no walls with any other rooms (cost: $525 a night). Favorite recipes of past presidents are on the menu at the *American Harvest* restaurant; cardiovascular fitness gear is available at the health club along with treadmills and a sauna. Secretarial and concierge assistance are available, and A/V equipment, photocopiers, and computers are on call for guests. Other pluses include 10 meeting rooms, a ballroom, 24-hour room service, and express checkout. 1400 M St. NW (phone: 429-1700 or 800-223-1146; fax: 785-0786). Expensive.

Washington Court – A 268-room luxury property with a 4-story atrium; the *Signature Room*, a moderately priced restaurant serving American food; picturesque views; complimentary limousine service; and other amenities, such as TV sets, phones in both bedroom and bath, and an exercise room with a sauna. There's also 24-hour room service, a concierge desk, secretarial services, A/V equipment, photocopiers, computers, 15 meeting rooms, and express checkout. Two blocks from the Capitol, 525 New Jersey Ave. NW (phone: 628-2100 or 800-321-3010; fax: 879-7918). Expensive.

Watergate – Though this modern hotel-apartment-office complex doesn't look too historic, appearances can be deceiving (as can small pieces of tape). This property boasts 235 large contemporarily furnished rooms, an indoor swimming pool and health club, the excellent *Riverview* restaurant (see *Eating Out*), a cocktail lounge, *Les Champs Shopping Mall* with even more dining possibilities, and a location adjacent to the *Kennedy Center*. There's a concierge desk and 24-hour room service, and business amenities include secretarial services, A/V equipment, photocopiers, fax machines, computers, Showtime, and express checkout. 2650 Virginia Ave. NW (phone: 965-2300 or 800-424-2736; fax: 337-7915). Expensive.

Willard Inter-Continental – Ten presidents-elect stayed at this Beaux Arts landmark while awaiting their inauguration, and Charles Dickens and Julia Ward Howe were regulars, too. But the "crown jewel" of Pennsylvania Avenue fell into disrepair (and was almost razed during the late 1960s). Managed by Inter-Continental (and the recipient of a $70-million renovation and modernization of all public spaces and its 365 rooms), it has been restored to its turn-of-the-century grandeur. Facilities include a mini-bar, direct-dial telephone, and hair dryer in all rooms. The hotel dining room, the *Willard Room*, is one of DC's most elegant eateries (see *Eating Out*). *Café Espresso* has been redesigned in Old World, turn-of-the-century style and is available for casual dining. Additional amenities include 24-hour room service, both concierge and secretarial services, 15 meeting rooms, A/V equipment, photocopiers, computers, an exercise room, and express checkout. Children under 15 free ($25 charge for a roll-away bed). Corner Pennsylvania Ave. and 14th St. NW (phone: 628-9100 or 800-327-0200; fax: 637-7326). Expensive.

Wyndham Bristol – There are 239 rooms (37 of which are suites) in the English-style hostelry. The *Bristol Grill* offers fine food. Amenities include turndown service, 24-hour room service, A/V equipment, secretarial service, fax machines, and access to a health club ($5 charge). Other pluses: 7 meeting rooms, a concierge desk, and express checkout. 2430 Pennsylvania Ave. NW (phone: 955-6400 or 800-822-4200; fax: 955-5765). Expensive.

Georgetown Dutch Inn – Near the C&O Canal and within a block of the best restaurants and shopping that Georgetown has to offer, this small inn has 47 housekeeping units. There is a meeting room, fax service, complimentary continental breakfast, and photocopiers. CNN is not available here. 1075 Thomas Jefferson St. NW (phone: 337-0900 or 800-388-2410; fax: 333-6526). Moderate.

Morrison-Clark Inn – This popular inn served as the hostel for the *Soldiers, Sailors, Marines, and Airmen Club* from 1923 to 1984. A 1988 addition to the two historic buildings comprises 41 of the 54 tastefully decorated rooms. There also is an excellent restaurant. Room service can be ordered until 11 PM, and there's complimentary breakfast. A concierge desk, 3 meeting rooms, secretarial services, A/V equipment, photocopiers, and computers also are available. Located 1 block from the *Convention Center* and 4 blocks from *Metro Center* (*Metrorail* stop) at Massachusetts Ave. and 11th St. NW (phone: 898-1200 or 800-332-7898; fax: 289-8576). Moderate.

Tabard Inn – On a charming semi-residential street near the heart of the business district. Guests enjoy an ambience rare in an American city; there is a library and small dining room on the first floor. The 40 rooms are furnished with antiques and some of them share baths (23 have private baths). CNN is not available here. In fact, there are no TV sets in the rooms. There is a meeting room, a banquet room, a concierge, photocopiers, fax machines, and complimentary breakfast. A restaurant serves breakfast, lunch, and dinner, and brunch on weekends. 1739 N St. NW (phone: 785-1277; fax: 785-6173). Moderate.

Washington – One of the city's older properties offering an incomparable view from its rooftop restaurant. Always comfortable, but great during an inaugural parade. The 370 rooms feature TV sets and bathroom phones; downtown shopping is nearby. Room service is available until 11 PM. 15th St. and Pennsylvania Ave. NW (phone: 638-5900; fax: 628-4275). Moderate.

Allen Lee – In the heart of the George Washington University campus near the downtown area. There are 85 rooms; half have private baths, all have TV sets. You can't always count on hot water, but it's a popular spot with young people. CNN is not available here. 2224 F St. NW (phone: 331-1224). Inexpensive.

Harrington – A 310-room, older establishment in the center of Washington's commercial area, it has seen better days but provides clean accommodations and is within walking distance of the Mall. Popular with high school and family groups, who are drawn because the *Kitcheteria* makes feeding the troops easy and inexpensive. No CNN. 11th and E Sts. NW (phone: 628-8140). Inexpensive.

Kalorama Guest House – Bed and breakfast (and complimentary afternoon sherry) in 6 comfortable, turn-of-the-century row houses (in two different locations) decked out with antique furnishings. Continental breakfast included. There is a TV set in each common room and guest phones in each house (no charge for local calls). CNN is not available here. Four units in Kalorama, 1854 Mintwood Pl. NW (phone: 667-6369), and two units at Woodley Park near the National Zoo, 2700 Cathedral Ave. NW (phone: 328-0860). Inexpensive.

Windsor Inn – Small and unpretentious, in the trendy Adams Morgan district. A magnet for relocating embassy employees as well as government workers who prefer a modest, homey atmosphere. All 46 rooms have color TV sets and air conditioning; the staff is personable and attentive. Continental breakfast comes with a newspaper; and for a European touch, afternoon sherry is served. 1842 16th St. NW (phone: 667-0300 or 800-423-9111). Inexpensive.

Windsor Park – Modest, but this 40-room property is within walking distance of the Woodley Park *Metro* station and near the French diplomats' residence and Chinese Embassy. Complimentary continental breakfast; cable TV in each room. Convenient and basic. 2116 Kalorama Rd. NW (phone: 483-7700 or 800-247-3064; fax: 332-4547). Inexpensive.

EATING OUT: Considering the international aspects of Washington — 2,000 diplomats and a large number of residents who have lived abroad and brought back a taste for foreign fare — it's not too surprising that the District can provide an international gastronomic tour de force. What is surprising is that this wasn't the case until just a few years back. The greatest local meals even 2 decades ago were served in private homes or in embassies (Thomas Jefferson was known to treat his guests to such delicacies as ice cream and imported French wines). The change began when the Kennedys brought a French chef to the White House, and this awakened a broad interest in food and spawned a restaurant boom that hasn't stopped yet. Though it's always helpful to have an ermine-lined wallet or, better yet, a generous expense account, those who have only the yen for good food needn't go hungry. Our restaurant selections range in price from $100 or more for a dinner for two in the very expensive restaurants to between $75 and $90 in expensive places, $40 to $60 in the moderate ones, and $35 and under in the inexpensive bracket. Prices do not include drinks, wine, or tips. Reservations are a must at the top-flight restaurants. All telephone numbers are in the 202 area code unless otherwise indicated.

Aux Beaux Champs – This handsome dining room in the *Four Seasons* hotel is distinguished by a highly creative menu that changes daily, specializing in *cuisine courante* — a mixture of French and California food, stylish service, and a very cosmopolitan clientele. Specialties include breast of quail stuffed with woodland mushrooms in a zinfandel sauce with wild rice and scallion cake, and stuffed lamb with pistachio crust and risotto fritters in a minted madeira glaze. Open daily. Reservations advised. Major credit cards accepted. 2800 Pennsylvania Ave. NW (phone: 342-0444). Very expensive.

Cantina d'Italia – Still the longest-running hit among Italian restaurants (northern Italian fare), the changing menu offers new culinary delights but retains the old showstoppers like *fettuccine con salsa di noci* (homemade noodles with puréed walnuts, pine nuts, and ricotta and parmesan cheese) and *vale de stana* (veal chops with prosciutto and fontina cheese). The only drawback is the small and somewhat confining basement location. A second location has opened in Georgetown (3251 Prospect St. NW; phone: 337-5130). Closed Sundays. Reservations necessary at both locations. Major credit cards accepted. 1214A 18th St. NW (phone: 659-1830). Very expensive.

Galileo – A revitalized menu has proved invaluable in this dining establishment's major comeback. The grilled porcini mushrooms are a must, as is the pigeon with balsamic vinegar. The highlight among the pasta dishes is the exquisite ravioli. The fresh bread and risotto are also excellent. Open daily. Lunch on weekdays only. Reservations necessary. Major credit cards accepted. 1110 21st St. NW, between M and L Sts. (phone: 293-7191). Very expensive.

Jean-Louis – Named for its chef, this is a small (only 14 tables) and elegant restaurant with gracious service and fine nouvelle cuisine. Fixed-price dinners. Closed Sundays. Reservations necessary. Major credit cards accepted. In the *Watergate Hotel,* 2650 Virginia Ave. NW (phone: 298-4488). Very expensive.

Le Lion d'Or – Reputed to have the finest French food in town, although some say that the service isn't up to par. Don't leave without tasting one of the spectacular desserts. Open Mondays through Fridays; Saturdays for dinner only; closed Sundays. Reservations at least 2 weeks in advance. Major credit cards accepted. 1150 Connecticut Ave. NW, between 18th and M Sts. (phone: 296-7972). Very expensive.

Le Pavillon – Though this place may have the highest prices in town, French chef Yannick Cam offers nouvelle cuisine to those who know and appreciate the best. Closed Sundays. Reservations necessary. Major credit cards accepted. 1050 Connecticut Ave. NW (phone: 842-0022). Very expensive.

L'Auberge Chez François – This Alsatian country inn, 30 minutes west of the District in northern Virginia's hunt country, is a perennial favorite. The service is attentive and the setting cozy, yet refined. There are several working fireplaces, antique grandfather clocks, a mounted elk's head, a staff dressed in Alsatian garb, and lots of other knickknacks from the Alsace region in France. And the fare draws upon the best of both worlds, blending the hearty proportions of Germanic cooking with French touches: excellent sauces, cheeses, and presentation. Owner François Haeringer's reasonably priced menu includes a number of Alsatian specialties, among them the famed *choucroute garnie,* a collection of sausages and duck atop heavily seasoned sauerkraut; Gruyère tart, an Alsatian version of cassoulet with sausages and lentils; stuffed rabbit; and chicken stewed in Alsatian riesling. The assortment of pâtés is renowned, and for dessert, we recommend the lime tart. Reservations necessary well in advance. 332 Springvale Rd., Great Falls, VA (phone: 703-759-3800). Expensive.

Bice – This northern Italian eatery, owned by the proprietors of the New York establishment of the same name, was named best new restaurant by *Washingtonian* magazine readers in 1991. Specialties include risotto, fresh pasta, fish dishes, and duck entrées. Only Italian and California wines are served (and French champagne). Open daily; closed Saturdays for lunch. Reservations advised. Major credit cards accepted. 601 Pennsylvania Ave. NW, between 6th and 7th Sts. (phone: 638-2423). Expensive.

Dominique's – Elegant French food, a lively and friendly atmosphere, and such exotic items as wild boar, rattlesnake, buffalo, and alligator tail. The kitchen also serves up an excellent version of Senate bean soup. For a great bargain, try the pre- and post-theater prix fixe menu. Open Sundays from 5 to 9:30 PM. Reservations advised. Major credit cards accepted. 1900 Pennsylvania Ave. NW (phone: 452-1126). Expensive.

Jockey Club – This *Ritz-Carlton* restaurant is a favorite meeting and eating spot for local movers and shakers. The decor looks more like New York's old *"21"* than the original (it once was managed by them). Besides soft-shell crabs, the food is French-influenced; new chef Fabrice Canelle was formerly with *Maxim's* in Paris. Open daily. Reservations necessary. Major credit cards accepted. 2100 Massachusetts Ave. NW (phone: 659-8000). Expensive.

Maison Blanche – The "in" spot since the Reagan years, where Washington's famous and powerful (assorted Kennedys and Art Buchwald) meet amid an elegant Parisian dining room decor. Classical French dishes are served, but there are touches of "nouvelle" as well. An extensive list of lunch and dinner specials is offered daily. Specialties include fresh Dover sole, rack of lamb with mustard and herbs of Provence, and lobster with saffron pasta. Closed Sundays. Reservations necessary. Major credit cards accepted. Special pre-theater prix fixe dinner at $24.95 served 6 to 7 PM. 1725 F St. NW (phone: 842-0070). Expensive.

Morton's of Chicago – One of the best places in Washington to get steaks with all the trimmings; seafood dishes are also available. Dinner only; closed Sundays. Reservations advised. Major credit cards accepted. 3251 Prospect St. NW (phone: 342-6258). Expensive.

Palm – Caricatures of Washington celebrities line the walls of this New York–style steakhouse, fashioned after the original in the Big Apple. Steaks are the specialty, although lamb chops, veal, excellent prime ribs, and Nova Scotia lobsters are available, too. Open weekdays for lunch and dinner; Saturdays for dinner only; closed Sundays. Reservations advised. Major credit cards accepted. 1225 19th St. NW (phone: 293-9091). Expensive.

Prime Rib – Named the best restaurant in the city by *Washingtonian* magazine readers in 1991, this is a first-rate establishment serving a spectacular rib that is perfectly cooked throughout its 2-inch thickness. The menu also includes a wide choice of fresh seafood dishes. The blackened swordfish is a must, and try the double chocolate cheesecake for dessert. An elegant atmosphere is accompanied by impeccable service. Open weekdays for lunch; Mondays through Saturdays for dinner; closed Sundays. Reservations necessary. Major credit cards accepted. 2020 K St. NW (phone: 466-8817). Expensive.

Red Sage – One of Washington's newest spots, it is accented with hand-blown chandeliers, silver and gold decor, and food that is as exquisite as the surroundings. Chef Mark Miller creates dishes with a Southwestern flavor that includes a stew of lobster, scallops, mussels, and clams. Also try *plum ancho* (glazed quail with jalapeño slaw and spoonbread). Open daily for lunch and dinner. Reservations necessary. Major credit cards accepted. 405 14th St. NW at F St. (phone: 638-4444). Expensive.

I Ricchi – One of the city's hottest eateries, where Chef Francesco Ricchi concocts fabulous Florentine fare such as broad noodles tossed with hare sauce, leg of rabbit with rosemary, and quail stuffed with homemade sausage. This trattoria has a warm homey feeling. Closed Sundays and lunch Saturdays. Reservations necessary. Major credit cards accepted. 1220 19th St. NW (phone: 835-0459). Expensive.

Sam & Harry's – This popular steakhouse located south of Dupont Circle has a clubby atmosphere with dark wood paneling and leather banquettes. The jazz-inspired artwork is done by local artists. Specialties include porterhouse and strip steaks; seafood dishes are also available. Open daily. Reservations advised. Major credit cards accepted. 1200 19th St. NW (phone: 296-4333). Expensive.

Sea Catch – A favorite among Washingtonians, this upscale wood-beamed restaurant boasts a long list of tasty seafood dishes. Chef Frederic Lange stresses the use of fresh, natural ingredients in the preparation of crab, lobster, and other fish. Try the special house-smoked fish or crabcakes. From the first of June through mid-August, the restaurant features the *Soft Shell Crab Festival* with specialties such as baked soft-shell crabs with creole mustard and bitter greens. Closed Sundays. Reservations advised. Major credit cards accepted. 1054 31st St. NW (phone: 337-8855). Expensive.

Willard Room – Bruno Bonnet, formerly of the *Lion d'Or* and the *Kennedy Center,* was named best sommelier on the East Coast in 1991 by SOPEXA (the French Food and Wine Association), and he creates delicious, regional American–style dishes all made from local produce. Try the rack of lamb, Dover sole, or Chesapeake Bay fish. Open for breakfast and lunch weekdays, nightly for dinner, and brunch on Sundays. Reservations advised. Major credit cards accepted. 1401 Pennsylvania Ave. NW, in the *Willard Inter-Continental* (phone: 628-9100). Expensive.

Riverview – Northern Italian and Mediterranean-French food are the specialties at this *Watergate* eatery. Risotto made-to-order and homemade pasta are favorites. Try the Kasu salmon made with the pulp of rice wine, the tournedos Rossini, and the foie gras. Pre-theater special available for $29.50. Open daily for breakfast, lunch, and dinner. Reservations advised. Major credit cards accepted. 2650 Virginia Ave. NW (phone: 298-4455). Expensive to moderate.

Adams Room – There's not a better place to start the day than this beautiful room with views of the White House and Lafayette Square. Breakfast choices range from croissants and fresh berries to pecan waffles or corned beef and eggs. Open daily for breakfast and lunch. Reservations necessary. Major credit cards accepted. *Hay-Adams Hotel,* 16th and H Sts. NW (phone: 638-6600). Moderate.

Allegro – This lovely dining room of the *Carlton* hotel is known for its fabulous business buffet lunch featuring jumbo shrimp, salmon, pâté, and carved roast of the day, and is perfect for those under time constrictions. Afternoon tea is accompanied by a harpist and Sunday brunch by a pianist. Breakfast might include assorted breads, healthy options such as Bircher Muesli and honey yogurt, and international offerings such as miso soup and grilled salmon à la Japanese. Dinner highlights include saffron ravioli with shiitake-morel sauce and asparagus tips, and curry oyster tempura with sake herb sabayon. Open daily. Reservations advised, especially for the business lunch and brunch. Major credit cards accepted. 16th and K Sts. NW (phone: 879-6900). Moderate.

American Café – A DC institution, popular for informal but imaginatively prepared meals of grilled fish, sandwiches, salads, and soup. There also are some luscious desserts and homemade breads. Open daily. Reservations unnecessary. Major credit cards accepted. Three of the establishment's six locations: 1211 Wisconsin Ave. NW, Georgetown (phone: 944-9464); on Capitol Hill at 227 Massachusetts Ave. NE (phone: 547-8500); and National Pl., 1331 Pennsylvania Ave. NW (phone: 626-0770). Moderate.

Austin Grill – Tex-Mex food is the star here, along with the best margaritas east of the Mississippi. Smoked duck quesadillas, grilled pork chops baked with Mexican hot peppers, fajitas, and enchiladas are some of the unbelievably good choices. Open daily. Reservations unnecessary. Major credit cards accepted. 2404 Wisconsin Ave. NW (phone: 337-8080). Moderate.

Bacchus – A fairly new eatery that serves excellent Lebanese food, offering a wide selection of vegetarian dishes and daily specials. Try the lamb and chicken kebabs, the grape leaves stuffed with rice, or the fresh rockfish. Closed Sundays. Reservations necessary. Major credit cards accepted. 1827 Jefferson Pl. NW (phone: 785-0734). Moderate.

Bombay Club – This local Indian hangout has unusual specialties such as spiced lobster seasoned with mild curries, lamb entrées, and tandoori baked salmon marinated with ginger, garlic, and yogurt sauce. Closed for lunch Saturdays; open for brunch Sundays. Reservations unnecessary. Major credit cards accepted. 815 Conn. Ave. NW (phone: 659-3727). Moderate.

Clyde's – Frequented by Georgetown students and local preppy types, it serves omelettes, pasta, fresh seafood, and steaks, but is known mostly for its terrific bacon cheeseburgers, great desserts, and its weekend brunch. They have their own lager — Clyde's Amber — on tap that's served at just the right temperature. Open daily. Reservations advised. Major credit cards accepted. 3236 M St. NW (phone: 333-9180). Moderate.

La Colline – Charming and reasonably priced, it serves adventurous French food and daily specials as well as wonderful desserts. Open daily for breakfast, lunch, and dinner. Try the bouillabaise and *choucroute alsacienne* (sauerkraut, sausages, pork). Reservations advised. Major credit cards accepted. 400 N. Capitol St. NW (phone: 737-0400). Moderate.

Donatello – This northern Italian dining spot offers both pre- and post-theater specials. Favorites include homemade pasta, seafood, and veal dishes. Open daily; lunch on weekdays only. Reservations advised. Major credit cards accepted. 2514 L St. NW, at Pennsylvania Ave. (phone: 333-1485). Moderate.

Fitch, Fox & Brown – Located in the *Old Post Office Pavilion*, it serves traditional American fare, including pasta, seafood, and steaks. Try the capital chicken prepared with crabmeat and spinach. Open daily for breakfast, lunch, and dinner; happy hour weekdays. Reservations advised. Major credit cards accepted. 1100 Pennsylvania Ave. NW (phone: 289-2048). Moderate.

Germaine's – Varied Pan-Asian menu — including Japanese, Korean, Vietnamese, and Indonesian fare. Specialties are pine cone fish, scallop salad, *satay*, and squirrelfish. Open daily; dinner only on weekends. Reservations advised. Major credit cards accepted. 2400 Wisconsin Ave. NW (phone: 965-1185). Moderate.

Hogs on the Hill – As the less-than-delicate name implies, the decor amounts to raw wood walls that are a porcine extravaganza: Signs, posters, drawings, and other paraphernalia pay homage to the pig in all its splendor. The food, however, is sublime. Greens, red beans and rice, and French fries accompany barbecued ribs bathed in tangy sauce. There's also a take-out counter around the corner. Open daily. Reservations unnecessary except on weekends. Major credit cards accepted. 732 Maryland Ave. NE (phone: 547-4553). Moderate.

Lafitte – Classic French and authentic creole specialties are served in an atmosphere reminiscent of 18th-century New Orleans. The New Orleans bread pudding is a must. Open daily. Reservations advised. Major credit cards accepted. 1310 New Hampshire Ave. NW (phone: 466-7978). Moderate.

Marrakesh – Walking into this restaurant, just minutes from Capitol Hill, makes diners feel as if they've entered another world. Fashioned after a Moroccan-style dining room, tapestries hang from the walls, and patrons sit on low banquettes around brass trays that serve as tables. A nine-course meal including chicken, salad, duck, couscous, and dessert is eaten entirely with your hands (helped along with some bread); dinner is accompanied by native music with a belly dancer as an added attraction during dessert. This spot is a must if you're looking for a truly unique eating experience. Open daily. Reservations advised. No credits cards, but checks are accepted. 617 New York Ave. NW (phone: 393-9393). Moderate.

I Matti – *Galileo* owner Roberto Donna opened this popular eatery in the Adams Morgan section of town a few years ago, offering both northern Italian dishes and Italian nouvelle cuisine. In 1991, it was rated by *Washingtonian* magazine as one of DC's best restaurants. Aromatic stews, pizza with paper-thin crusts, and meltingly wonderful ricotta cheesecake. Open daily. Reservations necessary. Major credit cards accepted. 2436 18th St. NW (phone: 462-8844). Moderate.

McPherson Grill – Contemporary American place featuring grilled seafood, meat, and poultry. Sandwiches, soups, and salads, as well as a variety of appetizers, are served all day. Try chicken with pears on walnut bread, skewered beef tenderloin with shiitake mushrooms and port wine sauce, and swordfish grilled with sesame and soy sauce. Closed Sundays. Reservations advised and major credit cards accepted at both places. 950 15th St. NW (phone: 638-0950). Moderate.

Mr. K's – Excellent food from four regions of China, including Peking, Hunan, both spicy and milder Szechuan, and classic Cantonese; favorites include beef mimosa, Peking duck, and any of several lobster dishes. This bustling place has four private dining rooms — very private, for the high-powered lawyers and lobbyists who have lunch or dinner here — decorated with impressive jade statues of dragons and a phoenix. At the end of the meal, there's a high-tech coffee urn that's wheeled out and delivers a delicious brew. Open daily. Reservations advised. Major credit cards accepted. 2121 K. St. NW (phone: 331-8868). Moderate.

Occidental – Sister restaurant to the *McPherson Grill,* this historic DC eatery has redesigned its dining room to create a more casual ambience, doing away with the starched drapes and portraits of presidents, and replacing them with a clubby brass-and-leather look. Specialties of chef Jeff Ruben include a swordfish sandwich, escalope of salmon *au poivre* with black bean purée, crab cakes, and varied meat, fish, and sausage dishes. There is an impressive wine list and a tempting dessert menu. Closed Sundays. Reservations advised. Major credit cards accepted. 1475 Pennsylvania Ave. NW (phone: 783-1475). Moderate.

Old Ebbitt Grill – An old-timer in an elegant Victorian setting. Tasty appetizers lead off a menu ranging from hamburgers to filet mignon. The menu choices change daily. Try the pecan pie or cheesecake for dessert. Open daily. Reservations advised. Major credit cards accepted. 675 15th St. NW (phone: 347-4801). Moderate.

Old Europe – Features the best German wine list in the District with some French and American labels; standard German dishes as well. Try the *jägerschnitzel* (veal steaks topped with mushrooms and brown sauce) or *zwiebel rostbraten* (rib steaks with roasted onions). Open daily. Reservations advised. Major credit cards accepted. 2434 Wisconsin Ave. NW (phone: 333-7600). Moderate.

Sfuzzi Washington – Northern Italian food with an American touch is served in this Union Station dining establishment, started by the owners of New York City's *Sfuzzi* restaurant. The grilled salmon is recommended, as are the pizza and pasta. Try the chicken *romano tagliatelli* (grilled chicken with gorgonzola cheese and noodles). There's an outdoor café in the summer and a happy hour on weekdays. Open daily. Reservations advised. Major credit cards accepted. 50 Massachusetts Ave. NE (phone: 842-4141). Moderate.

Tabard Inn – The nouvelle-influenced menu at this charmingly quirky inn is strong on fresh seafood such as grilled tuna and swordfish. The vegetables are shipped fresh daily from a nearby farm in Virginia. Sunday brunch is a popular affair, and there's a fire in the hearth in winter. Open daily. Reservations advised. Only Visa and MasterCard accepted. 1739 N St. NW (phone: 785-1277). Moderate.

Tout Va Bien – In the heart of Georgetown, this French bistro serves excellent duck, steaks, and lamb, also the shrimp and scallops Provençale. Open daily. Reservations advised. Major credit cards accepted. 1063 31st St. NW (phone: 965-1212). Moderate.

Veneziano – A northern Italian eatery specializing in risotto and seasonal fish dishes. Try the black risotto (made with cuttlefish ink) or the tripe. It also boasts the largest selection of grappas (Italian brandies) on the East Coast. Open daily for lunch and dinner; lunch only on Sundays. Reservations advised. Major credit cards accepted. 2305 16th St. NW (phone: 483-9300). Moderate.

Brickskeller – This down-home saloon claims to have the world's largest selection of beers (over 500 varieties from around the world). Steaks and burgers are served in the casual dining areas. Try the South Dakota buffalo steaks and the spicy chicken wings. Open daily. Reservations advised. Major credit cards accepted. 1523 22nd St. NW (phone: 293-1885). Moderate to inexpensive.

Dancin' Crab – A great place to enjoy a Chesapeake crab feast in a pleasant atmosphere. Open daily. Reservations advised on the weekends. Major credit cards accepted. 4611 Wisconsin Ave. NW (phone: 244-1882). Moderate to inexpensive.

Ernie's Original Crab House – Across the Potomac in Alexandria, this is an old favorite for crab lovers. Open daily. Reservations advised on weekends. Major credit cards accepted. Two locations: 1623 Fern St. (phone: 703-836-1623) and 7929 Richmond Hwy. (phone: 703-780-0100). Moderate to inexpensive.

Perry's – In trendy Adams Morgan, this sushi bar also has an open grill and roof deck lounge area. There's late-night karaoke on Mondays, Fridays, and Saturdays. Open daily. Reservations advised. Major credit cards accepted. 1811 Columbia Rd. NW (phone: 234-0618). Moderate to inexpensive.

Au Pied de Cochon – An informal place for a good meal at a decent price 24 hours a day. If *pieds de cochon* (pigs' feet) aren't your style, try asparagus vinaigrette, coq au vin, and other bistro specialties. No reservations. Open daily. Major credit cards accepted. 1335 Wisconsin Ave. NW (phone: 333-5440). Moderate to inexpensive.

Saigonnais – A Vietnamese dining spot in Adams Morgan serving food primarily from the southern regions of the country. Try lemon chicken marinated with coconut milk and served on rice, strip of tenderloin wrapped around scallions and rice vermicelli noodles, or catfish filet with turmeric and dill. Open weekdays for lunch; nightly for dinner. Reservations advised. Major credit cards accepted. 2307 16th St. NW (phone: 232-5300). Moderate to inexpensive.

America – The menu at this eatery (whose sister restaurant is in New York City) offers choices from all regions of the United States, from grits to Cajun shrimp to grilled tuna salad. Open daily. Reservations advised. Major credit cards accepted. 50 Massachusetts Ave. NE, in Union Station (phone: 682-9559). Inexpensive.

Bombay Palace – Specialties at this Indian spot include butter chicken marinated in saffron, cumin, and other spices and cooked in a clay oven, and the lamb kebabs. Open daily. Reservations advised. Major credit cards accepted. 1835 K St. NW (phone: 331-0111). Inexpensive.

Chadwicks – A favorite among the Georgetown crowd, this place serves great burgers, salads, and a popular weekend brunch. Open daily. Reservations advised. Major credit cards accepted. Two locations: 3205 K St. NW (phone: 333-2565) and 5247 Wisconsin Ave. NW, in Friendship Heights (phone: 362-8040). Inexpensive.

China Inn – In Washington's Chinatown, this eatery serves primarily Cantonese fare and some Szechuan dishes. Try the lemon chicken, butterfly shrimp, or sea bass dipped in boiling water and cooked with scallions, ginger and spices. Open daily. Reservations unnecessary. Major credit cards accepted. 631 H St. NW (phone: 842-0909). Inexpensive.

City Café – A warm, upbeat spot not far from Washington Circle in the West End with a blend of light and new American cooking, and organic food. Individual pizza topped with sun-dried tomato, onion, and goat cheese, or chicken, tomato, and mozzarella, are especially gratifying. Interesting soup, stir-fried scallops with vegetables, and hearty hamburgers are other worthy offerings. Closed Saturdays for lunch and Sundays. Reservations advised. Visa and MasterCard accepted. 2213 M St. NW (phone: 797-4860). Inexpensive.

Hard Rock Café – A relative newcomer to Washington, but already a legend, this outpost of the famous rock-music hangout serves hearty sandwiches, burgers, and salads. Open daily for lunch and dinner. Reservations advised for large groups. Major credit cards accepted. Corner of 10th and E Sts. NW (phone: 737-7625). Inexpensive.

House of Hunan – Among the finest Oriental spots in the city. Unusual appetizers include shrimp balls and vegetable curls, and special main dishes are crisp whole fish Hunan-style, and orange beef. Open daily. Reservations necessary for dinner. Major credit cards accepted. 1900 K St. NW (phone: 293-9111). Inexpensive.

Houston's – There's always a line at this popular Georgetown dining spot, known for its great burgers, sandwiches, and salads (though management sometimes can be less than helpful). Try the grilled chicken salad with peanut sauce. Open daily. No reservations. Major credit cards accepted. 1065 Wisconsin Ave. NW (phone: 338-7760). Inexpensive.

Iron Gate – A former stable now dedicated to Mediterranean food: shish kebab, couscous, and stuffed grape leaves. Speaking of which, there's a charming little grape arbor over the outdoor dining area where you can be served in warm weather. A private room with a fireplace is inviting during the winter months. Open daily. Reservations advised for larger parties. Major credit cards accepted. 1734 N St. NW (phone: 737-1370). Inexpensive.

Jaimalito's – Located in the *Washington Harbour* complex overlooking the Potomac River, this place specializes in Southwestern fare. Try the fajitas, enchiladas, or the grilled fresh fish entrées. Open daily. Reservations advised. Major credit cards accepted. 3000 K St. NW (phone: 944-4400). Inexpensive.

Madurai – Vegetarian Indian food is the specialty of this Georgetown establishment. Try the eggplant curry or the vegetable *biryani* (mixed vegetables cooked with rice). Open daily. Reservations advised. Major credit cards accepted. 3318 M St. NW (phone: 333-0997). Inexpensive.

Meskerem – The best of the Ethiopian eateries that line the Adams Morgan section of town. The dining room in front has conventional tables and chairs; in back there are woven straw tables called *mesobs*. Entrées arrive on huge plates of spongy Ethiopian bread, which is then torn off and used in lieu of utensils to scoop up the lamb, chicken, or vegetarian concoctions. Open daily. Reservations advised. Major credit cards accepted. 2434 18th St. NW (phone: 462-4100). Inexpensive.

Peyote Café – This new Southwestern bar and grill is located below *Roxanne's* in the heart of Adams Morgan. Try the chuck wagon beef and pinto bean chili, the mashed potatoes (with skins), and the Texas yardbird (barbecue chicken with melted Monterey Jack cheese). Open daily. Reservations advised. Major credit cards accepted. 2319 18th St. NW (phone: 462-8330). Inexpensive.

Red Sea – Enjoy casual, convivial dining at this popular Ethiopian eatery in Adams Morgan. The delicately seasoned dishes (*alechas*) are good starters. The hot ones (*berberes*) are not for the faint of heart (or stomach)! Traditional music on Fridays and Saturdays. Open daily. Reservations unnecessary. Major credit cards accepted. 2463 18th St. NW (phone: 483-5000). Inexpensive.

Restoran Indonesia Savinah Satay House – A new favorite among locals, this place specializes in Indonesian fare. Order the grilled chicken in coconut sauce, the *satay,* and the *gado gado* (salad with peanut sauce). Closed Mondays. Reservations advised. Major credit cards accepted. 1338 Wisconsin Ave. NW (phone: 337-2955). Inexpensive.

Roma – Solid Italian family-style place, best in warm weather when the large outdoor garden is open and musicians and singers add to the relaxed ambience. All the old favorites are here from pizza to pasta. Open daily. Reservations advised. Major credit cards accepted. 3419 Connecticut Ave. NW (phone: 363-6611). Inexpensive.

Roxanne's – Chef Phil DeMott worked with New Orleans's Paul Prudhomme for 5 years before coming to this Cajun-style eatery in Adams Morgan. Taste the barbecued shrimp, the blackened tuna, or the grilled lamb with white bean salad. Open daily. Reservations advised. Major credit cards accepted. 2319 18th St. NW (phone: 462-8330). Inexpensive.

Saigon Gourmet – A new Vietnamese dining spot that specializes in cooking from southern Vietnam. Taste the Saigon crispy noodles (fried noodles with a stir-fried mixture of chicken, beef, scallops, shrimp, and vegetables in a black bean sauce) or the ground pork wrapped in rice paper with rice noodles. Open daily. Reservations advised. Major credit cards accepted. 2635 Connecticut Ave. NE (phone: 265-1360). Inexpensive.

Star of Siam – This place reputedly serves the best Thai food in the district. Try one of the ten different kinds of curries, the crispy noodles, or the fish cakes. Open daily. Reservations necessary for parties of 4 or more. Major credit cards accepted. 1136 19th St NW, between L and M Sts. (phone: 785-2838/9). There's a second location in Rosslyn, VA, across the Key Bridge from Georgetown: 1735 N. Lynn St. (phone: 703-524-1208). Inexpensive.

Szechuan – Spicy Szechuan fare is the specialty here, with a touch of Cantonese and Hunan cooking. We recommend the crispy whole red snapper, the *kung pao* chicken (spicy chicken with peanuts and hot red peppers), and the crispy shredded beef Szechuan-style. Dim sum are served on Saturdays and Sundays. Open daily. Reservations necessary for four or more. Major credit cards accepted. 615 1st St. NW (phone: 393-0130). Inexpensive.

Tony Cheng's Mongolian – Mongolian barbecue is the specialty in this place where diners make their choices of vegetables, meat, and sauces that are then grilled in front of your eyes. The best part is that you can go back for seconds. Open daily. Reservations necessary for four or more. Major credit cards accepted. 619 H St. NW, in Chinatown (phone: 842-8669). Inexpensive.

Vietnam Georgetown – Small and intimate, this simple place serves the best Vietnamese food in town. Specialties include deep-fried crispy spring rolls, shrimp with sugarcane, and beef in grape leaves. Open daily. Reservations unnecessary. MasterCard and Visa accepted. 2934 M St. NW (phone: 337-4536). Inexpensive.

For the sweet of tooth, Washington has a homegrown ice cream empire founded by renegade attorney Bob Weiss. *Bob's Famous Ice Cream* has stores on Capitol Hill (236 Massachusetts Ave. NE; phone: 546-3860), near the Cleveland Park *Metro* station (3510 Connecticut Ave. NW; phone: 244-4465), and in Bethesda, MD (4706 Bethesda Ave.; phone: 301-986-5911). Bob's ice cream also is sold just above Georgetown at the *Ice Cream Shop* (2416 Wisconsin Ave. NW; phone: 965-4499).

DIVERSIONS

DIVERSIONS

For the Experience

Quintessential Washington

Many Americans at one time or another have stood — ice cream cones dripping down their sleeves on a typically hot and humid August day — in awe of Washington's white marble grandeur. As schoolchildren, we saw pictures in textbooks of our republic's eminent federal buildings and monuments — the White House, the Capitol Building, the Supreme Court, the Washington Monument — so in a way, the images are familiar. That is, until you come here. For whether home is Bangor or Bakersfield, a close encounter with the nation's capital brings the textbook dazzlingly to life; only here can you sense the vision of Washington, Jefferson, L'Enfant, and company who founded this city, hoping it would become both the workshop and showcase of American government that it is today.

There is much more to this major metropolitan area than its government, however — there are jazz clubs, ethnic restaurants, trendy shops, the *Redskins* — but the monuments, memorials, and marble façades are the magnets that draw upwards of 19 million visitors a year. Don't be reluctant to behave like a tourist — ask questions, ignore the ice cream on your sleeve, and buy a *Redskins* or Georgetown University T-shirt. Many of those who live and work here — senators, congressmen, and the like — are also tourists of sorts. It's just that they will stay a little longer (2 or 6 years, at least) before returning home.

NATIONAL ARCHIVES: Most of us take freedom for granted. We salute the flag and stand for the singing of the "Star-Spangled Banner," but few if any of us stop to think about how and why we live "in the land of the free and the home of the brave." The Archives, home to the sacred documents on which our nation was built — the Declaration of Independence, the Constitution, and the Bill of Rights — should be a required visit. There is little glitz to this exhibit, which essentially involves no more than hunching over a glass case and squinting at faded parchment paper. But for those who come to pay solemn tribute to these paper pillars of democracy (unlike those who just wander in to kill time before the movie begins over at the *Air and Space Museum*), it is refreshing to look beyond the *Fourth of July* fireworks to see what all the hubbub is about.

The shimmering white marble and pure classical design of the *National Archives* Building lend an air of security and permanence to what is in essence our nation's file cabinet. Walking up the steps on the Mall side (Constitution Ave.) and through the legion of Corinthian columns and 6½-ton bronze doors, you pass into the building's grand Rotunda. On a pedestal at the top of a set of steps inside are the documents, flanked on either side by the sweeping murals by Barry Faulkner depicting Jefferson presenting a draft of the Declaration of Independence to John Hancock, the President of the Continental Congress (left); and James Madison submitting the Constitution to George Washington and the Constitutional Convention (right).

First explore the exhibition hall that encircles the Rotunda, always a slice of Americana serving up such changing themes as Yankee ingenuity or the history of political cartoons. After clearing the metal detector and bag search, proceed up the steps for a look at the Charters of Freedom — visible (and readable) through several layers of laminated glass (which makes them look green) and special filters that protect them from the ravages of light. In addition, an electronic-sensored vault underneath the case is ready to seal up the documents for safekeeping if it senses trouble. Indeed, the security arrangement that protects against anything short of Armageddon reinforces the notion of our impenetrable commitment to preserving our freedom and its symbols.

CRAB FEAST: Just as refusing a lobster in Maine — the state's mascot and chief commodity — is, to some, grounds for deportation, so is passing up a crab, the Chesapeake Bay area's cherished crustacean, in the Washington area. There is no other dining experience, at least in this country and in this century, that compares with a traditional, unpretentious Chesapeake crab feast. Setting the tone for the proceedings is a crab house waiter who first places upon the table a brown paper tablecloth that functions as a drop cloth, preventing permanent damage to the property. Fast on its heels are the weapons: a wooden mallet and a stubby knife, followed by a tall pitcher of beer. Before long, a heaping mound of deliciously red, spiced steamed crabs is hoisted onto the table. Let the games begin. Some restaurants have placemats with instructions. Other places sell T-shirts that illustrate ten easy ways to approach a crab — and live to tell about it. Nevertheless, a brief tutorial is in order for the uninitiated since strategy is crucial for getting at the edible parts of the crab. (A good waiter or waitress should be of help in identifying the most succulent morsels.) Though ordinary appetites require only a half-dozen to a dozen crabs in order to be sated, a hearty appetite is recommended for a feast (normally $15 a head for all-you-can-eat — usually bushelsful). The best time for a crab orgy is from mid-March to November, since crabs are rarely taken from the Chesapeake during the winter (when they're flown up from the Carolinas). The sound of mallets pounding and the odd crab leg landing in your lap only add to the experience. A true crab aficionado will get down and dirty, emerging from the whole feast covered in spices and shards of shell. The ancient mariner of such feasts is *Ernie's Original Crab House,* across the Potomac in Alexandria (1623 Fern St.; phone: 703-836-1623; and 7929 Richmond Hwy.; phone: 703-780-0100). For a more upscale mallet mode try the *Dancin' Crab* (4611 Wisconsin Ave. NW; phone: 202-244-1882).

CHERRY BLOSSOM TIME: For those whose spirits are lifted by buds bursting, early April is the very best time to visit Washington. The *Cherry Blossom Festival* is this city's graceful and glorious rite of spring. In fact, the sight of cherry trees in bloom is the only happening known to stir Washingtonians more than does a *Redskin* victory or a juicy political scandal. The exact date the blossoms appear varies each year, depending on the weather (but usually between March 20 and April 17). When the trees — a gift from the Japanese government — are in blustery, full bloom, Washingtonians descend upon the Tidal Basin, an ordinarily tranquil body of water to the north of the Jefferson Memorial, its landscape now dressed in pale pink and white. Couples amble slowly amid the blossoms; artists dig in their easels, awash with inspiration; boaters paddle about, observing the spectacle from the water. One of the most colossal traffic jams of the calendar year ensues as motorists, who never seem to learn, clog the streets circling the Tidal Basin. The delicate beauty of the blossoms is best viewed up close amid the majesty of the nearby Lincoln and Jefferson memorials (see *Walk 1: The Mall and Monuments* in DIRECTIONS). The trees are of two varieties: Most are Akebeno trees, with delicate white blossoms, and scattered among them are Yoshino trees, with pale pink petals. Whether or not the blossoms have arrived, the *Cherry Blossom Festival* —

always held during the first week in April — proceeds as planned. Happily, nature usually obliges. The ceremonial lighting of the Japanese lantern, a stone lantern located among the trees, begins a week of festivities that includes a parade, pageants, concerts, and a marathon.

TEA AT THE WILLARD: In Washington's most historic hotel — known for many years as the "Residence of the Presidents" due to the distinguished company it used to keep (see *DC's Best Digs*) — the ancient English custom of afternoon tea is strictly observed. Tea here is an ideal way for guests and visitors to experience this restored Beaux Arts building. Washington's elite gathers in the L-shape *Nest* lounge to sip Earl Grey tea and daintily munch on the full complement of finger sandwiches, scones, Devonshire cream, and pastries. Strategically set on the mezzanine, the lounge sports a decidedly feminine decor, with light, marble-topped tables draped in white linen, small vases holding irises, pink-rose china, and soft blue drapes and carpeting adorning the floor and walls. The delicate touch is a throwback to an era when women were not allowed to swill spirits in the downstairs bar nor accompany their husbands as they imbibed. Instead, members of the fairer sex were banished up the spiral staircase to sip tea and chat amongst themselves. Today, the decor remains, but the crowd has changed. Tea at the *Willard* is a popular venue for movers and shakers to stop moving and shaking, business folks escaping the rigors of the office, baby and bridal showers, and the regular contingent of society ladies who sip champagne along with their tea. Tea is served daily from 3 to 5 PM. Everyone is welcome. Even men.

SENATE BEAN SOUP: Though few can explain its origin with any authority, a beige and rather bland bean soup has been the official dish and a trusty staple of the *US Senate Dining Room* since the turn of the century. Senate and culinary historians have boiled the blame (or credit) down to either Minnesota Senator Knute Nelson — whose affinity for a brimming bowl of bean soup was well documented — or Senator Fred Thomas Dubois of Idaho — who, using his inestimable clout as chairman of the Senate Restaurant Committee, cooked up a law ensuring that bean soup would enjoy special status on the *Senate Dining Room* menu. Though the controversy continues, bean soup is, in fact, made and served here each day by special order of Congress. In the cafeterias and dining rooms of the Senate office buildings and on the Senate side of the Capitol senators, staffers, and tourists alike sip, slurp, or spoon this most capital soup.

Though an able bowl of Senate soup is served (where else?) in the *Senate Dining Room,* the trouble for most of us is that one must get elected or be a personal guest of a US Senator to enter the sanctity of this exclusive room. For the tourist committed to experiencing this taste of pure Americana while on "the Hill," the *Capitol Refectory* (also called the *Senate Dining Room*) on the Senate side serves up a respectable bowl of bean soup on white linen tablecloths in a hurried, but rather pleasant, atmosphere. Pen-and-ink drawings of the Capitol Building adorn the walls and, since you're sitting so near the floor of the Senate, don't be surprised if a legislator or two happens to stride past. Bean soup receives star billing here and, indeed, leads off the menu (open Mondays through Fridays from 8 AM until the Senate is out of session, which sometimes lasts all night). Another good bean soup option on Capitol Hill is the admittedly character-less cafeteria in the Dirksen Senate Office Building (the middle of three Senate office buildings, located in the basement; phone: 202-224-7196). But perhaps Washington's best bean soup can be found down in the lowlands of Foggy Bottom. After finding the bean soup in the *Senate Dining Room* (the exclusive one) too watery for his tastes, restaurateur Dominique D'Ermo, owner of *Dominique's* (1900 Pennsylvania Ave. NW; phone: 202-452-1126), concocted a "better recipe" and now, with much fanfare, serves the steamy staple in his highly touted restaurant. Though not as good as the real thing, *Dominique's* canned version makes for a tasty souvenir.

A MOUNT VERNON AFTERNOON: Lovingly preserved, George Washington's Mount Vernon home is a far more meaningful monument to the man who was our first president than is the impersonal obelisk that bears his name. To spend a leisurely afternoon at Mount Vernon — a short drive south of Washington — is both a relaxing reprieve from the bustling city and a respectful glimpse into the life and times of this US patriot. Washington wrote about Mount Vernon that "no estate in America is as pleasantly situated as this home." Gazing out upon the wide sweep of the Potomac — from the Windsor chairs arranged on the mansion's portico, down the verdant Bowling Green that Washington himself laid out in 1785, and across the river to the Maryland hills that — thanks to private donations of land and the purchasing power of the federal government — preserves the area much as it was in Washington's day, it is clear that the proprietor's claim about the location of his home was no idle boast. But by Virginia Tidewater standards today, this colonial country house, like our first president's financial status at the time, is modest. Still, there is much to appreciate at Mount Vernon. First visit the mansion, preferably in the morning (the estate attracts some 10,000 visitors each day during the summer, and the line gets unwieldy in the afternoon). Inside this mid-Georgian style building with its columns and patio are some of the land- and riverscapes that recall Washington's interest in the commercial navigation of Virginia's waterways. There is an elegantly embellished Palladian window in the Banquet Hall. Elsewhere are found the Key to the Bastille, given to Washington by his chum Lafayette; a harpsichord he imported from England for his adopted daughter; a trunk Washington carried with him throughout the Revolutionary War; and the bed in which he died. But perhaps the real draw of Mount Vernon is its tranquillity. Yet its sylvan setting — Mount Vernon's spinning room, stable, open-hearth kitchen house, period garden, remaining slave quarters, George and Martha's burial vaults, and the shaded paths that connect them all — belies the fact that a 15-minute walk in any direction leads to an ugly suburban subdevelopment. But don't let that stop you. A visit to Mount Vernon has all the makings of a memorable afternoon.

A KENNEDY CENTER OPENING: Dust off your tux, shake out your mink, and prepare for a gala night out. Opening night at *Kennedy Center* is Washington at its glitziest. It's the place where people come to see and be seen, but more important, it's a staid, history-rich, red-tape-ridden city's salute to some of the finest theater this side of Broadway, with recent programs highlighting such hits as August Wilson's *Two Trains Running,* a smash revival of *Bye Bye Birdie,* and the premiere of the *Red Army Choir.* The opening-night experience begins with dinner at one of several choice local restaurants (see below); then it's time to mingle with the pundits, policymakers, and power brokers who exchange witty anecdotes, swap government gossip, and slap backs, all under the crystal chandeliers (a gift from Sweden) of the plush, red-carpeted Grand Foyer. Critics strut about, senators mingle with lobbyists, cabinet secretaries chat with White House aides, and veteran socialites exchange the latest scuttlebutt quietly among themselves. Often, the playwright may be in attendance, scanning the crowd for a friendly reviewer. An early arrival is imperative in order to drink in this social spectacle along with a glass of champagne from the refreshment concession. Before the curtain rises take a walk around the *Kennedy Center's* roof terrace, which offers a view of the Potomac in one direction and the glimmering capital city opposite. A leisurely terrace stroll takes about 15 minutes. On your way back into the theater, note the 7-foot bronze bust of John F. Kennedy in the Grand Foyer; it was Kennedy's plan for the performing arts center that stirred Washington out of its deep cultural sleep.

Fixed-price pre-theater dinner deals abound at the center's nearby restaurants. Book a table at *Maison Blanche,* near the White House, which specializes in French classics (phone: 202-842-0070); *Dominique's,* a favorite of Elizabeth Taylor (phone: 202-452-1126); or *Jean-Louis,* the *Watergate* complex's premier eatery and one of the most expensive in the lower forty-eight (phone: 202-298-4488). The *Kennedy Center* features its own excellent eatery, the *Roof Terrace,* which concentrates on regional food such as Maryland crab cakes (phone: 202-833-8870). Don't forget to protect your best bib and tucker.

THE GEORGETOWN EXPERIENCE: The spirited community west of Rock Creek that locals stubbornly call Georgetown (though its official name, according to the DC municipal government, is West Washington) is the city's adrenal gland. Through its main arteries, M Street and Wisconsin Avenue, flows the energy that makes this historic former tobacco port the city's most popular nightlife destination. Some of the folks who gravitate to Georgetown after sundown have a particular destination in mind. Perhaps they're hustling off to *Blues Alley,* a reformed hole-in-the-wall down a forgotten alley where cool jazz and Cajun food are the standard fare (is it coincidence that Duke Ellington grew up nearby?). Or possibly they're meeting friends (or an ambassador) at one of Georgetown's upscale ethnic restaurants (our favorite is *Dar es Salem,* offering a finger-licking-good Moroccan meal and entertainment by belly dancers); or just ruminating over a late-night coffee and dessert at *Au Pied de Cochon.* Other folks who deluge Georgetown's narrow streets on weekend nights have no particular destination in mind.

During daylight hours, like nomads, they cast about wherever their fancy takes them, popping into a tony boutique or bookshop here and a pub there, orbiting the corner of M Street and Wisconsin Avenue, Georgetown's nerve center. Georgetown is like that. Its real activity unfolds on the street, which is a bonanza for passionate people watchers. The full spectrum of personal style is on parade here. While waiting to cross an intersection, it is not unusual to find yourself flanked by black-garbed Existential types on their way to their favorite outfitter up Wisconsin Avenue and a gaggle of aged New Deal matrons off for tea and a chat about today's politics. Georgetown is a hodgepodge of students, socialites, Senate staffers, and street crazies (like the one who recently positioned himself as a tour guide outside the *Old Stone House* and convincingly told visitors that George Washington once entertained prostitutes there). After a lively tour of the main drags, wander among the residential back streets, where Georgetown's real cobblestone, colonial charm lies. The towpath of the C & O Canal (go there only by day), which slices through Georgetown, is another pleasant dimension to this once-tacky tobacco town.

DC's Best Digs

At any given time, Washington plays host to tens of thousands of tourists from around the globe. The guest population is composed not just of budget-conscious visitors or disgruntled folks who have come to America's complaints department to vent their spleens. Since Washington is the political hub of the Western world, it is not surprising that an extraordinary number of its visitors seek world class accommodations. Hosting the Queen of England and her entourage one week, the French prime minister and his retinue the next, and perhaps the Sultan of Brunei the following week, few other cities demand more from their hotels than does the nation's capital. Happily, many, especially those mentioned here, rise to the occasion.

FOUR SEASONS: If the difference between a good and a great hotel is in the details, this is one of the capital city's very best. The full spectrum of guest needs are given personalized attention. Each room is furnished with an ample number of chairs, a desk large enough to scatter papers over, juices, spirits, and chocolates in the armoire, plus a thick terry-cloth robe behind the bathroom door. In fact, if you lose your luggage or haven't time to unpack, each room contains enough toiletries and other accoutrements to ready you for a night on the town. And the town, Georgetown that is, unfolds to the west just outside the front door. The wisdom of this location is, indeed, unimpeachable. It is flanked by the Chesapeake & Ohio Canal, one of the country's first, and by Rock Creek Park, Washington's premier parkland (a run along the canal is a Washington ritual); in fact, most of the 197 rooms overlook the tranquil green space. The property is regal yet relaxed, attracting many entertainers and Hollywood types. Body-conscious guests can use the fitness club with a skylighted lap pool, a whirlpool bath, a sauna, and a steambath. Those who are not in retreat from the business world will find the hotel's fax machine, cellular phones, newspapers, and other business services useful. The *Garden Terrace,* a sunlit indoor room with flowered sofas and a piano, affords a view of the verdant park and canal area. The dining area serves nouvelle French cuisine and is notable for its afternoon tea, replete with scones, double Devonshire cream, and homemade preserves. The champagne breakfast is also gaining quite a following. The bar in *Garden Terrace* is a popular after-work cocktail spot. The main restaurant, *Aux Beaux Champs,* features classic and modern French food and excellent wines. *Le Petit Champs* is a private dining enclave with its own waiters and so-called dinner "captains," seating up to 14 for lunch, dinner parties, or breakfast meetings. Information: *Four Seasons,* 2800 Pennsylvania Ave. NW (phone: 342-0444 or 800-332-3442).

HAY-ADAMS: This architecturally stunning hostelry sits on some of DC's most prized real estate: Many of its 143 Edwardian- and Georgian-style rooms overlook Lafayette Square and the White House; others afford a point-blank view of St. John's Church, "the Church of the Presidents." Rooms are decorated with 18th-century period furniture and antiques. Designed in the Italian Renaissance style by a former palace architect of a Turkish sultan, the structure is built of white Indiana limestone, with a paneled lobby, Tudor dining rooms, and obsequious doormen dressed like Prussian generals. Rich in Old World charm, the hotel's Windsor and Lafayette Rooms — the reception areas just off the lobby — are certainly worth a peek. With their hand-painted wallpaper, antiques, and chandeliers, each is reminiscent of an old English manor house. Such well-known figures as Charles Lindbergh, Amelia Earhart, Sinclair Lewis, prominent heads of state, and foreign dignitaries have all stayed here. The *John Hay Room* offers classic French fare and an elegant afternoon tea with all the tasty trappings of this ancient British custom (from 3 to 5 PM daily). This restaurant and the informal subterranean *Eagle Bar and Grill* are where Ollie North and his cohorts wooed well-heeled potential contributors to their private Nicaraguan Contra fund. *The Adams Room* is a pleasant place to mull over breakfast and the day's events in the *Washington Post;* it also offers an excellent lunch and weekend brunch. Full concierge service, 24-hour room service, and valet parking round out the amenities. Information: *Hay-Adams,* 800 16th St. NW (phone: 202-638-6600 or 800-424-5054).

JEFFERSON: Federal-style understatement is the hallmark of this downtown establishment that has the feel of a British estate. The drawings of past presidents adorn the walls of the hotel and restaurant, and just out on 16th Street, the residence of the presidents can be seen to the right. Relatively intimate with 69 rooms and 35 suites, its room service never dozes nor refuses even the most extravagant of requests — even during the wee hours; and multilingual concierge service is ideal for arranging dinner reservations or theater tickets. Each guestroom has a fax line, and portable fax machines are available for the business traveler. One of the hotel's real gems is the *Hunt Club,* a restaurant and bar on the ground floor; painted fox-hunt red, it has original prints of political caricatures dating back to the 1700s. The *Club* (it's not private) has a wood-burning fireplace and lots of niches, ideal for a heart-to-heart or sensitive high-level discussions. The kitchen features American and French food, including such dishes as Jefferson macaroni (named after our third president, who, according to the hotel, introduced pasta to the US after his travels through Europe) and vegetable strudel. There is also a display of 18th-century historical prints and portraits (many of the originals hang in the White House). For those with an expensive thirst (and proof that this is an expense account–driven economy), an $800 bottle of Louis XIV brandy is locked in a glass case to the right of the bar. But don't be put off: You can order a single snifter for only $75! A cigar box containing fine complimentary smokes sits on a cherry-wood table near the exit. Enjoy a postprandial promenade by inspecting the various anterooms, chandeliers, and brass elevator railings in this sumptuously refurbished establishment, within walking distance of the White House. Information: *Jefferson Hotel,* 1200 16th St. NW (phone: 202-347-2200 or 800-368-5966).

RITZ-CARLTON: From the hand-carved mahogany headboards and embroidered English bedspreads to the quaint afternoon tea and the extra-dry martinis served amid the intimate alcoves of the *Fairfax Bar,* it is everything one would expect from the Ritz name. Washington's edition is deserving of Webster's description: ritzy, adj. (Ritz hotels, noted for their opulence) 1: fashionable, posh — from *Websters New Collegiate Dictionary,* 1973. Formerly the *Fairfax,* its new owners have worked wonders with the Georgian-style red brick building, already at a geographic advantage in the middle of tree-lined Embassy Row. It has the feel of an elegant — yet "understated" (as the staff is quick to add) — European home; Federal-style antiques complement the colonial decor. Amenities include 24-hour room service, in-room honor bars, morning delivery of the *Wall Street Journal,* fax, telex, and secretarial services, valet parking, and baby-sitting. There is a data base of customer profiles so that if a guest returns, the staff knows his or her preference for soft or firm pillows, chocolates, reading material, and other personal items to make the traveler feel at home. The *Jockey Club* reception room is filled with paintings of famous horses and the *Fairfax Bar* sports a good collection of equestrian-themed oils, wood-burning fireplaces, and afternoon tea (daily from 3 to 5 PM) with a full complement of various teas, house-smoked salmon, cucumber sandwiches on crustless bread, scones, Devonshire cream — the makings of a first-rate tea time. The *Jockey Club* restaurant (modeled after New York's famed "21") is steeped in clubby congeniality, the food French-influenced. New chef Fabrice Canelle was formerly with *Maxim's* in Paris. Soft-shell crabs have long been a staple here; and the city's power brokers and diplomatic crowd from nearby Embassy Row are its staple clientele. Information: *Ritz-Carlton,* 2100 Massachusetts Ave. NW (phone: 202-293-2100 or 800-241-3333).

STOUFFER MAYFLOWER: This historic and recently renovated property, one of the capital's treasures, has earned laurels over the years for catering to the world's movers and shakers with elegance and style. It has returned to its former exalted status — to a time when it hosted such world figures as Queen Elizabeth, West German Chancellor Konrad Adenauer, the Shah of Iran, Charles de Gaulle, and, on a daily basis in his day, J. Edgar Hoover. The yellow brick-and-limestone Beaux Arts building boasts a block-long lobby adorned with Italian marble, glittering chandeliers, and intricately carved, 23-karat gold leaf ceilings. Although under the Stouffer trademark and management, it's known simply as the "Mayflower" and its gradual 7-year renovation was more extensive — and expensive — than the cost of the original building. But despite its costly makeover, the hotel no longer charges only stellar rates (children under 18 stay free in their parents' room). Its central location in the heart of downtown is a premium for sightseers (not far from the White House and the Mall) and its nearly 700 rooms can accommodate legions of them. Guests can enjoy round-the-clock room service, valet parking, full concierge service, and some suites with wet bars. There also is a business center and a new health center. The Grand Ballroom — with its terraces, balconies, and Wedgwood-like bas-reliefs — recalls the splendor of a bygone era. The lush surroundings make the *Nicholas* restaurant a fitting place to feast on the latest in mid-Atlantic American fare, including swordfish with pineapple, Maine lobster, and veal chops with riesling and mushrooms. Jacket and tie are required. Information: *Stouffer Mayflower,* 1127 Connecticut Ave. NW (phone: 202-347-3000 or 800-HO-TELS-1).

WILLARD INTER-CONTINENTAL: A mid-1980s renovation converted this sprawling, imposing Beaux Arts building from being just another pretty façade to its full fin de siècle glory. Reopened in 1986 as part of the Inter-Continental chain, its lobby boasts the original chandeliers and oak paneling, reminiscent of the days when it was known as the "Residence of the Presidents." The carpeting, columns, and much of the furniture are historic reproductions based on photographs of the original decor. The 365 rooms are decorated in turn-of-the-century style.

A temporary home for no fewer than 10 American presidents-elect, including Abraham Lincoln and Warren Harding, perhaps its finest hour came in 1923 when a distinguished resident, Vice President Calvin Coolidge, had to assume the presidency following the death of Warren Harding. Until Mrs. Harding could clear out of the White House, this spot served as the temporary White House for Coolidge and, thus, the American flag flew overhead. It was here, after meeting a haggard and war-weary President Lincoln, that Julia Ward Howe wrote the "Battle Hymn of the Republic"; and where Dr. Martin Luther King, Jr., wrote his "I Have a Dream" speech. Since 1986 more than 50 heads of state have chosen the *Willard* as their home away from home. If its distinctive architecture and impressive history are not enough, the service is nothing less than superb. There is 24-hour room service, an exercise room, a café, two lounges, and the *Willard Room,* which serves contemporary American fare and regional favorites amid Edwardian decor. A special treat is superb afternoon tea (from 3 to 5 PM daily) served in the *Nest* lounge. *The Occidental,* one of the city's finest dining spots and a popular meeting place for primary powers, is adjacent to the hotel but not under the same ownership (see *Capital Dining*). A special staff assists guests with plane reservations, theater tickets, and transportation. Peacock Alley, an opulent, block-long hall with marble columns that connects the two entrances, was, according to legend, the very spot in which the term "lobbyist" was coined. As the story goes, on occasion, Ulysses Grant liked to escape the rigors of the White House and headed for the *Willard.* A legion of influence peddlers would follow him there and linger about as he enjoyed his brandy in Peacock Alley. (A few of the serge-suited species may still be spotted here pressing flesh and slapping backs.) A number of upscale shops are located in the refurbished building. Information: *Willard,* 1401 Pennsylvania Ave. NW (phone: 202-628-9100 or 800-327-0200).

Capital Dining

Washington's restaurant scene has made a quantum leap since its days as a sleepy, parochial southern city. Now almost as much of the nation's business is conducted over dinner tables in local eateries as across cluttered departmental desks. A stroll down most streets reinforces the notion that this influential capital city is geared to satisfy a global audience. And though Washington is still more provincial than New York City, its restaurants, many boasting first-rate French chefs, offer menus from around the world — from Afghanistan and Vietnam to Ethiopia and Thailand. Still, for many, the best DC dining experiences are in those places that provide food and atmosphere indigenous to its geography. Many spots are also developing favorable reputations for their wine lists: According to the American Wine Institute, Washingtonians consume more fine wines per capita than any other American city. But be advised: This city's expense-account crowd seems to gravitate to good food and grog and has driven the prices of some tabs into the realm of the absurd. The restaurants listed below offer some of DC's finer dining experiences.

L'AUBERGE CHEZ FRANÇOIS: According to the readers of *Washingtonian* magazine, this Alsatian country inn, 30 minutes west of the District in northern Virginia's
hunt country, is a perennial favorite. Everything from the attentive service to the cozy
yet refined setting of a country house and the sublime preparation of the Alsatian
specialties makes dinner here an enchanting experience. The decor alone is worth the
drive: There are several working fireplaces, antique grandfather clocks, a mounted elk's
head, lots of other knickknacks from the Alsace region in France, and a staff dressed
in Alsatian garb. And the fare draws upon the best of both worlds, blending the hearty
proportions of Germanic cooking with French touches: excellent sauces, cheeses, and
presentation. Owner François Haeringer's reasonably priced menu includes a number
of Alsatian specialties, among them the famed *choucroute garnie,* a collection of sausages and duck atop heavily seasoned sauerkraut; Gruyére tart, an Alsatian version of
cassoulet with sausages and lentils; stuffed rabbit; and chicken stewed in Alsatian
riesling. The assortment of pâtés is renowned, and for dessert, we recommend the lime
tart. The prices listed for the main course (from $27 to $32) include a selection from
the list of first courses, a house salad, a family-style serving of vegetables, and a dessert.
The reservation book is always filled, so plan far in advance (a well-kept secret among
the regulars is that no reservations are necessary for dining in the garden during the
warm months). Information: *L'Auberge Chez François,* 332 Springvale Rd., Great
Falls, VA (phone: 703-759-3800).

GALILEO: *Washingtonian* magazine ranks this as not only the capital's best Italian
dining spot, but possibly the best restaurant in town. (It is one of only two restaurants
to which the food scribes at the *Washingtonian* are willing to affix their coveted four
stars.) And no wonder. The simple, yet spacious new quarters give chef Roberto Donna
more room to apply his northern Italian ingenuity to the poultry, meat, and game
dishes — along with the city's finest breads, which accompany each meal. Try the
risotto or the homemade *agnolotti,* a pasta filled with spinach and ricotta. The rack of
veal with mushroom and rosemary sauce is also popular. Preferred seating is in the
Wine Room, a cozy alcove where the impressive selection of wine is stored. (In fact,
the wine list has earned a coveted Award of Excellence from *The Wine Spectator.*)
Portraits and reproductions of the writings of the Italian astronomer for whom the
restaurant is named adorn the walls. Perhaps the most endearing aspect of eating here
is the exuberance of the staff, who give each diner the feeling that his or her meal is
a cause for celebration. Unfortunately, reaching the heights of popularity results in
steeper prices. Bring lots of dough — and not for bread. Information: *Galileo,* 1110 21st
St. NW (phone: 202-293-7191).

MAISON BLANCHE: This elegant French dining room is so close to the White
House that even a snail could crawl over on its lunch hour. The only place you'll find
a snail in this place, however, is on a plate: Chef Christian Gautrois is well-known for
his exquisite escargot. Gautrois specializes in this and other French classics such as
bouillabaisse. Other favorites are his nouvelle version of Norwegian salmon in a vegetable sauce and shrimp with angel hair pasta. The wine list boasts over 350 labels. Elegant
decor — walnut, brown-velvet arm chairs, a crystal chandelier from Belgium, and a
remarkable carpet sporting a bouquet of 36 colors — and excellent cuisine make this
a favorite among lobbyists and White House staffers. It's also a haunt of newsfolk,
including no-nonsense — when eating — columnist Art Buchwald, who dines here
regularly. The prix fixe theater menu (available either before or after the performance)
is a bargain at $24.95. The *Kennedy Center* is a short drive or an 8-block walk away.
Information: *Maison Blanche,* 1725 F St. NW (phone: 202-842-0070).

MR. K'S: The strength of this bustling restaurant ridge (K Street) place lies in the
hushed competence of its staff — who arrive at tableside in threes — and the excellent
food that hails from four areas of China (northern from Peking, spicy Hunan and
Szechuan from central China, the milder Shanghai version from eastern China, and the
classic Cantonese dishes from the country's south). Favorites include beef mimosa,

Peking duck, and any one of several lobster dishes. There are four private dining rooms with impressive jade statues of dragons and a phoenix. The tables in the spacious main dining room are arranged with privacy in mind — a nod to the high-powered lawyers and lobbyists who frequent here. Keeping with the family tradition of Chinese dining, dishes can be placed on an elaborate, gilded "lazy Susan" and spun around for everyone's convenience. Surprisingly for a Chinese restaurant, a real treat awaits coffee aficionados at the end of the meal: A high-tech coffee urn is wheeled out, a burner lit underneath, and after the water in the pipes boils, causing quaking, burbling, and gurgling, a delicious brew issues forth (don't worry: They serve tea, too). Information: *Mr. K's,* 2121 K St. NW (phone: 202-331-8868).

OCCIDENTAL: This historic Washington eatery has recently transformed its stuffy, formal dining room upstairs. Gone are the starched drapes, the portraits of presidents, the impeccably dressed but stiff-necked staff, and the unnervingly repressed atmosphere that gave diners the feeling that the wrong choice of fork would result in instant banishment. Today, though still an archetypal DC dining place, the atmosphere is more casual. Fortunately, the first-rate fare hasn't changed. Longtime chef Jeff Buben's specialties include a super swordfish sandwich, escalope of salmon *au poivre* with black bean purée, crab cakes, and a selection of grilled meat, fish, and sausage. The wine list is impressive and the dessert list comprehensive. Given its proximity to the houses of American government, don't be surprised if you wind up rubbing elbows with a senator or a congressman, a White House aide, or a Supreme Court Justice or two. The walls of this clubby brass and leather dining room are covered with more than 3,000 signed photographs of statesmen dating back to the early 1900s. This spot has lived up to its reputation as the place "where statesmen dine." The mahogany bar on the lower level is a wonderful venue for a cocktail; always dense with legislators, it's popular among lobbyists, too. Another one of its contributions to history: The *Occidental* was the place where a Kennedy aide met with the Soviet ambassador to exchange messages between the president and Khrushchev during the Cuban missile crisis. Information: *Occidental Bar and Grill,* 1475 Pennsylvania Ave. NW (phone: 202-783-1475).

PRIME RIB: Washington's premier steak house; and why not? Anybody who can't stare down a 2-inch-thick cut of the signature entrée shouldn't be here. Nevertheless, the menu does offer, in addition to prime ribs, an impressive rack of lamb, crab Imperial, and other fish specialties, and the ambience — featuring soothing piano music from a baby grand against a motif of black and white and polished brass — evokes the mood of a 1940s New York supper club, but without the mammoth Manhattan prices. In fact, meals here are remarkably reasonable. Perhaps the city's best lunch value is an on-the-bone-cut of prime ribs served with two vegetables (and the aforementioned music) for $11.95. Dinner is more expensive, but still well priced, considering that you're getting some of the largest portions of the finest steaks in the area. Information: *The Prime Rib,* 2020 K St. NW (phone: 202-466-8811).

Antiques

To find the best concentration of antiques in the Washington area one must first locate the area's most historic districts. Old homes beget old furnishings. Thus, with the exception of lengthier trips to the Pennsylvania Dutch country or to Leesburg and the other Virginia "burgs" to the south, Georgetown and Old Town Alexandria are the antiques buff's best hunting grounds. These old Potomac port cities, rich in well-preserved 18th-century architecture, predate the nation's capital. In exchange for the hogsheads of tobacco that left these ports for England, ships returned carrying furniture, the latest fashions, books, and other trappings of European culture to fill the houses of the area's wealthy tobacco merchants who were part of the colonial aristocracy. In addition to the more austere American collectibles one might find in this area, there is usually a respectable selection of European antiques, too. All of the following offer shipping services for furniture and larger items.

MILLER & ARNEY ANTIQUES: The owner of this 20-year-old shop characterizes his inventory as a "general store of antiques." This place is a sort of one-stop emporium where many Georgetowners go to furnish their homes. Housed in a turn-of-the-century, 2-story Victorian building are American, English, and continental furniture and decorative objects from the 18th and 19th centuries. Owner Joe Miller says he is most proud of his English discoveries and personally travels to Great Britain to rummage and restock when the exchange rate is favorable. (Lately, he has had to concentrate on scouring for antiques in his own back yard.) Fortunately, Miller is known by local antiques mavens as much for his purchases as for his sales. He always seems to carry a selection of many mahogany desks, "occasional tables," standing clocks, and lamps of all ilks for traditional homes. One of Miller's prized possessions at press time was a massive 18th-century French china cabinet. If notified in advance, the shop will provide chauffeur service to and from downtown DC (an attractive feature since there is no public transportation to Georgetown). Information: *Miller & Arney Antiques,* 1737 Wisconsin Ave. NW, Georgetown (phone: 202-338-2369).

SUSQUEHANNA ANTIQUES COMPANY: The inventory of this spacious Georgetown shop, filling a 2-story house just off Wisconsin Avenue, includes mainly American and English furniture, paintings, and clocks. Among the vast collection of early American bracket and shelf clocks is a Federal-period standing piece made in 1790 by a clockmaster whose family held on to it for all of its 200-year history. Owner David Friedman, who is a third-generation antiques dealer, is an aficionado of American art; and his collection reflects it. Included here are works by Charles Warren Eaton, Paul Cornoyer, and Herbert Morton Stoops. The shop also features myriad antique brass andirons and a collection of pre-1920 quilts mainly from Maryland and Pennsylvania. The owner will let you have a peek at the stuff in his nearby warehouse (call for an appointment), which he uses as a workshop and place to store the overflow. Information: *Susquehanna Antiques Company,* 3216 O St. NW, Georgetown (phone: 202-333-1511).

THIEVES MARKET: This antiques mall, the first of its kind in the country when it opened 40 years ago, is a place to really get a steal (thus the name — it's also the namesake of a famous Parisian market). For example, this market sold the oldest painting of Abraham Lincoln, pre-beard, for $3 in the 1970s. A box filled with assorted papers was sold for $8 — much to the delight of the patron when he discovered that the box contained a rough draft of General Robert E. Lee's farewell address. Stories abound of customers walking away with ordinary antique desks and drawers and, after some inspection, finding secret compartments containing diamonds, emeralds, and rubies. One canny shopper paid $1,200 for an American-made table that fetched over $28,000 several weeks later at an auction. Though the presentation of its inventory might not be as demure as the more exclusive dealers', it is no coincidence that many dealers and decorators shop here. Turnover is so quick (the market attracts several thousand people every week) that it is difficult to list anything that is certain to be in stock. Owner Kaplan Cohen, a third-generation art dealer, offers American, English, and continental china, silver, crystal, armoires, antique paintings, Venetian chandeliers, bronze and marble statuary, 18th-century mahogany desks, and other unusual items.

Information: *Thieves Market,* 8101 Richmond Hwy., Alexandria, VA (phone: 703-360-4200).

WASHINGTON ANTIQUES CENTER: Housed in a plain, red brick office building that displays the wares of some 35 antiques dealers; the exterior of the center belies the venerable treasures inside. From an excellent collection of silver, in which 17th-century pieces can be found now and again, to furniture, rugs, books, porcelain, crystal, and fine arts, this gallery seemingly has it all. Among the dealers whose antiques are tastefully displayed here are Roberta Tankel, Washington's premier dealer in porcelain, *G & M Antiques,* which carries an unholy alliance of affordable retro (from the 1950s) and Victorian furniture; and a bookseller who specializes in collectible first editions. One showcase sparkles with vintage costume jewelry. The management has created the sophisticated mood of a gallery and is careful not to overwhelm the patron with bric-a-brac. Classical music serves as background, and the collections are carefully placed so as not to clutter the area as they do at a flea market. Information: *Washington Antiques Center,* 209 Madison St., Old Town Alexandria, VA (phone: 703-739-2484).

For The Body

Good Golf

The late President Dwight Eisenhower left cleat marks behind in the Oval Office from his frequent putting practices between foreign policy briefings. In recent years, President George Bush has conducted much of his business as the nation's commander in chief from the links, and Vice President Dan Quayle's obsession with and proficiency at the sport is well documented. From the top brass on down, Washingtonians love golf. With the exception of the *Redskins* during football season, golf is perhaps the most popular water-cooler conversation. To those who strive to fit into Washington life, teeing up is as important as having voted in the last presidential election. Perhaps this is the genius behind the area's many golf-equipment discount shops (just check the yellow pages). And in spite of hot-and-humid-as-hell summers and an occasional snowstorm, golf is played almost every month of the year at the area's many courses. There's municipal golf to be played inside the District of Columbia's city limits (36 holes at Hains Point, in East Potomac Park; phone: 202-554-7660; or 18 holes at Rock Creek Park; phone: 202-723-9832) but those who venture a little farther from the city will be rewarded with a high-caliber round. Here are a few of the better public courses within a reasonable drive of DC.

ENTERPRISE: This picturesque collection of holes is known among locals as the "*Augusta National* of area public courses." Though golfers must keep their eye on the ball, the azaleas, Oriental dogwood blossoms, and other colorful plantings are delightful distractions. These 18 holes occupy 160 acres of the former farm and estate of Captain Newton H. White, the first commanding officer of the USS *Enterprise*, a World War II aircraft carrier (hence the name). The captain's stately mansion has been carefully preserved and sits next to the course's modern clubhouse, which has a snack bar for light breakfast or sandwiches, and plenty of cold beer. Though there are two ponds, only one should come into play (unless your backswing goes awry). The 6,200-yard course is still fairly challenging; bunkers tightly flank most of the sprawling greens. A putting green is available, as is club rental (even for the southpaw), and both pull and powered golf carts. An odd tee-time system that forces players to arrange their cars in the parking lot on a first-come, first-served basis creates hours-long backups on weekends. Interestingly, one spirited soul arrives around 2:30 to 3:30 AM on Saturdays. For his efforts, he has been the first to tee off every Saturday for the past 2 years. Just 10 minutes north of DC. Greens fees at this par 72 course range from $15 to $20. Information: *Enterprise Golf Course,* 2802 Enterprise Rd. (off Rte. 214 east), Mitchellville, MD (phone: 301-249-2040).

HERNDON CENTENNIAL: Noted by area professionals for its thorough maintenance, this 18-hole, par 71 course features rolling, tree-lined fairways. A prominent design feature is the mysterious grassy mounds that have been molded along the fairway, often causing shots to veer sideways (which can either mean serendipity or doom, depending on which side of the mound the shot returns to earth). These mounds are reminiscent of the grand old game's Scottish origins — thankfully without the added heather hazard. With ample bunkers intruding on most tee shots and every green, the course presents over 50 opportunities to test one's mettle in the sand. Fortunately, the course's relative paucity of water (with the exception of three or four holes where it comes into play) and its forgiving length (5,865 yards from the men's tees) are enough to repair the ego if you're having a sandy day and getting some bad bounces. *Herndon* has a putting green and driving range, golf-club rental, and pull-cart and power golf cart rental. Clubhouse amenities include a golf shop, a snack bar, and a well-stocked 19th hole that encourages a more spirited recounting of the round's events or misadventures. Best to reserve tee times 1 week in advance. Greens fees are $22 for 18 holes; $17 for 9 holes. The city of Herndon is about 15 miles southwest of Washington. From Dulles Toll Road, take exit 2 to Route 657 north; Ferndale Avenue is on the left. Information: *Herndon Centennial Golf Course,* Ferndale Ave., Herndon, VA (phone: 703-471-5769).

RESTON: Big hitters will enjoy (or at least be challenged by) this well-maintained, classically designed course that is long (6,550 yards, par 71), lush, and rolling. Tall, mature oak trees line many of the well-groomed fairways, and attractive townhouses are just out of range (golfers hope) of this busy course's cross fire. The course contains a series of traps enclosing both the greens and those nettlesome fairway bunkers that can gobble up even the best-struck shot. Bring along a good sand wedge. For example, the 18th hole is pockmarked by no less than seven bunkers, five of them on the fairway. Also, the wind has been known to sweep away otherwise dazzling shots from their intended targets. (At least this can be your reasoning while replaying the round in the clubhouse's snack bar over a cup of soup, a sandwich, or a brew.) Tee times are not needed during the winter months but are an absolute necessity during peak season. For weekday play, call the pro shop starting at 8 AM on Wednesdays; for Sunday play, at 8 AM on Thursdays. Clubs, and pull and power carts, can be rented. Located about 15 miles southwest of Washington. Greens fees are $18. Information: *Reston Golf Course,* 11875 Sunrise Valley Rd. (off exit 3, Dulles Toll Rd. and Reston Ave.), Reston, VA (phone: 703-620-9333).

SWAN POINT: Though it's over an hour's drive into the Maryland countryside north of Washington, this 6,403-yard course (par 72) is well worth the trip. Due in part to the marshy natural surroundings with lots of old pine trees, ominous mounds, and plenty of sand, its classic Carolina feel is also a credit to its recent redesign and reconstruction by Atlanta-based golf course architect Bob Crupp, an adviser for the *Augusta National,* home of the *Master's* tournament. Most of all, the narrow fairways demand placement that may seem as difficult as threading a camel through the proverbial eye of a needle — though thankfully there aren't many fairway bunkers. The fairways are Bermuda grass (almost unheard of in this area) and the greens are bent grass — and are like putting on smooth ice. A quorum of the holes meanders through the marshland, and water could conceivably come into play on 13 of them (bring lots of extra balls). A driving range and putting green are also available. Golf carts are mandatory until 3 PM, and the greens fees are $43. A fancy clubhouse with restaurant and 19th hole was scheduled to open as we went to press. Tee times for weekday play should be arranged 1 week in advance; call on Thursdays beginning at 8 AM for weekend play. Greens fees, which include a cart, are $43 for 18 holes. Information: *Swan Point,* Swan Point Rd. (off Rte. 301), Issue, MD (phone: 301-259-4411).

Tennis

According to the *Washington Tennis Guide,* the definitive publication on local tennis, there are over 1,000 courts in the Washington area. As most of these courts are public, many have fallen into hopeless disrepair due to the ravages of time and neglect. Some of the better courts in the area require a fee and some insist on reservations. It is best to call in advance to check the regulations. Also, many private area courts may honor reciprocal agreements with members of other clubs. Check the yellow pages for a list of private clubs in the area.

CHINQUAPIN CENTER: Along with an Olympic-size swimming pool, a fitness room with Lifecycles and weights, this sports complex has 4 lighted, outdoor tennis courts. The courts are operated on a first-come, first-served basis with a log book for times when it gets especially crowded (usually in the summer). These are the only public courts in Alexandria that the park service recommends. Information: *Chinquapin Center,* 3210 King St., Alexandria, VA (phone: 703-931-1127).

HAINS POINT: This complex of 24 public tennis courts includes 5 heated and air conditioned indoor courts. Of the 19 outdoor courts, 10 are clay. Located on Hains Point and reasonably close to Capitol Hill, the courts have been known to attract members of Congress and count among their regular players Chief Justice William Rehnquist and HUD Secretary Jack Kemp. Courts should be reserved at least 1 week in advance. The fee is steep ($15–$24 per hour, depending on the day and time). Information: *Hains Point,* 1090 Ohio Dr., Washington, DC (phone: 202-554-5962).

WASHINGTON TENNIS CENTER: This collection of 17 soft-surface and 5 hard-surface courts are open from April through November. They are perhaps the District's best courts since they are in a particularly lovely area of Rock Creek Park north of the National Zoo. Reservations must be made. Information: *Guest Services, Inc.,* 16th and Kennedy Sts. NW, Washington, DC (phone: 202-722-5949).

WHEATON REGIONAL PARK & CABIN JOHN PARK: Here are two sets of what are the best of Montgomery County's (in Maryland) 235 public courts (for information on other courts, call 301-495-2530). Along with a number of outdoor courts in Wheaton Regional Park, just 10 miles from the District, there are 6 indoor courts that can be reserved for a charge. The rate, if reserved a day or two in advance, is from $10 to $23 per hour, depending on the day and time. The indoor courts are open until 1 AM. Also within the park is an ice skating rink, an indoor garden and conservatory, and horse stables. Cabin John Park features 6 indoor courts. Though these are a little busier, court time is ordinarily available from $10 to $23 per hour. Information: *Wheaton Regional Park,* 2000 Shorefield Rd., Wheaton, MD (phone: 301-649-4049); *Cabin John Park,* 7801 Democracy Blvd., Bethesda, MD (phone: 301-469-7300).

Bicycling

Biking in any major metropolitan area is akin to waging war with a peashooter; in Washington, it's more like firing off at the *Redskins'* offensive line (known as "the Hogs") with no more padding than a pair of dress slacks and a starched sports shirt. The menaces are many. Absentminded tourists in cars, preoccupied with monuments and parking spaces, weave about like the dragon in a Chinese parade. Bespectacled bureaucrats wander randomly into traffic. And because of the high turnover of its citizenry, few Washingtonians have really mastered the slants, one-ways, traffic circles, and perpetual road construction that comprise driving in DC. Downtown biking is best left to the couriers. Fortunately, however, a number of bike trails abound in the Washington area that afford the cyclist an opportunity to get an invigorating workout while drinking in the serenity of several choice suburbs. If you've come with your wheels, happy trails. If not, 3-speed, 10-speed, and kids' bikes can be rented from *Big Wheel Bikes* (M St., Georgetown; phone: 202-337-0254; and at 1004 Vermont Ave.; phone: 638-3301); mountain bikes, beach bikes, and tandems are available at *Thompson's Boat Center* (Virginia Ave. at Rock Creek Pkwy.; phone: 202-333-4861), as well as at *Metropolis Bike & Scooter* (709 8th St. SE; phone: 202-543-8900) and other area bike shops. The following are several of the best bike paths in the area.

C & O CANAL TOWPATH: This wide, packed-dirt trail borders the historic waterway that was supposed to revolutionize commerce in the early 19th century. Commerce was, indeed, revolutionized, but by the railroad instead. Thus, instead of being trod by mules towing barges, the towpath along the canal has become more famous for being trod by bikers and joggers. Conceivably, the entire length of the canal, from Georgetown to Cumberland, Maryland, can be biked (184 miles each way; some serious bikers make it a 3- or 4-day excursion). Though the towpath is an almost imperceptible incline, it is slightly uphill from Georgetown. There are camping facilities, historical points of interest, and a canal museum along the way. The Great Falls of the Potomac, a dramatic series of jagged falls which roar into a narrow gorge, is one of the most spectacular sights in the eastern US. There are plenty of walking trails that are ideal for mountain bikes. The National Park Service, for its part, has put up mileposts along the towpath for the 14 miles from Georgetown to Great Falls. (As in any large city, solo cyclists should take extra care.)

ARLINGTON CEMETERY TO ROCK CREEK PARKWAY: This 5-mile stretch of paved bike path runs from Arlington National Cemetery across the Arlington Memorial Bridge to the Lincoln Memorial. From here, head uptown on the lovely Rock Creek Parkway toward the National Zoo, a thickly wooded spindle of greenery that meanders along Rock Creek. Teddy Roosevelt used to go on brisk hikes up this corridor of wilderness between Georgetown/Northwest and Adams Morgan. A good place to access the trail is from *Thompson's Boat Center,* at the northwest end of Virginia Avenue where Rock Creek feeds into the Potomac. From here the path can be taken toward Arlington National Cemetery, where it links up with the Mount Vernon Bike Path, running south. Another option from the Lincoln Memorial is to continue south to either Ohio Drive or West Basin Drive, which borders the Tidal Basin, and then follow the path around this serene body of water. This is especially recommended in April when the cherry blossoms are in bloom.

MOUNT VERNON BIKE PATH: This is Washington's premier bike trail. From the Lincoln Memorial use the left side of the bridge across the Potomac and bear left once in Virginia. This well-maintained, paved path runs approximately 25 miles along the Potomac all the way to George Washington's stately home in Mount Vernon, where there are ample bike locks near the snack bar, across from the parking lot. Along the way, enjoy the views of the city skyline, National Airport, vistas of the Maryland hills, the Masonic Temple, and a number of marinas along the Potomac shores. Fortunately, the path is wide, since cyclists share much of the road with runners and rollerbladers. The path breaks up for a short stretch in Old Town Alexandria and cyclists must forge through the streets of Old Town; the route is well marked and resumes at the other end of Old Town.

Boating

Traversed by rivers, tributaries, canals, and reservoirs, Washington offers a fleet of boating options on its various waterways — from plush dinner cruises on the Potomac River to paddleboats on the Tidal Basin. Perhaps the most intriguing water transport idea was proposed by the capital city's chief architect, Pierre L'Enfant, whose original plan of Washington envisioned a canal running from a point near the White House to the Capitol Building: When he paid a visit to Congress, the president would simply get there via barge. (The idea never got beyond L'Enfant's drawing board.) Even though the canal was paved over and is now Constitution Avenue, visitors can still get a feel for what mule-drawn barge travel was really like on the C & O Canal (see below). In addition, the world's fastest and most expensive speedboats come to Washington in early June for the *President's Cup Regatta,* held off Hains Point. Aside from the speed demons who vie for the coveted *President's Cup,* the extravaganza includes canoe and rowing races. The following are popular area boating experiences:

TACKING THE POTOMAC: Though the Potomac is not generally known for its world class sailing — since sandbars seem to pop up all the time and floating timber is apt to get in the way — the Washington Sailing Marina (George Washington Memorial Pkwy. south of National Airport; phone: 548-9027) is the exception. The hazards are well marked in this intermediate, 3-mile zone between the Woodrow Wilson Bridge to the south and Hains Point to the north. Sailing here offers unique views of the capital. The marina rents Sunfish for novices ($10 per hour), 15-foot sloops ($15 per hour), and 17-foot Islanders ($17). Windsurfing boards are rented for $11 an hour. Adjacent to the marina is the *Potomac Landing* (phone: 548-0001), which serves up a bountiful catch of seafood — a fitting end for a sightseeing-skipper's nautical adventure. For really top-shelf sailing, an ideal day trip is a visit to historic Annapolis, Maryland (the home of the United States Naval Academy), and the Chesapeake Bay (a 45-minute drive from Washington). During the warmer months, boat rentals are available throughout the area. For further information, call 301-267-7205.

C & O CANAL BARGE: The 1½-hour floating trips on the mule-drawn *Georgetown* or *Canal Clipper* barges are a close encounter with early-19th-century canal life. Built to resemble the cargo barges of yore, the boats used by the National Park Service are 85 feet long and 13 feet wide. The two mules that provide the journey's horsepower (that's 2 hp) reach a top speed of 2 miles per hour (the canal's speed limit is 4 miles per hour, since higher speeds with a full load create a wake that would flood the towpath, resulting in a stiff fine equal to about half the owner's profits). Tour guides in 19th-century garb explain the fascinating history of the canal. Barges run from mid-April to mid-October. The *Georgetown* (phone: 202-472-4376) leaves from *The Foundry* at 30th and Jefferson Streets. The *Canal Clipper* (phone: 301-299-2026) embarks at Great Falls Park.

TIDAL BASIN: This quiet reservoir is one of Washington's treasured water venues.

Originally built to transfer water from the tidal Potomac to the Washington Channel, it is now the domain of Washington's beloved cherry trees, lovestruck couples who walk along its banks, and an armada of boats busily paddling hither and yon. In fact, there may be no more relaxing a spot in the District of Columbia than on these waters, where, though you can see it, the city seems light-years away. From this spot the marble steps of the Jefferson Memorial rise out of the water over the bow of the boat, and the Washington Monument, the Mall area, and the White House are visible beyond the stern. The morning hours, when the fog hovers over the water giving the reservoir a mystic feel, are the best time for boating. Rowboats, swan boat rides, canoes, and paddleboats are all for hire for a nominal fee at the north end of the Tidal Basin at Maine Ave. and 15th St. SW (phone: 202-484-0845).

POTOMAC DINNER CRUISE

In the tradition of Paris's *bateaux mouches,* a Potomac dinner cruise is a novel boating experience that affords a stunning view of America's luminous capital at night. One of the better such dinner cruises is aboard the *Dandy* (Zero Prince St.; phone: 703-683-6076), which leaves nightly from its dock in historic Old Town Alexandria and quietly makes its way up the Potomac. As dusk turns into night and dinner is served (a 5-course meal with choice of prime ribs, cornish game hen, or poached salmon), the *Dandy* passes the Jefferson and Lincoln memorials, the Washington Monument, the *Kennedy Center,* Georgetown, and the *Watergate* complex, and turns about at *Washington Harbour.* There's also dancing — of the cheek-to-cheek variety so as not to rock the boat. The *Dandy* also sets sail for less expensive lunch cruises. Dinner prices range from $45 to $55 per person (depending on the day of the week) and do not include bar drinks, tax, or service. Lunch ranges from $25 to $29 per person. Sunday brunch includes a complementary glass of champagne.

For The Mind

Memorable Museums

Think museums in Washington, DC, and the name that instantly comes to mind is *Smithsonian*. The largest museum complex in the world, this center of American arts and sciences offers enough diversity to satisfy almost any cultural appetite — from the history of the origins of man to man's first — and ongoing — explorations into space. For those who prefer Monets or Magrittes to mummies and machines, Washington also boasts several world class collections. All in all, museum-hopping in the nation's capital can be a heady experience.

NATIONAL GALLERY OF ART: In a John Russell Pope building whose 500,000 square feet make it one of the world's largest marble structures, this museum, built to introduce Americans to the cream of European art, is what one local critic called "the sort of place paintings would aspire to if masterpieces went to heaven." Columns of Tuscan marble, floors of green marble from Vermont and gray marble from Tennessee, and walls of Indiana limestone and Italian travertine produce an effect that is unadulteratedly sumptuous. Leonardo da Vinci's *Ginevra de' Benci* (America's only Leonardo), Jan Vermeer's *Woman Holding a Balance,* a Rembrandt *Self-Portrait,* Jean-Honoré Fragonard's *A Young Girl Reading,* Auguste Renoir's *Girl with a Watering Can,* and Claude Monet's *Rouen Cathedral, West Façade* are among literally thousands of breathtaking canvases and sculptures — gifts of hundreds of donors — housed in the original building and the striking East Building, designed as a grouping of interlocking triangles by I. M. Pei & Partners. It all can be a bit bewildering, so, as an introduction, you might want to join one of the regular tours, rent a tape tour, or pick up the excellent *Brief Guide.* Major exhibits scheduled for this year (dates were unavailable at press time; call ahead) include "Art of the American Indian Frontier: The Collection of Chandler and Pohrt," "Steiglitz in the Darkroom," "Helen Frankenthaler Prints," and the "Reinstallation of Twentieth-Century Art." A monthly calendar of events includes free films, lectures, and concerts. Closed *Christmas* and *New Year's Day.* No admission charge. Information: *National Gallery of Art,* 4th St. and Constitution Ave. NW, Washington, DC 20565 (phone: 202-737-4215).

SMITHSONIAN INSTITUTION: Completed in 1855, the red Gothic castle (where the museum's Information Center is located) on the Mall now functions mainly as office space for the staff that oversees the *Smithsonian's* scattered museums and galleries — nine on the Mall, five (including the National Zoo) in other parts of DC, two in New York City (the *Cooper-Hewitt National Museum of Design* and the *National Museum of the American Indian*), and a half-dozen scientific research facilities around the country. The total collection contains over 137 million items and gains almost 1 million more every year; only an infinitesimal percentage is displayed at any given time, so there's always something new to see. The museums of *American History, Natural History,* and *Air & Space* (see below) are among the most popular in Washington.

Information: *Smithsonian Visitor Information,* 1000 Jefferson Dr. SW, Washington, DC 20560 (phone: 202-357-2700).

NATIONAL AIR & SPACE MUSEUM: Despite its crowded, Egyptian bazaar atmosphere, this member of the *Smithsonian* complex draws more visitors annually than any other museum in the world. Housing America's aerodynamic treasures, the museum chronicles the history of manned flight from the early, humble efforts to the modern space probes that are exploring the outer reaches of our solar system and beyond. There are 23 galleries in this lofty building that covers several blocks of the Mall. A showcase of famous aircraft is displayed from the ceiling in the Milestones of Flight Gallery (immediately upon entering). Among the illustrious aircraft in this hangar are Charles Lindbergh's *Spirit of St. Louis,* the Wright brothers' *Kitty Hawk Flyer,* and the *Gossamer Albatross,* the first human-powered plane to cross the English Channel. In all, there are 240 aircraft and 50 missiles in the collection. The museum's *Albert Einstein Planetarium* is truly a cosmic experience and the *Langley Theater,* which projects films onto a towering 5-story-high theater, is the next best thing to having your own wings. Different films are featured periodically but the historic mainstay of the theater is *To Fly,* a hell-for-leather romp through the skies in everything from a hot-air balloon to a fighter jet. Other exhibits allow the visitor to design aircraft, observe the history of aerial photography, and inspect a model of Skylab — without the powdered meals. Admission charge only for movies. Open daily 10 AM to 5:30 PM; summer hours vary, so call ahead. Information: *National Air & Space Museum,* Jefferson Dr. and Independence Ave. SW (phone: 202-357-2700).

NATIONAL MUSEUM OF NATURAL HISTORY: This massive and imposing museum on the Mall is bloated with an uncanny 118 million items (only a fraction of which are on display) that tell the story of man and his environment. The exhibits cover the entire spectrum of the life sciences, a treasure trove that ranges from anthropology to marine zoology. Among the more popular exhibits are the Dinosaur Hall; exhibits on the evolution of man; fossils; a collection of beasts bagged by Teddy Roosevelt on his African adventures; the Insect Zoo (with the hissing cockroach); birds; plants; rocks; and gems the size of Brazil nuts. The gem collection contains the legendary Hope Diamond, smuggled out of India in the 17th century and reputed to bring tragedy to its owners (many ogling onlookers would love to try and break the hex on this 45.5-carat blue diamond, the largest in the world). The largest elephant on record, a giant Fenkovi African bush elephant that is over 13 feet tall, greets visitors in the museum's octagonal rotunda, where colorful banners lead to the worlds of Fossils, Birds, Mammals, Bones, and Geology of the Earth. Another favorite occupant is "Uncle Beazly," the life-size model of a triceratops dinosaur. The Sea Life Hall contains live aquatic specimens and a living coral reef, and the Discovery Room is a godsend to parents: Its touchable exhibits of elephant tusks and arrowheads, plus a costume room (which allows children to actually try on costumes from around the world), usually keep kids occupied. The museum's gift shops and *Associates Court* cafeteria are excellent. Open daily 10 AM to 5:30 PM. Information: *National Museum of Natural History,* Constitution Ave. at 10th St. NW (phone: 202-357-2700).

NATIONAL MUSEUM OF AMERICAN HISTORY: The wealth of Americana that fills this uniquely austere Mall museum includes George Washington's false teeth, the original Star-Spangled Banner that inspired the Francis Scott Key poem (that inspired the national anthem), the desk on which Thomas Jefferson wrote the Declaration of Independence, Eli Whitney's cotton gin, Alexander Graham Bell's telephone, and other prized possessions — such as an exhibit of mannequins wearing the gowns worn by the First Ladies, from Martha Washington to Barbara Bush, standing in authentic reproductions of rooms in the White House. The museum's ground floor is devoted to our nation's machinery, from railroad locomotives and a 1913 Model T to atom smashers and computers. The second floor focuses on our nation's people, home life, community life, and our relationship to the world beyond. The third floor is crammed with exhibits ranging from musical instruments to instruments of war. One of the more interesting exhibits is an entire pre–Civil War post office taken from Headsville, West Virginia, that is still in operation and accepts letters for mail, franking them with a unique *Smithsonian* seal. The museum's various galleries, from the 1776 Gallery to the Pain Gallery (in the Medical Gallery) offer demonstrations of the workings of the ham radio, methods of type founding and printing, and marbling — to name a few. For those inspired by this walk through American history and such a close encounter with greatness, the *Smithsonian Bookstore* (phone: 202-357-1784) has the area's best selection of American history books. Open daily 10 AM to 5:30 PM (closed *Christmas*). Information: *National Museum of American History*, Constitution Ave. at 13th St. NW (phone: 202-357-2700).

HIRSHHORN MUSEUM AND SCULPTURE GARDEN: One of the museums under the *Smithsonian's* wing and the most modern of the city's museums of modern art. The *Hirshhorn* houses the ever-astonishing collections amassed by Joseph H. Hirshhorn (1899–1981), who grew up in such poverty that he never even owned a toy. He spent much of the fortune he made in stocks and uranium buying art. The painting collection, much expanded and refined since the original Hirshhorn gift, focuses on American art and includes works by Estes, Golub, Gorky, Henri, Hopper, de Kooning, Noland, and Stella; modern European masters such as Bacon, Balthus, Kiefer, and Magritte also are represented. The extraordinary vitality of the sculpture collection reflects the greatness of Calder, Degas, Matisse, Moore, Rodin, Serra, and David Smith — many of whose works are displayed in the sculpture garden — and the innovations of more recent artisans. For this variety alone the museum would be fascinating; the building itself — circular and fortress-like — is intriguing as well. Closed *Christmas*. No admission charge. Information: *Hirshhorn Museum*, 7th St. and Independence Ave. SW, Washington, DC 20560 (phone: 202-357-3235).

PHILLIPS COLLECTION: In the best of all possible worlds this would be a model for all art galleries. Though the hushed solemnity of its entrance hall leads some visitors to believe that they've come to the wrong place, the unhurried and elegant mood in this Victorian brownstone mansion near Dupont Circle enhances the appreciation of the gallery's relatively small collection of modern art (of the 2,000 works only 250 are displayed at one time). The *Phillips Collection* is America's oldest museum of modern art, opened in 1918 in two rooms of founder Duncan Phillips's family home in hopes, Phillips said, that it would become "a joy-giving, life-enhancing influence, assisting people to see beautifully as true artists see." Indeed, it has become just that. The innovations of such masters as El Greco, Manet, and Chardin are shown together with their artistic progeny: Cézanne, Monet, Klee, O'Keeffe, Rothko, and many others. The pièce de résistance is Renoir's beloved *Luncheon of the Boating Party*. Other favorites are Cézanne's 1877 *Self Portrait* and O'Keeffe's *Red Hills and the Sun*. But the opportunity to view the masters of modern art in the intimate surroundings of sitting rooms and parlors (some paintings are displayed on the stairways), furnished with armchairs and couches, is for many the real draw. The mahogany-paneled Music Room features a tasteful selection of paintings and a long-standing Sunday evening concert series of chamber music (through May at 5 PM; admission charge). Open 10 AM to 5 PM Mondays through Saturdays, noon to 7 PM on Sundays (closed *July 4, Thanksgiving, Christmas,* and *New Year's Day*). Information: *Phillips Collection*, 1612 21st St. NW (phone: 202-387-0961).

CORCORAN GALLERY OF ART: In its gracious, skylit halls full of American art — among the finest collections of 18th- and 19th-century American art anywhere, in fact — are prestigious assortments of works by Sargent, Bierstadt, and Copley. You'll also find European paintings, however (some by Corot, some by the animal sculptor Antoine Barye, as well as Renaissance drawings), and a variety of changing exhibitions of contemporary art and photography. One block beyond the White House. Information: *Corcoran Gallery of Art,* 17th and E Sts. NW, Washington, DC 20006 (phone: 202-638-3211).

BUREAU OF ENGRAVING AND PRINTING: At the world's largest securities manufacturing establishment, you can watch the making of currency on 25-minute self-guided tours. Open Mondays through Fridays, 9 AM to 2 PM. Closed federal holidays and the week between *Christmas* and *New Year's Day.* No admission charge. Information: *Bureau of Engraving and Printing,* 14th and C Sts. SW, Washington, DC 20228 (phone: 202-874-3316).

Historic Churches

Unlike the God-fearing Puritans to the north who built churches with the zeal of the newly converted, the English immigrants who colonized Virginia were more devoted to the sanctity of their individual landholdings, commerce, and the development of a parliament that would protect their rights. Consequently, there are few venerable churches in Washington with a real past. L'Enfant's original design for the city targeted an area where a "national pantheon or church" would be located to function much like London's Westminster Abbey or Notre-Dame in Paris. Unfortunately, the Greek Revival temple that was finally completed in 1867 was a victim of poor timing. It was quickly diverted into use as a Civil War hospital, and after the war was further demoted into service as the US Post Office. Nevertheless, there is a small congregation of churches of considerable interest to Washington visitors.

WASHINGTON NATIONAL CATHEDRAL: This colossal Gothic cathedral which towers over Northwest DC from its perch on Mount St. Albans is formally named the Cathedral Church of St. Peter and St. Paul. The less pedantic just call it the National Cathedral. Consecrated in 1990, this dramatic, twin-towered house of worship has all the classical components of Gothic architecture: flying buttresses, gargoyles, grotesques, ample stained glass, and spires that seem to tickle the heavens. Inspired by George Washington's vision of a national cathedral, this church has been described as "the last of the great cathedrals." Built stone by stone over the course of 83 years, its design and building materials are true to 14th-century Gothic form: No structural steel was used. And its interdenominational services and events are true to George Washington's dream of a national church. But the cathedral is not entirely a throwback to an earlier era. Embedded in the large, stained glass Space Window is a moon rock brought back to earth by astronauts Neil Armstrong, Michael Collins, and Edwin Aldrin from Apollo 11. Interred here are President Woodrow Wilson, Admiral George Dewey, Cordell Hull (Secretary of State during World War II), and Helen Keller. No visit to the National Cathedral is complete without a stroll through the 12th-century Norman arch and into the Bishop's Garden, a network of paths among rose bushes, medieval herbs, flowers, and well-groomed shrubbery. The benches in this English garden are a tranquil spot for resting the feet and restoring the soul. The circular Herb Cottage is nearby and sells jams, tasteful souvenirs, and other knickknacks. The Pilgrim Observation Gallery (which closes daily at 3:30 PM) affords a panoramic view of Washington from its highest point. Open daily from 10 AM to 4:30 PM. Information: *Washington National Cathedral,* Wisconsin Ave. at Woodley Rd. NW (phone: 202-537-6200).

NATIONAL SHRINE OF THE IMMACULATE CONCEPTION: This architectural blend of contemporary, Byzantine, and Romanesque styles is the largest Roman Catholic church in the Western Hemisphere. It is also the seventh-largest religious building in the world. Interestingly, it is the only Catholic house of worship in America to which every single parish in the country has made a spirited contribution. Thus, the church administration actively encourages sacred pilgrimages. Its sheer expanse is awesome: It seats over 6,000 worshipers in its 57 chapels. Begun in 1920, the edifice is noted for its statuary, over 200 stained glass windows, and intricate mosaics depicting the history of Catholicism in America. A mosaic inside on the ceiling of the dome, *Christ in Majesty,* is reputedly the largest of its kind in the world. (One of the church's mosaics used up all the stone from an Italian quarry.) Though the church — appropriately located near Catholic University — was dedicated in 1959, decorative work in its interior is ongoing. Summer organ recitals on Sunday evenings are widely attended. Open November 1 through April 1, from 7 AM to 6 PM daily; from April 2 through October 31, 7 AM to 7 PM daily. Information: *National Shrine of the Immaculate Conception,* 4th St. and Michigan Ave. NE (phone: 202-526-8300).

ST. JOHN'S EPISCOPAL CHURCH: Every American president since James Madison has worshiped in this charming yellow church across the street from the White House on Lafayette Square. It is nicknamed the "Church of the Presidents," and Pew 54 is reserved for the president and his family. Several architects have contributed to the construction of this building but the one who deserves the most credit is Benjamin Henry Latrobe, a multi-talented fellow who not only designed the Greek Revival church, but served as its first organist and composed a hymn for its grand opening; Latrobe was also a church member. The spectacular stained glass was designed by the curator of the stained glass windows at Chartres Cathedral in France; their installation was overseen by James Renwick, architect of the "castle," the *Smithsonian's* flagship building, on the Mall. Gerald Ford came here before he announced his presidential pardon for the political sins of his predecessor, Richard Nixon. St. John's is worth a visit. There are free organ recitals every Wednesday, just after noon. Next door is the Parish House, a lovely French Second Empire–style building that hasn't lost a bit of elegance in its scaled-down size and seems to harmonize like a church choir with the church. The Parish House is the former home of Lord Ashburton, a British minister who negotiated the boundary between the US and Canada with Daniel Webster, who lived not far from here. Open daily from 8 AM to 4 PM. Services are held at 8, 9, and 11 AM, and 4 PM (the afternoon service is held in French). Information: *St. John's Church,* 16th and H Sts. NW (phone: 202-347-8766).

Washington Theater

Washington is America's third city of theater, according to *Variety* magazine. With New York City as the undisputed leader of the nation's theater scene and Boston a respectable but distant second, Washington, with its strong cast of over 20 professional stage theaters and a dozen professional dinner and community theaters in the area, is a major cultural force. Clearly, as its presidential namesake intended, it was the behemoth *Kennedy Center* that created the beginning of a theatrical renaissance in this once sleepy town. Today, boasting one of the country's premier stages and one of its finest Shakespearean theaters (the *Folger*), Washington has won a place on the theatrical map of America. For half-price, same-day performance tickets try *Ticketplace* (12th and F Sts. NW; phone:

202-TIC-KETS). If all else fails, a hotel concierge probably has some valuable insider information. The following is a list of Washington's most outstanding stages.

ARENA STAGE: One of the oldest and most consistently admired American theater companies and the first outside New York to receive a Tony for theatrical excellence, the *Arena Stage,* founded in 1950, is noted for developing American drama and for introducing foreign (particularly Eastern European) plays to the US. The theater's three stages seat 827, 514, and 180; the last is used for small musical revues and experimental works. Robert Prosky and James Earl Jones have performed here; past productions (some of which premiered here) include *After the Fall* by Arthur Miller, *Happy End* by Bertolt Brecht and Kurt Weill; *Women and Water* by John Guare, *A Lesson from Aloes* by Athol Fugard, *Tomfoolery* by Tom Lehrer, George Bernard Shaw's *Major Barbara,* and *On the Razzle* by Tom Stoppard. The company's most recent hit was the highly acclaimed musical *A Wonderful Life,* based on the Frank Capra film. Information: *Arena Stage,* 6th St. and Maine Ave. SW (phone: 202-554-9066; box office, 202-488-3300; TDD number for hearing-impaired patrons, 202-484-0247).

FOLGER THEATER: An evening at the *Folger* is the consummate Shakespearean-immersion experience. To some, this white marble building just behind the Supreme Court is primarily a library and a major center of scholarly research with holdings devoted to works by and about the immortal Bard. To others it is the *Folger Theater,* an Elizabethan innyard–style theater that is the closest thing stateside to witnessing a play in Shakespeare's hometown, Stratford-on-Avon. Though Shakespearean works dominate the repertoire, the company is also known for its thoughtful productions of classics, plus the occasional new play. Before the performance, take some time to review the latest exhibit of memorabilia from the library in the magnificent Tudor-style Great Hall. Information: *Shakespeare Theater at the Folger,* 201 E. Capitol St. SE (phone: 202-544-4600).

FORD'S THEATRE: The infamous theater in which Lincoln was shot has been faithfully restored to the way it looked that fateful April night in 1865. The flag-draped presidential box remains empty, a memorial to the slain president. The performances hosted by the theater these days are professional productions of contemporary plays and musicals, with such offerings as *Private Lives* and *Man of La Mancha.* After Lincoln's assassination the theater was closed for 100 years out of respect. Its basement houses a select collection of personal mementos, including the suit in which Lincoln died, the flag that covered his casket, and the derringer used by the assassin. Across the street is the Peterson House, where Lincoln succumbed to his wounds (Peterson House open daily from 9 AM to 5 PM). Information: *Ford's Theatre,* 511 10th St. NW (phone: 202-426-6924).

KENNEDY CENTER: Since its opening in 1971 the *Kennedy Center* has succeeded in attracting world-renowned dance, theater, and musical companies to its five theaters and concert halls. But this massive classical building is a tourist attraction all its own. Among the premier performances featured here over the years are *The Phantom of the Opera,* a revival of *Bye Bye Birdie, Grand Hotel, Tru, Buddy: The Buddy Holly Story,* the latest of August Wilson's plays, and the like. It has also been the venue for the American premiere of *Les Misérables* and the world premiere of *A Few Good Men.* Before attending a performance, come early to walk through the red-carpeted Grand Foyer, lit by 18 chandeliers, and a prime pre- and post-performance schmoozing area for VIPs and politicos. Original productions and Broadway-bound shows are held in the *Eisenhower Theater,* a comfortable and intimate house paneled with East Indian laurel. Other performances on the premises are held in the *Concert Hall, Opera House,*

Terrace Theater, and *American Film Institute Theater* (phone: 202-785-4600). An oft-overlooked feature of the *Kennedy Center* is the rooftop terrace, which offers a spectacular panorama of the Potomac and Washington. Check with specific theaters for events, showtimes, and ticket prices. Information: *The Kennedy Center for the Performing Arts,* New Hampshire Ave. and Rock Creek Pkwy. NW (phone: 800-444-1324 or 202-467-4600 for all theaters).

NATIONAL THEATER: Established in 1835, this is Washington's oldest operating community theater. Throughout its venerable career it has played host to every American president since Eisenhower (who was not known for being a culture vulture). Pre- and post-Broadway shows perform here, including such hits as *Cats, 42nd Street,* and *Dreamgirls.* The theater is now under the management of the Shubert Organization, who put this grand old building through an intensive 2-year restoration from 1982 to 1984 that recaptured its former glory. Visitors should be forewarned that this is the stomping grounds of a legendary phantom — the ghost of an actor whose stage name was John McCollough and who is said to roam the theater. McCollough, as the story goes, got into a fight with another actor while washing clothes; McCollough lost the fight, and the killer allegedly stuffed his body between the theater's old and new foundation walls — an area now known as the "cemetery." The late actor has been spotted a number of times and disappears when addressed. Several years ago, electricians found part of a musket, which is believed to have been the murder weapon. Life (or death?) is still more compelling than art. Information: *National Theater,* 1321 Pennsylvania Ave. NW (phone: 202-628-6161; Telecharge: 800-233-3123).

A Shutterbug's Washington

The ideal shutterbug in Washington is part tourist, part photojournalist, and part paparazzi. Also, beyond the photogenic white marble temples of our democracy is a charming tidewater city. From the trickling fountain in Dupont Circle, the cobblestone streets of Georgetown and Old Town Alexandria, and the lovely English Bishop's Garden next to the National Cathedral to the bright red, steaming mound of steamed crab in the austere setting of a crab feast (see *Quintessential Washington* in DIVERSIONS), photo ops abound in the area. And since a city like Washington can't help but be symbolic — with its statuary, monuments, and memorials — be on the lookout for that photograph that speaks volumes.

Even a beginner can achieve remarkable results with a surprisingly basic set of lenses and filters. Equipment is, in fact, only as valuable as the imagination that puts it into use. (For further information on equipment, see *Cameras and Equipment* in GETTING READY TO GO.)

Don't be afraid to experiment. Use what knowledge you have to explore new possibilities. At the same time, don't limit yourself by preconceived ideas of what's hackneyed or corny. Because the Lincoln Memorial has been photographed thousands of times before doesn't make it any less worthy of your attention.

In Washington, as elsewhere, spontaneity is one of the keys to good photography. Whether it's a sudden shaft of light bursting through the clouds and hitting the Potomac River just so, or park rangers hoisting the flags at the Washington Monument, don't hesitate to shoot if the moment is right. If photography is indeed capturing a moment and making it timeless, success lies in judging just when a moment worth capturing occurs.

A good picture reveals an eye for detail, whether it's a matter of lighting, of positioning your subject, or of taking time to frame a picture carefully. The better your grasp of the importance of details, the better your results will be photographically.

Patience is often necessary. Don't shoot a view of the Capitol Building if a cloud suddenly dims its glow. A rusted old Volkswagen in the center of your Georgetown Street scene? Reframe your image to eliminate the obvious distraction. People walking toward a scene that would benefit from their presence? Wait until they're in position before you shoot. After the fact, many of the flaws will be self-evident. The trick is to be aware of the ideal and have the patience to allow it to happen. If you are part of a group, you may well have to trail behind a bit in order to shoot properly. Not only is group activity distracting, but bunches of people hovering nearby tend to stifle spontaneity and overwhelm potential subjects.

The camera provides an opportunity, not only to capture Washington's varied and awesome beauty, but to interpret it. What it takes is a sensitivity to the surroundings, a knowledge of the capabilities of your equipment, and a willingness to see things in new ways.

LANDSCAPES AND CITYSCAPES: Washington's monuments and government buildings are most often visiting photographers' favorite subjects. But the Mall, the Potomac, and quaint Georgetown provide numerous photo possibilities as well. In addition to the Capitol, the White House, and the National Cathedral, be sure to look for natural beauty: Cherry trees that line the Tidal Basin, the lovely gardens in Dumbarton Oaks, the stately homes and buildings in the Embassy District, and the crew and sailboats that skim along the Potomac River are just a few examples.

Color and form are the obvious ingredients here, and how you frame your pictures can be as important as getting the proper exposure. Study the shapes, angles, and colors that make up the scene and create a composition that uses them to best advantage.

Lighting is a vital component in landscapes. Take advantage of the richer colors of early morning and late afternoon whenever possible. The overhead light of midday is often harsh and without the shadowing that can add to the drama of a scene. This is when a polarizer is used to best effect. Most polarizers come with a mark on the rotating ring. If you can aim at your subject and point that marker at the sun, the sun's rays are likely to be right for the polarizer to work for you. If not, stick to your skylight filter, underexposing slightly if the scene is particularly bright. Most light meters respond to an overall light balance, with the result that bright areas may appear burned out.

Although a standard 50mm to 55mm lens may work well in some landscape situations, most will benefit from a 20mm to 28mm wide-angle. The Mall, with the Washington Monument and Lincoln Memorial in the distance, for example, is the type of panorama that fits beautifully into a wide-angle format, allowing not only the overview, but the opportunity to include people or other points of interest in the foreground. A flower, for instance, may be used to set off a view of the Vietnam Veterans Memorial; or people can provide a sense of perspective in a shot of Dupont Circle.

To isolate specific elements of any scene, use your telephoto lens. Perhaps there's a particular statue that would make a lovely shot, or it might be the interplay of light and shadow on a cobblestone Georgetown street. The successful use of a telephoto means developing your eye for detail.

PEOPLE: As with taking pictures of people anywhere, there are going to be times in Washington when a camera is an intrusion. Your approach is the key: Consider your own reaction under similar circumstances, and you have an idea as to what would make others comfortable enough to be willing subjects. People are often sensitive to having a camera suddenly pointed at them, and a polite request, while getting you a share of refusals, will also provide a chance to shoot some wonderful portraits that capture the spirit of the city as surely as the scenery does. For candids, an excellent lens is a zoom telephoto in the 70mm to 210mm range; it allows you to remain unobtrusive while the telephoto lens draws the subject closer. And for portraits, a telephoto can be used effectively as close as 2 or 3 feet.

For authenticity and variety, select a place likely to produce interesting subjects. Georgetown is an obvious spot for visitors, but if it's local color you're after, visit *Eastern Market* on Capitol Hill, go to a game at *RFK Stadium,* walk around ethnic-rich Adams Morgan, or wander around Georgetown University campus. Aim for shots that tell what's different about our nation's capital. In portraiture, there are several factors to keep in mind. Morning or afternoon light will add richness to skin tones, emphasizing tans. To avoid the harsh facial shadows cast by direct sunlight, shoot in the shade or in an area where the light is diffused.

SUNSETS: Depending on where you are, you can see the sunset reflecting on the Potomac River, when the last golden rays shine off a lone sailboat, or when a fiery light hits the Jefferson Memorial with magical clouds of pink and lavender, purple and red.

When shooting sunsets, keep in mind that the brightness will distort meter readings. When composing a shot directly into the sun, frame the picture in the viewfinder so that only half of the sun is included. Read the meter, set, and shoot. Whenever there is this kind of unusual lighting, shoot a few frames in half-step increments, both over and under the meter reading. Bracketing, as this is called, can provide a range of images, the best of which may well be other than the one shot at the meter's recommended setting.

Use any lens for sunsets. A wide-angle is good when the sky is filled with color-streaked clouds, when the sun is partially hidden, or when you're close to an object that silhouettes dramatically against the sky.

Telephotos also produce wonderful silhouettes, either with the sun as a backdrop or against the palette of a brilliant sunset sky. Bracket again here. For the best silhouettes, wait 10 to 15 minutes after sunset. Unless using a very fast film, a tripod is recommended.

Red and orange filters are often used to accentuate a sunset's picture potential. Orange will help turn even a gray sky into something approaching a photogenic finale to the day. If the sunset is already bold in hue, the orange will overwhelm the natural colors. A red filter will produce dramatic, highly unrealistic results.

NIGHT: If you think that picture possibilities end at sunset, you're presuming that night photography is the exclusive domain of the professional. If you've got a tripod, all you'll need is a cable release to attach to your camera to assure a steady exposure (which is often timed in minutes rather than fractions of a second).

For situations such as a night tour of the monuments or moonlight boat cruises, a strobe does the trick, but beware: Flash units are often used improperly. You can't take a view of the tidal basin and Jefferson Memorial with a flash. It may reach out as far as 30 feet, but that's it. On the other hand, a flash used too close to a subject may result in overexposure, resulting in a "blown out" effect. With most cameras, strobes will work with a maximum shutter speed of 1/125 or 1/150 of a second. If you set the exposure properly and shoot within range, you should come up with pretty sharp results.

CLOSE-UPS: Whether of people or of objects such as antique door knockers, close-ups can add another dimension to your photography. There are a number of shooting options, one of which is to use a 70mm or a 210mm lens at its closest focusable distance. Unless you're working in bright sunlight, a tripod will be worthwhile. If you are very near your subject and there is a good deal of reflective light, it may pay to underexpose a bit in relation to the meter reading.

If you do not have a telephoto lens, you can still shoot close-ups using a set of magnification filters. Filter packs of one-, two-, and three-time magnification are available, converting your lens into a close-up lens. Even better is a special macro lens designed for close-up photography.

The following are some of Washington's truly great pictorial perspectives.

Tidal Basin – In the early morning the steam rises off this tranquil body of water just west of the Mall area, creating a mysterious veil for the Jefferson Memorial. Position yourself next to the boathouse on the east side next to the *Bureau of Engraving and Printing* and get as close to the surface of water as possible (try lying on the concrete rim of the basin). If several of the crusty fellows who fish the area near the bridge on the left are in the viewfinder, so much the better. If the cherry trees that line the Tidal Basin are in bloom (late March or early April), giving this pool a pinkish fringe, you've got a keeper.

Capitol's West Porch – Washington insiders who trod these paths every day swear that this rarely captured view is the best angle from which to truly appreciate the city. From here — on what constitutes the back patio of the White House — the Mall is in perfect alignment due west; the panorama extends toward the Reflecting Pool and, beyond it, the steps of the Lincoln Memorial. At a 25° angle to the right is Pennsylvania Avenue, America's Main Street, the tree-lined avenue that cuts its way through marble monuments and departmental monstrosities in its march to the White House. Every driver who has cursed Washington's street layout should study this photo. Though it may not calm the nerves, the aesthetic wisdom of L'Enfant's plan for a grid overlaid with broad avenues relieved by the intermittent traffic pinwheel is more easily understood from here.

Lafayette Park – Even if there are a zillion postcards depicting this scene, it is still a great photograph. From the northern edge of Lafayette Square face the White House. The dramatic equestrian statue of Andrew Jackson, the fountain on the front lawn, the president's residence as white as crisp, clean linen, the Stars and Stripes atop the portico, and the top half of the Washington Monument all come into view, creating a photo of remarkable balance. Early evening is the best time to capture this shot.

Street Scenes – If you've got a yen for historic street scenes, there are three places of note. Tree-lined O Street in Georgetown near Georgetown University is one of Washington's most endearing little thoroughfares, especially in the fall when the brilliantly colored Federal and Victorian townhouses are spruced up by the changing leaves. The trolley tracks embedded in the cobblestones are a vestige of a bygone era. Lower Prince Street in Old Town Alexandria is also a cobblestoned street, dating back to the late 18th century. A photo from atop Captain's Row (the corner of Prince and Lee Streets) — a block of Federal-style townhouses built by sea captains, with the Potomac and the Maryland hills in the background — is a must. Finally, *Washingtonian* magazine calls N Street, between Connecticut and Rhode Island Avenues, in downtown Washington the most charming street in the city. Photo buffs in search of a historic Washington, untainted by the urban jungle, will certainly agree.

DIRECTIONS

DIRECTIONS

Introduction

Like Canberra in Australia and Brasilia in Brazil, Washington was conceived as and built to be a capital city. And like the baseball field in the movie *Field of Dreams,* Washington's planners knew that if they built a city worthy of being a capital, tourists would come. Designed in the late 18th century by a Frenchman who had the network of broad, walker-friendly boulevards of Paris in mind — and at a time when walking was still a primary mode of transportation — Washington was created for the pedestrian.

In fact, most of the conventional tourist attractions in Washington — the fistful of *Smithsonian* museums, the Capitol, the White House, and most of the monuments — can be seen virtually without having to cross the path of motorized traffic. And that's probably just as well. Though most Washington drivers are accustomed to averting tourists wandering off track, automobiles aren't the major hazards. In a city driven by bureaucratic paper pushing, it's the bicycle couriers en route to the Department of Something or Other that pedestrians must really fear.

Unlike the condensed cities to the north where people crawl over each other to live, commute, and work, Washington, in true southern fashion, tends to sprawl out. In the District alone, an area of roughly 70 square miles, getting from one side of town to another by foot is a major cardiovascular feat. Adding in historic Old Town Alexandria, Virginia, to the south — without which no tour of these environs is complete — the Washington area that is the subject of these walking tours represents a good chunk of real estate — a good reason why comfortable shoes are a must. Remember, if you get too tired, Washington's *Metro* system is one of the finest in the world, and its taxis are relatively trustworthy. What's more, the alphabet streets (running east–west) combine with the numbered streets (running north–south) to give some semblance of order to what is otherwise a creative street plan.

The following walking tours have been designed to take the tourist past Washington's more familiar sites, along with stops at those often overlooked (but equally fascinating) places, all presented in manageable bits. These tours will coax the inquisitive up stairs, into nooks and near crannies, through hotel lobbies, under monuments, atop church spires, and within reach of many shops and cafés. But never fear: They also stop at the White House.

Be aware, however, that in addition to being the America's capital, Washington has the dubious honor of being the nation's crime capital as well. And although these walks will steer clear of the combat zones that plague every inner-city area (the only real concern should be around Capitol Hill), even on "safe" streets it's wise to keep your wits about you. As you would in any big city, pack your street smarts, walk purposefully, and watch your wallet. The rewards of walking through Washington are monumental.

The Mall and Monuments

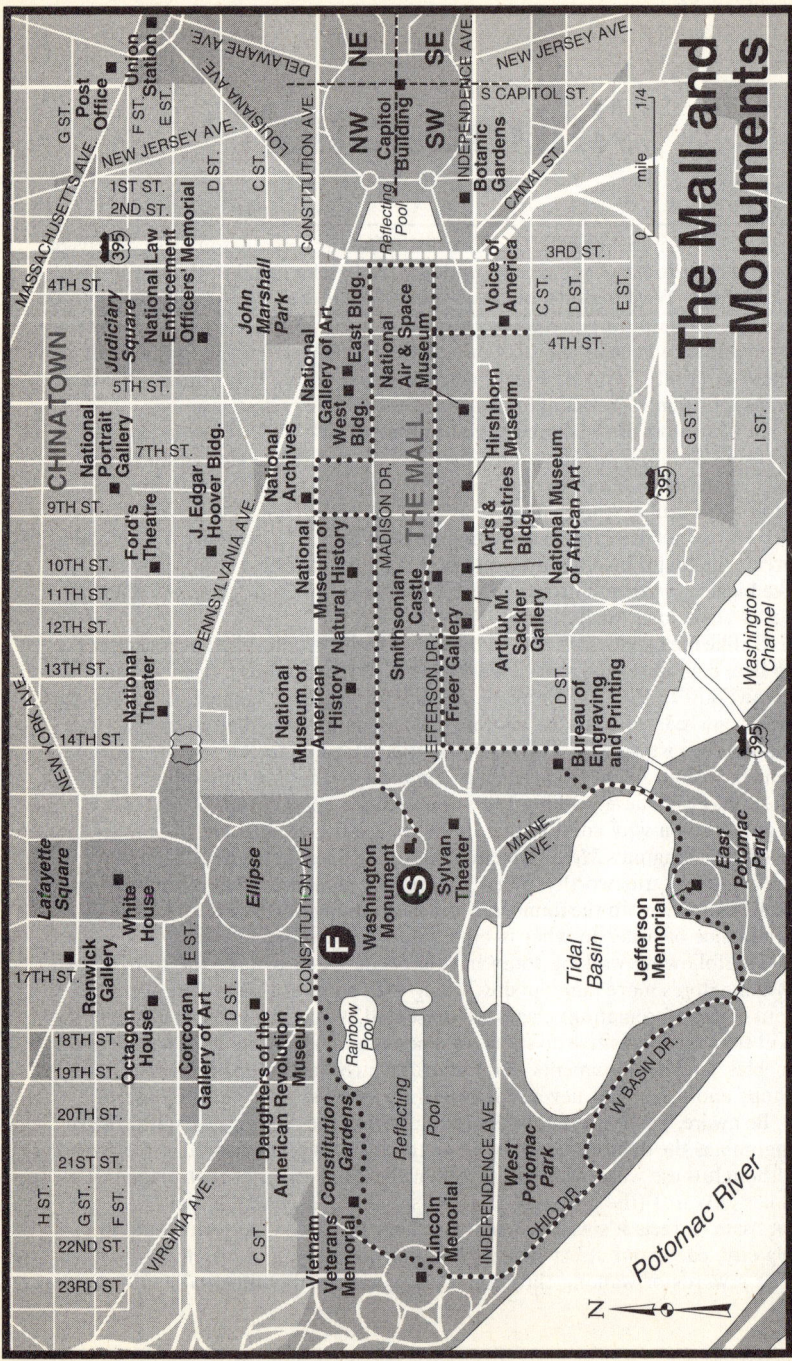

NE **SE**
NW **SW**

Union Station
Post Office
Capitol Building
Botanic Gardens
Voice of America
National Law Enforcement Officers' Memorial
John Marshall Park
National Gallery of Art West Bldg.
East Bldg.
National Air & Space Museum
Reflecting Pool
Hirshhorn Museum
National Portrait Gallery
National Archives
Ford's Theatre
J. Edgar Hoover Bldg.
Arts & Industries Bldg.
National Museum of African Art
National Museum of Natural History
Smithsonian Castle
Arthur M. Sackler Gallery
Freer Gallery
National Theater
National Museum of American History
Bureau of Engraving and Printing
Washington Channel
Lafayette Square
White House
Renwick Gallery
Octagon House
Corcoran Gallery of Art
Daughters of the American Revolution Museum
Ellipse
Washington Monument
Sylvan Theater
Tidal Basin
East Potomac Park
Jefferson Memorial
Rainbow Pool
Reflecting Pool
Constitution Gardens
Vietnam Veterans Memorial
Lincoln Memorial
West Potomac Park
Potomac River

CHINATOWN
Judiciary Square
THE MALL

Streets and Avenues

MASSACHUSETTS AVE.
G ST.
F ST.
E ST.
DELAWARE AVE.
LOUISIANA AVE.
NEW JERSEY AVE.
NEW JERSEY AVE.
S CAPITOL ST.
INDEPENDENCE AVE.
S ST.
CANAL ST.
1ST ST.
2ND ST.
D ST.
C ST.
CONSTITUTION AVE.
3RD ST.
C ST.
D ST.
E ST.
4TH ST.
5TH ST.
7TH ST.
G ST.
I ST.
9TH ST.
PENNSYLVANIA AVE.
10TH ST.
11TH ST.
12TH ST.
13TH ST.
14TH ST.
MADISON DR.
JEFFERSON DR.
D ST.
NEW YORK AVE.
MAINE AVE.
17TH ST.
E ST.
D ST.
C ST.
18TH ST.
19TH ST.
20TH ST.
21ST ST.
H ST.
G ST.
F ST.
22ND ST.
23RD ST.
VIRGINIA AVE.
INDEPENDENCE AVE.
CONSTITUTION AVE.
OHIO DR.
W BASIN DR.

1/4
0
mile

N

Walk 1: The Mall and Monuments

Washington's Mall area, the long rectangular strip of greenery that stretches from the Capitol Building through a canyon of museums to the Washington Monument, is both the nation's front lawn and its dusty storage attic.

In contrast to the sleepy ambience of many government buildings in the area and the sluggish pace of big government in general, the Mall is where most Washingtonians expend all the energy (and frustration) they have accumulated in the course of conducting the nation's business. Weather permitting, there is always something doing on the Mall, be it a combative game of congressional softball, jogging bureaucrats reversing the ravages of a sedentary lifestyle, souvenir and snack hucksters, a contentious political demonstration, distracted tourists precariously wandering into traffic, lovestruck picnickers, kite flyers, or more than likely, all of the above. The Mall is a playground with a bundle of physical and intellectual amusements and, much to the envy of Congress, it is always in recess.

The Mall is also the country's foremost repository of Americana and the cargo hold of our nation's collective bric-a-brac. On its fringe are nine sprawling museums devoted to everything from air travel and art to the evolution of the zebra. The country's pre-eminent museum complex, the *Smithsonian Institution,* accounts for the lion's share of the exhibits. Though the organization boasts a total of over 137 million objects in its possession, there is only enough space in its sprawling buildings to display 1% of its holdings (sending the family heirloom to Washington in a spell of benevolent patriotism would appear to have little more effect than to possibly ensure its eternal storage). However, the more than 1 million items on display are still enough to keep an alert tourist awash in exhibits for several full days. And unlike cultural exhibits in other major American cities, admission is free to most museums and monuments in the nation's capital.

The Mall tour begins from the easiest site in Washington to spot: the Washington Monument. The nearest *Metro* station is Smithsonian. The tour will take about 4 hours, allowing for a solemn moment at each of the monuments but only a stroll by the buildings of the *Smithsonian Institution.* At least a day, preferably longer, is recommended for inspecting the contents of these stately bastions to art and artifacts.

The mound on which the Washington Monument is built is an ideal place from which to observe and to reflect on the history of Washington's Mall. The Mall has not always been the hub of Washington activity. It originally was slated by city designer Pierre Charles L'Enfant as a grand avenue, à la Paris, lined with gardens and diplomats' mansions that would run from the Capitol

Building to the Washington Monument. But because the Washington administration was dissatisfied with his design and exasperated by his unyielding arrogance, L'Enfant was fired before he could execute his grand plan. And the Mall remained a no-man's-land, a simple common for pasturing cows until a grid of railroad tracks were built, filling the void and guiding trains that disturbed the peace and tranquillity and sent up periodic plumes of noxious air.

The railroad tracks, nearby lumber and coal yards, and years of neglect sent the Mall area into further decline before its fortunes could rise. In the mid-19th century, the proposal of the horticulturist Andrew Jackson Downing to create an English garden here was met with a collective yawn. The Mall was slowly becoming an unsightly industrial sinkhole. By the early 20th century, the area where the reflecting pool is now located had become home to a sort of shanty town of wood and stucco shacks and temporary office buildings.

Nearby Southwest DC, which was originally scheduled to be the city's primary commercial district, became an impoverished working class housing district instead. It looked as if L'Enfant's grand plan had been a grand failure. Gradually, however, the French planner's original idea began to germinate, taking root in 1902 in Senator James McMillan's Senate District Committee. It was here that more sophisticated heads eventually prevailed. A veritable brain trust of landscaping, architecture, and sculpting genius was assembled to carry out the plan devised by the committee to save the Mall. Renowned landscape architect Frederick Law Olmsted, architects Daniel Burnham and Charles McKim, and sculptor Augustus Saint-Gaudens teamed up to give what has been dubbed the "nation's town green" a thoughtful, utilitarian, and sanctified feel.

The railroad was transported from its location along the Mall to Union Station in 1908, a new terminal to the northeast. The conservatory of the Botanic Garden was removed from smack-dab in the middle of the Mall to its southeastern edge. The emotionally stirring Lincoln Memorial was built in the 1920s, staking out the Mall's western boundary, and the Jefferson Memorial, a little farther afield, was dedicated in 1943.

What formerly was a blight has been lovingly converted into an important attraction for tourists — not just because of the culture but also because the Mall is a great place from which to view, from a single spot, many of Washington's most familiar and famous buildings and monuments.

Possibly its most recognizable structure — and certainly its most striking — towers toward the sky: the Washington Monument. Though a relatively simple obelisk with a clean design by Robert Mills, the monument to our first president took over 100 years to build, weathering countless design changes, wrangling in Congress, sabotage, and neglect during the Civil War.

There will probably be a wait for the elevator that goes to the porthole atop the monument. While waiting, you may want to reflect on this famous spindle's history.

Perhaps it is the ultimate insight into the workings of Congress that the learned body approved a simple equestrian statue dedicated to George Washington in 1783 and that, 105 years later, the nation's taxpayers received a 555-foot, 2-toned, sinking obelisk with a steam-driven elevator. Considering the other suggestions made by our legislature — a crypt in the Capitol and a marble tomb were two of their more morbid suggestions — Americans should be thankful for Congress's decision to build an obelisk. And if attendance is any indicator — about 4,000 visitors per day ascend the monument during high season — they are.

The cornerstone of the monument was laid in 1848, using the same trowel that Washington had used to lay the Capitol cornerstone 55 years earlier. After construction began, the Washington Monument Society continued to solicit funds from individuals and from each state in the union. Because Alabama was short on cash, it sent a stone instead. The idea caught on and stones arrived from around the world — until a stone from Pope Pius IX arrived. In the small hours of March 6, 1854, a band of intruders from the virulently anti-Catholic "Know-Nothing" party set upon the monument, stole the "pope's stone," and reportedly threw it into the Potomac. A local paper called it "a deed of barbarism." When the night watchman was asked why he hadn't used his shotgun to sound the alarm, his response was that he didn't know why he did (or didn't) do what he did. (Perhaps he was a "Know-Nothing.")

Construction continued apace until the onset of the Civil War, when the nation's resources were diverted to the military. This stub of stone sat forgotten for 15 years, collecting rainwater, until building was finally resumed. Stone from a different stratum of the Maryland quarry was used, accounting for the discoloration between the bottom one-quarter and the rest of the monument.

By the time you've finished reading this history, the trip up the elevator should be imminent. When first opened in 1888 the Washington Monument was equipped with a steam-driven elevator. Whether it was sincere concern or not for the fairer sex, the elevator was deemed too dangerous for women. The men lived life on the edge and rode the sluggish elevator, which took 20 minutes to reach the top. As for the women, they *climbed* the 897 steps — some collapsing and even dying — as the men toasted them with wine and beer — from the top. The elevator is safe and quicker now, but more crowded and less convivial. On a clear day, the view from the top includes most of the District and parts of Virginia and Maryland. The stairs are off-limits except for Park Service–conducted "step tours" (descent only) on weekends (hours vary); 188 carved memorial stones that were donated by various states, nations, societies, and individuals can be seen. Open April through *Labor Day,* daily 8 AM to midnight; from September to March, 9 AM to 5 PM. No admission charge. 15th St. between Constitution and Independence Aves. NW (phone: 202-426-6839).

After returning to terra firma, notice the *Sylvan Theater* on the southeast side of the monument's quadrant. This outdoor theater with its massive lawn hosts military bands, Shakespeare festivals, and musicals. There is a concert every day during the summer, including performances indigenous to Washington — for example, a Jesse Jackson speech backed up by three gospel singers, a five-piece electric band, and a voter-registration drive.

Walk the path leading north from the monument to Madison Drive. The Ellipse should be in the foreground, the familiar south side of the White

House sitting beyond. Begin walking on Madison Drive toward the Capitol Building in the distance. The first building ahead on the Mall proper is the *National Museum of American History,* the primary reason for the *Smithsonian* museum's nickname, the "nation's attic." It houses all the things that we just can't bear to throw out, but can't stand to keep near.

The wealth of Americana includes George Washington's false teeth, the original *Star-Spangled Banner* that inspired the poem that inspired the anthem, the desk on which Thomas Jefferson wrote the Declaration of Independence, a pocket compass used by Lewis and Clark, a collection of First Ladies' gowns, Eli Whitney's cotton gin, Muhammad Ali's boxing gloves, a collection of campaign paraphernalia, and an antebellum post office taken from Headsville, West Virginia, in which you can still mail a letter that will be postmarked with a unique Smithsonian seal (also see *Memorable Museums* in DIVERSIONS). And there's more — much more — some of great historical significance and some with none whatsoever (such as the Fonz's leather jacket, Dorothy's ruby slippers, and Radar O'Reilly's teddy bear). The museum's primary purpose is to document American civilization's achievements in science, technology, politics, and culture (the jury is still out on the inclusion of memorabilia from the hit TV series "Happy Days"). Open daily 10 AM to 5:30 PM; 9:30 AM to 7:30 PM June through *Labor Day* (Constitution Ave. between 12th and 14th Sts. NW; phone: 202-357-2700).

The next museum along the way is the *National Museum of Natural History;* housing 118 million objects inside its barrel-chested, early-20th-century façade, it sprouted two wings in the 1960s. If forced to categorize its contents, "planet earth" is the best we could do. It is a veritable treasure trove of the life sciences, filled with dinosaurs, exhibits on the evolution of man, fossils, a collection of animals bagged by Teddy Roosevelt on his numerous African safaris, reptiles, birds, plants, rocks, and gems. Among the major attractions is "Uncle Beazly," the life-size model of a triceratops which reminds us pint-size humans that the extinction of the dinosaur wasn't so tragic after all; the Dinosaur Hall; the Insect Zoo, featuring thousands of live insects including the incredible hissing cockroach; the Hall of Gems, which is studded with 1,000 precious stones, making the contents of New York's *Tiffany's* seem like prizes in a Cracker Jack box; and the History of Life exhibit. To see just a fraction of the museum's contents is a good cultural workout. Open 10 AM to 5:30 PM daily. Constitution Ave. between 9th and 12th Sts. NW (phone: 202-357-2700).

At 9th Street, the *National Archives* is on the left, set back on Constitution Avenue behind an area that is a garden in the summer and an ice rink in the winter (skates can be rented nearby). The *National Archives* is the nation's file cabinet, containing the Declaration of Independence, the Constitution, the Bill of Rights (all in the Archives Exhibition Hall on the Constitution Avenue side of the building), and a blizzard of our nation's paperwork and documentation throughout its history. Many genealogy buffs find the *Archives* to be a crucial link in tracing their ancestry (the research rooms are reached from the Pennsylvania Avenue entrance and are open to the public). In addition to the billions of documents housed here, there are a few rather bizarre holdings. Along with President Gerald Ford's pardon of Richard Nixon and all the laws ever enacted by Congress, there is a brown paper bag containing a hamburger with one bite missing. It is the evidence in a case in Detroit in 1940 involving a sailor on the USS *Dubuque* and a young woman who came aboard with a hamburger — and a yen for men in uniform. After the sailor and the woman found privacy in a gun locker, she took a bite of the burger. She also had been sniffing chloroform to get high, and promptly died in the sailor's arms. The sailor was acquitted of involuntary manslaughter and rape charges — but the hamburger remains in custody (for your benefit it is not on display). Exhibition Hall open from April 1 through *Labor Day* from 10 AM to 9 PM, from September to March from 10 AM to 5:30 PM (phone: 202-501-5205).

Return down 7th Street to Madison Drive and turn left. The massive marble West Building of the *National Gallery of Art* occupies a good chunk of real estate on the left. This gallery, which contains 5½ acres of gallery space, deserves to be ranked among the finest in the world, with major works by all the Impressionist painters, one of the best collections of Italian art outside Europe, an extensive collection of American art, and works by Flemish, German, Dutch, Spanish, and British artists, plus many others.

Interestingly, the West Building (the original *National Gallery of Art*) was constructed from funds provided by the Pittsburgh banker and philanthropist Andrew Mellon. Given control of the family's bank at age 26, Mellon wasted no time in converting his interest in art into one of the most impressive privately held collections in the world. The Mellon collection concentrated on the Old Masters of 16th-, 17th-, and 18th-century Europe (he sent a paltry $6 million to a cash-strapped Soviet Union for a collection of classics including works by Raphael and Botticelli). After relocating to Washington to become Secretary of the Treasury in 1921, he delighted European visitors by inviting them to dinner at his 15-room apartment to glimpse some of the works produced by their own national ancestors. Those paintings are among the many others in the *National Gallery*'s West Building.

The dramatically angular East Building was designed by architect I. M. Pei, who was given the formidable challenge of building on a trapezoidal site between Madison Drive and a slashing Pennsylvania Avenue to the north, complicated by tennis courts and rose bushes planted by Lady Bird Johnson. His solution, a building shaped like two interlocking triangles made out of stone from the same Tennessee quarry as the West Building, is as unorthodox as it is ingenious. Whether you love it or loathe it, its galleries are a who's who of 20th-century art and are a delightful gambol amid greatness. Open daily (phone: 202-737-4215).

Along the underground concourse between the two buildings is a rather generic cafeteria, which serves salads, sandwiches, and soups, and the *Cascade Café,* with a waterfall that trickles down against a glass wall. Both are good places at which to relax over tea or coffee. Also, there are plenty of food vendors along the Mall hawking everything from killer hot dogs, giant pretzels, and candy bars to coffee, soft drinks, and snow cones. The benches along the Mall's gravel paths offer a pleasant perch for short culture breaks.

After reaching 3rd Street, turn right to get to the museums on the south side of the Mall. The view of the Mall from its east end over your right shoulder yields a stunning, linear view of the Washington Monument and the Lincoln Memorial beyond. Notice how the *Smithsonian* "Castle" building on the south side juts into the Mall. (This was built before L'Enfant's Mall plan had been resuscitated, and any area on the Mall was fair game for development.) Directly ahead beyond Jefferson Drive, between 3rd and 4th Streets, is the last vacant lot on the Mall. But probably not for long. There are tentative plans to build an American Indian museum here.

Now, begin walking down Jefferson Drive on the south side of the Mall toward the Washington Monument. Turn left off the Mall on 4th Street and cross Independence Avenue; walk south 1 block to C Street. The building on the left is the home of *Voice of America,* the government-operated radio station that broadcasts news throughout the world. At last count, *VOA* broadcasts in 44 languages, including Swahili, Armenian, and Urdu. The 45-minute guided tours explain the role of the *VOA* and its umbrella organization, the US Information Agency (USIA). Open Mondays through Fridays (phone: 202-485-6231).

Return up 4th Street to Jefferson Drive, and turn left. The first building on the left, the *National Air and Space Museum,* is Washington's most popular tourist attraction. Statistics bear this out. The museum, which chronicles the history of man's ageless quest to soar with the birds — with its many exhibits in 23 galleries that span several blocks of the Mall — hosted over 7.5 million visitors last year. Hanging from the ceiling of the main entrance are Lindbergh's *Spirit of St. Louis;* the *Gossamer Albatross,* the first human-powered plane to cross the English Channel; and the Wright Brothers' *Kitty Hawk Flyer* — as well as the *Apollo 11* and *Viking Lander.* The exhibits cover air travel from man's most humble efforts to the space probes that have been sent to the outer reaches of the solar system. The *Langley Theater* presents several memorable films about flight on its dizzying 5-story-high screen. Even a mildly curious visitor could easily spend a day here. Open daily. Admission charge to the films (phone: 202-357-2700).

The next building to the west on Jefferson Drive is the *Hirshhorn Museum,* a.k.a. the "Doughnut on the Mall." This round building (an astonishing array of sculpture is displayed in the "doughnut hole" and the plaza area) houses the rather copious art collection of a Latvian-born immigrant of the same name who made a fortune in the US running uranium mines. At a time when the art world revolved around Europe, Hirshhorn championed the cause of many contemporary American artists. His reward was a collection worth, by most accounts, $50 million when he went on to that great gallery in the sky. The entrance is on the Independence Avenue side. The collection includes works by Mark Rothko, Jackson Pollock, Georgia O'Keeffe, and Andy Warhol. Equally impressive are the sculptures — over 2,000 works. The *Hirshhorn* also boasts the definitive collection of Henry Moore sculpture, on display across Jefferson Drive in the sunken Sculpture Garden. Also in the garden are works by Henri Daumier, Alberto Giacometti, Auguste Rodin, and Pablo Picasso. Open daily (phone: 202-357-3235).

After wandering among the statuary in the garden, forge ahead to the next museum, the *Arts and Industries Building.* Along with the "Castle" next door, this Victorian structure, made of red sandstone with giant industrial trusses and balconies, represents the old-guard *Smithsonian* building. Built in 1881 to shelter the horse-drawn carriages, pistols, machinery, and furniture exhibitions at the *Philadelphia Centennial Exhibition* of 1876, this was the second of the two buildings. Across the street is a festive and carefully preserved carousel, always a hit with the kids.

The granddaddy of the Mall, though, is the "Castle," the original *Smithsonian Institution,* a dramatic building that is generally regarded as one of the best specimens of Gothic Revival architecture in the US. Not much need to go inside, though — except for the visitors' center — since today it comprises the *Smithsonian Institution*'s administrative offices and serves as the headquarters of the Woodrow Wilson International Center for Scholars. Also inside is the Crypt Room, containing the tomb of the institution's eccentric founder, James Smithson. Open daily (phone: 202-357-2700).

Smithson, a well-heeled British scientist in the early 19th century, never visited the US. He was the illegitimate son of a duke and was ostracized by English society for his shortcoming. His will, drafted 3 years before his death in 1929, left his entire estate to his nephew with the stipulation that, if his nephew should die without children, Smithson's entire fortune — worth $515,169 at the time — would go to the US "to found in Washington, under the name of the Smithsonian Institution, an establishment for the increase and diffusion of knowledge among men." Fortunately for the enrichment of knowledge among men, the nephew died young and without children. But the US Congress, which is known for its reluctance to change, took a full 11 years to decide whether it should accept the money.

Directly behind the Castle and underground is the Quadrangle, an underground complex that houses the Smithsonian's two newest additions, the *Arthur M. Sackler Gallery* and the *National Museum of African Art.* The *Sackler Gallery*'s three floors afford a tactful opportunity for the *Smithsonian* to show off its impressive holdings of Eastern art. The museum, along with a wealth of other art and artifacts, has Chinese bronzes that date back to the Shang dynasty (1523–1028 BC) and Chinese jades that date to 3000 BC. The museum library shelves over 35,000 volumes in Chinese and Japanese. Open daily (phone: 202-357-2700).

The *National Museum of African Art*'s 6,000-object collection is one of the finest of its kind in the world. Previously housed in the home of Frederick Douglass, the former slave, abolitionist, and writer, the museum's contents moved to their plush quarters on the Mall in 1987. Open daily (phone: 202-357-4000).

The wrought-iron benches, beds of bright flowers, and greenery between the entrance buildings of the *Sackler* and *Museum of African Art* comprise the Enid A. Haupt Garden, named after the New Yorker who contributed the money for its construction. The Fountain Garden, near the *African Art Museum,* is a godsend on sweltering August days in the District.

Finally, the *Freer Gallery of Art* on the west side of the "Castle" is an intimate museum with an impressive collection of art from the Near and Far East. It also boasts perhaps the finest cluster of paintings by American artist James McNeill Whistler, who was a friend of the museum's founder, plus a good many paintings by Winslow Homer and John Singer Sargent. The gallery was built to resemble a Florentine palace. Because the building is small and works are constantly being juggled, visitors can call to schedule an appointment to see anything not on display. Open daily (phone: 202-357-2104).

The remainder of the Mall to 14th Street is graced by the elegant white marble Department of Agriculture Building, one of the first structures to take root as a result of the McMillan Commission's resurrection of Pierre L'Enfant's plan. The Mall seemed an ideal location for this department since it was thought the ground in front of the department could be used as a garden for growing experimental crops. (It wasn't.) Etched in the cornices on this side of the building are symbols of some of the staples of this department's bureaucratic toil: grains and forests, flowers and fruit. The majestic, castle-like structure across 14th Street is the Auditor's Building which, in 1879, was the first building dedicated to the task of printing the nation's legal tender. Turn left on 14th Street and walk past Independence Avenue. Notice the bridge that spans this thoroughfare. Known as the "Bridge of Sighs," it is dedicated to a former secretary of agriculture as well as to Seaman Knapp, a distinguished warrior in the fight against the scourge of cotton, the dreaded boll weevil. The bridge connects the old and new buildings of the Agriculture Department.

Now, cross 14th Street and walk down to the Bureau of Engraving and Printing. This is where the nation's paper money, postage and food stamps, military certificates, and presidential invitations are printed. The 25-minute, self-guided tour is a favorite of out-of-towners and gives the tourist a good view of crisp sheets of currency coming hot off the presses, money being checked, overprinted with the treasury seal, cut, stacked, and bundled for transport. The bureau makes a cool $20 billion every year. An explanation of the process of making money is provided over a public-address system. Open 9 AM to 2 PM weekdays (phone: 202-874-3316). The tour finishes in the gift shop, where bags of money can be bought at an enormous discount (too bad it's shredded), on the Maine Avenue side of the building.

Walk down the bureau's steps; the Tidal Basin comes into view across the street. Cross Maine Avenue to reach the footpath that encircles this peaceful, inviting body of water. There is a boathouse at the entrance to the footpath that rents paddleboats — a favorite Tidal Basin pastime and a great way to spend a lazy summer afternoon (boats rent for $7 an hour; phone: 202-484-0206).

Walk south (to the left) on the footpath. Glimmering in the distance at the foot of the Tidal Basin's placid water is our next stop, the Jefferson Memorial. After crossing the Outlet Bridge continue on the footpath up to the marble dome that is the southernmost of Washington's major monuments. This lovely area, surprisingly, is land reclaimed from the mud flats of the Potomac.

It is no secret that Thomas Jefferson admired the dome motif of Rome's Pantheon. He adopted it for his Monticello, Virginia, home. He also worked it into the design of the University of Virginia in Charlottesville. And it is fitting that his memorial is also a dome. The 19-foot statue of our nation's third president — who was also drafter of the Declaration of Independence, a secretary of state, botanist, architect, and general Renaissance man —

stands firm in the rotunda, which is inscribed with some of his most compelling words. The memorial was dedicated in 1943 and is blanketed in the pinkish splendor of the cherry blossoms that bloom here in April. If you're interested in some reading material on Jefferson, try talking with the gregarious Jefferson scholar who works in the bookshop beneath the monument. The monument is always open. Sections will be blocked off for renovations, however, until sometime in 1996 (phone: 202-426-6822).

After leaving the Jefferson Memorial, take the footpath that clings to the Tidal Basin, leading to the Inlet Bridge. There are two bronze, human-headed fish sculptures on the inside of the bridge that spout water from their mouths. After crossing the bridge stay on the path that is the right prong of this fork at the foot of West Potomac Park (the left is a not-so-spectacular stroll along the Potomac). The undisputed main attraction in this area is the 600 Yoshino and Akebono cherry trees that were a gift to the American people by the Japanese government in 1912. During the 10 to 12 days in early April that they are in full blossom, they are absolutely gorgeous and jam traffic for miles.

Today's trees were actually a replacement bunch. The first batch of cherry trees sent by the Japanese in 1909 were besieged by insects and fungus. Consequently, the Department of Agriculture had them destroyed, and the Japanese graciously avoided an international incident by sending another batch with a better bill of health 3 years later. Incidentally, in the 1960s the US came to the rescue of Japan's pollution-ravaged native cherry trees by sending cuttings from these trees back to their homeland.

If you're so inclined, West Potomac Park during the spring and summer is a relaxing spot amid the cherry trees to laze, picnic, and feed the squirrels against the backdrop of the Tidal Basin.

Continue along West Basin Drive to the next fork in the road. Take the left prong as it curves back to Ohio Drive. Turn right on Ohio Drive to the northwest and continue to the Lincoln Memorial (also under renovation until 1996).

Though marble, like so many other buildings in Washington, something about the Lincoln Memorial is more inspiring and human than the rest. Perhaps it's the man. And perhaps it's his statue — a war-weary Lincoln sitting pensively on his monumental throne. The two best speeches delivered by our articulate 16th president, the Gettysburg Address and the Second Inaugural Address, flank his statue. Sculptor Daniel Chester French's statue in this Greek-style memorial (which resembles the Parthenon in Athens) goes a long way toward honoring this extraordinary man.

Interestingly, the artist had just finished a memorial to Thomas Hopkins Gallaudet, the pioneer educator of the deaf, before he began work on the Lincoln Memorial. Those who know sign language say that Lincoln's hands form his initials, A and L. Also, it was on the steps of the Lincoln Memorial, above the Reflecting Pool, that Dr. Martin Luther King, Jr., delivered his moving "I Have a Dream" speech. Walk down to the Reflecting Pool to confirm that Lincoln's statue, indeed, is reflected in this body of water. The monument is always open (phone: 202-426-6841).

Now, walk to the left (north) of the Reflecting Pool to the somber Vietnam Veterans Memorial. Architect Maya Lin's unorthodox design — two below-ground, polished black granite walls forming an outstretched "V," with the names of all those killed or missing in the war etched in the stone — was fervently criticized at first; it is now widely admired by vets and former protesters alike. Critics also were mollified by Frederick Hart's bronze sculpture of three soldiers, and a flagpole, nearby. Another statue commemorating the women who gave their lives in Vietnam is scheduled for completion this year and will be situated near the present monument. Few walk away from the memorial without being moved. The monument is always open (phone: 202-426-6841).

Continuing east (toward the Washington Monument) through the rather undistinguished Constitution Gardens, eventually work your way north to Constitution Avenue. L'Enfant's original city plan envisioned a grand canal that would stretch roughly from where the Lincoln Memorial is now to the Capitol Building and then south to the Anacostia River. The French planner even envisioned the president riding from the Capitol to the White House on a barge. One wonders how Jimmy Carter would have handled this dilemma, since he insisted on eschewing official transportation after his inauguration by walking. The canal, where Constitution Avenue is now, never captured the hearts and minds of sensible Washingtonians and, by the Civil War, this putrid waterway (it was also prone to flooding) was filled in and converted into a street. At the corner of Constitution Avenue and 17th Street is the last stop on the Mall/Monument walking tour: a tiny and well-maintained stone building that was the home of the canal's lock keeper.

Walk 2: Capitol Hill

The majestic building that sits firmly atop Capitol Hill appears to fit in as naturally in its present location as the Parthenon atop Athens's Acropolis. It is hard to imagine the imposing edifice elsewhere.

Nevertheless, its present location at the crest of Jenkins Hill — a name rarely heard these days since giving way long ago to being called Capitol Hill or just "the Hill" — was really the third choice of the men who founded America's capital city. James Madison favored Shuter's Hill, a mound west of Old Town Alexandria (which was part of the original District of Columbia), present site of the George Washington Masonic National Memorial (see *Walk 7: Old Town Alexandria*). Thomas Jefferson agreed with Madison until he discovered another hill overlooking what is now Foggy Bottom. But President Washington, feeling that Virginia had received her full share of the honors in launching the new republic, insisted that the seat of government should indeed be on the Maryland side of the Potomac.

With these parameters in mind, Pierre L'Enfant, the original city architect, set about surveying the area for the site of the principal government buildings. When he laid eyes upon Jenkins Hill he remarked: "It's a pedestal waiting for a monument." Atop this pedestal now sit the Capitol Building, the Library of Congress, the Supreme Court Building, Union Station, congressional office buildings, and one of the city's most charming residential neighborhoods. The walking tour of Capitol Hill — with only brief forays into the aforementioned buildings (which are best left for another time) — takes approximately 3 hours.

The wisdom of Washington and L'Enfant's vision for Capitol Hill was probably lost on the first batch of congressmen who arrived in 1800 from Philadelphia, the former capital. There was only one sidewalk, made from chips left over from the Capitol; it cut the shoes of pedestrians in dry weather and covered them with white mortar when wet.

When some disgruntled representatives realized that the nearest tavern was in Georgetown, they moved there and commuted by coach to Capitol Hill. National newspapers echoed the grumblings of the new inhabitants. One reported that Capitol Hill has "few houses in any place, and most of them are small, miserable huts." The national press began a campaign to encourage the government to move yet again, to a more populated and more civilized city. The campaign culminated in a resolution that was actually introduced in Congress, was brought to a vote — and nearly passed.

As a result of hearing these discouraging words, members of the Supreme Court were sluggish in leaving their beloved Philadelphia for this remote village that seemed more like a refugee camp than a national capital. They also were not eager to shack up in the Capitol Building with a Congress that eyed the Court suspiciously (the first chief justice, John Jay, had resigned 5

Capitol Hill

0 mile 1/4

N

M ST.

NEW JERSEY AVE.

1ST ST.

N CAPITOL ST.

3RD ST.

L ST.

K ST.

I ST.

H ST.

G ST.

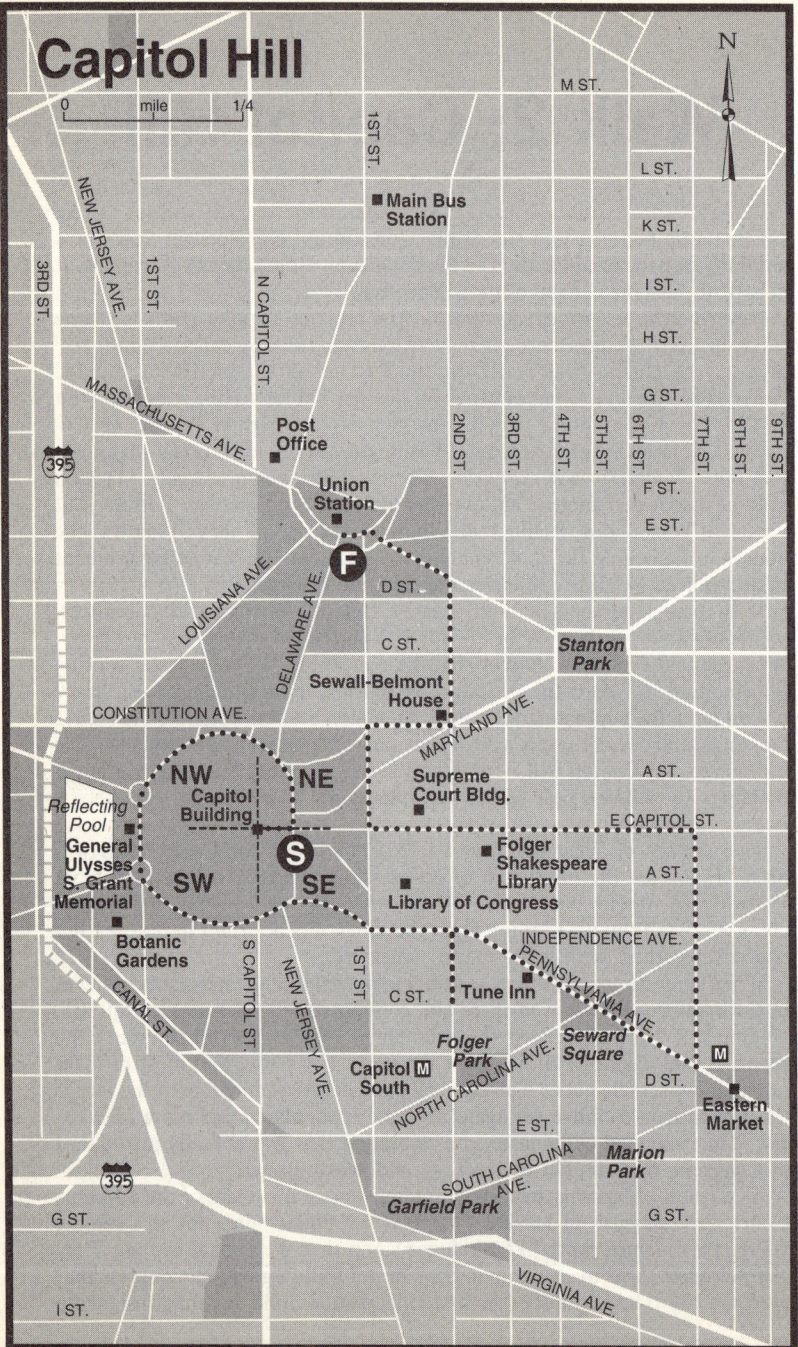

■ Main Bus Station

MASSACHUSETTS AVE.

395

Post Office

Union Station

2ND ST.

3RD ST.

4TH ST.

5TH ST.

6TH ST.

7TH ST.

8TH ST.

9TH ST.

F ST.

E ST.

F

LOUISIANA AVE.

DELAWARE AVE.

D ST.

C ST.

Stanton Park

Sewall-Belmont House

CONSTITUTION AVE.

MARYLAND AVE.

NW
Capitol Building

NE

Supreme Court Bldg. ■

A ST.

E CAPITOL ST.

Reflecting Pool

General Ulysses S. Grant Memorial ■

SW

SE

S

Folger Shakespeare Library ■

A ST.

Library of Congress ■

Botanic Gardens ■

CANAL ST.

S CAPITOL ST.

NEW JERSEY AVE.

1ST ST.

C ST.

INDEPENDENCE AVE.

PENNSYLVANIA AVE.

Tune Inn ■

Seward Square

M

Folger Park

Capitol South M

NORTH CAROLINA AVE.

D ST.

Eastern Market ■

395

E ST.

Marion Park

G ST.

SOUTH CAROLINA AVE.

Garfield Park

G ST.

I ST.

VIRGINIA AVE.

years earlier because he thought there wasn't enough support for the Court to uphold their decisions).

While you're "on the Hill" — which, incidentally, is a popular code used by lobbyists meaning a visit to the offices of select members of Congress — consider just how far our national capital has come. And if by chance you wander too far toward the east — where crime is rampant — consider how far it has to go.

Where else to begin this walking tour of Capitol Hill than the Capitol Building (Capitol South is the closest *Metro* station; then just walk uphill on 1st Street).

The east side — the front — is the most familiar view of this building since L'Enfant mistakenly thought affluent Washington would gravitate toward the east and the Anacostia River. The design of the Capitol Building is the result of Thomas Jefferson's desire for a classical Greek structure. A competition was held in 1792, and the impressive design submitted by a physician named William Thornton was the winner; his award for setting the tone of the city's architecture was $500.

The Capitol in its early days, however, looked nothing like the imposing, dome-shaped structure — the culmination of various remodelings, additions, and fire — that is seen today. When Congress arrived in 1800 the Capitol was a 2-story square building. By 1807 a similar edifice had been built for the House of Representatives. The two buildings were connected by a wooden walkway — an arrangement that worked well until the British invasion of Washington in 1814. During the attack on the Capitol Admiral Cockburn, a British officer, mounted the speaker's dais in the House of Representatives and called a mock session of Congress to order. The business was brief, putting the question to vote: "Shall this harbour of Yankee democracy be burned?" The roar of "ayes" from his men was unanimous and the insurgents immediately set fire to the building, including a bonfire of written records and volumes from the Library of Congress (then housed in the Capitol Building). The Capitol was spared total destruction by a sudden summer rainstorm.

Before advancing on the Capitol, notice the Statue of Freedom atop the dome. Though this 19-foot statue looks like an American Indian, the sculptor said he had a freed Roman slave in mind — and to prove the point, he topped off the figure with a liberty cap, the kind worn by freed Roman slaves. Jefferson Davis, then in charge of construction, objected to the antislavery implication and had the design changed. Davis went on to become the President of the Confederacy. If a flag is flying above the House (on the left or south) or the Senate (on the right or north), it means that respective body is in session.

Enter the Capitol's East Front up the steps where presidential inaugurals have been historically held (Ronald Reagan, however, decided to have his first inaugural on the West Front). It was here that Franklin Delano Roosevelt told a depressed America that "the only thing we have to fear is fear itself" and John F. Kennedy urged Americans to "ask not what your country can do for you, but what you can do for your country." It was also here that William Henry Harrison delivered in a drizzly downpour the longest inaugural speech on record — only to die of pneumonia a month later.

The 10-ton bronze Columbus Doors lead the way to the Rotunda, the starting point for 40-minute guided tours of the Capitol, which include access to the visitors' galleries of Congress. Though this is America and you're free to wander about, even the most savvy veteran of the "Hill" reports getting gloriously lost in the complex labyrinth that is the hallowed halls of Congress. The tour is the best way to explore the Capitol. But you'll have to go it alone to ride the monorail between the House and Senate or to sample the famous bean soup in the *Senate Dining Room* (see *Quintessential Washington* in DIVERSIONS). Capitol open daily from 9 AM to 4:30 PM (the last tour is at 3:45 PM). 1st St. between Constitution and Independence Aves. (phone: 202-224-3121).

Return to the East Front of the Capitol Building. Ahead is East Capitol Street, which slices between the Library of Congress (on the right) and Supreme Court Building (on the left). Before wandering over to other branches of government, first inspect the Capitol grounds. The best way to approach this is to turn left after descending the steps of the East Front; this is a popular broadcast spot for TV reporters and a setting for filming congressmen's campaign ads. On the left, just past the Senate chamber and a guard post, is a path that winds downhill to the Capitol's west side. Follow the path as it bends to the left and pass the Spring Grotto, a charming little hideaway designed by Frederick Law Olmsted, creator of New York's Central Park. If the day is sultry this stone grotto is a pleasant place for a cool reprieve.

The path intersects with 1st Street and Pennsylvania Avenue at a traffic rotary (in Washington all roads lead to the Capitol) with the Peace Monument at its axis, a marble memorial to the sailors, marines, and naval officers who died in the Civil War. The figure of America cries on the shoulder of history; and written in America's book is a reference to Lincoln's Gettysburg address: "They died that their country might live." Just off Pennsylvania Avenue is a short path which leads to the spectacular General Ulysses S. Grant Memorial, a moving series of statues that is known for its realism and its condemnation of war. As you enter, the first group of statues is the Cavalry Group, featuring seven mounted men ready to charge (actually one is not so ready, as he is falling headlong off his horse into the mud). A 17-foot bronze of Grant, the commander of the Union troops, is in the middle; the Artillery Group is to the south — three horses pulling a cart with a cannon, and three men each displaying a different face of battle.

This spot west of the Capitol affords perhaps the best perspective of the engaging structure; thanks to some impressive landscaping, the gentle slope up to the Capitol Building enhances its marbled stateliness. Broad flights of steps with intermittent marble terraces ascend this grassy slope — once used by neighborhood residents as croquet grounds.

This part of the grounds used to be enclosed by an iron fence and gates that were shut in the evening by watchmen; congressmen working late would have to call the guard at the gates in order to exit the Capitol from this direction. Since some chose a more expedient means of departure by smashing the gate locks with stones, the iron fence was finally removed. The very best view of the city — from the terrace on the West Front of the Capitol — illustrates what that flamboyant Frenchman who designed this city had in mind (see also

A Shutterbug's Washington in DIVERSIONS). Take the steps up to that vantage point.

After lapping up this exceptional view of the Mall, which gives way to the Washington Monument, the Reflecting Pool, the Lincoln Memorial, and beyond, walk south toward the House of Representatives' side of the Capitol and around again to the East Front. From here you can take either of two paths around the egg-shape park area on the southeast of the Capitol which leads to 1st Street and the front of the Jefferson Building of the Library of Congress — the world's largest library.

This massive temple to the written word is constructed in an American version of Italian Renaissance. It is so spacious (470 feet wide) that it may require neck-craning for a complete view of its front façade. It is difficult to imagine that our nation's library began as a one-room reference collection for Congress. Grasping the breadth of its current literary holdings is like trying to calculate infinity.

There are nearly 90 million items in the library, including around 6,000 books printed before the year 1500, one of only three remaining Gutenberg Bibles (the first great book to be published with movable metal type), the world's finest collection of folk music recordings, and five Stradivarius violins which are used for a concert series in the *Coolidge Auditorium* (1st St. SE and Independence Ave.; phone: 202-707-5502). In the minute you spend standing before this building, it has added about seven books to its stacks; it increases its holdings by 400 every hour. The Great Hall features an enormous dome, columns, statues, murals, and carved balustrades. Another real treat is its Main Reading Room, a domed octagon which hovers over 212 reading desks and a veritable sea of reference volumes. Since this library is widely used by researchers, there is an acute seriousness of purpose here. Adults are welcome to use the facilities, and visitors of all ages may tour the exhibit halls. Renovations began on the Jefferson Building in 1988 and are expected to be completed sometime this year. Until then, the library part of the building is not accessible to the public. When renovations are complete, it will be open daily from 8:30 AM to 9:30 PM; Saturdays from 8:30 AM to 5 PM; and Sundays from 1 to 5 PM. The corner of 1st St. SE and Independence Ave. (phone: 202-707-5000).

Catercorner from the Jefferson Building are the House office buildings (Rayburn, Cannon, and Longfellow), three white marble structures named after former speakers of the House of Representatives.

Around the corner to the left on Independence Avenue (across the street) is the Madison Building, a 46-acre Library of Congress annex. This primarily houses the library's extensive photo collection of over 12 million items that spans the history of photography. Upstairs on the sixth floor of this white marble building is the *Madison Building Cafeteria,* one of the city's best restaurant bargains. Sizable portions of good-quality (it's still a cafeteria) soups, salads, sandwiches, and entrées are served in a handsome setting with a panoramic view of Capitol Hill. The lunchtime crowd is dense with congressional staffers — giving the constituent (a designation for anyone outside the Beltway) who just pops in for lunch a feel for who is really deciding our fate. 101 Independence Ave. SE (phone: 202-707-8300).

At the corner of 2nd and Independence, just behind the Jefferson Building, is the rather austere, white Georgian marble John Adams Building, the first Library of Congress annex.

Cross the street and walk south down 2nd Street. On the left in the historic, Federal-era brick Watterston House is the Cato Institute, an independent public policy think tank. At the end of the block on the left is the *Capitol Hill* hotel, an intriguing former apartment building that has been converted into moderately priced luxury suites with fully equipped kitchens (200 C St. SE; phone: 202-543-6000). Returning back up 2nd Street to Pennsylvania Avenue, take note on the right of a petite French bakery and café, *Le Bon Café* (210 2nd St. SE; phone: 202-547-7200).

Turn right on Pennsylvania Avenue and make your way through the morass of dense shops along this thoroughfare. Perhaps because of the youngish crowd of interns and students who frequent this area, there are several excellent bookstores and music shops along the way. Take time to browse.

Follow Pennsylvania Avenue as it veers off of Independence at 2nd Street. The next several blocks are thick with shops, restaurants, pubs, and other commercial establishments serving the Capitol Hill crowd. Among the more interesting are *Tavern The Greek Islands* (307 Pennsylvania Ave. SE; phone: 202-547-8360), a Greek restaurant serving reasonably priced moussaka, souvlaki, and stuffed grape leaves; *Toscanini* (313 Pennsylvania Ave. SE; phone: 202-544-2335), offering good northern Italian dishes; and the *Hawk and Dove* (329 Pennsylvania Ave. SE; phone: 202-543-3300), a Hill treasure that is one of those quintessentially dark, brooding bars filled cheek-to-jowl with an eclectic mixture of bureaucrats, Congressional staffers, and barflies. Perhaps the most beloved Capitol Hill institution is the *Tune Inn* (331½ Pennsylvania Ave. SE; phone: 202-543-2725), which offers a hearty barbecue feast, greasy burgers, curly-Qs, and plenty of cheap beer. The help is notoriously surly — and patrons wouldn't have it any other way.

Continue down Pennsylvania Avenue through Seward Square, named after the former Secretary of State famous for purchasing land from Russia for $7 million in a secret deal that became known as "Seward's Folly." That "big lump of ice" was mineral-rich Alaska. After reaching 7th Street turn left to *Bread and Chocolate* (666 Pennsylvania Ave. SE; phone: 202-547-2875), a popular tearoom that features soups, salads, and French-influenced entrées.

Now, saunter a block or two down 7th Street to the long green overhang of *Eastern Market,* the pavilion on the left, which shelters the stalls of the Virginia, Maryland, and Pennsylvania farmers who sell their produce, flowers, cider, and other wares outside. Inside, greengrocers and butchers hawk fresh foods, and the *Market Lunch* is a densely populated luncheonette that is renowned for its hearty Saturday breakfasts, crab cakes on homemade fresh bread, and lines that snake out the door (phone: 202-547-8444). The wildest, wooliest, and best day to visit is Saturday. By Sunday, the market mysteriously converts to a flea market. The only one still remaining, *Eastern Market,* was once one of four District markets — along with *West, South,* and *North* markets.

Across the street are several well-reputed antiques dealers. Perhaps the best is *Architectural Artifacts* (216 7th St. SE; phone: 202-546-2811), a shop that specializes in high-quality antique furniture without the highbrow atmosphere or prices. 8th Street also is home to several good antiques shops.

Two blocks up 7th Street is East Capitol Street, the thoroughfare that divides the northeast quadrant of the city from the southeast. In Washington it is crucial to pay strict attention to the quadrant designation since, for example, C Street NE is 6 blocks from C Street SE. Don't feel that you're the only one who's confused: the city's alphabet soup of street names is also the scourge of many a DC driver. Turn left here amid some of Capitol Hill's early residential architecture.

Four blocks ahead on the left is the Folger Shakespeare Library, a white marble building with nine bas-reliefs that feature various Shakespearean scenes. This library and theater, founded in 1930 by Standard Oil executive and Shakespeare aficionado Henry Clay Folger, is pure heaven for scholars of the Bard. It contains the world's best collection of rare books, manuscripts, and research materials devoted to the famed English playwright. The library is a handsome oak-paneled and barrel-vaulted Elizabethan palace that, along with its vast literary holdings, contains a model of London's *Globe Theatre*. The theater on the premises is an Elizabethan innyard–style theater replicating the Shakespeare theater in Stratford-upon-Avon in England; it hosts performances of Shakespeare as well as other classics. Open Mondays through Saturdays from 10 AM to 4 PM. 201 E. Capitol St. (phone: 202-544-4600).

Return to East Capitol Street and turn left, facing the East Front of the Capitol Building head-on. After walking just over a block back to 1st Street, take a sneak preview of the Supreme Court Building on the right. Cross the intersection with care: The pandemonium wrought by droves of youngsters visiting here on field trips can easily distract even a mild-mannered pedestrian. Also, bus drivers delayed while unloading large groups of people on the Capitol steps tend to speed down East Capitol Street to make up for lost time.

It is appropriate that the massive classical structure that houses our nation's Supreme Court pays homage to ancient Greece, the birthplace of democracy, reason, and the Socratic method. The Supreme Court occupied seven different locations within the capital between 1800 and 1935, until it found a permanent home in this neo-classical building designed by Cass Gilbert and completed in 1935. The main entrance, on 1st Street, is noteworthy for its 15 marble columns that support a pediment with the inscription "Equal Justice Under Law." This entrance is flanked by two seated statues representing "The Contemplation of Justice" and "The Guardian, or Authority, of Law." Among the inside attractions are the Great Hall, lined with the busts of former chief justices; an exhibition of cartoon art depicting the Supreme Court and other Court photographs and memorabilia on display on the ground floor; courtroom lectures; and a film featuring the chief justice and several associate justices who are uncharacteristically candid in their description of the inner workings of the Court and its history. When the Court is in session from October to April (2 weeks on for oral arguments and 2 weeks off for deliberation and opinion writing), it is open to the public for hearings (Mondays and Tuesdays). Check the *Washington Post* or *Washington Times* for listings and times of cases to be heard. The building also has one of the best government cafeterias, but closes to the public three times each day (from 10:30 to 11:30 AM, noon to 12:15 PM, and 1 to 1:10 PM). The Supreme Court is open Mondays through Fridays from 9 AM to 4:30 PM. 1st and East Capitol Sts. NE (phone: 202-479-3000).

After descending the steps of the Supreme Court, a popular area for demonstrations, follow 1st Street to the right until reaching Constitution Avenue. The white marble building to the left of this intersection is the Russell Senate Office Building, one of three such buildings containing the offices of senators, their staff, committee hearing rooms, and the offices of committee staff. The building to the right is the Dirksen Senate Office Building. The general public is ordinarily invited to attend committee hearings — for a close encounter of government activity (though many who frequent these hearings contend "inactivity" is a better characterization). Check the *Washington Post* or *Washington Times* for the daily schedule of hearings in such forums as the Senate Foreign Relations Committee, the Senate Finance Committee, and others. Hearings that don't feature a financial scandal, a testifying celebrity (Oprah Winfrey and Victoria Principal are recent examples), or a Supreme Court nominee generally draw an audience composed of congressional staff, lobbyists, aides to those testifying, and others with a stake in the proceedings. Nevertheless, ordinary folk have a civic right to attend, regardless of how boring the topic and how monotonous the questioning.

Located on the Constitution Avenue side, the guest entrances to the Senate Office Buildings are well marked. Committee protocol dictates that spectators form a queue outside the committee room well in advance. Lobbyists often leave their briefcases to hold their place in line as they go off for a cup of coffee or to use the phone.

Walk to the east (right from 1st Street) on Constitution Avenue to the next building — adjoining the Dirksen Building — which is the Hart Senate Office Building. This modern office complex is the newest of the Senate Office Buildings and contains an attractive, sunlit atrium with an assortment of modern statuary. As with all congressional office buildings, visitors must clear a metal detector before entering.

At the corner of 2nd Street NE and Constitution Avenue is the historic and stately *Sewall-Belmont House,* a museum of women's political achievements that is owned by the National Women's Party. The building has undergone so many additions and remodelings that it's a patchwork quilt of architectural styles. Nevertheless, part of it dates back to 1680, making it the oldest house on Capitol Hill. Albert Gallatin, Jefferson's and Madison's Secretary of the Treasury, is said to have hammered out the Louisiana Purchase in this house; and the only resistance to the 1814 British invasion of Washington originated here. The British responded by setting the house ablaze, damaging its front section. Displays — which range from suffrage to the present — commemorate, among other noteworthy women, Alice Paul, author of the original Equal Rights Amendment. Open Tuesdays through Fridays from 10 AM to 3 PM; Saturdays and Sundays from noon to 4 PM. 144 Constitution Ave. NE (phone: 202-546-3989).

Turn left on 2nd Street and walk past the driveway entrance of the Hart building. Just 2 blocks up, hugging Massachusetts Avenue, is a cluster of restaurants and watering holes that are in a prime location for after-hours hobnobbing and alfresco lunches for Senate staffers. The darling of this pack is the *American Café* (227 Massachusetts Ave. NE; phone: 202-546-7690), part of a beloved local chain that serves inventive American cuisine and features a bustling outdoor patio in the summer. Across the street is *Bob's Famous Homemade Ice Cream* (236 Massachusetts Ave. NE; phone: 202-546-3860), "designer" ice cream by Bob, a former high-powered Washington lawyer–turned–ice cream entrepreneur. Also in this block is *La Brasserie* (239 Massachusetts Ave. NE; phone: 202-546-6066), which features excellent nouvelle and classic country fare such as rabbit and quiche.

Just up Massachusetts Avenue (to the northwest) is Union Station, Washington's recently renovated railway terminal. The exterior of the Beaux Arts building has been restored to its original state; statues aplenty, gold leaf, and columns, plus an overwhelming, grand façade (adorned during the *Christmas* season with wreaths larger in size than many Pacific atolls). The new Union Station serves its original purpose as a train station, but with over 100 upscale shops, a food court, a movie theater, and a spectacular barrel-vaulted interior, its transport function seems almost secondary. 50 Massachusetts Ave. (phone: 202-383-3078).

With the possible exception of a jaunt over to two of Washington's most spirited Irish pubs — the *Irish Times* (14 F St. NW; phone: 202-543-5433) and the *Dubliner* (520 N. Capitol St. NW; phone: 202-737-3773) — Union Station is the end of the line on the Capitol Hill walking tour.

Downtown

0 mile 1/4

N

U ST.

T ST.

S ST.

R ST.

Q ST.

CORCORAN ST.

NEW HAMPSHIRE AVE.

VERMONT AVE.

RHODE ISLAND AVE.

P ST.

O ST.

N ST.

Dupont Circle

CONNECTICUT AVE.

17TH ST.

Scott Circle

National Firearms Museum

Logan Circle

14TH ST.

13TH ST.

12TH ST.

11TH ST.

10TH ST.

9TH ST.

8TH ST.

7TH ST.

M ST.

Thomas Circle

Mayflower

21ST ST.

20TH ST.

19TH ST.

18TH ST.

National Geographic Society

15TH ST.

Farragut Square

K ST.

16TH ST.

L ST.

MASSACHUSETTS AVE.

Farragut West

M

I ST.

McPherson Square

M

Franklin Square

Mt. Vernon Square

Washington Convention Center

CHINATOWN

PENNSYLVANIA AVE.

Decatur House

St. John's Church

NEW YORK AVE.

H ST.

Renwick Gallery

Lafayette Square

G ST.

National Portrait Gallery

Old Executive Office Building

17TH ST.

S

White House

F ST.

National Theater

Peterson House

Ford's Theatre

Corcoran Gallery of Art

E ST.

Peacock Alley

Freedom Plaza

J. Edgar Hoover Bldg.

VIRGINIA AVE.

D ST.

Ellipse

15TH ST.

PENNSYLVANIA AVE.

C ST.

Daughters of the American Revolution Museum

Old Post Office

National Archives

F

CONSTITUTION AVE.

National Museum of American History

National Museum of Natural History

Rainbow Pool

Reflecting Pool

Washington Monument

THE MALL

MADISON DR.

Smithsonian Castle

Sylvan Theater

JEFFERSON DR.

INDEPENDENCE AVE.

1

Freer Gallery

Hancock Park

Tidal Basin

D ST.

Walk 3: Downtown

Washington's downtown area contains a veritable patchwork quilt of sites that should be of interest to tourists. This section of the District of Columbia is anchored by the White House and Lafayette Park. Bordered by the Mall to the south, Foggy Bottom to the west, Capitol Hill to the east, and a sliver of Adams Morgan to the north, the most accurate statement that can be made about this densely developed area is that it begins where the others end. A question about downtown's parameters from ten different people would probably elicit as many responses. And this area resembles the traditional urban downtown area only in name: There has long been a building code that restricts building higher than the Capitol and district's monuments.

Downtown is home to Washington's chicest shops, especially along lower Connecticut Avenue, the capital city's Rodeo Drive. Several blocks to the south is K Street, an area of impersonal buildings known as Lawyers Canyon, which houses the highest concentration of lawyers anywhere in America. The country's chief executive is a resident of downtown; also here are the historical homes, museums, churches, hotels, and green spaces that surround the White House. Pennsylvania Avenue (known among locals as "the Avenue"), which connects the Capitol with the White House and serves as the ceremonial parade route for inaugurals and other national events, defines the downtown's southern border. To the north are take-out restaurants, colorful shops, and the distinctly Asian feel of Chinatown. Also carving out a niche are the hip music clubs, art galleries, and bohemian feel of the area just west of the *Washington Convention Center,* the city's premier exhibition and entertainment complex.

The logical starting point for a tour of downtown, a walk that should take approximately 4 hours, is the familiar white residence at 1600 Pennsylvania Avenue which must have as high (if not higher) a turnover as any Washington residence: the White House. The nearest *Metro* stations are McPherson Square and Farragut West.

Many interesting anecdotes accompanied George Washington's tireless efforts to secure land for the capital city from District landowners who were reluctant to part with their plots. Some of the most stubborn resistance came from the previous owner of the land on which the White House and Lafayette Park now sit, a canny Scot named David Burns. It is said that Burns held out so long that Washington had to appeal in person to him. After pointing out the financial windfalls Burns stood to gain from selling his coveted land, Washington added: "But for this opportunity, Mr. Burns, you might have died a poor tobacco planter."

"Aye," replied the unflappable Scotsman, "and had ye no married the widow Custis" — Custis was Martha Washington's maiden name; her family was rather well-to-do — "ye'd ha been a land surveyor the noo, and a mighty poor one at that." Despite his reluctance to sell, Burns finally came to realize that if he didn't accept Washington's generous offer his land would be seized for the public good — not doing him much good at all.

This elevated spot overlooking a bend in the Potomac, with a view of Alexandria to the south, was chosen for what was originally called the Presidential Palace. It was designed by James Hoban, an Irish architect who modeled the house after Dublin's Leinster Hall. The president's residence and office was not originally white, having been built with a sort of pinkish Virginia sandstone. It was only after the British set fire to it during their invasion of the capital in 1814 that the palace was painted white (to cover the damage). Over the years, the White House has undergone a number of renovations and reconstructions before evolving into the house we know today.

After a stroll through Lafayette Park (officially known as Lafayette Square) and its occasionally rambunctuous assortment of demonstrators attempting to catch the president's eye, approach the White House from the north. The Main Portico on Pennsylvania Avenue is the First Family's front door (though rarely used except by tourists). From this side, this esteemed residence appears tranquil, small, and as white as freshly laundered linen. The tall, black wrought-iron fence is a striking contrast to the white façade — an imposing reminder that, though this is a free country, uninvited guests are frowned upon. This scene is especially pleasing in the evening when the bustle of Pennsylvania Avenue has died down and the trickle from the White House fountain can be heard. After crossing Pennsylvania Avenue, walk to the left along the sidewalk toward the east side of the White House.

After reaching the open gate on the east side (it is always overseen by a watchful guard), turn right into East Executive Park (open from 5 AM to 11 PM). This thin strip of green space features a series of lovely shrubs and fountains that cut a path between the White House and the rather self-important Department of Treasury building on the left.

The first gate within the park on the right (known as the East Gate) is the entrance for White House tours. The tour of the White House focuses on the lower floor's majestic public rooms. Tourists are not permitted entrance to the offices, kitchen, pressroom, or private living quarters of the president, located on the upper floors. Though glimpses of the president are possible, they are rare.

Visitors will be led past the Library; the Vermeil Room, with its extensive collection of gilded silver; into the China Room for a glimpse of the china chosen by past presidents and their wives; and to the Diplomatic Reception Room, a Federal-period parlor where foreign diplomats present their credentials to the president and where Franklin D. Roosevelt delivered his legendary "fireside chats." The next floor up is the State Floor, on which the East Room, the largest room in the White House, is situated. In the East Room, press conferences, receptions, and other ceremonies are held under the elaborate glass chandeliers which date from 1902. Seven presidents have lain in state here; and the *Harlem Globetrotters* once played a game of basketball on its parquet floor during the Carter administration. The other rooms on this floor that are part of the White House tour include the Green Room, a reception room that formerly was Thomas Jefferson's dining room; the Blue Room, furnished to represent the period of James Monroe and often thought to be the building's most beautiful; the Red Room, beloved by First Ladies; and the State Dining Room, which seats 140 guests. Carved into the fireplace mantel is a quotation by former President John Adams: "I Pray Heaven to Bestow the Best of Blessings on This House and All that shall hereafter Inhabit it. May none but Honest and Wise Men ever rule under this roof." Regardless of how one rates the results of this blessing, Adams's sincerity is unimpeachable.

The White House tour, which ends on the Main Portico facing Pennsylvania Avenue, is a favorite tourist attraction. To avoid the crowds, the best strategy is to call your senator or congressmen in advance for a guided VIP tour, held early in the morning before the White House is open to the general public (call far in advance for tours during the spring and summer months). Otherwise, the White House is open Tuesdays through Saturdays from 10 AM to noon. Tickets can be obtained at the East Gate in East Executive Park. From *Memorial Day* to *Labor Day* tickets with a specific time are issued beginning at 8 AM from a booth on the Ellipse just south of the White House. No admission charge. 1600 Pennsylvania Ave. NW (phone: 202-456-7041 or 202-472-3669).

After exiting the executive residence return to East Executive Park and continue along the east side of the White House. Pass through another gate to where East Executive Street meets E Street. Straight ahead is the Ellipse and the Washington Monument. It is on the north section of the Ellipse just ahead that the national *Christmas* tree is placed each year, drawing a festive crowd for its lighting by the president. Also on the 32-acre Ellipse are a number of softball fields.

The view from the south side of the White House is perhaps the best and most familiar. It was here that President Nixon boarded the presidential helicopter one last time after resigning his post in 1974. And it was here that we remember seeing President Kennedy scooping up his children after returning from a journey; and the image of President Reagan cupping his ears to the questions of newsmen as he boarded a helicopter waiting to whisk him off to California or Camp David.

Continue around the south lawn, hugging the sidewalk just outside the black iron fence. The 18-acre spot of greenery that surrounds the White House is also known as President's Park and is home to over 80 varieties of trees planted over the years by almost every presidential family. The giant elm within the central oval (on the south side) was planted by John Quincy Adams — a seedling from his home in Massachusetts. There is Andrew Jackson's magnolia from Tennessee, planted as a memorial to his wife. Gerald Ford's white pine and Richard Nixon's giant sequoia can be seen within the central oval. Even Amy Carter's tree house has survived two Republican administrations, shielded by a huge silver Atlas cedar.

A favorite of the White House grounds is the Kennedy Rose Garden, a re-creation of an 18th-century garden that was planted in 1913. Within the garden are osmanthus, boxwood hedges, tulips, chrysanthemums, and a number of other plantings. One can romp through the rose garden only during White House garden tours (in mid-April and mid-October) and during the annual *Easter Egg Roll,* when the White House grounds are deluged by children 8 and under bearing hard-boiled eggs and boundless energy (for more information, call 202-456-2200).

After rounding the south lawn to the gate of West Executive Drive (closed to the public), follow E Street to 17th Street. On the right is the rear of the Old Executive Office Building (OEOB), an extravagant French Second Empire structure that is one of Washington's most recognizable buildings. People either love it or hate it, with no small contingent representing the latter category (see below). On the left is a memorial obelisk dedicated to the army's First Infantry Divisions that served in World War II and Vietnam. Across the street is the *Corcoran Gallery* (see *Walk 5: Foggy Bottom*).

At 17th Street turn right. It will be a short jaunt back up to Pennsylvania Avenue from E Street. Notice the Federal Deposit Insurance Corporation (FDIC) across from the OEOB (Washingtonians love to speak in acronyms). The FDIC is the government agency that satisfies the claims of depositors when banks fail — unfortunately, the agency has been very busy of late. Also on the left, before Pennsylvania Avenue, is the Office of the US Trade Representative, which is responsible for setting trade policy and negotiating trade treaties with other nations. At Pennsylvania Avenue turn right. This stretch of sidewalk offers a better view of the OEOB.

Formerly hosting the Navy and the departments of War and State, this almost whimsical-looking structure was so disliked by sober Washingtonians at the time of its completion that nobody wanted to pay the architect, Alfred Mullett, his fee. But in time, the city developed a taste for the busy architectural vision of its creator. Today the OEOB is used for the offices of senior-level White House officials. Notice the two 5-inch brass trophy guns next to the front entrance. They were captured from the Spanish in Manila Bay by the US Navy as America successfully fought the Spanish for control of the Philippines, in 1898. A tour of the building's Victorian interior, various libraries, and treaty rooms requires some foresight, but is highly recommended. Reservations for Saturday tours should be made 2 weeks in advance on weekday mornings between 9 AM and noon (phone: 202-395-5895).

Across the street in the distinctive Second Empire–style building is the *Renwick Gallery,* the *Smithsonian Institution*'s showcase for American designs, crafts, and decorative arts. But overshadowing these exhibits — which are almost secondary by comparison but still no less interesting — are the second-floor galleries (the Octagon Room and the Grand Salon), which mimic a Victorian parlor from the late 19th century and include several oil paintings that are as big as highway billboards. Ease back into one of the sofas and take it all in. Many of these paintings are from the collection of William Corcoran, for whom the structure was built. However, Corcoran's collection grew so large that it had to be moved down the street to its present location on 17th Street. Open daily from 10 AM to 5:30 PM (phone: 202-357-2531).

Walking back toward Lafayette Square (opposite the White House), notice the cluster of early-19th-century townhouses on the left. The Blair-Lee Houses are brimming with history but, alas, as they are ideal guesthouses for the executive mansion, are open only to official guests of the president. Robert E. Lee was offered command of the Union army here by Abraham Lincoln, and refused; and when the White House was deemed unsafe for human habitation, Harry Truman lived in Blair House during the renovations.

Back to Lafayette Square. This pleasant park was designed by Pierre L'Enfant as the president's front yard. Thomas Jefferson, however, decided 80 acres were enough (and perhaps a bit too much to mow) and deeded much of the executive mansion's front yard to the city for use as a public park. Though named after George Washington's faithful sidekick, the real star of this park is Andrew Jackson, around whose prominent equestrian statue everything else in the park revolves (see *A Shutterbug's Washington* in DIVERSIONS). The Marquis de Lafayette's diminutive statue, depicting the fiery Frenchman standing before the French people asking them to support the American Revolution, is on the southeast corner. Other monuments in the park include ones commemorating Major General Comte de Rochambeau, another Frenchman who distinguished himself in the American Revolution at Yorktown; Brigadier General Thaddeus Kosciusko, the Polish-born hero responsible for the fortifications at West Point; and Baron Von Steuben, a Prussian who organized, trained, and drilled the army beginning at Valley Forge.

The row of townhouses along Jackson Place are attractive, and their proximity to the White House is no coincidence. The Carnegie Endowment for International Peace is at No. 700; the President's Drug Advisory Council at No. 708; and a public service organization that owes its name to a much-mocked line from an acceptance speech at a presidential convention, the Points of Light Foundation, is at No. 734. On the corner is the Decatur House (748 Jackson Pl. NW), one of the original homes built along Lafayette Square. This early-19th-century townhouse was built by the naval hero Commodore Stephen Decatur, who coined the line: "Our country! In her intercourse with foreign nations, may she always be in the right; but our country, right or wrong." Walk-in tours to see the spiral staircase, handsome woodwork, and Federal-period furniture are conducted every 30 minutes. The home's second-floor ballroom is a real treat. Admission charge (phone: 202-842-0920).

To the right on H Street is the US Chamber of Commerce Building, yet another of the city's ubiquitous Roman monstrosities, this one distinguished by the flags of nations. Formerly on this site facing Lafayette Square was a mansion in which Daniel Webster lived while he was Secretary of State. A bit farther down H Street on the other side of 16th Street is the charming, yellow St. John's Church, also known as the Church of Presidents, since every president since James Madison has attended services here (see *Historic Churches* in DIVERSIONS). Open daily. No admission charge. 16th and H Sts. NW (phone: 202-347-8766).

Return to Connecticut Avenue, on the northwest corner of Lafayette Square, and turn right. This leads to Farragut Square; surrounded by office buildings and *Metro* stops, it is one of the city's busiest areas. Crowds of professionals migrate around lunchtime and flood this tiny park. (It might as well be called Courier Square, since the city's fearless bike couriers also seem to congregate here.) On the square is the *Map Store,* which sells cartography covering every inch of the globe (1636 Eye St. NW; phone: 202-628-2608). Just before Farragut Square is the *Bombay Club* (815 Connecticut Ave. NW;

phone: 202-659-3727); a good Indian restaurant, it is a favorite among the local professional crowd for its central location and its kabob platter and green chili chicken.

After walking through Farragut Square, follow 17th Street due north for 1 block. At the corner of 17th and L Streets is the *Capitol Coin & Stamp Co.*, a wonderfully cluttered little shop that has a comprehensive assortment of political memorabilia (campaign buttons, posters, recorded speeches, photos, and presidential china) in addition to its staple of rare coins and paper money (phone: 202-296-0400).

In the next block on the left is the sumptuous, yellow-brick-and-limestone *Mayflower* hotel (see *DC's Best Digs* in DIVERSIONS), with its ornate, block-long lobby that will be this tour's passageway back over to the ritzy section of Connecticut Avenue. Pass through the *Mayflower* doors on the left into the lobby. If the Italian marble, the grand chandeliers, or the ornate ceilings and 23-karat gold leaf fail to impress, certainly the length of this lobby will not. Along the way to Connecticut Avenue is the hotel's *Café Promenade* and a display of photographs documenting the dignitaries who have chosen the *Mayflower* for their Washington stay, including Queen Elizabeth, de Gaulle, Churchill, the Shah of Iran, and Will Rogers. After reaching the other end of the lobby, note the hotel's resident *Cartier* shop, which sets the tone for what will be encountered on Connecticut Avenue. Walk to the right up Connecticut. There are a number of pricey emporia over the next several blocks.

Walk up to where Rhode Island Avenue and M Street split off of Connecticut Avenue. Turn right on M Street. The red brick cathedral with the green dome and intriguing mosaic over the entrance is St. Matthew's Cathedral, the seat of Washington's Catholic archbishop. But this Renaissance-style cathedral's most familiar association was with President John F. Kennedy. This is where Kennedy frequently worshiped and where his funeral mass was held (an inscription marks the spot of the casket). Open daily from 7 AM to 6 PM (phone: 202-347-3215). In the next block on M Street, between 17th and 16th Streets, is the *National Geographic Society Explorers Hall* (see *Museums* in THE CITY), the world headquarters of the society that funds global exploration and publishes the enormously popular journal, which has hardly changed over the last 100 years. The modern structure that houses the offices of the society also contains Explorers Hall and other exhibits of interest to the tourist. Within Explorers Hall are a number of items, including the sled Admiral Robert Peary used to reach the North Pole, dioramas depicting the lives of Southwest American cliff dwellers, and the giant, 11-foot, hand-painted, freestanding globe that has become the symbol of the Society. Just completed is "Geographica," an interactive center for the study of geography. Also, the publication desk has a world class selection of maps, atlases, and photography books. Open Mondays through Saturdays from 9 AM to 5 PM, Sundays from 10 AM to 5 PM. No admission charge. 17th Sts. and M Sts. NW (phone: 202-857-7588).

From the Explorers Hall, turn right on 17th Street and cross Rhode Island Avenue. On the right is the *B'nai B'rith Klutznick Museum,* which contains one of the largest collections of Jewish history in the US. Among the items on display are thousand-year-old coins and a 16th-century Torah wrapper. Open Mondays through Fridays and Sundays from 10 AM to 5 PM. Closed on Jewish holidays (phone: 202-857-6583).

From here a left on N Street is like stepping into a different era. *Washingtonian* magazine calls this the best block in the city. For a moment, the chaos of the surrounding thoroughfares is overshadowed by the elegance of this charming, tree-lined street, which hasn't heard — it seems — that Washington has turned into an urban jungle. On the left is the *Iron Gate Inn,* a former 19th-century stable now dedicated to Mediterranean cuisine. For ambience, this place can't be beat. The former stable — which once served the 19th-century buildings on the street — features the original horse stalls and hay racks, now converted into dining booths. The original fireplace is still intact and General Nelson Miles, one of the youngest generals ever — and a former owner of the buildings — is said to haunt the place. Mysteriously, a candle is oftentimes found burning at his table, and he frequently nips from the bottle of Southern Comfort behind the bar. The outdoor terrace is the crowning glory of the restaurant, with a grape arbor overhead and a clear view of the dome of St. Matthew's Cathedral. On any given night you may find one or several of Washington's political pundits (from "Face the Nation," the "Capitol Gang," or the "McLaughlin Group") dining here. It is also a favorite of controversial biographer Kitty Kelley. 1734 N St. NW (phone: 202-737-1370).

Across the street is the *Tabard Inn* (see *Checking In,* THE CITY), the oldest continuously operating hotel in Washington. Named after the famous hostelry in Chaucer's *Canterbury Tales,* it is a classic bed and breakfast establishment with 40 rooms, some with pianos, and many with working fireplaces. But the real treat for those who are not guests of the inn is the dimly lit, creaky-floored parlor filled with overstuffed sofas and chairs, antiques, and oil paintings. The inn's restaurant is casual, crowded, and continental, and emphasizes healthy, inventive dishes. The restaurant's produce comes from the *Tabard*'s own farm in Middletown, Virginia (1739 N St. NW; phone: 202-785-1277). Next door is the *Canterbury* (1733 N St. NW; phone: 202-393-3000 or 800-424-2950), an elegant and comfortable hotel that is on the site of the Little White House — the residence of Teddy Roosevelt. Each room has a comfortable sitting area and dressing room, and many other amenities.

Follow N Street west back to the bustling intersection of 18th Street, Connecticut Avenue, and N Street. Before heading up Connecticut to Dupont Circle, have a look into *Rand McNally,* one of the more fascinating shops on Connecticut Avenue. A wood-paneled enclave that is a veritable universe of maps, globes, travel literature, and sundry knicknacks with the globe motif, the shop carries anything and everything that is geography (1201 Connecticut Ave.; phone: 202-223-6751). Next door is *Joe & Mo's,* a favored Washington eatery among the power-lunch crowd. This basement restaurant features industrial-size steaks (1211 Connecticut Ave. NW; phone: 202-659-1211).

Now, make an about-face and follow Connecticut Avenue into Dupont Circle, which has been many things to many people through the years. Presently, it is a premier residential and commercial center along with being the nucleus of Washington's arts community, gay community, and a stomping ground of the local avant-garde. The circle is graced by the Dupont Fountain; it replaces a statue of Civil War Admiral Samuel Francis Dupont which was taken back to Delaware in the early 1900s by the Dupont family. Dupont Circle's benches, when not overrun by rogues and scalawags, are the domain of musicians, chess players, and political demonstrators. There is such a brimming cornucopia of shops, cafés, and galleries in this area that to do them justice would require a lengthy scroll. Certainly one stop should be at *Kramerbooks & Afterwords,* a bookstore and café that is open all night on weekends (1517 Connecticut Ave. NW; phone: 202-387-1400). Otherwise, spend some time wandering the area before exploring Massachusetts Avenue and the northern reaches of this downtown walking tour.

Massachusetts Avenue leads southeast from Dupont Circle to Scott Circle, which interrupts 16th Street in its path to the White House. Along the stretch of Massachusetts between 18th and 17th Streets on the right is the SAIS (School of Advanced International Studies), the arm of Johns Hopkins University for graduate students interested in international studies. Also in this block are several embassies and embassy chanceries: the Chilean Chancery, the Turkish Chancery, and the embassies of Trinidad and Tobago, and Peru. After passing by the statue of the great legislator Daniel Webster on the right, the confusion visible ahead is the intersection of Massachusetts and Rhode Island Avenues. On the right is the headquarters of the National Rifle Association (NRA), one of the strongest lobbying associations in America. The NRA works to fight against any form of gun-control legislation or restrictions on the right of Americans to bear arms (the relevant passage in the Constitution appears on the building's front). Regardless of what side of the issue you stand, a browse through the *National Firearms Museum* (which allows no smoking, by the way) may be of interest. On display is President Eisenhower's 20-gauge shotgun, a collection of muskets, competition firearms, and the mounted heads of wild boars, lions, and such that to their chagrin found themselves in the path of someone exercising his or her constitutional right to bear arms. Open daily from 10 AM to 4 PM. 1600 Rhode Island Ave. NW (phone: 202-828-6000).

Continue down Massachusetts Avenue through the circle, pausing for a few moments on the bridge spanning 16th Street. Look to the south down 16th Street: The White House can be seen in the distance. Lafayette Square is in the foreground, the Washington Monument in the background. With cars bounding up an incline to a traffic light in the immediate foreground, this is one of those Washington street scenes wrought with uncanny balance and symbolism.

After crossing over the intersection of Massachusetts Avenue and 15th Street, the *Madison* hotel will be seen on the right (see *DC's Best Digs* in DIVERSIONS). It's worth a short detour to stroll through its public rooms, rich with antique treasures. In the lobby is a rare Chinese Imperial altar table, black lacquered and inset with a porcelain plaque; and a Louis XVI palace commode, cartel clock, and gold leaf girandole mirror. This spot is a favorite of visiting heads of state and features a top-security floor, once favored by Soviet delegations. 1177 15th St. NW (phone: 202-862-1600).

Go left out of the *Madison* and continue down 15th Street. Across the street are the offices of one of America's most respected newspapers, *The Washington Post.* Its dogged investigative coverage during Watergate — a scandal that the *Post* was largely responsible for breaking to the American people — and its publication of the Pentagon Papers boosted the newspaper into national prominence. Forty-five-minute tours through the building for individuals or groups include the newsroom, pressroom, and museum. Tours are available Mondays and Thursdays from 10 AM to 3 PM. 1150 15th St. NW (phone: 202-334-7969).

At L Street turn right and go back 1 block to 16th Street, and then turn left (toward the White House). There are several points of measured interest in this next block. The *Jefferson* hotel (see *DC's Best Digs* in DIVERSIONS) with its Federal-style façade sits proudly on the right. The hotel's *Hunt Club* is a preferred venue for an early evening cocktail (16th and M Sts. NW; phone: 202-347-2200). On the opposite side of the street is the stately Russian Embassy, a charming old ivy-covered, stone building that is much more active now than when its Soviet diplomats adopted the bunker mentality for the Cold War.

On the corner of the next block is the *Capital Hilton,* a good hotel that is centrally located. On the north side of the hotel on the lower level is *Trader Vic's,* replete with this worldwide chain's traditional decor of jungle kitsch. 16th and K St. NW (phone: 202-393-1000).

Continue down 16th Street. On the right just off of 16th Street (it's actually at 1600 Eye Street) is the Tuckerman House, a late-19th-century Romanesque dwelling. Before reaching Lafayette Square there is the *Hay-Adams,* thought by many to be Washington's best hotel (see *DC's Best Digs* in DIVERSIONS). Few dispute this point. The location, amenities, ambience, and staid history make this Italian Renaissance building, which is a pleasure to behold, top flight by anybody's standards (16th and H Sts. NW; phone: 202-638-6600). After reaching Lafayette Square again, turn left on H Street. At the corner of H Street and Madison Place is the Dolley Madison House, another original building on the square (not open to the public), which was the home of the widowed former First Lady until she died in 1849. The building is now part of the Claims Court complex.

Instead of turning right on Madison Place, cross over it by remaining on H Street until reaching 15th Street. Notice the Southern Building just across the intersection, designed in 1912 by the renowned American architect Daniel Burnham. Though Burnham displayed great restraint with this building, he seemed to channel his creative energies into its wildly decorative cornice. The Southern Building is now an office building. Walk down 15th Street (to the right).

On the left is *Prime Plus,* a restaurant featuring new American food such as grilled venison, and a slew of salmon dishes. Within a short walk of the *National Theater,* the pre-theater dinner at this rather formal restaurant is first-rate (727 15th St. NW; phone: 202-783-0166). Farther down 15th Street is the modern incarnation of a true Washington institute, the *Old Ebbitt Grill* (see *Eating Out,* THE CITY). The *Old Ebbitt* in one form or another — it has been a boarding house, a saloon, and a restaurant — has been wandering around Washington like a nomad since its founding in 1856. It was acquired in 1970 by the Clyde's restaurant chain — along with its collection of antique beer steins and animal heads (reputedly bagged by Teddy Roosevelt). It then became the *Old Ebbitt Grill* — and has prospered ever since. This place is definitely worth a visit for breakfast, Sunday brunch, dinner, or just a gander at the big game. 675 15th St. NW (phone: 202-347-4800).

The Italian Renaissance building that sits on the corner of the next block down (Pennsylvania Avenue) is the *Washington* hotel, a grand matron of Washington hostelries. Possibly every 20th-century American president and scores of national and international dignitaries have stayed here. One of its best features is its rooftop terrace, the *Sky Terrace,* which offers great views of the White House, the Treasury, and the Mall area — a delightful backdrop at cocktail time or any time. 515 15th St. NW (phone: 202-638-5900).

Turn left at Hamilton Place onto Pennsylvania Avenue. Ahead towers one of Washington's cherished landmarks: the *Willard Inter-Continental* hotel (see *DC's Best Digs* in DIVERSIONS). The intricate craftsmanship that went into this imposing marble Beaux Arts building is awe-inspiring. This establishment has played almost as important a role in the affairs of the executive branch as has its neighbor, the White House — it has served as the temporary home for 10 presidents-elect. Have a look at Peacock Alley, where the term "lobbyist" was coined (15th St. and Pennsylvania Ave. NW; phone: 202-628-9100). Before reaching the canopied entrance, but still in the *Willard* complex, there is the *Occidental Bar & Grill* (see *Capital Dining* in DIVERSIONS), a watering hole for power brokers. The grilled swordfish is a staple in the diet of our nation's legislature (1475 Pennsylvania Ave. NW; phone: 202-783-1475). The upscale shops in this complex are worth a look. Venture over to the appealing tuft of green in front of the hotel. Pershing Park has a glimmering pool that becomes a skating rink in the winter, a cluster of trees, and a kiosk. Beyond this park is the District Building, an overblown Beaux Arts affair that houses the administration of the District of Columbia.

Walk through the passageway that houses the shops of the *Willard* complex, and turn right on F Street. On the right side of the next corner is the National Press Club Building which, with the recent installation of shops formally called *The Shops at National Place,* is known now as much for its consumer spending opportunities as for a forum where the Fourth Estate — the press — comes in contact with the members of the first three estates (1331 Pennsylvania Ave. NW; phone: 202-783-9090). After returning to the street, follow 14th Street back down to Pennsylvania Avenue. On the left is *J.W. Marriott* (1331 Pennsylvania Ave. NW; phone: 202-393-2000), the flagship of this locally based hotel chain, which stares down its rival, the *Willard,* across 14th Street.

Just past the *Marriott* is the *National Theater* (1321 Pennsylvania Ave. NW; for tickets, call 800-233-3123; for information, call 202-628-6161). First established in 1835, the *National* is one of the oldest continually operating theater organizations in America. Nevertheless, it wasn't until a comprehensive renovation in 1984 that the theater's earlier glory was recaptured. Though it specializes in musicals, recent performances have included Joan Collins in *Private Lives* and Raul Julia in *Man of La Mancha* (1321 Pennsylvania Ave. NW; phone: 202-628-6161; also see *Washington Theater* in DIVER-

SIONS). Next to the *National* is the *Warner Theater,* which began as a venue for vaudeville but later became a movie house and now stages concerts under its gilded ceiling.

Return to Pennsylvania Avenue via 13th Street on the east end of an intriguing, block-long plaza known as Freedom Plaza. It is here that Pennsylvania Avenue comes into full view. This street has borne witness to the emotional rollercoaster ride of American history, from the victory parade following World War I in which Union and Confederate veterans marched together for the first time, and the parade led by Dwight Eisenhower after victory in World War II, to the riderless horse leading the slain John F. Kennedy's funeral cortege. It has hosted demonstrations of angry farmers, blacks, women demanding equality, and many other groups feeling betrayed by Washington. It is also along this path that the president rides — or walks, in the case of President Carter — between the Capitol and the White House on inauguration day.

Indeed, it was largely one inauguration journey in particular that contributed to the avenue's rebirth, after its post–World War II decline. Looking out upon a combat zone of liquor stores, abandoned buildings, and downtrodden masses, President Kennedy commented to an aide on the deplorable state of the avenue. And setting the tone for the New Frontier, he added: "Fix it."

Pennsylvania Avenue's renaissance was inspired by Kennedy's conviction, and the conviction of many others to follow, who believed this American Champs-Elysées should indeed be transformed. A centerpiece of this redevelopment is the Old Post Office Building, the gorgeous Romanesque edifice across the street, with the clock tower. In addition to the government offices that remain on the upper floors, the building's pavilion has been converted into the city's most dazzling indoor mall (called the *Old Post Office Pavilion*). Definitely worth a look (1100 Pennsylvania Ave. NW; phone: 202-289-4224). Directly behind the Old Post Office is the dreaded Internal Revenue Service (IRS).

Just past the Old Post Office is 10th Street. A slight, 1½-block diversion up 10th Street from Pennsylvania Avenue leads to the infamous *Ford's Theater* (511 10th St. NW; phone: 202-426-6924; also see *National Theater* in DIVERSIONS) on the right, where President Lincoln was assassinated. After that fateful night in April 1865, the theater was closed for 100 years. It was reopened in the late 1960s and today hosts professional productions of contemporary plays. The box in which Lincoln sat when he was shot is draped with a flag. In the basement is a collection of personal mementos of the slain president and his assassin, including the murder weapon, the suit of clothes that Lincoln wore when shot, and the flag that was draped over his casket. Across the street is the Peterson House, the house in which Lincoln died. Self-guided tours of the house's first floor, which is decorated in period furnishings, are available. Open daily from 9 AM to 5 PM. 516 10th St. NW (phone: 202-426-6830).

Farther up 10th Street and to the right on F Street are a number of hip and progressive music clubs, including the *9:30 Club* (930 F St. NW; phone: 202-393-0930), in a dilapidated storefront; and the *Fifth Column* (915 F St. NW; phone: 202-393-3632), a 3-story juke joint and art gallery. On E Street is DC's favorite bohemian hangout, *DC Space,* a bar and café with great live jazz/blues/punk music and good burgers and vegetarian dishes (443 7th St. and E St. NW; phone: 202-347-1445). If you're not in the mood for slam-dancing, return to Pennsylvania Avenue for the completion of this downtown walking tour.

The rather institutional building on the left after returning to Pennsylvania Avenue is the J. Edgar Hoover Building, just across from the monolithic Department of Justice. Headquarters of the Federal Bureau of Investigation, one of Washington's favorite tours is conducted here. The free tour includes a visit to high-tech laboratories, exhibitions chronicling the FBI's history from the Dillinger days to today's techniques, plus a popular firearms demonstration by a special agent. Tours are Mondays through Fridays from 8:45 AM to 4:15 PM. Enter on E St. (phone: 202-324-3447).

And, finally, diagonally across Pennsylvania Avenue toward the Capitol is a stout building that marks the end of this walking tour of downtown. The *National Archives,* in addition to being our nation's file cabinet and safe deposit box, is the resting place of the great documents that are the cornerstone on which our republic is founded: the Declaration of Independence, the Bill of Rights, and the US Constitution (see *Quintessential Washington* in DIVERSIONS and *Walk 1: The Mall and Monuments*). Open daily from 10 AM to 5:30 PM in the fall and winter, and from 10 AM to 9 PM from April to *Labor Day.*

Walk 4: Northwest/Embassy Row

As the beneficiaries of the golden age of capitalism began to prosper as never before, the capital city's upper crust needed a district in which to distance themselves from their harried offices and the more cramped dwellings of downtown — while remaining within a croquet shot of civilization. Undoubtedly, it was their occasional outings to the pastoral northwest that led them to think this area wouldn't be a bad place to build. And what homes they built. The northwest quadrant of DC was, until well into this century, the city's backyard. Development was slow. For most of the 19th century, Northwest (now recognized by its capital letter) was an enormous picnic ground that was only now and again crisscrossed by dusty, desolate paths. It was an ideal place to cavort amid its gently rolling hills, throw a spread, and ignore, if just for an afternoon, the enormous in-basket of the nation's business.

President Grover Cleveland, in a tradition set by President Martin Van Buren, "summered" in Northwest. He was so taken with the tranquillity of the cool breeze that comes with the elevation that, during his administration, he bought a country house to escape the fabled heat and humidity of the District. Washington summers are characterized by an oppressive stickiness that has caused many presidents to flee the White House for long stretches during the hottest months. Though Cleveland wanted to keep his anonymity, his neighbors welcomed his arrival with fanfare, naming the area Cleveland Park (more about this later). The president's name lent a certain cachet to the area — the first iron truss bridge was built over Rock Creek, allowing trolley cars to cross — and the rush for development was on. Northwest is now home to a historic residential district, the sprawling National Zoo — home to two of Washington's most popular residents, the pandas — and the Washington Cathedral, the city's highest building, on Mount St. Albans. Cleveland Park represents the outer limits of this rather long walking tour, which will require about 5 hours.

A row of dazzling Beaux Arts dwellings and masterful mansions emerged west of Dupont Circle. Custom-built for lavish living and entertainment, each was a testament to the carefree era before FDR had to apply the brakes of regulation to the runaway freight train of free enterprise. This area is known as Kalorama, the name of the area's first estate and country house, built in 1807 by businessman and diplomat Joel Barlow (US Consul to Algiers from 1795 to 1797). The name "Kalorama," taken from the Greek word meaning

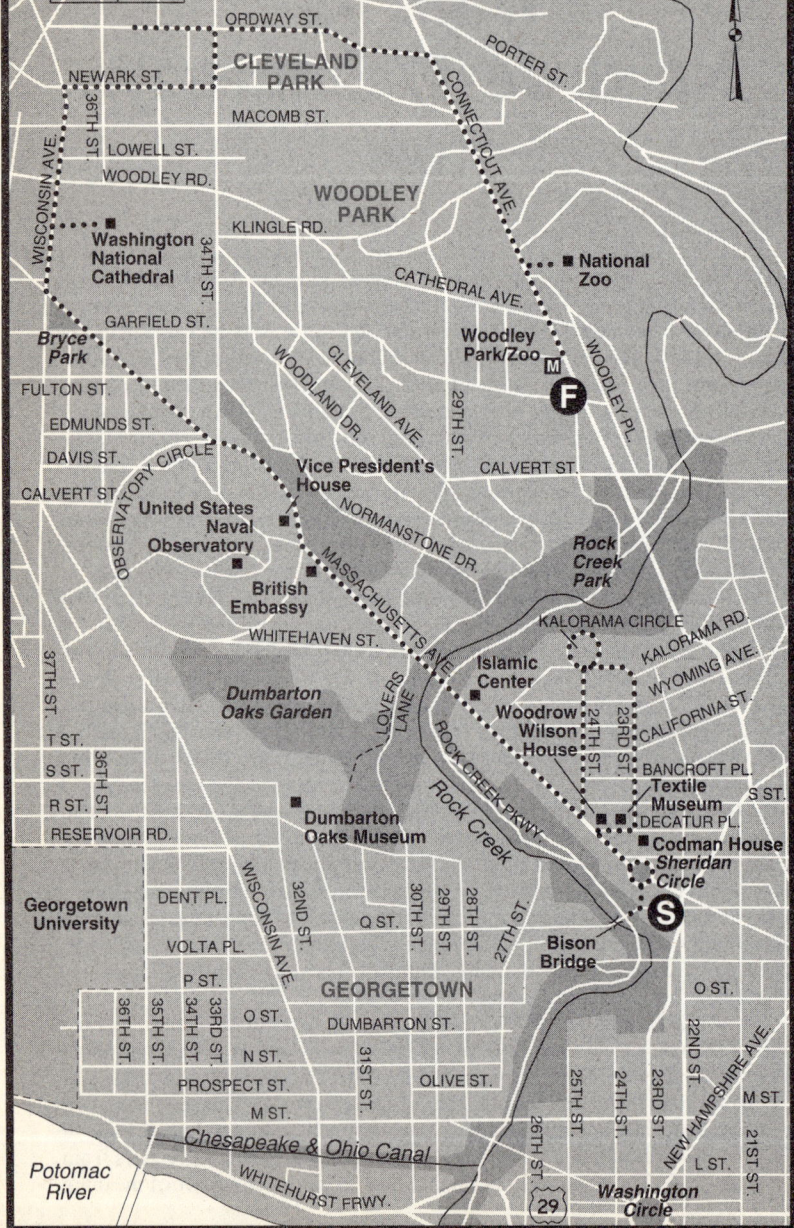

Northwest/Embassy Row

N

0 — miles — 1/4

ORDWAY ST.

PORTER ST.

CLEVELAND PARK

NEWARK ST.

MACOMB ST.

36TH ST.

WISCONSIN AVE.

LOWELL ST.

WOODLEY RD.

WOODLEY PARK

KLINGLE RD.

CONNECTICUT AVE.

CATHEDRAL AVE.

■ National Zoo

Washington National Cathedral

34TH ST.

Woodley Park/Zoo

M
F

WOODLEY PL.

GARFIELD ST.

Bryce Park

FULTON ST.

EDMUNDS ST.

DAVIS ST.

CALVERT ST.

WOODLAND DR.

CLEVELAND AVE.

29TH ST.

CALVERT ST.

Vice President's House

OBSERVATORY CIRCLE

United States Naval Observatory

NORMANSTONE DR.

Rock Creek Park

British Embassy

MASSACHUSETTS AVE.

WHITEHAVEN ST.

KALORAMA CIRCLE

KALORAMA RD.

WYOMING AVE.

37TH ST.

Dumbarton Oaks Garden

LOVERS LANE

Islamic Center

CALIFORNIA ST.

T ST.

S ST.

R ST.

36TH ST.

Woodrow Wilson House

24TH ST.

23RD ST.

BANCROFT PL.

Textile Museum

S ST.

RESERVOIR RD.

ROCK CREEK PKWY.

DECATUR PL.

Codman House

Dumbarton Oaks Museum

Rock Creek

Sheridan Circle

S

Georgetown University

DENT PL.

WISCONSIN AVE.

32ND ST.

Q ST.

30TH ST.

29TH ST.

28TH ST.

27TH ST.

Bison Bridge

VOLTA PL.

P ST.

O ST.

22ND ST.

O ST.

NEW HAMPSHIRE AVE.

36TH ST.

35TH ST.

34TH ST.

33RD ST.

GEORGETOWN

DUMBARTON ST.

31ST ST.

25TH ST.

24TH ST.

23RD ST.

22ND ST.

M ST.

N ST.

OLIVE ST.

PROSPECT ST.

21ST ST.

M ST.

L ST.

Chesapeake & Ohio Canal

WHITEHURST FRWY.

26TH ST.

29

Washington Circle

Potomac River

"beautiful view," is apt, since the area looked out across the capital and the Potomac River to northern Virginia.

The Stock Market crash of 1929 and the ensuing Depression severely depleted the bank accounts of many of these proud homeowners. A number of the palatial mansions were sadly divided into apartments or, less regrettably, sold intact for use as embassies. In fact, the influx of foreign delegations was so pervasive that today the corridor along Massachusetts Avenue is known as Embassy Row. It is from Sheridan Circle, the heart of Embassy Row, that this walking tour begins.

Sheridan Circle is just a few blocks to the northwest from Dupont Circle, up Massachusetts Avenue. This main thoroughfare slices diagonally through 3 blocks between Dupont and Sheridan Circles. Though it was not conceived by Pierre L'Enfant, it represents everything the French city planner revered in a circle. It is a small, prim park at the nucleus of radial avenues that branch off in all directions. In the center is an equestrian statue of the circle's namesake, General Philip Sheridan, Commander of the Union Army of the Shenandoah. The statue's sculptor, Gutzon Borglum (who also carved the presidential portraits on Mount Rushmore), features Sheridan sitting atop his favorite mount.

Begin to orbit the circle along the outside sidewalk, noting the subdued splendor of the architecture of the surrounding mansions. There was little that was subdued here on September 21, 1976. It was here that Chilean Ambassador Orlando Letelier and his aide Ronni Karpen Moffitt were killed when a remote-controlled bomb destroyed their car. The Chilean secret police and army officials were later implicated in the assassination. A small memorial rests on the outside curb of the southeast quadrant of the circle.

Walk just short of one revolution around the circle and note the Turkish and Romanian embassies with their mammoth antennae; reminiscent of designs from their homeland, they look like enormous beach umbrellas stripped of their fabric.

You may want to take a jaunt down to Q Street, the same direction General Sheridan seems to be gazing. Spanning Rock Creek and leading into Georgetown is the impressive Bison Bridge (its official name is Dumbarton Bridge), which features four sculpted bison. (That's bison, not buffalo. Exacting paleontologists will tell you with a sniff that the massive beast that native Americans drove over cliffs in herds is actually a bison.) From here you can see the Washington Monument poking above buildings on the left; the spires of the Washington Cathedral are visible on the right. The perpetual hum of traffic of Rock Creek Parkway is underneath.

The bridge's arches are supported by copper Indian heads in full headdress, sculpted by Glenn Brown from a life mask of Sioux Indian Chief Kicking Bear. Don't attempt to dangle over the side to find them (remember what happened to the bison); they are more safely visible from the green handrail just to the right before reaching the bridge, or from Rock Creek Parkway, below.

Head back to Sheridan Circle, noticing the stately Turkish Embassy on the left, a villa originally built for Edward Everett, the inventor of the bottle cap. Conveniently, Massachusetts Avenue separates the Turkish and Greek embassies, which are at an uncomfortable proximity to each other considering their historical animosity. And the embassy of Cyprus, the Aegean island that has long been the focus of dispute between these two countries, lies equidistant from the Turks and the Greeks on R Street. On the right is the attractive Romanian Embassy and an adjoining chancery building.

After reaching the circle, walk left on the outer sidewalk. On the left is the Mediterranean-style *Barney Studio House* (2306 Massachusetts Ave.; phone: 202-357-3111), which features the works and artifacts of bohemian/heiress Alice Pike Barney and her artist friends. At the turn of the century, Barney complained that America's capital city was a cultural wasteland — and decided to do something about it. Her home, the second to be built on Sheridan Circle, became a meeting place for Washington's cultural elite.

After rounding Sheridan Circle to the left, start up Massachusetts Avenue to the northwest. This is Embassy Row's Main Street. Though security is tight and the limos, blue suits, and attaché cases are aplenty, stroll through this neighborhood slowly; enjoy its splendid and occasionally eclectic architecture, its cosmopolitan feel, its United Nations of national banners, the aromas of a cornucopia of cuisines, and, perhaps, pedestrians sporting a turban, an African gown, or exotic footwear of jewelry from the far reaches of the globe. Embassy Row is truly a global village.

On the right when heading up Massachusetts Avenue are the Chilean, Haitian, and Pakistani embassies. Before going right on Decatur Street, notice the Cameroon Embassy (2349 Massachusetts Ave.). This ornate mansion — with a cone-shaped turret, extraordinary detail, and always a fleet of limousines out front — is one of the most overwhelming buildings on Embassy Row. The showiness is limited to the structure, however: Cameroon is a West African nation from which rarely a peep is heard.

Walk down Decatur Place about a block to a delightful stone and concrete staircase framed by gas lamps on either side and crowned by a quietly trickling lion's head fountain. The staircase is known as the Decatur Terrace Steps (also referred to by some area residents as the Spanish Steps because of its vague resemblance to the Piazza di Spagna in Rome).

But before heading up the steps, have a look at the mansion to the immediate right. This is the Codman House (2145 Decatur Pl.), built in 1907 as a Washington residence for Miss Martha Codman, a spinster until the age of 72 when she married a Russian tenor who was half her age. Codman was "of Boston and Newport" — a delightful designation that was the seal of good breeding in her day. Codman House is a deep-red brick, 4-story townhouse with stone panels of festoons between the second- and third-floor windows. The house was later sold to Dwight Davis, who aside from being a former Governor of the Philippines is best remembered for donating the *Davis Cup* to the sport of tennis. Scheduled for "condo-ization" in the late 1970s, the house was fortunately bought by a neighbor and now is in the safe harbor of the National Register of Historic Places.

Climb the steps to S Street. Ahead is the exclusive Kalorama district. Architecture buffs should walk the length of 23rd Street ahead to a Tudor mansion built in 1911 for the mining magnate W. W. Lawrence. One of the more spectacular buildings in this posh area (2122 Kalorama Rd), today, it is the residence of the French ambassador. Proceed left down Kalorama Road to Kalorama Circle for a real *kalorama* (beautiful view), in the Greek sense, down into Rock Creek Park. Return to S Street via 24th Street.

There are two museums to the left, the *Woodrow Wilson House* and the *Textile Museum,* which will allow you to dawdle a bit before the long march deep into Northwest Washington.

After their years as the nation's chief executive — what Thomas Jefferson called "splendid misery" — most American presidents can't get far enough away from the White House. Just consider our living presidents. Reagan and Nixon fled to California. Carter went to Georgia. And Gerald Ford rarely steps off the golf course. Woodrow Wilson, the nation's 21st president, is the only commander in chief to stay in Washington after leaving the White House. The Georgian Revival house in which he and his wife lived after serving 2 terms — during which he led the country through World War I — is on the right (2340 S St.; phone: 202-387-4062). Considering Wilson's tireless effort in establishing the League of Nations and his efforts at expanding America's role in international affairs, it is altogether fitting that he relocated in the Embassy Row district. On display are his library, the dining room, bedrooms, a solarium overlooking a garden, and many personal effects such as the typewriter he used to compose speeches. Only guided tours are available and take roughly 45 minutes. Open Tuesdays through Sundays from 10 AM to 4 PM.

Several doors down from the *Woodrow Wilson House,* on the same side of the street, is a great temple to the art of weaving. The *Textile Museum* (2320 S St.; phone: 202-667-0441) features woven goods of both artistic and archaeological significance. It is one of only two museums in the world devoted entirely to woven rugs and fabrics, and the sundry exhibits will keep the Oriental/Navajo/Persian rug aficionado enthralled with the endless yarns that have been spun about things woven. Even if your interest in the field runs no deeper than getting a good buy on something to cover that stain on the den rug, this may be the place. (The prices may cause you to knit your brows, though.) Return past the *Woodrow Wilson House* to Massachusetts Avenue. On the left at the intersection is a statue of the Irish patriot Robert Emmett, dedicated in 1966 to mark the 50th anniversary of Irish independence. Make a right on Massachusetts, the broad avenue that will lead past the Japanese Embassy, the British Embassy, the vice president's home, and up Mount St. Albans to Washington National Cathedral.

Just past the intersection with California Street, the Japanese Embassy is on the left. (Try to ignore the gray, colossal, and rather ugly administrative building next door.) The plans the American architects conjured up for this neo-Georgian embassy house, with a cobblestone courtyard surrounded by a row of trees and a concave arch above the balcony that suggests the rising sun, were submitted to the emperor himself for approval. The Son of Heaven gave his nod to this headquarters on foreign soil, which harmonizes a touch of Nippon into the surroundings.

The street signs along here are instructive, noting the embassies that are located on the adjoining side streets.

Farther up Massachusetts Avenue on the right is still another architectural style from yet another corner of the globe. The *Islamic Center,* a.k.a. "the Mosque," is the most distinctive building on Embassy Row and provides a place of prayer for the diplomatic missions in Washington that represent nearly 40 predominantly Islamic countries. The faithful are called to prayer five times a day. Anybody is invited into the mosque, which faces Mecca; its lush interior is replete with thick Persian carpets (there are no chairs) and intricate Turkish tiles that grace the walls. Visitors must keep with custom, though, for this is a house of worship. No shoes (leave them at the entrance), shorts, short sleeves, or bare female heads. Head coverings are provided before entering (2551 Massachusetts Ave.; phone: 202-332-8343).

After crossing over Glover Bridge, which spans Rock Creek Park and pokes into what is officially the Northwest, note a series of Latin American embassies on the left. The most striking — some would say appalling — is the Brazilian Embassy. This strange building looks like a top-heavy ice cube that somehow keeps from melting.

The British Embassy is not far along on the left. A statue of Winston Churchill, giving the "V"-for-victory sign while flashing his impish grin, extends greetings and salutations. Interestingly, this statue places the former British prime minister straddling the boundary between British and American territory. According to several choice United Nations treaties, Churchill's right leg is in America, his left leg is in the United Kingdom. Sir Winston considered the idea smashing; after all, his mother was an American, his father a Brit. The British Embassy, with its Queen Anne architecture and stately English country house look, is the quintessential diplomatic residence. The elegance of the building — home to the second-largest diplomatic mission in the world — and the Rolls-Royces parked out front may understandably leave one humming a few bars of "Rule Britannia." Notice the authentic, fire-engine red British telephone booth in front of the embassy annex next door.

Across the street is a garden and fountain dedicated as a memorial in May 1991 to the Arab poet and philosopher Kahlil Gibran. His book *The Prophet,* which has sold millions of copies, is a moving contribution to cultural and religious understanding. Among the passages inscribed in stone is this one: "We live only to discover beauty. All else is a form of waiting." If you have yet to behold the beauty of the surroundings from this memorial, just wait on a circular bench. It should come to you very soon. After spending a few pensive moments drinking in Kahlil's poignant prose, continue up Massachusetts Avenue.

Just beyond the British Embassy is the visitors' entrance to the United States Naval Observatory — unfortunately, an often overlooked Washington attraction. In addition to maintaining the plush, pastoral surroundings, the work of the observatory is to provide the most accurate time and astronomical information for air, space, and sea navigation. Tours include a look at the clocks that keep the most accurate time on the planet (a good place to set your own watch) and the telescopes that track planetary positions. Due to the sensitivity of some of the instruments, Massachusetts Avenue gives the Naval Observatory a wide berth, ensuring that the occasional rumbling dump truck won't send the world's navigation into disarray. 34th St. and Massachusetts Ave. NW (phone: 202-653-1543).

Follow Massachusetts Avenue uphill as it rounds the Observatory grounds. The vice president's house comes into view on the left — a late Victorian mansion with a turret, dormers, and a surrounding porch the size of an Indiana corn field. First occupied by the superintendent of the Navy Observatory when completed in 1893, it became the home of the Secretary of the Navy in 1928. It wasn't until 1974 that it was officially designated the residence of the VP. Since Nelson Rockefeller, Jr., preferred to live in his own rather comfortable area home, Walter Mondale was the first vice president to live here full-time. After an appropriation of over $300,000 for repairs, the Bushes discovered that the roof still leaked.

After an additional $240,000 in repairs during his residence — and at least $578,000 in repairs recorded during the Quayles' stay — rumor has it that the ceiling no longer drips and the damp streaks have disappeared from the living room wall. After the enormous anchor at the employee entrance of the Naval Observatory, you will reach Wisconsin Avenue, which begins the climb up Mount St. Albans toward Washington National Cathedral.

The chunk of terra firma at the intersection of Massachusetts Avenue and Wisconsin was thought to yield the best view of the capital city, according to James Bryce, a British ambassador in the early part of this century. That was before a cluster of rather unseemly townhouses took root. After a glowing magazine article that he wrote about the spot was recently uncovered, a triangular park was named for him here. Bryce Park is an excellent place to rest after having made the gradual — but persistent — climb to the District's highest point.

Before venturing into the many treasures of the Washington Cathedral (which must have caught your attention by now), you may want to first explore the treasures of one of several good restaurants in the next block of Wisconsin Avenue. First up on the left is *Primavera,* a rather pricey Italian place with both indoor dining and an inner courtyard. Recommended dishes include fried calamari, swordfish, and *tiramisù* (3700 Massachusetts Ave.; phone: 202-342-0224). Much less expensive and certainly less formal is the *Zebra Room* which, true to its name, is clad in zebra wallpaper. The *Zebra Room* has featured half-price pizza every Tuesday and Thursday evening since the early 1960s and is usually packed with a loyal clientele. A memorial plaque for a late customer tells it all: "Every Tuesday night he enjoyed beer, his friends, and pizza here. In that order" (3238 Wisconsin Ave.; phone: 202-362-8307). Across Macomb Street is the *Cactus Cantina,* offering laudable Tex-Mex food in a festive, neon-saturated environment (3300 Wisconsin Ave.; phone: 202-686-7222). For classic Thai cuisine, try *Thai Flavor* next door (3709 Macomb St.; phone: 202-966-0200).

Now, return down Wisconsin Avenue to the piéce de résistance of the Northwest walking tour: the Cathedral Church of St. Peter and St. Paul. Never mind the highfalutin' moniker. Ordinary folks in these parts just call it the National Cathedral. There is nothing ordinary about the building, though. It is a dramatic, twin-towered Gothic cathedral that is the closest thing to a national church in the US. Originally the idea of George Washington, it took nearly 100 years to germinate and nearly 100 more to be fully realized.

A fund drive began in 1893 and actual construction began in 1907 by a firm that, over the years, always maintained a stable of technicians able to build with limestone in the Gothic style of the 14th century. The cathedral, which is the sixth-largest in the world, was finally consecrated in September 1990. It's got everything for the Gothic-lover: gargoyles, grotesques, flying buttresses, stained glass, and spires that tickle the heavens. Don't miss the observatory in the west tower, a stroll in the Bishop's Garden (to the south), or a browse in the Herb Cottage (Wisconsin Ave. at Woodley Rd.; phone: 202-537-6200; see also *Historic Churches* in DIVERSIONS).

Amble up Wisconsin Avenue several blocks to Newark Street, and turn right. This area is the Cleveland Park Historic District, one of the District of Columbia's loveliest neighborhoods.

Home now to well-to-do lawyers, bureaucrats, and journalists (the city's three main professions), it was on Newark Street that President Grover Cleveland built a country house (now long gone). By the turn of the century, Cleveland Park became a full-time suburban community, attracting several noteworthy architects who built the gorgeous, large frame houses with front and back porches, an occasional turret, and gazebos that can still be seen today.

Walk down to 3501 Newark Street. This farmhouse, built by General Uriah Forrest, dates from 1740. Known as Rosedale, it was where George Washington and Major L'Enfant dined when they were working on the boundary plans for the 10-square-mile federal district.

Turn left on 34th Street, and left again on Ordway Street. On the right is a bizarre dwelling (3411 Ordway; it may take some searching to find) that was designed by architect I. M. Pei as a favor to his friend and business partner, William Slayton. Some locals claim that it is a testament to Pei's genius and benevolence that he kept this house out of view. A cluster of houses at the end of the block, built by the Faulkners, a family of architects, is worth a look.

Return down Ordway Street east to Connecticut Avenue. Go right on Connecticut; the next block features a number of pubs, restaurants, bookstores, and the *Cineplex Odeon and Uptown Theater* (just *Uptown Theater* to locals), which features blockbuster classics such as *Gone With the Wind, Lawrence of Arabia,* and other epics where they were meant to be shown — on the big screen (3426 Connecticut Ave.; phone: 202-244-0880). Farther down the street is *Ireland's Four Provinces,* a cavernous drinking haunt with Gaelic musicians, Harp beer on tap, and plenty of corned beef and cabbage (3412 Connecticut Ave.; phone: 202-244-0860). Across the street is *Roma's,* an Italian restaurant with a Romanesque courtyard, bubbling fountain, and tables shaded by a grape arbor. Weather permitting, request to sit outside (3419 Connecticut Ave.; phone: 202-363-6611). *Vace,* near the end of the block on the left, is an Italian deli with fresh pasta, sauces, pizza, and the wine to wash it all down (3504 Connecticut Ave.; phone: 202-363-1999).

Continue down Connecticut Avenue past the DC branch library on the right to the last stop on the Embassy Row/Northwest walking tour. Several blocks down on the left — the signs will guide you in — is the National Zoological Park (better known as the National Zoo). Located in Rock Creek Park (where, incidentally, Teddy Roosevelt used to take his strenuous walks), the expansive, 163-acre zoo is one of Washington's most prized treasures.

Relatively humane — since its enormity gives its 4,000 residents plenty of room to move about upon land and water that simulate their natural habitats — the zoo boasts a population of elephants, giraffes, gorillas, jaguars, and the Great Flight Cage, filled with exotic birds. But the undisputed celebrity inhabitants are Ling-Ling and Hsing-Hsing, two giant pandas that were gifts of the People's Republic of China. Washingtonians have kept a close eye on the pair through numerous tries (and failures) at parenting. In fact, there is even a photo display of the two trying to procreate in all sorts of X-rated positions! Entering from Connecticut Avenue, a brief walk leads to their home, to the *Panda Café,* and to a shop with a wealth of panda paraphernalia (3000 block of Connecticut Ave.; phone: 202-673-4800). To return to the vicinity of where the walk began, turn left after exiting the zoo on Connecticut Avenue. Several blocks on the right is the Woodley Park/Zoo metro stop on the red line. You are just one stop from Dupont Circle.

Foggy Bottom

0 mile 1/4

P ST.

O ST.

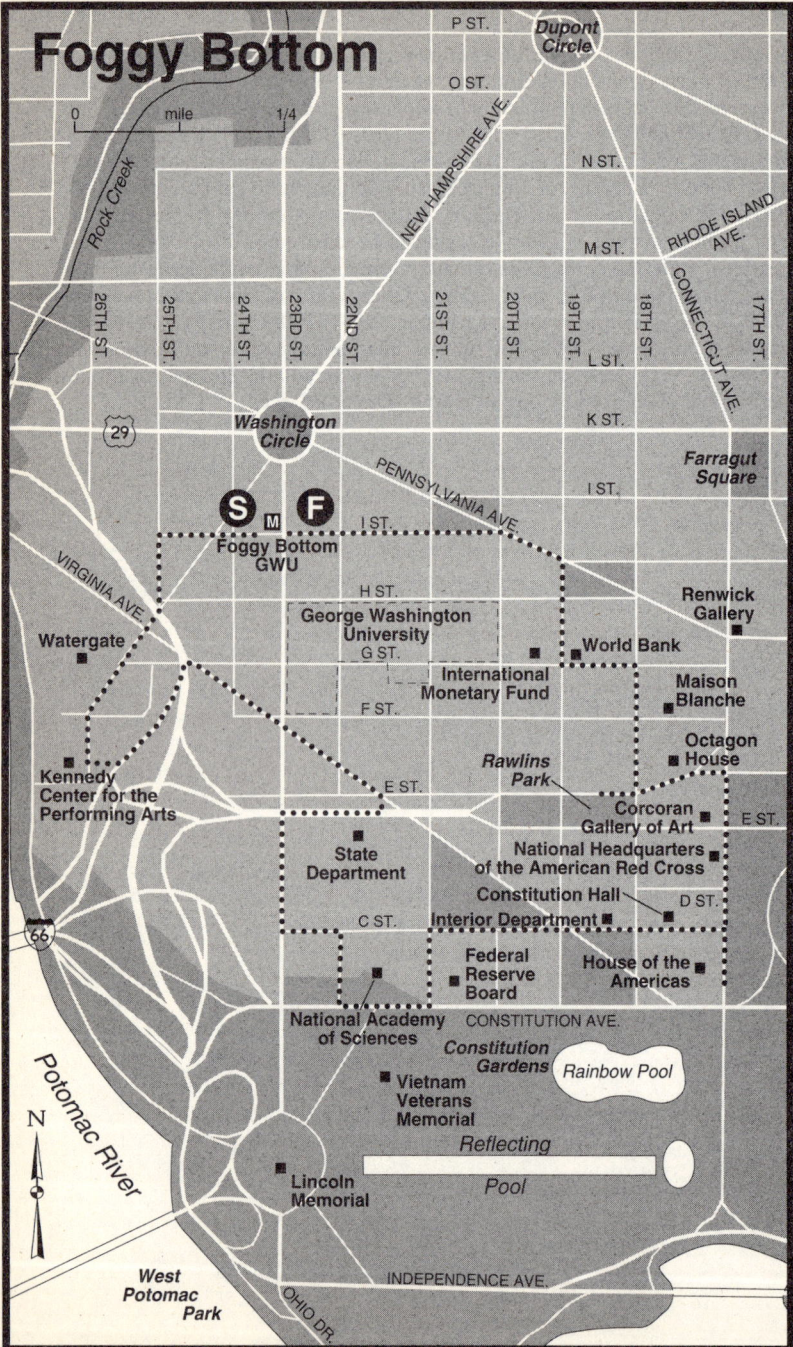

Dupont Circle

N ST.

NEW HAMPSHIRE AVE.

M ST.

RHODE ISLAND AVE.

Rock Creek

26TH ST. 25TH ST. 24TH ST. 23RD ST. 22ND ST. 21ST ST. 20TH ST. 19TH ST. 18TH ST. 17TH ST.

CONNECTICUT AVE.

L ST.

K ST.

Washington Circle

29

PENNSYLVANIA AVE.

I ST.

Farragut Square

S M F

I ST.

Foggy Bottom GWU

VIRGINIA AVE.

H ST.

George Washington University

Renwick Gallery

Watergate

G ST.

World Bank

International Monetary Fund

Maison Blanche

F ST.

Octagon House

Kennedy Center for the Performing Arts

E ST.

Rawlins Park

Corcoran Gallery of Art

E ST.

State Department

National Headquarters of the American Red Cross

66

Constitution Hall

Interior Department

D ST.

C ST.

Federal Reserve Board

House of the Americas

National Academy of Sciences

CONSTITUTION AVE.

Constitution Gardens

Rainbow Pool

Vietnam Veterans Memorial

Reflecting

Potomac River

N

Lincoln Memorial

Pool

West Potomac Park

INDEPENDENCE AVE.

OHIO DR.

Walk 5: Foggy Bottom

America was spared a potentially embarrassing misstep when Thomas Jefferson's idea of locating the Capitol Building on a bump of land rising out of a malarial swamp was ignored. According to the early outline of the city, the hill upon which the ordinarily lucid Jefferson originally planned to place the Capitol would have been located in a town on the banks of the Potomac in the District's southwest. Named Hamburg, the town was founded by a German immigrant named Funks. Congress just narrowly escaped being dubbed Hamburgers or Funksters (the town was also know as Funk).

This mosquito-ridden community was later known by the less attractive but well-deserved nickname Foggy Bottom. It may have been Jefferson's intention to plop Congress down at the crest of this inhospitable district to distract the legislators with poor visibility and soggy shoes from meddling in the affairs of the executive branch. Or maybe he just hadn't ventured over to Jenkins Hill, the lovely spot where the Capitol was finally situated. We'll never know. The area is dominated by the imposing structures of the *Kennedy Center,* the *Watergate* complex, and George Washington University buildings. This low-lying area offers excellent views of the Potomac, especially from the Roof Terrace of the *Kennedy Center.* The broad avenues are home to numerous government buildings, shops, and restaurants.

Foggy Bottom, the mention of which usually causes visitors to chuckle, earned its memorable name from the omnipresent bank of "fog" that hung over this low-lying area when it was the city's industrial center. In contrast to the marble monuments, museums, and governmental offices that comprise the area today, it was then home to such installations as a glass factory, a coal depot, a brewery, and wharves. The brewery spewed forth enough beer to make its founder, Christian Heurich, a millionaire many times over, and the factories spewed forth enough smog and foul stench to ward off middle class development until after World War II. Throughout the 19th century, Foggy Bottom was home to Irish, Italian, and German immigrants who were starting anew in this erstwhile grim enclave of the New World.

The factories eventually moved along and Foggy Bottom began to emerge from its proletarian squalor. It was the building of the new State Department after World War II that cleared the way.

A process of gentrification ensued, and many of the small but charming row houses that comprise the Foggy Bottom Historical District (an area clearly marked with signs) were saved from the wrecker's ball. The *Watergate* complex, posh before it was notorious, was built along the Potomac, as was the *Kennedy Center,* a monstrous theater complex that was intended to enliven the capital's modest arts scene.

The 3½-hour walking tour of Foggy Bottom begins on the plaza area of the Foggy Bottom/GWU *Metro* station on the western fringe of George Washington University.

To the south and east of the *Metro* station is George Washington University (GWU). George Washington really had hoped that a national university equal to Oxford and Cambridge — endowed with funds from his stock in the Potowmack Canal Company — would be founded after his death. Congress couldn't decide what role government should play in the university and, in making no decision, forfeited Washington's stock. Nevertheless, the Baptist Church founded the non-sectarian Columbian College in 1821 which, a century later, would become George Washington University, locate in Foggy Bottom, and become instrumental (with its enormous assets, it is the second-largest landholder in Washington next to the federal government) in the area's redevelopment. The university has snatched up and restored many of Foggy Bottom's fine old homes.

Across 23rd Street and to the north is the GWU Hospital. You may recognize the rear entrance through which Ronald Reagan was rushed into surgery after being shot in March 1981.

Begin walking down I Street to the right. After crossing 24th Street and New Hampshire Avenue, notice some of the colonial-style, wooden homes of the factory workers that are located here on this tree-lined street. Lumped into the Foggy Bottom Historical District, they have gone markedly upscale as the neighborhood has been gentrified and university professors and administrators have moved in. Turn left on 25th Street, where a row of some of the most charming houses can be seen on the left side of the street between Nos. 813 and 803.

Before crossing the traffic circle at Virginia Avenue, note an otherwise ordinary and rather humdrum *Howard Johnson Motor Lodge* to the right. It figures prominently in the notoriety of the *Watergate* complex, the serpentine, upscale residential monstrosity across the street. From their room at *HoJo's* (Room 723), Nixon aides G. Gordon Liddy and E. Howard Hunt monitored the break-in by five men at the Democratic National Committee Office on the sixth floor of the *Watergate* building (you'll find a doctor's office there now). After their detection and a bungled cover-up that is firmly etched in the nation's conscience, the event led to the eventual resignation of Richard Nixon. The *Watergate* office/apartment complex is one of the choice addresses of Washington's power elite. Also in the complex is the *Watergate* hotel, with contemporary-style rooms and balconies that open up on the Potomac for spectacular sunrises; arguably one of the capital's better (and pricier) restaurants, *Jean-Louis* (see *Eating Out*, THE CITY), a stronghold of nouvelle cuisine (phone: 202-298-4488); and a collection of exclusive shops. (The complex gets its enigmatic name from the steps leading up from the river behind the Lincoln Memorial.)

After exploring the *Watergate*, cross the traffic circle — which is anchored by a statue of Benito Juárez, the 19th-century Mexican revolutionary hero and president — to the east entrance of the *John F. Kennedy Center for the Performing Arts* (or just the *Kennedy Center* to locals). Though the building itself has been criticized for being droll and unadorned, the center put a hitherto unsophisticated Washington, DC, on the cultural map. Featuring opera, dramatic productions that use their Washington performances to rev up for Broadway, film, ballet, musicals, and concerts, the *Kennedy Center* is also a ceremonious stage for the city's power brokers to see and be seen as well-rounded, arts-supporting culture vultures. Housing theaters, several restaurants and cafés, a roof terrace, an atrium, long halls, and countless souvenir encampments, the center is impressive if only for its sheer size. Even if you're not going to a performance (tickets for some performances can be purchased on the same day), visit the Hall of Nations. This long gallery displays the flags of every nation recognized by the US government (they may have to open a new wing for all the former Soviet republics). But the most impressive feature about the *Kennedy Center* is the panoramic view from its rooftop terrace. The Potomac and Roosevelt Island can be seen to the west; *Watergate,* Georgetown, and the Cathedral to the north; the Capitol and Washington Monument to the east; and the Jefferson and Lincoln memorials to the south. Open daily; no admission charge; guided tours from 10 AM to 1 PM (phone: 202-416-8341).

Now exit the building to the east (opposite the Potomac) from either the Hall of States or the Hall of Nations, two grand halls that separate the *Kennedy Center*'s major theaters. To avoid the phalanx of streets ahead take the paved path that circumvents them and leads to Virginia Avenue, a major thoroughfare that slices through Foggy Bottom (to get to the path, follow the sign with a trolley on it labeled "Columbia Plaza Path and Tram").

Walk to the right, down Virginia Avenue, several blocks to E Street and an equestrian statue of Bernardo Galvez, Spain's Governor of Louisiana in 1776. It was dedicated in 1976, in commemoration of the *Bicentennial,* and conveys appreciation to the Spanish for their unwavering support in the struggle for American independence.

Across the street is the State Department, confined to a remarkably uninspiring, stolid building with all the charm of a midwestern post office. This is where our country's (some would say equally stolid) foreign policy is made. Our government's first Cabinet department, the State Department was founded in 1789 and, prior to decamping to Foggy Bottom (the State Department itself is sometimes referred to as Foggy Bottom), was housed in the Old Executive Office Building, one of the capital city's more impressive structures, located near the White House.

In addition to rows of anonymous office space, behind its undistinguished exterior are the splendidly furnished, artistically excellent Diplomatic Reception Rooms. Located on the eighth floor, these stately salons contain an outstanding collection of 18th- and 19th-century American art and furniture; much of it is historically significant. Foreign diplomats are received here — as are visitors who have the foresight to make a reservation for a tour. Call a week in advance to schedule a tour, offered Mondays through Fridays at 9:30 and 10:30 AM, and 2:45 PM (phone: 202-647-3241). Moving counterclockwise, circle the State Department building.

After a left on 23rd Street and another left on C Street, turn right on 22nd. The Constitution Gardens and Vietnam Veterans Memorial are ahead. The white, Greek-style building on the left is the National Academy of Sciences, an organization that got its start during the administration of Abraham Lincoln and functions as a link between science and government. The Academy can mobilize thousands of scientists in a nanosecond to provide scientific information to the government or synthesize conflicting information for lawmakers. Though the inside of this building is rarely visited by tourists, its Great Hall, dome, and Foucault pendulum (which represents the earth spinning on its axis) are worth a look. Open Mondays through Fridays, 8:30 AM to 5 PM (phone: 202-334-2000).

The well-groomed grounds of the National Academy of Sciences are nice for a stroll. Of particular interest is the Einstein Memorial, in the back of the building on the southwest corner. A path that plunges into a clump of bushes leads the way to this intriguing, bigger-than-life statue dedicated to Albert Einstein. The pensive genius sits, tousled hair and all, with a tablet that contains mathematical equations summarizing three of his most important scientific contributions: the photoelectric effect, the theory of general relativity, and the equivalence of energy and matter. The statue was sculpted in the characteristic "mashed potato" style of Robert Berks. Children love to sit in Einstein's lap.

Walk out to Constitution Avenue, formerly B Street and before that a putrid canal that extended from the Potomac to the Capitol Building. Turn left on the sidewalk. A few paces will lead to 21st Street; turn left again.

The stolid, immovable, and deeply conservative building on the right is home to the Federal Reserve Board. The conduit for the nation's cash, the Fed — America's central bank — sets the nation's monetary policy (interest rates, cash flows, and so on) and wields enormous clout in financial circles. The Fed's board ordinarily meets on Wednesdays at 10 AM — and for those who might be interested in hearing technical and obscure disputations on monetary policy, the meetings are usually open to the public. (For a list of the topics to be discussed, call 202-452-2478). There is a 45-minute tour (on Thursdays or by appointment; phone: 202-452-3149) replete with film that explains the Federal Reserve. Also, the building contains a respectable collection of 19th- and 20th-century paintings and sculpture. Gallery open Mondays through Fridays, 11:30 AM to 2 PM (phone: 202-452-3000).

Turn right on C Street and walk between the old (on the right) and new buildings of the Federal Reserve. C Street will curl around to the left, in front of the Office of Personnel Management, an agency that sets government personnel policy and manages, so to speak, the civil service.

Directly across Virginia Avenue is the continuation of C Street. To the right is an attractive statue of Simon Bolívar, the Great Liberator of much of South America. Spanning 2 blocks, the building on the left is the Interior Department. The *Interior Department Museum* (housed in the same building) contains exhibits covering the breadth of the Interior Department's purview which, for example, includes the National Park Service, land reclamation, geological survey, Indian affairs, land management, wildlife preservation, and a dense forest of other duties. The centerpiece of the museum is its portrayal of the opening of the Wild West, illustrated by bounties, patents, paintings, photos, and original land grants. Also on display and for sale is an impressive collection of Indian crafts and artifacts. Open Mondays through Fridays, 8 AM to 5 PM (phone: 202-343-2743).

Continue down C Street across 18th Street toward the Ellipse, which is straight ahead. On the left is the Romanesque *Constitution Hall.* Built in 1930 by John Russell Pope, this was the city's premier concert venue until the *Kennedy Center* stole the scene. Seating 4,000, it still attracts such renowned performers as actor Stacy Keach and pianist André Watts. Toscanini thought the concert hall's acoustics were remarkable. Watch the newspapers for concert announcements (phone: 202-638-2661). The ornate Beaux Arts building connected to *Constitution Hall* that extends all the way to 17th Street is the headquarters of the Daughters of the American Revolution (DAR), an elite group of women who trace their lineage back to the American colonies' struggle for independence.

On the way to 17th Street, you will walk by a vast portico supported by Ionic columns. This building, also known as *Continental Hall,* features the *DAR Museum:* 34 rooms that commemorate each original colony and various later states. Included are the Oklahoma Room, a prairie farm kitchen; and the Steamboat Parlor in the Missouri Room. *Continental Hall* is also one of the world's largest genealogical archives (there's a small charge to use it). The museum is open and tours on a walk-in basis are available Mondays through Fridays, 8:30 AM to 4 PM, Sundays from 1 to 5 PM (phone: 202-628-1776).

After reaching 17th Street, see an unsung but noteworthy tourist destination housed within the majestic, Beaux Arts building on the right. The House of the Americas (formally called the Pan American Union Building) faces 18th Street as well as Constitution Avenue and is made of white Georgian marble and black Andean granite. This is the headquarters of the Organization of American States (OAS), the oldest international political organization (since 1890) with which the US has been steadily associated. It links the US with the countries of Latin America and the Caribbean, and through its symposiums, lectures, and general precepts tries to promote better political and trade relations. For example, the OAS was involved with the celebration of the 500th anniversary of Columbus's voyage to the New World. Note the statue of Queen Isabella I as you enter. Also inside are the Hall of Heroes and Flags; the Hall of the Americas; several Louis Tiffany chandeliers; and the Aztec Gardens, a year-round tropical spot that is overgrown with exotic plants sent here from the member nations of the OAS. Open Mondays through Fridays, 9 AM to 5:30 PM (phone: 202-458-3000). Directly behind the main building is the *Art Museum of the Americas,* featuring paintings and sculpture from that region. Open Tuesdays through Saturdays from 10 AM to 5 PM (phone: 202-458-6016).

Retrace your steps up 17th Street. Just past *Continental Hall* on the left, in a building as white as hospital sheets, is the *National Headquarters of the American Red Cross.* The American branch of this international organization was founded in 1881 by Clara Barton in an attempt to humanize an increasingly hostile world. The administrators who work here coordinate the more than 3,000 Red Cross chapters across the country which provide vital services ranging from disaster relief and blood banks to children's swimming lessons. The Red Cross is known best for its brave and selfless service tending the wounded through a Civil War, a couple of world wars, and countless other conflicts. Consequently, the centerpiece of the building is a marble, closed atrium that commemorates the women who ministered to the Civil War wounded. A century of Red Cross uniforms is on display, as is a retrospective of recruitment posters. A trilogy of Tiffany stained glass windows brightens the lobby on the second floor. It's worth a look. Open Mondays through Fridays, 8:30 AM to 4:45 PM (phone: 202-737-8300). Continue the trek up 17th Street.

The next point of interest up 17th Street is the *Corcoran Gallery of Art*, just past E Street on the left. The Beaux Arts building that houses this fine American collection has flourishes of the clean lines characteristic of American architecture (it was Frank Lloyd Wright's favorite building in Washington). Inside is one of the oldest and broadest collections of American art — from early portraiture to minimalism. The *Corcoran* is a privately funded museum — separate from the *Smithsonian* dynasty — and hosts many exhibits (some controversial) such as the works of local contemporary artists. No admission charge. Open Tuesdays through Sundays, 10 AM to 5 PM, Thursdays to 9 PM (phone: 202-638-3211; also see *Memorable Museums* in DIVERSIONS).

The oval, northern edge of the *Corcoran* is rimmed by E Street, which slashes back to the southwest. Follow E Street to the corner of 18th Street. On the right is the Octagon House, an 18th-century building that was spared the sacking and burning by the British during their invasion of Washington in 1814. It may have been spared because the French ambassador had been living here since the outbreak of the War of 1812 and the French tricolor was flying over the house. It later provided a safe haven for President James Madison and his wife, Dolley, since the pink house (the presidential palace that was the predecessor of the White House), along with the Capitol, had been burned. They resided here until 1815.

For one awkward moment in 1814, the President of the United States was homeless. He was also in danger of being friendless: Seen as responsible for declaring an unpopular war and for being sluggish in foreseeing the danger of a British attack on Washington, his popularity among the populace had plummeted. The following year (1815), on the second floor of the Octagon House, President Madison signed the Treaty of Ghent with Britain, ending the War of 1812.

The American Association of Architects — whose headquarters are adjacent to Octagon House — saved the building from deterioration almost a century ago; they also periodically restore it. Oddly, the Octagon House is a misnomer since it has only six sides. Nobody seems to know how it got its name. Tours are available. Open Tuesdays through Fridays, 10 AM to 4 PM, weekends from noon to 4 PM (phone: 202-638-3105).

A just reward for doggedly following this tour awaits the tuckered-out tourist in Rawlins Park, just past 18th Street on the left. This park is soft and inviting — despite being named after Ulysses Grant's hard-bitten chief of staff and, later, secretary of war. The park's two pools are home to goldfish and, when the season is right, blooming water lilies. Lingering about on spring days amid the tulip-tree magnolias is a favorite pastime of visitors and locals alike.

After relaxing in the park return to the Octagon House and head north up 18th Street. Cross F Street; *Maison Blanche,* the favorite restaurant of the movers and shakers of the Reagan administration, is on the right. Just a jelly bean's throw from the White House, this rather pricey restaurant features classic French cooking (the bouillabaisse and veal stew are favorites) in a luxurious setting. Newspaper columnist and humorist Art Buchwald is a regular fixture here. 1725 F St. NW (phone: 202-842-0070).

Where 18th Street meets G Street (just 1 block past *Maison Blanche*) turn left. Then turn right on 19th Street. Towering on both sides of this shady thoroughfare are the twin pillars of world finance and development, the International Monetary Fund (IMF) and World Bank. Both institutions, which received more than their share of bad press during the Third World debt crisis in the mid- to late 1980s, were established as the foundation of the postwar economic order in 1944 by Britain, the US, and their wartime allies. Though their roles have changed dramatically since then, they remain two of the most powerful institutions in the world, controlling tens of billions of dollars and the economic policies of the countries that receive their loans. Until recently their roles were clearly defined. The IMF would provide low-interest loans in exchange for the recipient adopting a package of monetary policies, and the World Bank granted loans for specific project development. But lately these duties have blurred. Some banking experts contend that the two institutions will eventually merge into one.

Nevertheless, walking this area around lunchtime is like strolling around the base of the Tower of Babel. The mixture of languages heard on 19th Street reinforces the fact that these are truly global institutions. Drop in on the IMF Visitors' Center (700 19th St.) which features an art gallery, crafts from Third World countries, a film series, a constant and full slate of cultural events, a library, reading room, and a lecture series on international economic issues (phone: 202-623-6869).

Just a quarter of a block past H Street, 19th Street meets Pennsylvania Avenue. But this tour does not head in the direction of the influential residents at No. 1600 who make this street famous (see *Walk 3: Downtown*). Instead, follow Pennsylvania Avenue left as it turns to the northwest. Walk through the canyon of "federal buildings" (amateur Washington tour guides are quick with this catch-all description when they are absolutely stumped by the identity of yet another marble building).

At the corner of Pennsylvania Avenue and 19th Street is *Dominique's,* a Washington dining institution. Famed for its exotic game dishes (rattlesnake, alligator), ultra-rich chocolate truffles, freely flowing champagne, and proximity to the *Kennedy Center, Dominique's* has long been a favorite of the theater crowd — audience and actors alike. Elizabeth Taylor has been a frequent visitor; there's even a chocolate truffle dessert named after her. Its $14.95 fixed-price pre- and post-theater dinners are a bargain (phone: 202-452-1126).

In another block up Pennsylvania Avenue, I Street veers off to the left (it's actually parallel with the other alphabet streets). This first block of attractive townhouses is known as "Lion's Row." It underwent a brilliant renovation in the early 1980s that thankfully preserved the brick façades. A petite mall within a couple of the townhouses contains several shops (*Ciao,* a sandwich shop; *Tower Records;* a newsstand; the *Gap;* and so on). There are two restaurants of note along this block. *E.E. Wolensky's Bar and Grill* features a courtyard café and lively bar with burgers, salads, and regular café fare at moderate prices (phone: 202-463-0050); the *Devon Bar and Grill* also has a lively bar and is popular among grilled-seafood aficionados (phone: 202-833-5660). Also, a 1 block stroll up 21st Street brings the walker with an appetite for Italian food to *Primi Piatti* (2013 I St. NW; phone: 202-223-3600), an establishment that specializes in simple, delicious pasta dishes.

Just a short stroll down I Street leads to the Foggy Bottom *Metro* station and the conclusion of this tour.

Walk 6: Georgetown

Though Washingtonians are quick to claim the historic area in west Washington as their own — the municipal government in its ravenous search for revenue is particularly proprietary on this score — the people of Georgetown would rather just be left alone.

Formerly a booming Maryland tobacco port and now Washington's oldest neighborhood, Georgetown is home to the city's stateliest Federal-era architecture. Georgetown lost its Maryland identity in 1790 when it was incorporated into the newfangled District Territory by George Washington and city architect Pierre L'Enfant; it became part of the federal territory but remained an independent town.

After years of decline that followed as a result of the Potomac filling in with silt, Georgetown lost its pre-eminent port status to Alexandria (Virginia) and Baltimore (Maryland) and was finally swallowed whole by the capital city in 1871. This full annexation meant that the District got its comeuppance: Georgetown was a seething hotbed of seccessionist fervor throughout the Civil War, and since the federal city couldn't risk keeping a heretic on its flank, it was better to bring it into the fold.

Initially, it was hoped that this acquisition would stave off Georgetown's economic power slide. Instead, because of suburban flight, the District was entering an era of decline, and Georgetown found itself aboard a sinking ship. Furthermore, as part of the District of Columbia, the town lost its congressman and its right to vote for president.

Against the vehement protests of the locals, its colonial street names such as Water Street, Fishing Lane, and the Keyes were turned into the anonymous and impersonal alphabet soup of street letters to conform with L'Enfant's plan and the rest of the city. The neighborhood was brought to its knees.

In desperation, Georgetown attempted to regain its slumping property values and to escape the creeping blight of the District by asking Maryland to take the town back, as Virginia had done with Alexandria in 1843. No such luck. "Georgetownians," in response, hunkered down like herefords in a snowstorm until, ironically, it was the fanatics of 20th-century federalism themselves, the New Dealers, that discovered this historic district and breathed life back into its decaying mansions, crumbling townhouses, and bumbling business district.

Today, Georgetown, with its brimming cornucopia of shops, colonial architecture, world class university, fine restaurants, and a thriving nightlife that makes it the place to be after sundown, has clearly benefited from its association with Washington and the federal government.

But the average Georgetown resident won't admit it. The people of Georgetown refuse to accept their community being called West Washington — the district's official label — and are known to use Georgetown, DC, for their

Georgetown

0   mile   1/4

N

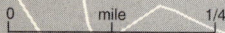

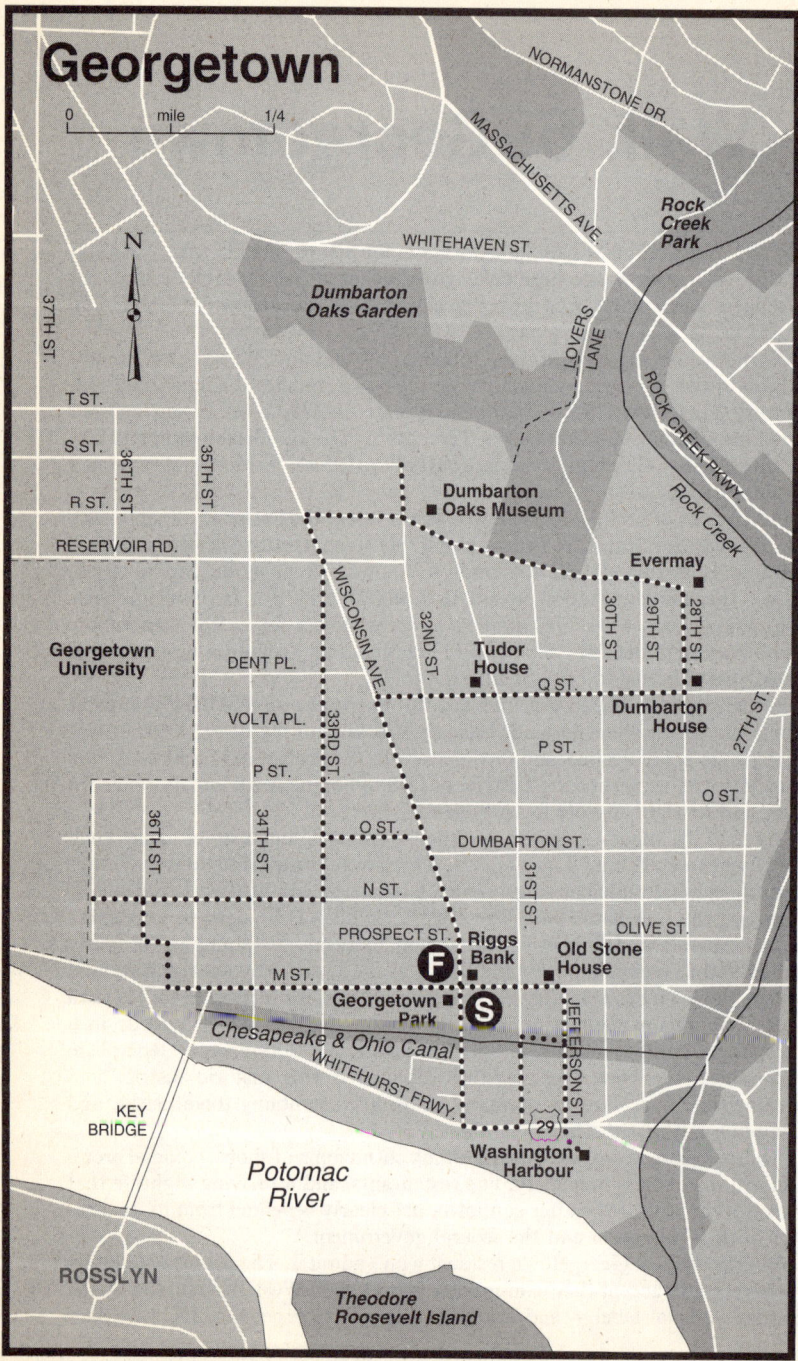

NORMANSTONE DR

MASSACHUSETTS AVE.

Rock Creek Park

WHITEHAVEN ST.

Dumbarton Oaks Garden

LOVERS LANE

ROCK CREEK PKWY.

Rock Creek

37TH ST.

T ST.

S ST.

36TH ST.

R ST.

35TH ST.

RESERVOIR RD.

Dumbarton Oaks Museum

Evermay

30TH ST.

29TH ST.

28TH ST.

WISCONSIN AVE.

Georgetown University

DENT PL.

32ND ST.

Tudor House

Q ST.

Dumbarton House

27TH ST.

VOLTA PL.

33RD ST.

P ST.

P ST.

DUMBARTON ST.

O ST.

36TH ST.

34TH ST.

O ST.

N ST.

31ST ST.

OLIVE ST.

PROSPECT ST.

Riggs Bank

Old Stone House

F

M ST.

Georgetown Park

S

JEFFERSON ST.

Chesapeake & Ohio Canal

WHITEHURST FRWY.

KEY BRIDGE

29

Washington Harbour

Potomac River

ROSSLYN

Theodore Roosevelt Island

postal address. Never mind that Georgetown was really named after one George Boone, a simpleton farmer who happened to purchase a chunk of land in this area in the early days (and not King George II as some contend). Georgetownians are fiercely independent. Much to the chagrin of tourists — barhoppers and the dinner crowd alike — they rejected the construction of a *Metro* route through their community and chose not to allow DC lottery tickets to be sold in Georgetown (indeed, property owners and trust-fund beneficiaries in this wealthy district don't need to win a lottery).

Georgetown has gotten away with its separate-and-better status by its sequestered geography. It is flanked by the Gothic campus of Georgetown University to the west and the Potomac to the south; Rock Creek is an ideal buffer zone between Georgetown and the rest of Washington. There is no threat to the north since the northern parameter of Georgetown gives way to the posh Cleveland Park residential area. In fact, Wisconsin Avenue is the only thoroughfare that makes its way into Georgetown unencumbered by parkland or greenery.

Our walking tour of Georgetown begins at the intersection of M Street and Wisconsin Avenue, a bustling corner around which all of Georgetown revolves. The crush of pedestrians on weekends here is almost as dense as during a papal visit or at a *Redskins* game at *RFK Stadium* (we exaggerate, but you get the point). Though the golden-domed building on the northeast corner looks as if it might have some historical significance, it doesn't. It is the Riggs Bank, which is a useful landmark and a reliable meeting place; gracing its tower is a trusty clock.

On business days libating lobbyists, politicos, and other serge-suited power brokers can be seen from the street dining in the clubby atmosphere of *Nathan's* (3150 M St.; phone: 202-338-2000), a popular Georgetown dining spot with a good Italian kitchen specializing in fresh pasta and seafood dishes. The front bar's impressive selection of champagne and understated atmosphere draws a sophisticated crowd.

Just up Wisconsin Avenue — one of the few remaining streets that predates L'Enfant's master plan for the capital city — is the *American Café* (5252 Wisconsin Ave.; phone: 202-363-5400), a DC institution. Founded in 1977, this is the flagship restaurant that has thus far spawned 18 franchises from Richmond to Baltimore. No visit to Washington is complete without a lunch stop here. Try the mushroom pesto lasagna, Baja flour-tortilla rolls, or tarragon chicken salad.

Begin walking east on M Street (in the direction of the Riggs Bank side of Wisconsin Avenue). If you need to stock up on smoking supplies, or simply enjoy a quick jaunt through a tobacco store to take in a complexity of aromas and view the intricate tobacco paraphernalia, nose your way into *Georgetown Tobacco & Pipe Stores* (3144 M St.; phone: 202-338-5100). The late Egyptian President Anwar Sadat used to smoke out this shop during his Washington visits for its special blend of pipe tobacco. At the corner of M and 31st Streets is *Bistro Français* (3128 M St.; phone: 202-338-3830), an authentic French bistro with reasonably priced *boeuf* in a romantic setting that gives francophiles a taste of *la belle France* — without the hefty airfare.

Across the street is *Glory* (3139 M St.; phone: 202-337-3406), a new restaurant and pub in which one is most likely to have a sighting of Elvis in the Washington area. The staff swears up and down that "the King" frequents this place — which serves excellent burgers and beers along with other fancier items — and hunches down on the end stool at the bar where he savors a sassafras and his anonymity. Even if the rock legend does not waddle in while you're there, a gaudy ceramic likeness of his majesty sits behind the bar, keeping the faith alive.

Continue down M Street to a 2-story stone cottage on the left. This is the *Old Stone House* (3051 M St.; phone: 202-426-6851), which is thought to be the only surviving pre-Revolutionary building in the District. Built by Pennsylvania cabinetmaker Christopher Layman in 1764, this house has been many things to its residential and commercial occupants over the years. Currently, the registered historical site's proprietor is the National Park Service, which keeps the house's furnishings — including solid beds, simple tables, and spinning wheels — true to its 18th-century colonial heritage. After inspecting its interior, walk around to the house's subdued garden, rich with fruit trees. No admission charge. Open Wednesdays through Sundays from 8 AM to 4:30 PM.

Now cross M Street to Jefferson Street. For some time, the area south of M Street (formerly Bridge Street, it was named after the bridge that spanned Rock Creek to the east) was a working class neighborhood, home to the manual laborers, tradesmen, and merchants of this once-thriving port and industrial city. Today these once-modest dwellings — most of which have undergone major refurbishment — sell for upwards of $400,000. Several of these upscale remnants can be seen on Jefferson Street — at Nos. 1069, 1067, and 1063 (with plaster covering the brick of the latter). Constructed by the Irish navvies (construction workers) who built the Chesapeake & Ohio Canal, these three red brick Federal houses, just past the *Georgetown Dutch Inn,* have weathered the test of time and the rumbling blight of the Whitehurst Freeway ahead. But before you reach them, note the 2-story building at No. 1083 which was built around the time of the Civil War as a stable for the horses and hearses of an undertaker who lived nearby. A hoist to lift hay, wood, and other supplies to the second floor can be seen above a window to the far right. Part of the building is now occupied by a frame shop.

Walk down Jefferson Street to where it crosses the C & O Canal. The bridge crossing this trickling artifact of a bygone mode of transportation is a good place from which to view the locks of the canal.

Completed in 1850, the Chesapeake & Ohio Canal kept Washington accessible to shipping after the Potomac filled with silt. The C & O was the brainchild of George Washington, who first advanced the idea of water traffic between the Potomac and Ohio rivers and crossing the Appalachians. Consequently, Georgetown represents the eastern end of this canal which extends 184 miles to Cumberland, Maryland — a little short of its destination. By the time this stretch of the canal was completed, the *B & O Railroad* (*Baltimore and Ohio*) had virtually derailed its usefulness.

The canal consisted of 174 locks and a towpath on both sides for the mules that methodically pulled the barges. Today, the C & O is a historical and aesthetic complement to Georgetown. Supreme Court Justice William O. Douglas saved it from the concrete madness of the 1950s, preventing it from being turned into a four-lane highway. From early spring to late autumn the *Georgetown,* a mule-drawn canal barge, carries passengers down the waterway. Tickets can be purchased just across the canal at the *Foundry Mall* (1055 Thomas Jefferson St.; phone: 202-472-4376). For now, complete the trip on foot down Jefferson Street, crossing K Street under the Whitehurst Freeway.

The riverfront commercial haven that opens before you is *Washington Harbour,* built by Arthur Cotton Moore in 1986. Though it certainly makes no contribution to environmental purity, the fact that it replaced an ugly, foul-smelling foundry makes this ritzy complex an improvement to the area. Top floors house office buildings and luxury apartments. The first floor is monopolized by a column of rather pricey restaurants; a few of the better ones include *Leonardo da Vinci's* for Italian food (on the right overlooking the Potomac; phone: 202-944-4881); *Tony and Joe's Seafood Place* (on the left overlooking the Potomac; phone: 202-944-4545), featuring fresh seafood with an unbeatable view of the river, especially from the vantage point of outdoor seating; *Hisago* (on the right; phone: 202-944-4181), an authentic Japanese restaurant (with such authentic prices you may conclude it's priced in yen); and *Jaimalito's* (on the left; phone: 202-944-4400), a reasonably priced eatery with an unmistakable Santa Fe feel — try the enchiladas with blue corn tortillas, black bean soup, or any of the many mesquite-grilled dishes. If you're not lured by the restaurants, walk around the fountains out to the promenade that runs along the Potomac and enjoy the splendid view of the *Kennedy Center* and the *Watergate* down the river to the left. On the way out of *Washington Harbour* tip your cap to the statue by J. Seward Johnson, Jr., of a workman on his lunch break.

Once out of *Washington Harbour,* cross K Street and walk back up Jefferson Street; cross over the C & O Canal, and follow a path on the left which leads parallel to the canal and past a jumble of inexpensive eateries. When you reach 31st Street, turn left and cross the canal again. Toward the end of the block and the intersection with K Street, *La Ruche* is on the left (1039 31st St.; phone: 202-965-2684), a cozy coffee shop that serves excellent desserts and various coffees.

Though it might take some snooping to find it — with the current construction going on in this area — there is a plaque commemorating the spot on which *Suter's Tavern* stood, on the left side at the corner of 31st and K Streets. The tavern was the watering hole where, in 1791, George Washington convinced the men who owned the tobacco farms and marshes east of Georgetown to sell their land to the federal government so that work could begin on forging the capital city. If not for the consent of this tough crowd (George must have won them over with one too many beers), Washington, DC, as we know it might never have been.

It was also because *Suter's Tavern* had the market cornered on libations at the turn of the 19th century that many senators and congressmen settled in Georgetown after the federal government moved from Philadelphia to Washington. One particularly cranky member of Congress wrote that "there was only one good tavern within a day's march" of Congress. Thus, many members lived nearby and were driven to and from the daily sessions of Congress in a rickety coach.

The buildings along K Street — which along with the Whitehurst Freeway

Now begins the ascent to higher ground. Just past the old brick Streetcar Barn (a row of offices that is still labeled as such), on the right, are the so-called "Exorcist Steps," a favorite site where locals congregate on *Halloween* or after yet another viewing of the eponymous movie that was filmed in and around the red brick Georgetown University building at the top and to the left of the stairs (3600 Prospect St.). The exorcist, as you may recall, met an unpleasant, head-over-heels fate on these 75 steps in the movie's final scene. Watch your step. The Georgetown University crew team runs up and down these stairs several times daily for a helluva workout.

After climbing the steps and taking a breather, walk up 36th Street. On the left in a nondescript 18th-century house is *1789* (1226 36th St.; phone: 202-965-1789), a restaurant that features game, salmon, caviar, oysters, and other well-prepared American dishes. With its working fireplace, etchings, and solemn atmosphere, the dining room would have been an ideal setting for FDR's fireside chats. Indeed, after you see the check you may wish the well-heeled late president was here to pick up the tab.

Down a flight of steps is *The Tombs* (1226 36th St.; phone: 202-337-6668), a markedly more informal dining experience that is a favorite among Georgetown University students and their professors.

After reaching N Street, turn left and walk the short distance to the campus of Georgetown University (37th St.; phone: 202-687-5055), a world-caliber institution of higher learning known for its preponderance of international students (from over 90 countries), the nation's only foreign-service program, renowned graduate programs in law and medicine, and an often near-legendary basketball team. Founded in 1789 by John Carroll, the first American bishop, the university is the oldest Jesuit school in the US. Take some time to walk about the campus and experience its Old World, scholarly charm. Most notable are the Old North Building, the school's original edifice built in 1792, and the Healy Building (built in 1879), a brooding yet redoubtable German Gothic structure with a spire that seems to puncture the heavens.

Now, retrace your steps down N Street to the corner of 34th and turn right. At the end of the block, across the street and on the right, is the majestic Halcyon House, built in 1783 and named by Benjamin Stoddert, the first secretary of the Navy. Though the interior today features nothing of interest, there is a gorgeous view of the Potomac from here. Appropriately, the street that runs east-west, parallel to M Street, was named Prospect Street because of its particularly mesmerizing vista — especially at sundown.

Return to N Street and turn right. Halfway down the next block on the left is a row of Federal houses built in 1817 by John Cox, the former Mayor of Georgetown. Hence their collective name, Cox's Row. In the late 1950s, the simple, red brick house at 3307 N Street was the home of then-Senator John F. Kennedy and his family before they moved into the more spacious quarters at 1600 Pennsylvania Avenue.

The next block is the intersection with 33rd Street. Walk up 33rd almost to the next block. On the left is an intriguing barn-red, stone house with a tiny white steeple atop it (you can't miss it) that was the former stable of the statelier house on the corner. More than 150 years old, the house still has the wooden gable that was used to hoist hay to the second-floor loft. The stained glass windows are said to have come from the Persian Embassy.

Now begins the ascent to higher ground. Just past the old brick Streetcar Barn (a row of offices that is still labeled as such), on the right, are the so-called "Exorcist Steps," a favorite site where locals congregate on *Halloween* or after yet another viewing of the eponymous movie that was filmed in and around the red brick Georgetown University building at the top and to the left of the stairs (3600 Prospect St.). The exorcist, as you may recall, met an unpleasant, head-over-heels fate on these 75 steps in the movie's final scene. Watch your step. The Georgetown University crew team runs up and down these stairs several times daily for a helluva workout.

After climbing the steps and taking a breather, walk up 36th Street. On the left in a nondescript 18th-century house is *1789* (1226 36th St.; phone: 202-965-1789), a restaurant that features game, salmon, caviar, oysters, and other well-prepared American dishes. With its working fireplace, etchings, and solemn atmosphere, the dining room would have been an ideal setting for FDR's fireside chats. Indeed, after you see the check you may wish the well-heeled late president was here to pick up the tab.

Down a flight of steps is *The Tombs* (1226 36th St.; phone: 202-337-6668), a markedly more informal dining experience that is a favorite among Georgetown University students and their professors.

After reaching N Street, turn left and walk the short distance to the campus of Georgetown University (37th St.; phone: 202-687-5055), a world-caliber institution of higher learning known for its preponderance of international students (from over 90 countries), the nation's only foreign-service program, renowned graduate programs in law and medicine, and an often near-legendary basketball team. Founded in 1789 by John Carroll, the first American bishop, the university is the oldest Jesuit school in the US. Take some time to walk about the campus and experience its Old World, scholarly charm. Most notable are the Old North Building, the school's original edifice built in 1792, and the Healy Building (built in 1879), a brooding yet redoubtable German Gothic structure with a spire that seems to puncture the heavens.

Now, retrace your steps down N Street to the corner of 34th and turn right. At the end of the block, across the street and on the right, is the majestic Halcyon House, built in 1783 and named by Benjamin Stoddert, the first secretary of the Navy. Though the interior today features nothing of interest, there is a gorgeous view of the Potomac from here. Appropriately, the street that runs east-west, parallel to M Street, was named Prospect Street because of its particularly mesmerizing vista — especially at sundown.

Return to N Street and turn right. Halfway down the next block on the left is a row of Federal houses built in 1817 by John Cox, the former Mayor of Georgetown. Hence their collective name, Cox's Row. In the late 1950s, the simple, red brick house at 3307 N Street was the home of then-Senator John F. Kennedy and his family before they moved into the more spacious quarters at 1600 Pennsylvania Avenue.

The next block is the intersection with 33rd Street. Walk up 33rd almost to the next block. On the left is an intriguing barn-red, stone house with a tiny white steeple atop it (you can't miss it) that was the former stable of the statelier house on the corner. More than 150 years old, the house still has the wooden gable that was used to hoist hay to the second-floor loft. The stained glass windows are said to have come from the Persian Embassy.

Continue up 33rd Street to O Street and take a little time to ramble up and down this street. The Federal and Victorian architecture on O Street is some of Washington's most endearing. The townhouses are brilliantly colored (tasteful light yellows next to distasteful fluorescent greens next to bright red houses with bright blue trim, and the like). They seem to instill ebullience in the spirit and a spring in one's step. Also, notice the trolley tracks and the cobblestones in O Street that make Georgetownians swell with pride.

Several blocks east on O Street (east of 33rd St.) is St. John's Episcopal Church (3240 O St. NW; phone: 202-338-1796), built in 1809 by Dr. William Thornton, the same architect who built the Capitol Building. Though the church was altered drastically in 1870 to appear more Victorian than Federal, the Capitol resemblance lingers ever-so-slightly in the dome-shape structure, with its extending wings on either side.

Return to 33rd Street and turn right. This thoroughfare cuts through the location of some of Georgetown's nicer homes. The residences become increasingly sprawling as you walk north. Follow 33rd Street 5 blocks to the intersection with Wisconsin Avenue. Though we will be crossing Wisconsin and swinging around the imposing Georgetown Library on R Street, there are several shops that might pique your curiosity on Wisconsin.

For sheer shock value slink into *Commander Salamander* (1420 Wisconsin Ave.; phone: 202-337-2265), which attracts the "leather-and-attitude" crowd along with some customers who are content to stare at the shop's unabashed weirdness. If in need of leather, chains, leopard skin garments, or rhinestone sunglasses, this shop is pay dirt. (Open until midnight on Fridays and Saturdays.) Another entertaining clothing store is *Up Against the Wall* (3219 M St. NW; phone: 202-337-9316). *Urban Outfitters* also offers offbeat clothing and accessories (3111 M St. NW; phone: 342-1012). After browsing, walk up Wisconsin to R Street and turn right.

The handsome building on the right is Georgetown's public library, part of the DC library system. Continue to 32nd Street and turn north (left). Though it's not immediately apparent, over the brick wall is *Dumbarton Oaks* (1703 32nd St.; phone: 202-342-3200 or 202-338-8278); a painstakingly preserved 19th-century estate, it is one of Washington's truly special places. The badly dilapidated mansion and grounds were bought in the 1920s by Robert Woods Bliss, former Ambassador to Argentina, and his wife. They quickly set about creating the present museum and gardens. The name *Dumbarton Oaks* is familiar, as it was the site of a crucial, groundbreaking series of meetings to form the United Nation's charter; held in the estate's lavish mansion in 1944, the meetings were attended by representatives of the US, Great Britain, China, and the Soviet Union.

Franklin Roosevelt's strategy for holding the talks at *Dumbarton Oaks* was made plain when he said during one of the meeting's press conferences: "If you can get the parties into a room with a big table and make them take their coats off and put their feet up on the table, and give them a good cigar, you can always make them agree." *Dumbarton Oaks* laid the groundwork for the San Francisco Conference the following year at which the United Nations was formally founded.

The surrounding gardens are a foliage fanatic's nirvana, and a walk among the intricate network of arbors, gardens, pools, fountains, and terraces is one of Washington's most delightful outdoor experiences. Access to the garden is through the R Street entrance (31st and R Sts.). The museum, which the Bliss family sold to Harvard University, contains a world-renowned collection of pre-Columbian and Byzantine art, displayed in nine glass cylinders.

Return to R Street and turn left. North of R Street are town parks, *Dumbarton Oaks,* and Montrose Park, which lie east of the Bliss estate and were formerly part of the Bliss's holdings. Farther east on R Street, where it turns sharply right, is Evermay (1623 28th St.), long considered one of Washington's most elegant homes. Now occupied by heirs to the DuPont fortune, this Georgian manor has been restored to its former opulence and the grounds are occasionally open for garden tours.

R Street angles right and intersects with Q Street. A few paces left on Q Street is *Dumbarton House* (2715 Q St.; phone: 202-337-2288), not to be confused with *Dumbarton Oaks.* This 19th-century Georgian home was built by the Capitol architect Dr. William Thornton, and features oval rooms and Federal furnishings that are maintained by the *National Society of the Colonial Dames of America.* Fine collections of silver and china are on display. Many famous figures have stayed here, including Dolley Madison, who is said to have lodged here while fleeing Washington and its sacking by the British in 1814. It's worth a look. Open daily. Admission charge.

This walk ends at M Street and Wisconsin Avenue, where it began. To get to Wisconsin, walk west on Q Street. On the way back, between 31st and 32nd Streets, note *Tudor House* (1644 31st St.; phone: 202-965-0400) which, despite its name, is a neo-classical mansion; built in 1816, it was first occupied by Martha Washington's granddaughter and her husband, Thomas Peter, son of Georgetown's first mayor. Because of the link with the nation's first First Family, *Tudor House* contains many furnishings and items from Mount Vernon. The house remained in the same family until 1983, when, after the death of its last Peter family occupant, a foundation was established to refurbish the house and open it to the public. Tours are available Tuesdays through Saturdays at 10 and 11:30 AM, 1 and 2:30 PM. Admission charge.

Return to Wisconsin Avenue, turn left and walk (downhill, thankfully) 4 blocks to M Street.

Old Town Alexandria

FIRST ST.

MONTGOMERY ST.

MADISON ST.

0   mile   1/8

N

WYTHE ST.

PENDLETON ST.

Potomac River

F

ORONOCO ST.

■ **Lee-Fendall House**

PRINCESS ST.

QUAY ST.

Lloyd House and Library

QUEEN ST.

■ **Christ Church**

CAMERON ST.

Torpedo Factory Art Center

To George Washington Masonic National Memorial

■ **City Hall** ■ ■ **Carlyle House**

Market Square

⑦

KING ST.

■ **Ramsay House**

←

■

S

■ **Stabler-Leadbeater Apothecary Shop**

Lyceum

PRINCE ST.

COLUMBUS ST.

WASHINGTON ST.

ST. ASAPH ST.

PITT ST.

ROYAL ST.

FAIRFAX ST.

LEE ST.

UNION ST.

②③⑥

DUKE ST.

■ **Old Presbyterian Meeting House**

WOLFE ST.

① ④⓪⓪

WILKES ST.

GIBBON ST.

FRANKLIN ST.

Walk 7: Old Town Alexandria

Virginia's rich colonial history is carefully sustained in Old Town Alexandria, the heart and soul of a sprawling suburban city just south of the District of Columbia. Old Town, as Washingtonians affectionately call it, has masterfully harmonized its cobblestoned streets, historic public buildings, and painstakingly preserved private residences with the neighborhood's newer — and livelier — additions: chic restaurants, pubs, clubs, and shops.

Old Town was founded in 1749 by a spirited band of Scottish merchants on land purchased by Scotsman John Alexander in 1699. Still represented today by shops selling tartans, bagpipes, and kilts, and at least one restaurant called *Scotland Yard* (728 King St.; phone: 703-683-1742) featuring venison and finnan haddie, Alexandria's Scottish forefathers are not forgotten by the city's modern-day residents. Their spirits really return to life in early December, when the Scottish *Christmas March* down King Street heralds the *Christmas* season.

In an era when tobacco was Virginia's cash crop and centuries before the surgeon general's warnings and the rights of nonsmokers were acknowledged, Alexandria's Potomac port was a center of colonial commerce. In exchange for the hogsheads of tobacco shipped to England from Virginia's burgeoning plantations, schooners returned to Alexandria laden with such things as the latest fashions, musical instruments, tea, books, exotic spices, and the trappings of European culture imported by the wealthy tobacco merchants who comprised the colonial aristocracy. Consequently, stately mansions were built, sophisticated shops carrying goods unavailable elsewhere in the colonies were opened, and luxurious inns were established.

Like the ancient Egyptian city after which it is named, Alexandria attracted the area's best and brightest. It was a popular meeting place for the likes of an ambitious land surveyor named George Washington and "Light Horse" Harry Lee, whose son, Robert E. Lee, led the Confederate army during the Civil War. Alexandria is imbued with the memory of both families. Indeed, Alexandria is home to more than one venue in which the claim "George Washington slept here" is not just an idle boast, unsubstantiated by history. But then, the same can be said about Presidents Thomas Jefferson and John Adams, and George Mason, renowned for his efforts in drafting the Bill of Rights.

Perhaps to its advantage, Alexandria narrowly avoided becoming the nation's capital in the late 18th century. The idea, promoted for a short time by Thomas Jefferson and others, was vetoed by George Washington. His Mount Vernon home dangerously near, the canny Washington probably wanted to maintain his distance from the fragile new federal capital — and canny he was: Less than 2 decades later the capital was overtaken and sacked by the British. Nevertheless, because of its charm and proximity to Washington, Alexandria has inherited a teeming population of the American government's prodigious barnacle: the lobbyist. Over 170 associations, ranging from the Snack Food Association of America to the National Helicopter Association, are headquartered here.

Everything worth seeing in Old Town Alexandria can be seen on foot. The historical buildings, quaint shops, and cobblestone streets are concentrated in a manageable, 3-hour walk.

The Old Town tour begins at Ramsay House (221 King St.; phone: 703-838-4200), also known as the visitors' center. Alexandria's oldest building (1724), the house was shipped upriver by barge from Dumfries, Virginia, around 1750, off-loaded, and dragged to its present location by its owner, William Ramsay, a founder of Alexandria, its first postmaster, and lord mayor. The house contains many of Ramsay's original possessions; the visitors' center (on the first floor) offers a bounty of brochures on the city. The center also shows a film about the town that, though generally uninspiring, contains a cameo appearance by Lt. Col. Francis Slate, Alexandria's official town crier. A distinguished Alexandrian who belts out the news from a compact, colonial-clad frame, Slate earned the distinction of being the world's loudest town crier at a recent competition in Nova Scotia. You also can pick up a parking pass at the Ramsey House that is good for 72 hours of metered parking (at 2-hour meters only). After parking, request a pass from the House and be sure to place it on your windshield. Remember, meter attendants in the Washington area are known — and feared — for their precision timing and quick ticket writing.

Walking north from King Street, turn the corner on Fairfax Street to *Carlyle House* (121 N. Fairfax St.; phone: 703-549-2997), another remnant of Alexandria's Scottish heritage. Designed to resemble a Scottish stone manor house, it was one of the first homes built in the fledgling town. This grand, mid-Georgian dwelling — home of Scottish merchant John Carlyle — dates from 1752. Perhaps its finest hour, though, was when it was chosen by General Edward Braddock and five colonial governors as their headquarters for planning the early campaign strategy and funding for the French and Indian War. Some of the Carlyle family's personal belongings are on display, rescued from dormant privy shafts and trash chutes by an unflappable band of archaeologists during the building's restoration in the 1970s. Though the contents are what one would expect to find in a flea market, the house is impressive and is best seen on guided tours, scheduled every half hour. Closed Mondays. Admission charge except for children under 10.

Turn right out of Carlyle House, then left on Cameron Street, and walk 1 block to Royal Street. On the corner is *Gadsby's Tavern* (138 N. Royal St.; phone: 703-548-1288), formerly the old *City Tavern and Hotel,* a crossroads of 18th-century political, business, and social life, and a favorite haunt of George Washington. At nearly 200 years old, the restaurant offers historic ambience — plenty of pewter, an original Hogarth painting in one of the three dining rooms (the first room entered was originally the tavern), and waiters and waitresses in colonial garb — and a menu that features game specialties, prime ribs, and some of the finest pecan pie this side of Georgia. A note to patrons from the "Tavern Keeper" explains why it's all right to have left home without your *American Express* card: "The tax upon this establishment by American Express was more repressive than the tax on tea imposed by the King. We therefore have thrown American Express over the side with the tea. We apologize if any of our customers get wet because of this, but we are sure you applaud this act against tyranny."

Next door to the tavern is *Gadsby's Tavern Museum* (134 N. Royal St.; phone: 703-838-4242). Built in 1770, it contains the second-floor ballroom in which George Washington attended gala birthday celebrations. The room is actually a reproduction, since the original (in its entirety) is now housed in New York's *Metropolitan Museum of Art* in its American Wing. A celebration of George Washington's birthday, called the *Night Ball,* is held here annually the weekend of or before Washington's birthday. Around the back are several original outbuildings, including a brick coffeehouse, a stable, a kitchen, and outdoor seating for the restaurant during the warm months.

Return 1 block to King Street, Alexandria's leading thoroughfare, and turn left. The block on the left is Market Square/City Hall. Two half-acre parcels of land were reserved in 1749 for the city marketplace, Town Hall, and courthouse. George Washington became a trustee of the market in 1766 and encouraged its growth by sending wagons of produce from Mt. Vernon to be sold here every week. With all that has changed over the years — including the addition of schools, jails, whipping posts, and a clock and bell tower, as well as several fires — this block's service to the city remains unchanged. A farmer's market (the longest continuously operating market in the country) is open every Saturday from 5 to 9 AM, with a mixed bag of early-risers peddling produce, meats, baked goods, and handmade crafts from the arcades on the south plaza of City Hall. A stoically early arriver (before 7 AM) is rewarded with free hot coffee and ham biscuits (phone: 703-838-4770).

A right turn on Fairfax Street leads to the doorstep of the *Stabler-Leadbeater Apothecary Shop* (107 S. Fairfax St.; phone: 703-836-3713), a charming remedy to the sanitized, impersonal feel of today's mega-drugstores. This unassuming little shop is the second-oldest apothecary in the country, and, in its time, contributed to the health of the Washington and Lee families. At one point, the shop was distributing its own medicines and cosmetics to customers in seven states. Now a museum, it offers a dose of history that includes an impressive collection of antique drugstore furnishings and apothecary bottles (some still filled with their original contents), a note from Martha Washington for a quart bottle of the proprietor's "best castor oil and the bill for it," and an 1861 entry in a logbook by an excited shop clerk reading: "Alexandria taken by US forces this morning at 5 o'clock; Ellsworth killed, great excitement, stores generally closed." Also, it was here in 1859 that Lt. Col. Robert E. Lee received orders to move to Harper's Ferry to head off John Brown's insurrection. The spot where Lee stood upon hearing the fateful news is marked by a plaque.

Return to King Street and walk east toward the Potomac. The blocks past Ramsay House are dense with restaurants, bookstores, boutiques, and more.

There are more than 200 shops within walking distance of Ramsey House; most are individually owned and operated, featuring all manner of unique and specialty merchandise. There are art galleries, fancy food stores, and shops selling jewelry, cookware, pipes and cigars, and more. The French Quarter meets the Scottish Quarter at *219 Basin Street Lounge* (219 King St.; phone: 703-549-1141), a better-than-average creole restaurant with cool, traditional jazz played upstairs. Next door is the *Scottish Merchant* (215 King St.; phone: 703-739-2302), an emporium selling kilts, tartans, bagpipes, and the best (and only) collection of Scottish music (cassettes only) in the Washington area. The shop does more than a "wee little" business among the ancient local clans.

Across the street is a collection of shops that feature Civil War books and memorabilia, foods and wines, and a café with excellent coffees. Farther along is the *Small Mall* (118 King St.; no phone), with shops offering American craftworks by artists from across the country. Back across the street is the *Fish Market* (105 King St.; phone: 703-836-5676), located in an 18th-century warehouse used to store ships' cargo. This is one of Old Town's most bustling watering holes and is an ideal location to savor a plate of oysters, chowder, broiled scallops, crabs prepared in every conceivable way (the restaurant's motto is: "We serve shrimps, crabs, tall people, and a lot of nice people, too"), and a schooner of beer — the swimming pool–like glasses for which the spot is well reputed.

At the corner of King Street (at the top) is Union Street, which runs parallel to the Potomac, whose waters are visible beyond the pier straight ahead. On the northeast corner is one of Alexandria's treasures, the *Torpedo Factory Art Center* (105 N. Union St.; phone: 703-838-4565). Formerly a munitions plant where naval torpedoes were manufactured for World Wars I and II, this spacious, restored building is now devoted to a rather more docile effort. Though it remains as industrious as it was when serving the war effort, it now does artistic duty as the studio and gallery for more than 175 professional artists, including painters, jewelers, photographers, sculptors, and textile designers. All the workshops are open to visitors, and most of the work can be purchased at reasonable prices. In the same building is the museum and laboratory of *Alexandria Archaeology* (phone: 703-838-4399), an organization that conducts explorations around Alexandria and displays objects that have been uncovered from as far back as 3000 BC.

For a better view of the Potomac, walk around behind the art center to a recently constructed waterfront area that includes — jutting out over the river — the *Chart House* restaurant (1 Cameron St.; phone: 703-684-5080), with its solid menu of prime ribs, fresh seafood dishes, and the always bodacious 67-item salad bar for which this chain is famous. The restaurant's Capitol Room affords a view of the Capitol Building up the river, in Washington. The area is also home to numerous fast-food eateries.

Now, walk south (back across King St.) on Union Street. Between King and Prince Streets in a brick building on the right is the *Union Street Public House* (121 S. Union St.; phone: 703-548-1785), a pub/restaurant usually well-stocked with patrons and good cheer. It is one of the Washington area's finest settings for swilling high-performance brewery beer (try the Virginia Native, brewed by the Virginia Brewing Company exclusively for the pub), and features a mishmash of good American food with a southern flair.

Follow Union Street south 1 block to Prince Street. Turn right and begin climbing this picturesque cobblestone street. The first block is known as Captain's Row because of the charming homes built by old sea captains in the late 18th century. Though the homes occupy the same block, their different sizes, building materials, and façade decorations bear witness to the fierce independence of the salty dogs who built them.

The cobblestones in the street, according to legend, were laid by Hessian mercenaries who fought for the British during the Revolutionary War and who were later imprisoned in Alexandria. Watch your step; it's easy to twist an ankle here. The Greek Revival *Athenaeum* (201 Prince St.; phone: 703-548-0035) sits solidly at the corner of Prince and Lee Streets. Built in the mid-19th century to house the Bank of Old Dominion, it served its fiscal purpose for over a century. In the 1950s, this reddish-brown building was purchased by the city of Alexandria for use as an art museum and cultural-activities center. It frequently features original exhibitions of contemporary art. The string of townhouses from Lee to Fairfax Streets beyond the *Athenaeum* is known as Gentry Row, a series of private residences all built in the mid-18th century. The houses are all in the colonial style — brick and painted in traditional but vastly different colors. It's fun to walk down this cobblestone street at night and peek in the windows. The curtains in these houses are intentionally left open.

At Fairfax Street, turn left. Less than 2 blocks down Fairfax on the right, just beyond Duke Street, is the Old Presbyterian Meeting House (321 S. Fairfax St.; phone: 703-549-6670), a popular meeting place built by and for the Scottish patriots in the Revolutionary War. Built in 1774 and still a functioning church, this somber-looking building was the place where George Washington's funeral service was held. A weathered tombstone in a small cemetery in the back honors the Unknown Soldier of the American Revolution. Open Mondays through Fridays, 8:30 AM to 4:30 PM; services Sundays at 8:30 and 11 AM.

Walk south 1 block from the meeting house to Wolfe Street. At Wolfe, make a right and stroll the several blocks to Washington Street, one of Old Town's main thoroughfares; turn right again into Washington Street.

Just over a block down Washington Street on the left is the *Lyceum* (open Mondays through Saturdays, 10 AM to 5 PM and Sundays 1 to 5 PM; 201 S. Washington St.; phone: 703-838-4994), an early-19th-century building that is yet another repository of this city's treasured past. In this Grecian-style building, Alexandria's history unfolds in the form of etchings, photographs, original documents, and video presentations.

A bit farther down Washington Street are *Geranio* (722 King St.; phone 703-548-0088) and *Terrazza* (710 King St.; phone: 703-683-6900), a pair of tantalizing Italian dining spots featuring northern Italian dishes. At the corner (King and Washington Sts.) is *Scotland Yard* (728 King St.; phone: 703-683-1742), a restaurant that features finnan haddie, quail, venison, and other Caledonian favorites. Its bar stocks the area's best selection of single malt Scotch whisky. Don't be alarmed to see plainclothes British bobbies hanging around; and be sure *not* to mutter wisecracks about the Irish Republican Army. Officers from London's Scotland Yard — in Washington in an exchange program with the FBI — occasionally dine here.

Stay on Washington Street; just past King Street is Christ Church (118 N. Washington St.; phone: 703-549-1450), an English country-style church that was once the house of worship of George Washington and, later, Robert E. Lee. In fact, George Washington plunked down over £36 — a good chunk of change at the time — for a pew (salvation wasn't cheap — even in colonial times). His pew (No. 60) is marked with a plaque, as is the pew of the Confederate general (No. 46), who grew up just down the street. The current president is invited to attend services on the Sunday closest to Washington's birthday. The interior features a dazzling chandelier that was imported from England at George Washington's expense. Before returning to Washington Street, circle the church to see the surrounding cemetery, which contains some of the earliest sculptured gravestones in the area.

Continue north on Washington Street past the Lloyd House and Library (220 N. Washington St.; phone: 703-838-4577) on the left. Built in 1779, this excellent example of late-Georgian architecture was saved from demolition at the 11th hour by Alexandria's feisty preservationists. Today it houses a wealth of documents and books on Virginian history. Visitors are welcome; open Mondays through Saturdays, 9 AM to 5 PM; admission charge.

Forge ahead 2 more blocks, noticing cobblestone Princess Street on the right with its collection of 18th-century buildings, to Lee Corner, at the intersection of Washington and Oronoco Streets. At one time, the Lee family had the intersection occupied on all sides — a Lee family house stood on all four corners. The one that is well-marked on the immediate right, the Lee-Fendall House (614 Oronoco St.; phone: 703-548-1789), is one of two Lee houses remaining. It was the home of Richard Henry Lee, whose moniker graces the Declaration of Independence, and "Light Horse" Harry Lee, a cavalry commander and father of Robert E. Lee. The 19th-century town-house across Oronoco Street is the boyhood home of Robert E. (607 Oronoco St.; phone: 703-548-8454), where he lived until decamping to West Point in 1825. His first glorious steed, a prized rocking horse, is on display here. Both homes welcome visitors; open Mondays through Saturdays from 10 AM to 4 PM and Sundays from 1 to 4 PM; admission charge.

Though this completes the walking tour of Old Town Alexandria, a three-quarters-of-a-mile jaunt up King Street to the George Washington Masonic National Memorial (King St. at Callahan Dr.; phone: 703-683-2007) is recommended. This tower, based on the design of the Pharaoh's Lighthouse in ancient Egypt's Alexandria, is as much a temple of Masonic lore as it is a tribute to George Washington, one of the society's most prominent members. Though there are many who think it's an eyesore, at the very least, it makes for a distinctive landmark. The tower's observatory does yield a splendid view of Alexandria and the Potomac.

Index

212   INDEX

Drinks
Program
mail bills
wash car
pizza
ribbon
Roast buf
wash clothes
P. cheese
Ham
→ Motel regist.

Chocolate Cake

Call:
Missy
M.S.
Chip